MARK W. GOLDSTEIN

The

EPIPHANY

GUIDING THE MIND TOWARD DISCOVERING THE SOUL

As the hummingbird draws nectar from a variety of flowers,
So shall we draw knowledge from a variety of sources.

MARK W. GOLDSTEIN

The EPIPHANY

GUIDING THE MIND TOWARD DISCOVERING THE SOUL

VOLUME I

EVOLUTION OF HUMAN CONSCIOUSNESS AND THE
FORM IT MANIFESTS

Illustrated by Cynthia A. Goldstein

This book is dedicated to

My Beloved Wife
Cynthia

For her love and support,
Her artwork and edits,
And her inexplicable way of
Knowing when things are right.

In Memory of

My dearly departed Brother
Melvyn S. Goldstein

Who lived the life of a lawyer
With the heart of a poet.

VOLUME I

Evolution of Human Consciousness and the Form it Manifests

TABLE OF CONTENTS

PREFACE

I wrote this book because it is the book I wanted to read and it hadn't been written yet. Much of the teachings and tenets contained within this book have been written and taught before, and by some of the most knowledgeable and enlightened minds of all times. I know this to be true as I have spent the entirety of my adult life searching out these teachings and studying their profound lessons. Even though these teachings were abundantly available, what seemed to be missing was a book that endeavored to compile this vast array of knowledge into a single work. Furthermore, it was my intention to blend this diverse array of ideas and teachings into a harmonious, multidisciplinary study with a coherent, unbiased message. In doing so, I strived to avoid the competitive and sanctimonious debates that are so distracting, yet characteristic, of such discourse.

It may be said that the guiding motif of this book is *unchurched spirituality.* In layman's terms, unchurched spirituality refers to the phenomenon of spirituality beyond the context of religion. Historically, religion has been the custodian of spirituality; some even assert that the two terms are synonymous. And, for those people, it is only natural that they would perceive spirituality and religion as one and the same given that religion has always been their source of spirituality. For our purposes, however, we will separate these two hallowed concepts in order to focus our undivided attention on the undefinable and indescribable wonder of spirituality.

This may be an appropriate time to introduce one of the fundamental tenets of spirituality. When it comes to our spiritual education, there stands one overarching rule of thumb: *Just as the language of religion is expressed in words, and the language of science is math, the language of spirituality is direct personal experience.* Given this overriding principle, we must always bear in mind that *spirituality can neither be taught nor learned, it must ultimately be experienced firsthand*. Of course, the teachings of the great Saints and Sages, Masters and Prophets, are instrumental and invaluable in guiding us toward the spiritual experience in question. Even the Buddha referred to his 84,000 teachings as merely a raft to cross the turbulent waters of maya (illusion) and darkness (ignorance) until we reach the shores of Enlightenment (awakening and realization). And once reached, we mustn't lug the raft up onto the shore and carry it with us. Instead, we are meant to explore our new home with new eyes and discover, for the first time, who we are and who we have always been.

Just as the spiritual hypothesis proclaims: *to be human is to be more spirit than flesh—more Soul than body*. If, indeed, our true identity is that of an immortal Soul having a mortal, physical experience, isn't it time for us to discover this age-old truth for ourselves? As the ancient Hindus taught over four thousand years ago, the two greatest needs of all humans are the *need to be* and *the need to know*. It appears that our need to be is covered by our mutually endowed and inherently held survival mechanism. In the final analysis, there seems to be no amount of exertion too great when it comes to preserving our own mortal life. On the other hand, when it comes to knowing the meaning and purpose of our mortal existence, many of us simply have better things to do with our time.

Even though I pondered these time-honored questions throughout the course of my life, I had yet to commit myself to any kind of sustained, prioritized approach to discovering my own spiritual nature. This pivotal moment came in the autumn of 2004 while attending my mother's funeral. My father had passed twenty-two years earlier, leaving me orphaned at the age of fifty-five. Not that I felt lost and bewildered by my mother's passing, but I was inexplicably confronted by my own mortality. Similar to my feelings as a young child when my grandfather died, I felt haunted by the notion of being *gone forever*. It all seemed so cruel. Why are we given this precious gift of life, only to have it snatched away forever? To say nothing of the fact that, at age fifty-five, I was just beginning to get the hang of it. Without realizing it at the time, my committed quest toward discovering my elusively veiled Soul, and the seed of my own immortality, had just begun.

From a research perspective, however, the more fundamental and less challenging question regarding the spiritual hypothesis was when and where did it begin? After endless hours of research, the best answer I can provide is that there doesn't seem to be a time, throughout all of human history, when the spiritual hypothesis was not in question. It is well-established that this hypothesis was a major component of the shamanic teachings and practices of the *hunting-and-gathering* cultures over 30,000 years ago. And it has continued throughout the generations right up to our current multitude of books and teachers on this topic, along with such media-venues as the popular Emmy Award-winning TV series, Super Soul Sunday.

By design, the first part of this book, explores how the spiritual hypothesis has had such an extensive and continual influence on our species' worldview from its earliest origins. Many of the greatest minds throughout history have pondered the big questions and arrived at equally big answers. Their exploration lays the groundwork for our own. Although we can benefit greatly from the world's renown spiritual explorers, it is only through our own direct experience that we come to know our true spiritual nature—the discovery of our living Soul—Self-realization.

This brings us to the essential purpose of this book, which is more experiential than informational. Succinctly stated: ***The content of this book has been selected and orchestrated to guide its readers to their own spiritual experience.*** Bear in mind, I can only provide the map; ultimately it is your navigational skills that will bring you to the long-awaited treasure. And perhaps your greatest navigational skills are rooted in your ability to patiently keep an *open mind* while maintaining a *hungry heart*. In other words, don't rush to judgment until you have achieved a true and unbiased understanding. Any conclusion regarding spirituality comes from expanded awareness and enhanced perception, which then generates an experience that was previously beyond our capability. Our awakening to the presence of the Soul is revealed gradually until it is suddenly realized, as opposed to being the result of jumping to quick conclusions that are rationalized and intellectualized without the benefit of expanded awareness and enhanced perception.

However, for readers desiring more rational explanations and evidence-based theories, I have included the findings from many of the foremost quantum physicists and neuro-scientists as well as numerous key teachings from the field of psychology. Also included are the findings of Duke University's Center for Spirituality, Theology and Health, which has compiled over 2400 studies regarding the impact of spiritual beliefs on the anatomy of the aging brain and its association to general mental health. All of these teachings suggest the potential of a modern, emerging worldview that can be characterized as a *scientific spiritual worldview.*

While Part One of *The Epiphany* explores the collective consciousness of humanity at large, Part Two focuses directly on raising our own individual consciousness. Part Two also introduces the *Spiritualization Process*, which, if followed, gives rise to the expanded awareness and enhanced perception necessary to attain the spiritual experience. This process allows for the raising of our individual consciousness to the level where we are able to perceive our spiritual nature through the veil of its concealment. We are blessed to be alive in such a rare moment in history when somewhat ordinary people can achieve the heightened states of consciousness that were traditionally only available to the great Saints and Sages; the Masters and Prophets. Self-realization (the mind realizing the Soul) is truly the idea whose time has come; and we are the fortunate people to whom it is coming.

There is an ancient saying amongst the spiritually enlightened: **Reality and our perception of reality are not the same.** Our perception of reality is altered by our previous experiences and conditioning, along with the influence of our incessant pursuit of pleasure and power, plus our ego's need to always be right while making others wrong. It is not easy for us to get a glimpse of truth in the midst of such nar-row-minded obstacles. Nevertheless, if we remain persistent and open, while allowing the content of the chapters ahead to guide our minds, we just might begin to feel the *sensations of expanded awareness* guiding us toward the discovery of the Soul; i.e., spiritual awakening.

This book was written for those who are just beginning to dip their toe in the spiritual waters, as well as those who are advanced swimmers. For many, this will not be an easy read; for some, it will feel like healing waters to a parched and thirsty land. The epiphany in question is nothing less than the realization of our true nature as spiritual beings having a physical experience.

I have spent the last nineteen years compiling many of the most noteworthy teachings by some of our species' most revered teachers on this topic of our human/spiritual nature. These teachings are presented in the chapters ahead—some quoted in their original form, others contemporized and para-phrased for a modern audience. The validity of these teach-ings and tenets is discovered and realized through our own direct personal experience of their truth. This *spiritual expe-rience* comes through expanded awareness and enhanced perception of who we are and who we have always been. Wait for this experience to emerge before jumping to any impetu-ous conclusions.

In closing, let's consider two quotes found in the pages ahead, from opposite ends of the spiritual spectrum. The first quote is from a mystical teacher of the ancient traditions and focuses on a common flaw in the character of the human ego: ***The wise expand their understanding to meet reality. Fools reduce reality to meet their under-standing.*** Our second quote is from a 20th century Nobel

Prize winning theoretical physicist and focuses on a fundamental aspect of reality, which most of us never considered: *Not only is the Universe* [reality] *stranger than we think, it is stranger than we <u>can</u> think.* These are profound lessons taught by two renown teachers—one mystical, the other scientific. The words of both will significantly set the tone for what lies ahead.

Experiencing the presence of the Soul is the primary objective of this book. This spiritual experience comes through a capability that for most of us remains dormant until properly awakened. Like the physical capabilities of hearing and sight, if never experienced previously it would be difficult to fully comprehend them through mere explanation. Spiritual capabilities are much more complex and more rare than our vast array of physical skills and abilities. Furthermore, as with the physical capabilities of seeing and hearing, if after never experiencing sight and sound previously, we suddenly awaken to these vital abilities being fully intact, the experience alone becomes the defining truth about their nature. This book is about the process of awakening our capability to experience our own Soul and that which has brought it into being.

In the chapters ahead, you will be introduced to a multitude of mind-expanding spiritual tenets—some from the mystical and some from science. If properly probed and processed by the reader, the mind will gradually rise to higher frequencies of expanded awareness and understanding. I have designed our approach to include spiritual novices initiating their first spiritual quest. However, *The Epiphany* is focused on providing the advanced spiritual seeker guidance and reinforcement toward higher frequencies they have yet to encounter. It is now time for all those having the ability and inclination to advance our precious planet's collective consciousness to join the effort. For this is clearly the path toward serving and saving the future of humanity.

Mark W. Goldstein
October 2023

ACKNOWLEDGEMENTS

With deep and sincere appreciation, I wish to acknowledge those who supported and encouraged the writing of this book.

When it comes to my eternal gratitude and appreciation, first, and foremost, is you, Cynthia, my beloved wife of 35 years, my partner, my best friend, my guide and very often my redeemer. Not only could I *not* have written this book without you, it is unlikely that I could have navigated my way through the turbulent waters of the past nineteen years. You showed me where to step when I was lost and you held me close when I faced those times of fear. I have never known such a selfless person as you, who doesn't even recognize or mention the sacrifices you make. Your exquisite drawings are an inspiration to me as they bring my characters and their concepts to life. Over the years, you have spent endless hours combing through every square inch of text—editing what needed editing while deleting the extraneous. Most importantly, you have taught me the meaning of the ancient tenet of Soulmates, where two Souls become as one and their human counterparts are able to explore the sacred pinnacle of selfless love where egos are forbidden.

My undying gratitude extends to you, my dearly departed brother, Melvyn Goldstein, for all the time and effort you spent providing your editing skills and keen understanding of this book's topic. I cherish the memories of our long, profound, philosophic discussions regarding the meaning and purpose of our lives and the true nature of our reality. Speaking of memories, I fondly remember the day when you were showing us your beautifully artistic travel photographs. As fate would have it, unexpectedly and in the same moment, Cynthia and I both knew that we just discovered the cover photo for our book. Mel, you joined me in a new level of spiritual exploration at our mother's funeral, which ultimately resulted in this book. And, you remained with me through every page of my manuscript until your untimely death right in the midst of the final chapter—a book that began at our mother's funeral and concluded with yours. I will never forget your words when, on your deathbed, I asked if you feared what lies ahead. You calmly told me that you did not; then added that it was covered extensively in the book and your *epiphany* had already come.

I am also grateful to you, Mel, for your loving daughter, our niece Mindy. Thank you, Mindy, for stepping in, at such a crucial time, to provide support and enthusiasm in your father's name. Mindy, you have always been more than a niece to Cynthia and me. And now that both your parents have passed on, we share an even stronger and more meaningful bond. The unique qualities of your mother and your father are endearingly reflected in you. Your continual inquiries into the progress and struggles we faced taking the completed manuscript to the next level of publishing and the launching of the book is reminiscent of the constant stream of support given by your father. I am certain that the profound feelings of loss and sorrow over your father's passing will stay with me for the remainder of my days. However, this new blossoming of our connection with you is a source of great delight for both of us. We are more than family; we are best friends.

And, speaking of family becoming best friends, this is the perfect time to acknowledge and express my appreciation to you, Kathleen Ryan—our *little sister*. I would be remiss if I did not acknowledge the contribution you've made, using your graphic skills, to prepare Mel's photograph for our book cover. You are one of a very small and select group who sampled *The Epiphany's* Preface and Introduction prior to its publishing. Your valuable feedback regarding their impact on you, and the enthusiasm you experienced, was much appreciated during a stressful and difficult time.

Now that I have acknowledged family becoming best friends, let me acknowledge friends becoming family. Looking back, there were those who seemed to be guiding me toward writing this book even before I knew I was heading in that direction. At the top of the list is you, Dr. Bruce Clark, my dear friend of nearly 40 years, who has become a brother to me. Between 2004 and 2022, I engaged in 6-8 hours of daily spiritual study and exploration. During the first 4½ years, my only writing was within the thousands of pages written in my notebooks. Bruce, our early 2009 chance encounter at Trader Joe's lasted over an hour and led to a series of illuminating, follow-up conversations. Prior to these discussions, I had only spoken with Cynthia and Mel regarding what I was learning and, ultimately, experiencing. As Age Wave colleagues and IPG partners, you and I worked together for years. Though our focus was on presenting data and its implications to clients, I recognized your unique ability to get to the essence of a topic without allowing personal biases or self-serving agendas to alter your perception of truth. I could always trust the validity of your keen insights and impartial evaluations. Admittedly, the decades of experience and expertise we cultivated careerwise paled in comparison to the vast, unlimited and unknown mysteries we faced when confronted by our own spiritual nature. It wasn't long before I detected your ravenous appetite for this topic of *unchurched spirituality* and the *spiritualization process* that leads to its discovery.

Bruce, your random request to provide you with a list of key points pertaining to our discussions (eventually weighing in at twenty-two pages), inadvertently became the origin of this book. You contributed to the starting of this book, you have been a part of its development and you recently contributed generously to its publishing. Had you not recognized the value of what I was exploring and experiencing, subsequently making space to participate in our weekly 2-hour sessions (over the next fourteen years), this book may not have developed as it did—and, undoubtedly, it would not have been nearly as much fun.

I am honored to acknowledge the role played by my dear friend, employer and often mentor, Dr. Ken Dychtwald—gerontologist, psychologist, author, founder and CEO of Age Wave. Of course, I am not alone. It seems, Ken, that you have had a significant influence on all of us whose paths have intersected with yours over the years. For those of us who were fortunate enough to be a part of the Age Wave experience, you will always be recognized as *The Boss*—the way Bruce Springsteen has held that moniker since the late sixties.

I am forever grateful for that Monday evening on December 27th, in 1982 when we met at your home in the hills of Berkeley, California to discuss my working with you as a speaker and seminar leader. That evening emerged into a pivotal moment in my career and in my life. You became more than an employer; you became my mentor and lifelong friend. I worked for you first at Dychtwald and Associates and then at Age Wave over the next twenty-two years. The quality and significance of our work always gave me a profound sense of pride. It was a thrilling adventure and we made a real difference in so many lives.

You have been instrumental in schooling me toward researching, understanding, and communicating complex topics to varied audiences in a manner that not only educates, but also entertains. As a professional, you recognized my strengths and weaknesses before I did; as a friend you guided me toward becoming the author who wrote this book. To say that you are a powerful and influential force in my life would be an understatement. On one hand, you knew Jonas Salk on a first name basis and received his personal calls to your home. You've met five US presidents and became close friends with Jimmy Carter. You testified before congress as to the trends that would become major crises in our nation's future. While at the same time, when Cynthia and I recently found ourselves facing the most terrifying crisis of our lives, there you were, Ken, at our side, making the right call to the right doctor on our behalf. When I count the blessings of my life, you, my brother, are in a class of your own.

Of course, that right doctor is you Suzanne LeBlang, MD, Co-Chief Medical Officer of the Focused Ultrasound Foundation, and the Medical Director for the Fibroid Education Center. Beyond your vast education and experience, Dr. Susie, you possess and express extraordinary compassion and empathy to those that you serve. This quality alone has the power to bring hope and healing to those who have the good fortune to be heartened by you. A while back, Ken referred to you as a godsend. For Cynthia and me, there could be no better word to describe you. You mean the world to us; and without your unremitting kindness and support, I am not sure this book would have been finished. Your expertise and friendship are a blessing.

Speaking of the blessing of friendship, I must acknowledge you, Katie Bowles, my dear friend of forty years. Over those years, we have worked together and we have played together; we shared our joys and we were there for each other in times of sorrow. And through it all, there has always been a common thread of *fighting the good fight.* As the sacred Gita has taught for thousands of years, we are all engaged in the battle within; a battle that rages between our egoistic nature and our altruistic aspirations—to say nothing of the intense conflicts emerging between these opposing forces. However, the world *within* can be a lonely place. I am eternally grateful to have such a friend as you, Katie, who has been there for me in resolving the conflicts that challenge my peace of mind and stunt my growth. You have participated in my seminars and you have read my book and you are still hungry for more. Your belief and support in my work is invaluable. Although the scenery and climate has continually changed, this path that we follow is one of lifelong friendship where our bond has always persisted unchanged.

A little over six years ago, Bruce Clark told me about his friend who has been fascinated by our discussions. He wanted to know if this friend could be included in our next session. I was somewhat tentative about bringing in someone new (i.e., an unknown factor) as our process had been going very well and gaining momentum. Nevertheless, I believe things often happen for a reason and that meeting someone new to discuss the topic and content of my book could be quite illuminating and enjoyable.

It was on that Monday morning, January 22, 2017, that my life became vastly enriched upon making your acquaintance, Jon Jeffries. In those two hours of sharing the content of *The Epiphany* with you, while you so generously shared your experience, we three officially became The Stumbling Scarecrow, The Rusted Tin Man and The Cowardly Lion on our Journey toward Oz. And now, after the 320 Monday morning sessions that followed, it could not be more obvious that you were always meant to be included. It was clear from the start that you have been on your own spiritual quest for decades and that the core message of *The Epiphany* was yours for the taking. And, like all sincere spiritual seekers, your perspective greatly enhances ours.

Aside from your weighty contribution made to our weekly group discussions, your thoughtful gift of spending five days with Cynthia and me, professionally spray-painting our kitchen cabinets, literally enhanced our experience of having to be stuck in the house over the following three years.

I would also like to acknowledge and express my appreciation of you, Michael Rybarski (Founder of LifeChange Strategies, former senior editor at Houghton Mifflin, author, coworker at Age Wave), my dear friend, for your involvement in my writing *The Epiphany*. I am ever so grateful for those inspiring conversations we have had over the years, in downtown Danville, regarding the writing and publishing of my book. Your knowledge and expertise on the book business have guided some of my key decisions. Michael, few people have such profound knowledge and understanding of religion, philosophy, and the teachings of the great teachers, as you do. You proved your recognition of the spiritual, my friend, when it was tested by your own devastating medical diagnosis. All of us who have witnessed your ordeal are amazed by the tenacity of your faith and your ability to remain positive and committed in the most difficult of times.

Clearly, one of your most significant contributions to my book, Michael, is the organizing of our online Zoom class which has continued for years from a variety of venues including your home in Texas, your hospital bed, skilled nursing facilities, rehabilitation, and physical therapy centers, all the while maintaining your unwavering commitment to the healing of your body and the nurturing of your Soul.

And in that Zoom class, Michael, was yet another of your significant contributions—Dr. George S. Sayre. You, George, my kindred spirit, were born and raised not far from where I was born, right around the same time. In our youth, we travelled down many of the same streets, ate at the same restaurants and hung out at the same clubs, yet it was not until we became septuagenarians that we actually met and became the closest of friends. As a 30-year seasoned meditator, you received your teaching and mantram directly from your personal friend, Professor Eknath Easwaran, one of the twentieth century's greatest spiritual teachers. Professor Easwaran, Founder of the Blue Mountain Center of Meditation and the originator of Passage Meditation, vastly expanded your knowledge and experience of the ancient Eastern traditions; thereby allowing your endorsement to bring greater validity to my book. George, you have selflessly supported me in completing my manuscript and you have generously supported me in the publishing of my book; while at the same time, you have sustained me during my darkest and most devastating hours of need. Few people have entered my life and ascended to the level of friendship and relevance that you have done in these past few years. From my perspective, your presence in my life is nothing short of a true blessing. Thank you, George, for all that you are and all that you have been for me and for Cynthia.

And finally, I would be remiss if I did not acknowledge the expert guidance and patient understanding provided by your sincere and caring nature, Kimberly Hitchens, owner of Booknook.Biz. From the first time that I landed on your website, I knew that you were not just another eBook conversion and formatting business; rather you provide a total education for new authors hoping to self-publish their work. While so many of your competitors' websites provide little more than a glorified Yellow Pages ad, your site is nothing less than an entire library of relevant information—all given before the point of sale. I have relied on you, and your team, countless times, Hitch, during this arduous journey, and you have yet to let me down. That, my friend, is rare in today's business setting. It seems fitting that this acknowledgment of your support is the last addition to my manuscript before submitting it into your highly capable hands.

INTRODUCTION

The underlying topic of this book is *Unchurched Spirituality*: the esoteric, mystical noumenon of spirituality viewed outside the more familiar context of religion. For some, this separation proves to be quite a challenge, since many consider the two terms, spirituality and religion, to be synonymous. Should this be the case, it may take some time and effort to recognize and understand spirituality as independent and free of the more apparent phenomenon of religion. Just as the physical and psychological aspects of our nature are deeply related, they can also be recognized and considered separately.

The most familiar spiritual aspect of a human being has become known as the Soul. Although this term is universally used, it defies all physical description or identification. The eyes can't see it and the ears are unable to hear it. None of the senses are able to notice the Soul as we do the person next to us waiting for a bus. If the physical body is unable to perceive the Soul, we must rely on the mind to make its acquaintance. However, before the mind is able to recognize the presence of the Soul, it must first gain independence from the limitations of the brain. And to achieve such liberation for the mind, we must first distinguish it from the brain. This begins the gradual and lengthy process of spiritual awakening.

The Epiphany: Guiding the Mind toward Discovering

the Soul, and the course within, is designed and composed to introduce the reader to the *spiritualization process*. Or, for some readers, to support the spiritualization process they have already begun. As a working definition positioned this early in the book, *spiritualization is the process that leads the mind toward discovering the presence of the Soul.* Said another way, it is the process that leads us toward discovering our spiritual nature. Either term, *Soul* or *spiritual nature*, requires greater understanding in order to expand our awareness of the meaning of such esoteric concepts.

In our fast-paced, modern world, the very notion that we simultaneously exist in three dimensions (physical, psychological and spiritual) is, for many, a somewhat baseless and unconfirmed concept. When this spiritual hypothesis shifts from a concept to an experience, it is a pivotal moment unlike any previous—a moment that impacts all moments that follow. It is not unusual for us to make this shift from *idea* to *experience* without even initially detecting that it's taking place. Typically, this is the result of our having preconceived notions of what the spiritual experience *should* be and how it occurs. For our purposes, it is best to let go of such notions in order to allow the spiritual experience to reveal and define itself. Consequently, it is recommended that we cultivate our skill of introspection in lieu of our active imagination and need for immediate conceptualization.

For many of us, our first profound and intentional, introspective moment arises when the path we've been following, often randomly and ill-conceived, blows up in our face. We can actually hear our mind rebuking itself: *What was I thinking?* Herein lies a big part of the problem—we weren't thinking. We were too busy *doing*. This standard operating procedure of doing at a faster rate than thinking has become all-too-common within our fast-track, overextended life-styles.

Speaking of thinking, most of us navigated our youth and education years never realizing the link between the rambling stream of our thoughts and the way our lives unfold. We certainly didn't understand that the form our lives take is actually sourced by those random thoughts incessantly rattling around in our head. Even though the prophets and philosophers of old revealed it to us, and more recently, psychology and neuroscience explained it to us, we have yet to make this metamorphic piece of the human puzzle our personal guiding light to: *what-you-think-is-what-you-get*.

Hinduism, recognized as the world's oldest religion, speaks of humanity's two most fundamental needs: the *need to be* and the *need to know*. While the first need is our need to exist, the second is our need to know *why*. Because our need *to be* is inexorably linked to our innate survival instincts, it runs on autopilot— often undetected. Our need *to know why we exist* is philosophic, multifaceted and mysterious rather than practical. For millennia, our species has been overwhelmed with its need to survive, leaving little time nor inclination to ponder the fundamental truths of *why*. Furthermore, the question of *why we exist* brings up the equally significant question of *what are we* and the true nature of our existence.

However, beyond the masses, and since the early days of our cave-dwelling ancestors, there have been those rare human beings who did ponder our true nature. Even before our early ancestors had a common language, their cave drawings reflected their interest in understanding the *whys* and *whats* of our existence. Early European, Asian, African, Australian and Indonesian cave art dates back some 40-45,000 years. Far beyond the depiction of animals and hand tracings, cave art shows the earliest beginnings of spiritual interest and religious sophistication. Shamanism is often represented as the origin of religion and the shamans as the first artists.

It is apparent that regardless of our generation or culture, we must inevitably decide for ourselves the validity of the age-old, underlying spiritual hypothesis: ***To be human is to be more spirit than flesh, more Soul than body.***

The epiphany referred to in the title of this book is the moment of insight that validates this spiritual hypothesis. In the ancient Eastern traditions, this insight is termed Self-realization. It begins when the mind becomes consciously aware of the presence of the Soul. It is the grand unveiling of the immortal essence of our mortal existence. The path that leads to this spiritual realization is the *spiritualization process*— the study, exploration and discovery of our spiritual nature. This book is an advanced course in spiritualization, and our teachers are some of the greatest and most renowned spiritual geniuses in human history, along with numerous eminent philosophic and scientific minds.

However, it is important to note that the teachings of this, or any book, are secondary; they are simply a means to an end. Although this book is a compilation of many teachings and extensive information, its primary purpose is not educational, rather it is experiential. While the *spiritualization process* begins with gaining knowledge and expanded understanding regarding our spiritual nature, it is ultimately designed to bring about the *mystical experience* of our spiritual nature. In other words, to lead the mind toward the discovery of the Soul. Although these two companions, mind and Soul, have been roommates throughout our lives, the Soul remains hidden behind closed doors. It requires an *act of will*, initiated by the heart and undertaken by the mind, to break through its veil of concealment in order to gain access to the ultimate teacher already residing within, waiting to be realized.

Bear in mind that words such as Soul, spirit, mystical and the like, carry a great deal of baggage in contemporary life. It's highly unlikely that we can even have the spiritual discussion, let alone engage in the spiritualization process, without hitting the tripwires of endless spiritual baggage. This baggage may, in fact, become the key obstacle blocking our path toward spiritual awareness. Such terms as God, Oneness, spiritual, etc. are words we use to communicate the ineffable. Like the Taoist taught centuries ago: *That which is truly spiritual cannot be translated into worldly terminology.* Such *worldly* communications are, at best, misrepresentations of that which they attempt to represent. Therein lies the reason for its accumulation of baggage; the true spiritual experience is unrecognizable after being conceptualized, interpreted, analyzed, evaluated, judged and spoken.

The *only* way to know the spiritual is through direct, personal experience of the spiritual. And even then, it takes keen mental discipline not to conceptualize the experience into ideas and words that are deficient and misleading. What else can the mind do with an utterly unique and novel experience but associate it with something more familiar from its past, stored in the brain's memory? This was demonstrated by Ebenezer Scrooge in Charles Dicken's *A Christmas Carol*, when he conceptualized his encounter with the spirit of his late partner, Jacob Marley. Here, Scrooge mistakenly associates the unprecedented experience with something more familiar, asserting to Marley's ghost: *You may be an undigested bit of beef, a blot of mustard, a crumb of cheese, a fragment of underdone potato. There's more of gravy than of grave about you, whatever you are!* Scrooge interpreted that profound spiritual moment as nothing more than indigestion.

This isn't uncommon; it is what the brain does—it interprets all that it encounters. The basis of these interpretations is from previous conditioning, previous experiences and previous data stored in its memory—all faulty at best. Needless to say, if these interpretations form the foundation of our perceptions in life, we are courting disaster.

Nobel Prize laureate Dr. Roger Sperry and Dr. Michael Gazzaniga are celebrated for their breakthrough work in split-brain research, cerebral lateralization and cognitive neuroscience. These doctors were involved with some of the most experimental and revealing brain surgeries in medical history.

In his 1998 book, *The Left-Brain Interpreter*, Dr. Gazzaniga discloses how their research determined that the left-brain provides explanations and reasons for what takes place in our lives and our world. In this way, it acts as an *interpreter of reality*. Even more astonishing, their work revealed that this interpreter was very often completely and utterly wrong in its findings. As you can imagine, this little fly in the ointment leaves us with a misperception of the reality in which we exist. As complicating as this is in our physical interactions, it is a major obstacle regarding our spiritual awakening.

The mystical experience that reveals our spiritual nature has no parallel in our previous memory, conditioning or experience; therefore, all of our initial mystical moments are misinterpreted. The more untainted we hold our initial spiritual experiences (without conceptualizing, interpreting or judging) the more they reveal to us. If this sounds confusing and frustrating, it is only because we are discussing the mystical experience without benefit of the *state of bliss* that accompanies it. All doubt and frustration melts away in the presence of such clarity and joy.

Key to reading this book (as well as all spiritual exploration) is to approach its teachings with an open mind and a willing heart. Remember, the teachings, like the experience they lead to, exist just beyond the current content and understanding of the brain. It will require *insights of expanded awareness* to bring about enhanced perception. Spiritualization is a gradual process. Be patient and trusting. Wait for the understanding, expanded awareness and greater clarity that ultimately leads to spiritual realization. Once realization has enlightened the mind, our spiritual nature will have revealed itself beyond any guesswork and interpretation. This is the only reliable source.

The Epiphany is an *advanced* course in spiritualization not because it is meant exclusively for advanced seekers, but rather because the course objective is advanced. The objective of this course is nothing less than a direct, personal experience of our spiritual nature. If, as the spiritual hypothesis suggests, we are a living Soul having a physical life in a material world, the discovery of this truth is a total game changer. Imagine yourself struggling to make ends meet in a dead-end life when you receive word from an emissary of the king and queen proclaiming that you are their long-lost child. Total game changer, right? And yet, even the benefits of discovering your royal heritage pale in comparison to all that comes with being an immortal Soul having a physical life.

However, the significance of this analogy is not so much about *benefits* but about truth. Whether our reality is about being a member of the royal family or the manifestation of an immortal Soul, it is about ignorance and awareness. If you are the lost child of the royal family living as a pauper, this hidden aspect of your identity is probably the most significant. Likewise, it is the most significant aspect of one who is a spiritual being having a physical experience, yet totally unaware of it. Just like going from being a pauper to becoming royalty, being ignorant of our spiritual nature and then becoming aware of it, is nothing less than a *Road to Damascus* epiphany.

This is not an exaggeration. It has been said that humans who attain full awareness of their spiritual nature are so much more advanced than those who remain ignorant of it that they will eventually be recognized as a new species. Furthermore, when humanity collectively realizes its spiritual nature, we will exist in a new reality—one that is not dominated by our conflict psychology, unnecessary chaos and behavior that is an expression of self-interest.

Although every individual approaches the spiritual hypothesis differently, we all eventually arrive at the same place—the realization of our true and everlasting spiritual nature. Of course, the vast majority of us do not arrive anywhere near this sacred destination, as most of us never take the journey that leads to it. Why? Because it is not even an item on our to-do list. It has no urgency or immediacy, and has no perceived benefit attached. On the surface, it does not appear to be useful information with a practical application to our already overextended material lives.

For many, spiritual knowledge is useless in the material world. What power, wealth or pleasure does it bring? We typically think that the time we would spend making sense of ancient mysteries could, and should, be put to better use. In our materialistic culture, *better use* is most often associated with the pursuit of worldly success, status, pleasure and material gain. This is not to say that such goals are immoral or wrong, rather to say that they should not be considered the exclusive focus of our attention. Moreover, they can become harmful if their pursuit becomes fixated and obsessive, especially at the cost of our spiritual curiosity and awareness. This point was immortalized by one of humanity's greatest spiritual geniuses when Jesus asked the ultimate question concerning worldly versus spiritual treasures, as recorded in the Gospel of Matthew (16:26) and Mark (8:36): *What good is it for someone to gain the whole world, yet forfeit their Soul?*

From the spiritual perspective, the measure of our lives is not based on what we *obtained* in life, but what we *became*. This is not to say that a person is wrong to obtain a successful worldly life. It is to say that if the process of gaining material success caused us to forfeit our intellectual and spiritual development—we missed the mark.

Often the knowledge associated with practical applications, which are germane to our pursuit of power and pleasure, has priority over knowledge rooted in philosophic and spiritual development. Although cultivating one's intellectual and spiritual acuity may not initially appear to have great relevance to one's immediate physical needs, their insights and perceptions often hold the key to our destiny.

Some time ago, this salient point was emphasized in an essay published in the October, 1939 issue of Harper's Magazine. The essay, "The Usefulness of Useless Knowledge" was written by Abraham Flexner (1866-1959), the founding director of the Institute for Advanced Study (IAS) in Princeton, New Jersey. The IAS brought together many of the greatest minds throughout the world to collaborate on intellectual discoveries and research, including Albert Einstein, Julius Oppenheimer, Hermann Weyl, Kurt Gödel, John von Neumann and others. Flexner's guiding principle as founder of the Institute is *knowledge for the sake of knowledge*. This guiding principle is an echo of the ancient mystics who asserted *spirituality for the sake of spirituality*—i.e., no personal agenda.

According to Dutch theoretical physicist and IAS Director, Professor Robbert Dijkgraaf, the unforeseen usefulness of the *useless* knowledge being explored at the Institute, came faster than expected. It became clear to Dijkgraaf that *Flexner unintentionally enabled the nuclear and digital revolutions*. In the midst of World War II, when the nuclear bomb program required large-scale numeric modeling, Professor John von Neumann put together a team of engineers at the Institute to begin designing, building and programing electronic digital computers. In 1946, Dr. von Neumann stated: *I am thinking about something much more important than bombs. I am thinking about computers.*

Like science, spirituality requires us to periodically disengage from the *angry current of daily life* (the practical application of useful knowledge in the incessant pursuit of material gain), to cultivate our spiritual perspective in order to recognize the underlying order and profound meaning of mundane life. This *stop and smell the roses* approach to life is nothing new; an ever-changing version of it is expressed by philosophers and poets of every generation.

If this is the case with regards to science, philosophy and academic studies, how much more so when it comes to the pursuit of spiritual knowledge? Spiritually speaking, curiosity is the initial awakening of our innate *need to know*. This is particularly true when it comes to curiosity regarding the meaning and purpose of our lives. Without question, the spiritualization process is initiated during the learning phase, i.e., gaining new knowledge that results in greater understanding, expanded awareness and enhanced perception.

From the material perspective, we certainly have the need to maintain our physical lives and perhaps even achieve some degree of comfort and enjoyment. However, should our pursuit of pleasure and power become the entirety of our life's purpose and the very basis of our identity, we will have sorely missed the point of a life that embraces both human desires and spiritual aspirations—flesh and spirit intertwined.

To be human is to live on two paths simultaneously—the path of material success and the path of spiritual development. Material achievement and success are essential aspects of our physical life. But, so too, are the aspects of impermanence, aging and death fundamental characteristics of physical life. In spite of our ability to ignore our impermanent nature during our youth, as we age, the veneer of our denial wears thin. Fortunately, these distinctive, perishable traits of our physical nature are mercifully counteracted by the contrasting features of our spiritual nature, which are undying and perpetual.

If this sounds a lot like immortality, that's precisely what it is. If the notion of being immortal is beyond your current experience, it is only because it is not recognized through your previous experience. Most of us only recognize and identify with the *little self*; we have yet to experience ourselves as the *Big Self*. Little "s" self and big "S" Self are references of the ancient Eastern traditions for the mortal self and the immortal Self. While exclusively living as the little self, we are utterly unaware of the big Self. Just as the caterpillar lives her life unaware of her future beauty, grace and soaring skills, we, too, are unaware of our future metamorphosis as spiritual beings having a physical life. Perhaps when the weary caterpillar enters her confining cocoon, she mistakes it for her coffin and thinks of it as death.

Although we may hide our inescapable fears from the forefront of our awareness, especially if we keep ourselves engrossed and busy, they still remain unchallenged in the deeper recesses of our mind. These fundamental fears of mortal man wait patiently for that unguarded moment or the hidden trigger that opens the floodgates for them to burst forth. Or, as is the case for most of us, the slow water torture of aging loosens the restraints that have held these fears of mortal impermanence in check.

It may be comforting to know that the deeper questions of our existence have been embedded in our consciousness (factory installed on our hard drives) to guide us toward the meaning and purpose of our lives. And they are far too integral and imperative to remain unnoticed throughout the span of our days. In fact, it is the unchecked, curious mind, often led by its own fears, that ultimately cracks the sacred mystery. The source of such questions is, indeed, the source of their answers. But this source is not accessible without first entering the mystical domain of the Soul.

Until we are in direct communication with the Soul, we are dependent on the mind (under the influence of the brain) as our interpreter. Unfortunately, the brain's interpretations of the spiritual are erratic and unreliable, as it is often preoccupied and tainted by its obsession with all things physical—distracted while in hot pursuit of power and pleasure. Any exertion of the brain toward gaining knowledge that will not advance its quest for success and status, power and pleasure, is rendered useless. And yet, as Flexner asserted, some of the world's greatest advances and achievements have been born out of *useless knowledge.*

When the Soul no longer requires an interpreter to communicate to the mind, we have arrived at a pivotal moment in spiritual awakening. Such a moment lifts us into a new reality; one that feeds our curiosity while wiping away our tears and fears. According to the great spiritual teachers, the eternal Soul has access to far greater knowledge than is stored in the insufficient memory bank of the brain or the limited range of the mortal mind's comprehension. Needless to say, the Soul's endless stream of knowledge is untainted by the demands of the mind's fixation on pleasure and power as well as the influence of the brain's previous conditioning and personal biases and beliefs.

For many novice Soul seekers, the initial venture into the spiritualization process simply involves making time for the habitual thought process to be put on hold while creating the space for brand new insights to emerge.

What is this habitual thought process needing to be put on hold? It is nothing more than the brain and mind grinding away incessantly in an attempt to conceptualize every new moment of *now*. In a manner of speaking, the brain and mind are *telling* each new moment what it is. After conceptualizing the moment, this enterprise of the brain and mind attempts to determine the meaning of that moment and whether it is a support or a threat to their current agenda. The spiritualization process begins by stopping this unremitting cerebral chatter long enough for reality to reveal itself as it truly is, without self-imposed standards and cognitive biases. While the mind is driven by pleasure and power, the spirit distinguishes between the sacred and the profane. From the spiritual perspective, the mind is considered to be in ill-health when it exclusively views the world in material form and accepts the profane as its provider of pleasure and power.

Beyond the habitual thought patterns of the mind and the previous conditioning of the brain, our own values, perception and behavior are heavily influenced by the *worldview* into which we were born. This worldview is the lens through which the world is viewed by the collective generations of our time. For the greater part of human history, the worldview was characterized as a *Religious Spiritual Worldview*. Beginning with the Scientific Revolution of the 16th Century, the worldview began to shift, leaning toward the discoveries of science and the theories of Copernicus, Galileo, Newton, Kepler, Descartes and others. During this time, science emerged with developments in mathematics, physics, astronomy, biology, human anatomy and chemistry.

This launched the beginning of the *Scientific Materialistic Worldview*. While the earlier worldview was rooted in religion, driven by faith and superstition (founded on the model whereby God is the ultimate authority), the latter worldview was based on reason as the primary source of authority and legitimacy (rooted in science), which came to play a leading role in the Age of Enlightenment. In turn, the Enlightenment movement allowed scientists to pursue their work and method without interference from church or state.

Nobody could have predicted what followed. In his landmark book, *The Structure of Scientific Revolutions*, Thomas S. Kuhn (1922-1996), considered one of the most influential 20th century philosophers of science, states that what started showing up were anomalies that could not be explained by classical Newtonian mechanics—the gold standard in physics since the 17th century. These anomalies began a revolution in scientific thought, leaning toward an entirely new way of understanding and viewing our physical reality. According to Professor Amit Goswami, theoretical nuclear physicist and author of *The Self-Aware Universe*, in this new philosophy, it is consciousness, not matter that is fundamental. Dr. Goswami states: *Both the world of matter and the world of mental phenomena, such as thought, are determined by consciousness.... Thus, consciousness is the only ultimate reality.*

Professor Goswami uses Plato's *Allegory of the Cave* (*The Republic, Book VII*), written 2,400 years ago, to describe our inability to see beyond *apparent* reality in order to realize *ultimate* reality, which encapsulates the basic premise of this book. Here, Plato imagines a group of prisoners held captive since birth, in an underground cave. They're chained in a manner in which they are unable to move, only able to look straight ahead at the cave wall. Behind the prisoners, burns a fire projecting shadows on the wall before them. Prison guards occasionally hold up objects and puppets in front of the fire's bright light to manipulate those shadows. Because those shadows are all the prisoners have seen since birth, they believe that this is all life has to offer. Consequently, the guards control the prisoner's perception of reality—day after day, year after year.

One day a prisoner managed to break free of his chains, stand up and move about. This was the first time a prisoner had seen the fire burning behind them and the objects casting the shadows. He realized that the shadows were being cast by the objects projecting them, rather than the shadows being the true reality. Walking about the cave, the newly freed prisoner eventually discovers its opening. He walks out into the daylight to experience the world for the first time.

He discovers that this outer world is the greater reality as opposed to the shadows seen on the cave wall. Clearly, there is so much more to life than he previously perceived. At that moment, he remembers his fellow prisoners still chained in the cave. He pities them for they are lost in ignorance of the greater reality he now perceives. The unbound prisoner decided to return to the cave in order to enlighten his friends of the greater reality beyond the cave. But because he challenged the only reality they knew, the prisoners were unable to understand or trust what he was saying. Eventually, they became angry and threatened to kill anyone else who would dare to leave the cave.

Here Plato suggests that we are basing our perception of reality on what we see and hear, not really knowing the greater truth. This perceived reality may be nothing more than the shadows of a greater reality we have yet to discover. In this allegory, the prisoner who escaped and discovered the greater reality beyond the cave is representative of the philosopher—the spiritual seeker of truth beyond what is physical and apparent. But when the prisoner returns to the cave to bestow greater awareness to the others, he is mocked and ridiculed by those who have no knowledge of this greater truth.

In keeping with the allegory of the cave, Plato demonstrates that like the prisoners, we, too, are kept in a state of *perpetual ignorance*, unaware of any reality existing beyond what is taking place before us and perceived by our eyes, ears and other senses. Also, like the prisoners, we are oblivious to our own ignorance. And, as such, we resist any notion that points out the deficiencies of our current awareness and the limitations of our current knowledge, especially philosophic or spiritual ideas that challenge our perception of reality. Are we to become seekers of truth or creatures of habit? A question that is fundamental to the purpose of this book.

This book is for those who have pondered and asked the big questions: *What does it all mean? What happens when we die? What is the purpose of our existence? And, what is the pathway to fulfilling this purpose?* These are the age-old questions that cannot be answered *for* us; however, the answers can be discovered and realized *by* us.

The path to spiritual awakening and Self-realization has gone by many names throughout history. In this book, it is referred to as the **spiritualization process**. In simple terms, this means *to purify and separate our spiritual perception from the corrupting influences of the physical world.* Initially, this process is a mental exercise that eventually leads to the direct personal experience of our spiritual nature—i.e., spiritual awakening and Self-realization.

In the following pages, are compiled the insights and teachings of some of the greatest spiritual teachers in human history. Some of these teachings are mystical, some philosophical, some are scientific and some are right out of contemporary pop culture. Often these teachers are quoted directly for authenticity, while some teachings are contemporized for better communication and understanding. All of the teachings are meant to lead the reader to their own ultimate, spiritual teacher—that which abides within their own human heart.

In many ways, the spiritualization process is analogous to a jigsaw puzzle, where each new spiritual tenet, idea and principle is a piece to that puzzle. The big picture, hidden within the small pieces, begins to take form and the great mystery is gradually revealed. And, like a puzzle, each new spiritual piece we add provides for the next piece. The fundamental spiritual hypothesis provides the straight edge, border pieces of the puzzle—namely, man and woman are more spirit than flesh.

All of the other spiritual tenets referred to in the pages

ahead, relate back to this essential, underlying premise that all humans are more spiritual than physical. To validate this primary spiritual theory for ourselves is the ultimate objective of the spiritualization process. Moreover, we must approach it with an open mind and a willing heart. The key is to reserve any conclusions of true or false and, instead, focus entirely on understanding. After all, a person who interprets and passes judgement prior to achieving understanding on any issue is, by definition, careless and foolish.

Thus, spiritualization is the process toward spiritual awakening, Self-realization and Enlightenment. The Buddha referred to this as *seeing things as they really are*. It has always been a prevalent blunder to attempt to understand the spiritual while viewing it through the physical lens of the material world. Such a common, yet imprudent mistake is tantamount to performing open-heart surgery wearing kaleidoscope glasses. Even though our perception is designed to recognize and ultimately realize the spiritual, it is distracted and tainted by our human need to see things as we *want* or *believe* them to be. This distraction by, and obsession with, the physical is the most challenging obstacle preventing us from exploring and experiencing our true spiritual nature.

For centuries, the physical lens of mankind has been rooted in the scientific worldview, whereas the spiritual lens has been rooted in the religious worldview, often demeaned and considered to be superstition. With the advent of the 20th century, science entered a new field of reality found at the quantum level. Here, science was able to see how atoms work, along with the fundamental workings of chemistry and biology. Science entered the subatomic level of reality and encountered what Einstein called *spukhafte fernwirkung* (spooky stuff). Spooky because the quantum level did not behave in accordance with the laws of classical physics where time, space and matter are fundamental.

Nobel Prize laureate, Max Planck, laid the foundation for quantum theory by his discovery of *energy quanta*. He changed physics and our understanding of the world, declaring:

> *There is no matter as such. All matter originates and exists only by virtue of a force which brings the particle of an atom to vibration and holds this most minute solar system of the atom together. We must assume behind this force the existence of a conscious and intelligent mind.* **This mind is the matrix of all matter.**

In a manner of speaking, what's being said here is that *universal* mind exists beyond the individual mind of man and woman. Furthermore, this universal mind is *thinking things into being.* And *we* are, in fact, an example of those things that have been thought into being. However, unlike the minerals, plants and lower animals, we humans are equipped with our own version of universal mind—that is, individual mind. Through the fully equipped human mind, we are endowed with similar creative powers to universal mind. Unfortunately, this highly complex system of human technology did not come with an owner's manual. Without proper guidance, we are left to fend for ourselves.

Once brought into being, we are given the power and free will to weave the tapestry of our lives. With or without our consent, our mind is manifesting our lives. All too often, our minds operate randomly and without proper discipline or supervision. In fact, the minds of most of us are governed almost exclusively by our brain's egoistic need to be right while making others wrong and our incessant craving for pleasure and power. These underlying forces are the inherent instincts born into our species. The earliest ancient scriptures caution us to train and discipline the mind or it will turn against us.

One such treatise is the sacred scripture in Hinduism, the *Bhagavad Gita*. Dating back to around the fifth to the second century BCE, *Bhagavad Gita* translates as the *Song of God*. It is described as God providing mankind with advice and guidance. Chapter 6, Verse 6, provides a profound insight into the *care and feeding* of the mind: *For one who has conquered the mind, the mind is the best of friends; but for one who has failed to do so, his very mind will be the greatest enemy.* The ancient Vedic philosophy (the original spiritual knowledge of India) emphasizes the ramifications of our thoughts. Whether we are considering our health, prosperity, relationships, or any aspect of our lives, what we harbor in the mind, manifests in our world. It is within the confines of our own mind that life's battles are won or lost. Furthermore, it is within the collective mind (consciousness) of humanity that our world's destiny is determined.

Interestingly, the challenges that lie ahead for those who seek higher consciousness and greater spiritual awareness coincide with the very same challenges that determine the future of humanity. In the early summer of 1983, at Brockwood Park in southern England, a series of now celebrated conversations took place between J. Krishnamurti (widely regarded as one of the greatest spiritual teachers of our time) and David Bohm (considered one of the most significant theoretical physicists of the 20th century) to discuss our collective future. The starting point of these discussions was the question: *What is the future of humanity?* Later Dr. Bohm recalls:

> *This question is by now of vital concern to every-one, because modern science and technology are clearly seen to have opened up immense possibili-ties of destruction. It soon became clear as we talked together that the ultimate origin of this situation is in the generally confused mentality of mankind, which has not changed basically in this respect throughout the whole of recorded history and probably for much longer than this. Evidently, it was essential to inquire deeply into the root of this difficulty if there is ever to be a possibility that humanity will be diverted from its present very dangerous course.*

Krishnamurti questioned the adequacy of humanity's knowledge and thoughts as a means of dealing with its prob-lems. Or whether, for that matter, our *own* personal knowl-edge and intelligence is up to the task of dealing with the issues of our *own* future. This question of our future, both individual and collective, led to yet another question of whether the mind is tethered to the limitations of the brain and the collective brain of mankind with its age-old accumulated knowledge and conditioning. After all, explains Krishnamurti, it is this same accumulated knowledge that has produced this *"irrational and self-destructive programme in which the brain seems to be helplessly caught up."* He went on to say that he does not regard the limitations of the brain's knowledge and its inherent conditioning to be inevitable limitations of the mind. Rather, he emphasized that the mind can essentially be free of the distorting biases and conditioning of the brain. Furthermore, with insight, arising through proper attention, the mind can change the cells of the brain and remove the destructive conditioning. Here, Krishnamurti's theory is supported within the words of modern science spoken by Dr. Bohm:

> *At this point, it is worth remarking that modern research into the brain and nervous system actually gives considerable support to Krishnamurti's statement that insight may change the brain cells. Thus, for example, it is now well known that there are important substances in the body, the hormones and the neurotransmitters, that fundamentally affect the entire functioning of the brain and nervous system. These substances respond from moment to moment, to what a person knows, to what he thinks, and to what all this means to him. It is by now fairly well established that in this way the brain cells and their functioning are profoundly affected by knowledge and thoughts, especially when these give rise to strong feelings and passions. It is thus quite plausible that insight, which must arise in a state of great mental energy and passion, could change the brain cells in an even more profound way.*

Clearly, as we consider the future of humanity, we must face the question of whether we can get past the *irrational and self-destructive programme in which the brain seems to be helplessly caught up*. Thus, it is not a question of new technology or greater resources needing to be developed, but, rather, liberation from the brain's previous conditioning, thereby, initiating a transformation in consciousness—both individual and collective.

Ironically, when Max Planck asserts that *consciousness is fundamental and that matter is a derivative of consciousness*, this notion of underlying consciousness being the source of all that exists has an uncanny resemblance to the teachings of ancient mystics who proclaim: *To think is to create*. In fact, this parallel is so apparent that currently an entire genre of books has been written on this very topic.

One of the earlier books exploring this parallel of physics and mystics is the 1975 bestseller, *The Tao of Physics*, written by physicist Fritjof Capra. This study into the parallels between modern physics and ancient Eastern mysticism has been published in 43 editions and 23 languages. There has been so much attention and study on this topic that we now find ourselves moving toward the unprecedented territory of the **Scientific Spiritual Worldview**. It appears that quantum theory has brought together the strange bedfellows of modern physics and ancient mystics—although now the teachings of the mystics are not based solely on intuition and superstition, but also on the sound foundation of scientific methods and precise experimentation. In the words of Dr. Fritjof Capra:

If physics leads us today to a world view which is essentially mystical, it returns, in a way, to its beginning, 2,500 years ago.... This time, however, it is not only based on intuition, but also on experiments of great precision and sophistication, and on a rigorous and consistent mathematical formalism.

The book you're now reading is a compilation of a vast and historic selection of spiritual, philosophic and scientific teachings, contemporized and personalized into a comprehensive narrative designed to bring the reader to his or her own direct spiritual experience. This direct personal and mystical experience, often referred to as Self-realization or spiritual epiphany, ultimately provides us with irrefutable evidence of our true nature as *spiritual beings having a physical experience.*

This single experience will be perceived as the culmination of all experiences and the answer to those haunting questions pondered by all advanced thinkers: *What is the meaning and purpose of my life, and how may I fulfill it?* This pivotal moment of clarity is so profound that many religions refer to it as *being born again.* It cannot, however, be taught or learned; rather we must experience it for ourselves in order to decide for ourselves. Bear in mind, it is not through intellectual knowledge but through experiential awareness that the spiritual becomes known. Although learning and gathering knowledge may initiate the process and point the direction, it is through insight, intuition and raw emotion that the spiritual dimension is entered. As the age-old proverb states: *The proof of the pudding is in the eating.*

Like the great Saints and Sages of religion (such as Jesus in Luke: 17:21) asserted many centuries ago—the spiritual realm is not found in a different place or in a different time, rather it is here and now, albeit in a concealed dimension. It is not easy to grasp the notion of another dimension, let alone experience it; yet, once realized it will never be forgotten.

Just as the education of the mind cultivated the psychological dimension of mankind, lifting humanity from caves to skyscrapers, from sharpened stones to guided missiles, from drawings on cave walls to hand-held devices that send live streaming images around the world in the blink of an eye, the realizations of the mind will usher in the spiritual dimension. It is the mind that will form the bridge to the Soul in the same way that the mind has been the source of achievement in our physical life.

The renowned 19ᵗʰ century philosopher, psychologist and Father of American psychology, William James, went so far as to say: *The greatest revolution of our generation is the discovery that human beings, by changing the inner attitudes of their minds, can change the outer aspects of their lives.* We have now benefited from over a century of discoveries regarding the science of mind.

Today, the idea whose time has come (and has been coming for some time) explores the transcendental nature of human consciousness. Particularly, its hierarchy and progression. Furthermore, the higher our consciousness rises, the greater our perception of reality becomes; and, the greater our awareness and perception of reality become, so too, the better our experience of reality becomes. In short, it is within our human capacity to alter and enhance the reality in which we exist. This central spiritual tenet is endorsed and taught by many of the great philosophers as well as religious and spiritual scriptures. For example, it is a fundamental teaching found in the Book of Proverbs, chapter 23, verse 7: *As a man thinketh in his heart, so is he.*

The progression of our *knowing* and *being* is controlled by our *free will* through which we determine the focus our mind's concentration and our heart's passion. From the spiritual standpoint, there is no more important an object of the mind's focus and concentration than that of the Soul. When the mind takes on the quest to discover the Soul, it has begun the process of spiritualization; when the mind makes contact with the Soul, it has arrived at Self-realization.

Take into consideration the most significant of the spiritual tenets, and the epiphany on which this book is based:

*to be human is to be both flesh and spirit, matter and con-
sciousness, body and Soul.* Correspondingly, this is the mission of all self-evolving creatures—to raise our awareness and
perception high enough to recognize our true nature as a living Soul in human form. As stated in a variety of ways and by
numerous teachers, this is not a truth that can be learned or
taught; it is a truth that is experienced in that pivotal moment
when the mind makes contact with the Soul.

However, before the mind can make contact with the Soul,
it must first make contact with (and distinguish itself from)
the brain. The importance of this initial connection is to facilitate the mind in gaining liberation from the brain's previous
conditioning, biases and beliefs. In other words, the mind
must become opened to what it is about to encounter without
the obstacle of the brain's preconceived notions and previous
conditioning. As long as the mind is perceived as a function
of the brain, it remains limited by the current content of the
brain. Spiritual awakening, transcendental consciousness
and Self-realization are experiences yet to be experienced for
most. Therefore, we must open to the possibility of entering
uncharted territory—entering the spiritual dimension while
at the same time maintaining our presence in the physical.

When the mind is untethered and open to all possibilities, and the heart is eager and yearning, we are poised for a
quantum leap into greater understanding. The teachings of
the great spiritual geniuses, Saints and Sages, Masters and
Prophets of previous days, revealed a key piece of the mystical puzzle: *we are not only two-dimensional (physical and
mental), rather we are, indeed, three-dimensional (physical, psychological and spiritual) creatures.* The time has
now come for us to recognize and cultivate the powers of the
third aspect—our spiritual nature. Recognition of the spiri-

tual dimension is so new and novel that there are no words available to describe it; hence, we must borrow from the language of religion, which has been all over this topic since day one—literally.

Today, our minds are totally aware of their relationship with the physical (i.e., brain), yet, completely unaware of their connection to the spiritual (i.e., Soul). This is certainly understandable, since the entirety of our focus and concentration is on our physical life playing out in the material world. Given that the physical obscures the spiritual, it is no wonder that we are obscured from perceiving the spiritual, let alone experiencing it. According to one of the leading theologians and philosophers of the 20th century, Professor Abraham J. Heschel, we are enamored by the *stuff* of our physical lives and the *things* of the material world:

We are all infatuated with the splendor of space, with the grandeur of things of space. Thing is a category that lies heavy on our minds, tyrannizing all our thoughts. Our imagination tends to mold all concepts in its image. In our daily lives we attend primarily to that which the senses are spelling out for us: to what the eyes perceive, to what the fingers touch. Reality to us is thinghood, consisting of substances that occupy space; even God is conceived of us as a thing. The result of our thinginess is our blindness to all reality that fails to identify itself as a thing... —Abraham J. Heschel

This is not to suggest that *things* are wrong and that we must escape the *thinghood reality* in which we find ourselves. Such a far-reaching withdrawal from the physical would not only be counterproductive, it sounds a lot like death. This is not about separation and elimination, rather it is about amalgamation. It is not that one way is right and the other is wrong. When we draw a bath, is the hot or cold water right and the other wrong? We arrive at perfection by combining both. So, too, it is with the spiritual and physical—we arrive at perfection by combining both. Although often imagined as a battle, the union of flesh and spirit is more like a dance of two strong-willed lovers—not conflict, but art—the *art of being*, as the Maharishi defines it.

Even though the Soul is more vast and powerful, it cannot initiate the relationship with the mind or impose its will into the physical world. Such an act would nullify our inalienable human right to free will. Like all that is spiritual, the Soul must remain in concealment until the mind, of its own free will, chooses and develops the path toward spiritual awakening.

Just as the laws of nature govern the phenomena of the physical world, the spiritual domain has its own fundamental principles to which we must adhere. Perhaps one of the most significant and overarching of these principles is also one of the most challenging: ***We cannot see the spiritual while looking through our physical lens***. Those who view reality exclusively through the physical lens make the classic spiritual mistake of looking at a two-sided coin and seeing only one side.

Remember, our physical lens is generated by the five physical senses and the brain's biased interpretations of the data they send. Through the physical lens, we see only that which is here and now, in present time. Even with support from the brain's memories, our recollections of the past and imaginings of the future are faulty at best. According to the findings of modern neuroscience (discussed further in the chapters ahead), the majority of our memories of the past, our conjectures of the future and our interpretations of what is going down in real time are seldom precise and more often utterly wrong. Even though our brain is highly analytical, the thought process is under the influence of previous conditioning, personal biases and the egoistic agenda of our self-serving nature. On the other hand, the spiritual lens is detached, impartial and has *Big Picture* vision. It sees the connection and continuity of past, present and future as well as insights and understanding, motives and consequences.

Because the spiritual is concealed from the physical, we encounter the first big challenge faced by all spiritual seekers, namely, cultivating the spiritual lens. *How is this accomplished?* In simple terms, we cultivate the spiritual lens by becoming less physical (egocentric) and more spiritual (altruistic), i.e., spiritualization. We must gain more spiritual knowledge in order to know more so that we may understand more and eventually realize and experience the spiritual for ourselves.

Key to progressing along the spiritualization process, is to reserve any form of conceptualization, interpretation or judgment until we have first attained sound understanding. This type of profound spiritual understanding naturally follows direct personal experience. Without achieving direct experience, our thinking and judgments will be the product of our current beliefs and previous experience, both falling short when dealing with all that is unprecedented and unparalleled.

Too often, we impose judgement on a situation, idea or object based upon our first encounter with it—long before we know what it actually is or have any true understanding of what it means. This is foolish enough when applied to the material world; it is an immediate disqualifier in spiritual terms. We are not required to accept unworldly spiritual theories blindly; we are, however, required to recognize that the problem might be the fallibility of our understanding rather than the validity of the theory.

Like a piece to a jigsaw puzzle, each spiritual tenet reveals its own portion of the big picture. If the tenet facilitates our *seeing* more of the big picture, it is valid; it did its job. The Buddha taught that all teachings and beliefs are like rafts helping us navigate the turbulent waters of obliviousness toward the distant shores of Enlightenment. Therefore, embrace all spiritual tenets without prejudice: study them, learn their stories, discover their deeper meaning and search out their hidden potency. Make a special space in your mind to store these tenets as you carry them with you throughout your day. Give these spiritual tenets vitality, significance, prominence and preeminence until the mind is blessed with *spiritual vision* and the heart is sanctified by *sensations of expanded awareness.*

Even though a grand moment of spiritual epiphany may seem as if it comes out of the blue, this is rarely the case. The mystical experience in question is the crescendo of a gradual, lengthy course of pondering, calculating and discovery. Truth ascends gradually and follows a carefully designed process. It alters and enhances the very reality in which we live. Many of the great philosophical and spiritual teachers emphasize this point: **We live in the reality we perceive**. This is the teaching of Plato's Allegory of the Cave—our perception of reality has a significant impact on how we experience reality. For the most part, our perception is under the influence of our senses and the brain's previous conditioning.

However, even beyond the sensitivity of our senses, reality is perceived subjectively through the brain's interpretation of all that it encounters. In this way, our perception is always changing. Furthermore, the brain has no *sensory* perception of the spiritual, as the spiritual has no object to be seen, heard, smelled or touched. In order for the mind to gain perception of the spiritual, it must expand its awareness of the spiritual. The expanded awareness is the result of greater understanding, which comes from increased learning of both spiritual and self-knowledge. This is the spiritualization process explored in the chapters ahead—learn more in order to understand more, thus expanding our awareness and enhancing our perception of the spiritual. Like the prince or princess living as a pauper, the most significant aspect of who we are is yet unknown to us.

Of course, in the ancient mystical traditions of the East, this is known as the practice of raising our consciousness. This rather complex idea is explored in great detail in the chapters ahead. For now, I will attempt a brief paraphrased and contemporized explanation of the 7 Levels of Consciousness rooted in the Yoga Sutras, written by Yoga Master Patanjali around 400 BC. In the words of Patanjali: *When you are inspired by some great purpose, some extraordinary project, all your thoughts break their bonds; your mind transcends limitations; your consciousness expands in every direction; and you find yourself in a great, new and wonderful world. Dormant forces, faculties and talents become alive, and you discover yourself to be a greater person by far than you ever dreamed yourself to be.*

First, let's consider the indefinable term consciousness. The dictionary says that consciousness is awareness. But then we must define awareness. Neither term can easily be defined in spiritual terms, especially considering they both are deeply rooted in another indefinable term—God. For our purposes, in this illustration, let's think of consciousness as a form of perception; the higher our consciousness, the more we are able to perceive things as they really are. This holds true if we think of consciousness as awareness also. The greater our awareness, the more we are able to perceive. Let's now explore the Seven Levels of Consciousness.

All of humanity, for all of our mortal lives, exists on the lower three levels of consciousness. At the lowest level, where both body (the five senses) and mind (thoughts and emotions) are inactive (i.e., sleep), there is no perception—we are unable to observe anything (internal or external). At the next level, the body remains inactive, however the mind becomes active (i.e., dream). At the third level of consciousness, both body and mind are active (i.e., awake). All human life, whoever we are, exists within these three levels of consciousness—sleep, dream and awake. Whether we are Ted Bundy or Mother Teresa, we continually move from level one to level three and back again. We are not required to evolve and elevate our consciousness to navigate our way through the first three levels of consciousness.

Over two thousand years ago, Patanjali (and earlier than that, the Buddha and the Bhagavad Gita) spoke of higher levels of consciousness where a person becomes aware of the Greater Reality that is imperceptible at the lower levels. The first of these high levels of consciousness is the Fourth Level: Transcendental Consciousness. Some say that the mind transcends the limitations of the brain at this level. This typically comes from the experience of the mind "observing" the person and the person's life from a higher vantage. At the Transcendental Level the mind becomes the observer, NOT the observed.

At this level of consciousness, the quality of observation is heightened; we are not perceiving through the lens of the senses (physical seeing, hearing, smelling, etc.), rather we are perceiving through the lens of "knowing." In a manner of speaking, we are not "seeing" the way things really are, we are "knowing" the way they are. And, along with this greater awareness and perception, the mind comes to recognize that it is not the highest authority on the topic of True Reality (i.e., the way things really are). It recognizes this truth as it comes to recognize that it is in the presence of a higher authority.

The mind is not intimidated by this higher authority because it also recognizes the bond it has with it—undying love—mutual love. Unlike human love, this love hasn't even a hint of vulnerability. It is a love that grows based only on the mind's capacity to receive it. Furthermore, the mind increases its capacity to receive this spiritual love as the heart begins pouring out its own love in return. With each cycle of *pouring out* and *receiving back* this growing love, the mind expands its knowing into the Realization that it is both giver and receiver. In fact, the mind realizes that it is loving and being loved by the Soul.

At this moment, the mind has entered the Fifth Level of Consciousness: Self-realization or Cosmic Consciousness. The mind and the Soul are One. But there is more... the Soul and God are One. With this realization, we have entered the Sixth Level: God Consciousness. But there is still more... If I am One with the Soul, and the Soul is One with God... Yep, there it is... staring us right in the face. The Ultimate Realization: God, the Soul and I are One. Here we find ourselves at the Seventh Level of Consciousness: Unity Consciousness (i.e., Oneness). In the words of Jesus: *The Father and I are One; and you and I are One.*

For those who have difficulty with the religious tone and language of the ancient teachings of the Eastern tradition regarding the raising of consciousness, the same points can be made outside the context of religion. Theoretical physicist and Nobel Prize laureate, Max Planck, used the term *Universal Mind* to describe the consciousness that is the source of our physical world: *I regard consciousness as fundamental. I regard matter as derivative from consciousness. We cannot get behind consciousness. Everything that we talk about, everything that we regard as existing, postulates consciousness.* Planck continues: *All matter originates and exists only by virtue of a force which brings the particle of an atom to vibration and holds this most minute solar system of the atom together. We must assume behind this force the existence of a conscious and intelligent mind.* **This mind is the matrix of all matter.**

We humans have our own individual minds or consciousness that is heavily influenced by the previous conditioning and content of the brain. Unlike the brain, our mind is not organic—not made of matter. Our mind has the ability to operate independent of the brain in order to form a bridge with universal mind (i.e., pure consciousness). This is a highly illuminating and enlightening experience that raises our consciousness, expands our awareness and enhances our perception.

The objective of the spiritualization process, and that of all spiritual seekers, is to reach the fourth level of consciousness—**Transcendental Consciousness.** Here, we are able to perceive beyond the physical structure of life and attain our first glimpse into the spiritual. Once we have reached this coveted and blessed state of awareness, the mind is poised to gain entry into the higher three echelons of consciousness.

Our great challenge is to rise above the mundane and highly restrictive awareness found on the lower three levels. At the transcendental level, we are granted a personal escort to guide our steps on the path toward Enlightenment—the Soul. Until we reach the transcendental level of consciousness (of our own effort and free will) all that is spiritual is kept behind the veil of concealment.

This elevation of consciousness is not possible as long as we cling to the notion of physical exclusivity. As stated previously, we are not required to accept the existence of the spiritual structure, we are simply required to accept its possibility. Without this open-mindedness, all spiritual learning will be shrouded in doubt. In the words of American attorney, author, mystic and pioneer of the New Thought movement, Yogi Ramacharaka (aka William Walker Atkinson): *One must eradicate from the mind the idea that physical life is everything. Such an idea prevents one from recognizing the fuller life of the Soul, and makes this particular life in the body the whole thing, instead of merely a grain of sand on the shores of the everlasting seas. One must grow to feel that he will always be alive, whether he is in the body or out of it, and that this particular physical 'life' is merely a thing to be used by the Real Self, which cannot die.*

After we have realized our spiritual nature and it becomes the new normal, life becomes an expression of spirit dwelling within flesh. Herein lies the next phase of human evolution: the human expression of its indwelling Soul, as opposed to the human expression of its self-serving ego. This single shift from *taker mentality* to *giver mentality* is the necessary component for human redemption and humanity's salvation. For the one having this epiphany, it comes with a new identity—that of *a spiritual being having a physical experience.*

Summary of Part One: Historic Development of the Spiritual Hypothesis

Part One explores the evolution of humanity's collective consciousness and the form that it manifests. Whether characterized as a reflection of harmony, intellectual development and peace, or hostility, ignorance and violence, it is the outward expression of our world's collective consciousness (both current and past). This exploration pays particular attention to one vital aspect of our collective consciousness—it tracks the history of the spiritual hypothesis: *to be human is to be both spirit and flesh, immortal and mortal, Soul and body.* Although the information provided in these first six chapters is relevant, the primary purpose is to familiarize the reader with the spiritual hypothesis in order to prepare for the spiritual experience.

CHAPTER ONE: *The Epiphany*
Chapter One deals directly with the epiphany referred to in the title of this book. The spiritual hypothesis simply states: ***to be human is to be more spirit than flesh—more Soul than body, more immortal than mortal***. This is the basic truth of the human condition; we are spiritual beings embedded in a physical creature. Eventually we must all decide for ourselves where we stand on this ancient hypothesis. Even though we are all challenged by this spiritual truth, for most, it remains unexplored and, thus, unresolved.

The experience of this truth is nowhere to be found on the physical dimension. We must enter the spiritual realm to discover its whereabouts. Experience is the language of the spiritual the way math is the language of science. Our task is not to *find* the spiritual realm, our task is to *recognize* it, as it is already present—although masterfully concealed, the spiritual dimension has been here all along.

We begin by exploring the spiritual epiphany through the ancient teachings of the Hindu scriptures, the Buddha's Sutras, the mystical traditions of the Abrahamic religions and the sacred words of Saints and Sages, which all point toward a separate reality that remains hidden until we gain access to higher levels of awareness and perception.

The early teachings of *The Science of Mind* established the mind as the gateway to the Soul, paving the way for the birth of human psychology. Additionally, Chapter One introduces the astonishing parallel emerging between the teachings of ancient mystics and the discoveries of modern physics.

Because the spiritual dimension is beyond sensory perception, we become aware of its presence through direct personal experience. This is the topic and purpose of this book: To learn and engage the *spiritualization process* in order to achieve the *spiritual experience.*

CHAPTER TWO: *Is Spirituality the New Religion?*
In this chapter, we separate the subtle and novel occurrence of spirituality from the well-known and highly recognized institution of religion. This separation is for illustrative purposes in order to gain an unbiased view of *unchurched spirituality* (the underlying topic of this book), without the additional distraction and confusion brought by the multifarious agendas of religious packaging.

Spirituality has always been the essence of religion. Religion is the container in which spirituality has been kept. Religion is the outward expression of the inward spiritual essence. Religion is also the historic path that spirituality has taken in our world—its events and stories; its heroes and its villains. Spirituality is far more intricate and obscure than religion—far more difficult to identify, describe, or detect. Whereas spirituality is most often a private affair reflecting personal experience, religion is far more public—a congregation of people adhering to shared denominational doctrines while participating in communal rituals.

According to the teachings of numerous Prophets, Saints and Sages, the interest and pursuit of religion is, and has always been, about attaining the *sacred spiritual experience*—i.e., experiencing the spiritual while existing on the physical plane. The *sacred experience* is the primary focus of this book—*what it is* and *how to have it*. In the chapters ahead, you will come to realize that the only true way to know what the spiritual experience is, is to have it for yourself. Furthermore, once you have it, you will sense that it has been with you all along. Hence, the issue is not about making the spiritual experience happen, the task at hand is to recognize its inexhaustible presence.

CHAPTER THREE: *The Influence of our Modern World-view on Spirituality*
This chapter explores the impact that the current, collective worldview is having on our ability to realize our own true spiritual nature. Since the sixteenth century, the *scientific materialist worldview* has dominated our species' understanding and perception of reality. For centuries, humanity has moved toward viewing reality from a materialistic understanding, thereby maintaining a materialistic perception and an exclusively physical experience of reality. This became the fundamental cognitive orientation of society. Furthermore, it is the worldview that most of us entered at our time of birth.

In the words of renowned 19th century spiritual teacher, Yosef Lieb Bloch: *The wise expand their understanding to meet reality. Fools reduce reality to meet their understanding.* Simply stated, the mind is designed to protect what is already believed to be true. Such is the case with numerous abominable *reduced realities* of the past such as inequality, slavery and the repression of women. What starts as an idea, later becomes a conviction. But if the new idea (such as civil rights or feminism) is closer to truth than previous beliefs, it will morph into a movement that eventually expands our collective worldview. Equality, liberty, human rights, opportunity, justice and democracy were all ideas that turned into movements that changed the governing of the world. Today's *idea whose time has come*, is the spiritual hypothesis: **to be human is to be spirit formed into flesh**—consciousness manifesting as matter. The Big Picture vision of tomorrow is a world populated by *spiritual beings having physical lives*.

Never has the time been so ripe for spiritual awakening as it is at this very moment. For one thing, we have the benefits of advanced technology and higher education. For another, we have gained exponentially from the evolution of human consciousness over the previous millennia. The teachings of the sacred scriptures, Saints and Sages were typically beyond the comprehension of earlier societies. The words of the Prophets were always geared more toward an educated, advanced 21st century audience than the masses of the first centuries. Were this not the case, history would have recorded the ushering in of the *New Era of Enlightenment* long ago.

Chapter Four: **The Historic Shaping of Our Modern Worldview**

Now that we have established how the worldview influences

humanity, this chapter will explore how humanity shapes the worldview. It is a reciprocal arrangement whereby both parties influence the other concurrently. Spiritually speaking, individual consciousness impacts collective consciousness while collective consciousness is impacting the individual. In many ways, our worldview is an expression of our collective consciousness. It is not static; rather, it is ever-evolving toward greater understanding. Dr. James W. Sire defines worldview as *a fundamental orientation of the heart where we hold the basic constitution of reality*. This is, however, a double-edged sword. Although our worldview is useful in providing a necessary commonality for people to relate to one another and for defining our cultures, it can also be counterproductive by narrowing and limiting our thinking and ostracizing those who hold a contrasting perception of reality.

Chapter Four is an exploration of the *big ideas* (and their teachers) that have shaped our worldview. We will hear from ancient Greek philosophers such as Pythagoras and Socrates, as well as the Christian mystic Swedenborg who inspired Emerson and Thoreau to call for a revolution in human consciousness—the Transcendental Movement. We will explore *The Science of Mind* with Ernest Holms and the New Thought Movement coined by Dr. William Henry Holcombe, which set the stage for Wilhelm Wundt and William James in establishing modern psychology. From here, we will look into the groundbreaking work of Freud and Jung; Alfred Adler and Viktor Frankl; the three Viennese schools of psychotherapy. Also included, are the *Three Forces* of psychology: psychoanalysis, behaviorism and humanistic psychology with the work of Carl Rogers and Abraham Maslow. From the teachings of the ancient philosophers, to the discoveries of modern psychologists, the spiritual hypothesis continues to permeate the story of humankind, ever growing and evolving.

We won't be debating or rating these ideas or their teachers—we are simply setting the stage for what will follow. The *spiritual journey* is a quest for truth—Absolute Truth. This truth, the Buddha called *the way things really are.* Long before we reach the summit of Absolute Truth, we must climb through endless passages of relative truth—truth that points us in the right direction but does not necessarily get us to our ultimate destination. Chapter Four ends on the powerful notion of *human potential*, the ultimate path of *self-actualization.*

CHAPTER FIVE: *Actualizing the Human Potential*
The long and winding road exploring the mysteries of the mind led to a key universal message for all who navigate this life: there is untapped power and unbounded delight that lives within. The treasures of a greater version of ourselves hidden in the form of human potential is yet to be discovered—and yet to be actualized. The instrument designed to discover and actualize this hidden potential is the mind. Certainly, as evidenced by the small percentage of people who actually achieve their full potential, this path is not for the faint of heart. In the words of Abraham Maslow: *We fear to know the fearsome and unsavory aspects of ourselves, but we fear even more to know the godlike in ourselves.*

By the 1960s, a profound shift emerged in the field of psychology. Traditionally, treatment had been confined to those plagued by psychological disorders—the mentally ill. After the acceptance of Maslow's *Theory of Human Motivation*, there began a shift in focus from those burdened by a stunted ability to produce results to those recognized as high achievers. Humanistic psychology espoused the notion of hidden potential just waiting to be tapped and the power of human will to overcome one's limitations.

Also in 1960, Aldous Huxley, an English author, professor and philosopher, delivered a speech at the University of California, San Francisco Medical Center, where he discussed what he called *Human Potentialities*—the hidden potential within each of us, waiting to surface under the proper conditions. He asked his unique and savvy audience: *What should be done now and in the immediate future to actualize the many and great potentialities which in most individuals still remain latent?* He further challenged them to develop the necessary mechanisms and techniques that would provide the conditions in which their latent potential might become actualized.

As fate would have it, two Stanford graduates, Richard Price and Michael Murphy, were in attendance and took Huxley's challenge very seriously. The result? The Esalen Institute—a 120-acre retreat on the mountainous Pacific coast in Big Sur, California. Esalen was, and still is, a response to Huxley's challenge to provide people with the conditions that promote the exploration and actualization of their latent potential. This wasn't merely clever pop culture marketing, rather Esalen became a key component of something much grander and more profound—the launch of the Human Potential Movement.

Beyond the academic approach that is characterized by the Esalen Institute and its impressive list of distinguished philosophers, psychologists, artists, scientists, professors, religious scholars and even some well-known rock stars, there emerged a correlation between the pursuit of human potential and the awakening of our spiritual nature. At the same time, there were a number of 60's spiritual explorers who ingested entheogenic plants and chemicals *to produce a nonordinary state of consciousness for religious or spiritual purposes*—i.e., the *mystical experience*. Perhaps the most famous explorers of drug-based spiritual awakening were the Harvard professors Timothy Leary and Richard Alpert—both teachers at Esalen. And, perhaps the most well-known of the experiments concerning entheogenic plants was the Harvard Psilocybin Project.

The phenomena of the *mystical experience* were also explored by Dr. Walter N. Pahnke, who was awarded his MD from Harvard Medical School, his MDIV from Harvard Divinity School, and his PhD from Harvard Graduate School of Arts and Sciences. Dr. Pahnke published a paper entitled *Drugs and Mysticism* in The International Journal of Parapsychology, where he compiled a typology of nine categories defining *the universal phenomena of the mystical experience*. It is fascinating to recognize that the conclusions and characteristics compiled by modern science regarding the mystical experience brought about by entheogenic plants and those identified by Zen Master D.T. Suzuki regarding *satori* (the mystical experience of sudden enlightenment) are closely related, and compared in this chapter.

Within no time, a third avenue emerged for the Human Potential Movement to gain momentum—Large Group Awareness Training (LGAT). Another Englishman, Alexander Everett, was inspired by Huxley as well, especially after reading his *The Perennial Philosophy*. Here, Huxley states: *Knowledge is a function of being. When there is a change in the being of the knower, there is a corresponding change in the nature and amount of knowing.* By the same token, when there is a change in the nature and amount of what a person knows—an expansion and elevation of their knowledge—there is a change in their being. He goes on to say that it is the responsibility of every human being to discover for themselves the truth of who they truly are at their most fundamental core—to know the spiritual ground of things within us and outside of us. In 1968, Everett launched the beginning of another channel of the Human Potential Movement—self-awareness seminars.

From Abraham Maslow's *Theory of Human Motivation* to Aldous Huxley's *Perennial Philosophy*; from the Harvard Psilocybin Project to the Beatle's chance encounter with the ancient mystical traditions of the East; and from Large Group Awareness Trainings to Oprah's Super Soul Sunday, our evolving spiritual awakening, with its Human Potential Movement, has undergone a collective growth spurt. And, like the growth and development of the body, spiritual growth comes with its fair share of aches and irritations.

The 20th century became the turning point in the ancient battle between science and spirit. Although science and religion have traditionally viewed the world through their own separate lenses, they have focused on the same reality. Perhaps one of the most significant coalescences of modern time is that of science and the spiritual; the physical and the mystical; matter and consciousness. In Chapter six, we explore the link, or interdependency, between these two grand movements in forming a new and unprecedented worldview.

CHAPTER SIX: ***The Noosphere and the New Worldview***
Nobel laureate, Albert Einstein, once stated: *The most beautiful and profound emotion we can experience is the sensation of the mystical.... To know that what is impenetrable to us really exists... this knowledge, this feeling, is at the*

center of true religiousness. This, coming from the man who once said: *Two things are infinite: the universe and human stupidity; and I'm not sure about the universe.* It certainly appears that many of the great scientific geniuses of the 20th century had a change of heart regarding the teachings of the ancient mystics. Furthermore, this shift in attitude was the result of scientific discovery rather than a religious conversion.

Science began impacting the worldview of humanity as far back as the ancient Sumerians and Greeks. Aristotle (384-322 BC), is recognized as the first true scientist. Nicolaus Copernicus (1473-1543), a Polish mathematician and astronomer, triggered a major shift in the worldview by formulating a new model of the heliocentric universe, challenging the Aristotelian model that places the earth at the center of the universe. This shift in worldview (begun by Copernicus) would eventually lead to the Scientific Revolution—overhauling our entire view of society and nature. The shifting worldview during the Age of Reason, or Enlightenment, was characterized by the continuing face-off between the theories of science and the beliefs of religion. It's not surprising that a number of Enlightenment philosophers were exiled or imprisoned, and it wasn't long before the revolutionary ideas of the Enlightenment were expressed by bullets and cannonballs. There were so many revolutionary wars throughout the 18th and 19th centuries that it became known as the Age of Revolution.

Twentieth century scientists made the greatest contributions to physics in human history. Their discoveries would lead to nothing short of a technological revolution in how we live our lives. But the revolutions in information and communication technology, as well as medical innovations that would change healthcare, had to wait in line while science fulfilled a more urgent priority—death and destruction. Before the innovations of mass preservation would get a chance to emerge, the new discoveries of science would expose the world to weapons of mass destruction— the new normal— ***acceptable atrocities***.

Through the age of revolutionary wars, followed by a century of world war and cold war, hostility, violence, war, government sponsored genocide and military sanctioned rape have dominated the collective consciousness of man. These are the *accepted atrocities* of man. Just as Freud exposed the dark and murky details of what lurks within the individual, unconscious *id* of our human psychology, we must also recognize the shaping of our collective consciousness born out of the thoughts and behavior of who we have been. In the words of physician and author, Rosalie Matilda Chou (pen name Han Suyin): *We are all products of our time, vulnerable to history.* And, judging by the small slice of history that we have just come through over the past century, our collective consciousness is indeed vulnerable.

Our understanding of collective consciousness took a quantum leap forward in the first part of the 20th century when Vladimir Ivanovich Vernadsky (Ukrainian scientist considered one of the founders of geochemistry) and Pierre Teilhard de Chardin (French Jesuit priest, scientist, theologian and philosopher) developed and popularized the philosophical concept of the *noosphere*. Merriam-Webster's dictionary defines noosphere as *the sphere of human consciousness and mental activity especially in regard to its influence on the biosphere and in relation to evolution.* Teilhard defined noosphere as *a state of interconnected awareness among all minds, postulated as resulting from humanity's biological and cultural evolution.*

In the original theory of Vernadsky, *the noosphere is the third in a succession of phases of development of the Earth, after the geosphere (inanimate matter) and the biosphere (biological life).* In Teilhard's 1955 book, *The Phenomenon of Man*, he writes that in the *conception of the evolution of the species, a collective identity begins to develop as trade and the transmission of ideas increases. Knowledge accumulates and is transmitted in increasing levels of depth and complexity. This leads to a further augmentation of consciousness and the emergence of a thinking layer that envelops the Earth. Teilhard calls the new membrane the noosphere.... to denote the sphere of mind... acting as a transforming agency promoting hominisation.* In ancient philosophy, "hominization" referred to the ensoulment of the human fetus, the moment when the Soul is said to enter the fetus at some point after conception.

Sir Julian Huxley (who wrote the introduction of Teilhard's book) explains that he would have used the phrase *progressive psychosocial evolution* to describe the hominization process by which potential man realized more of his possibilities. Teilhard extends this evolutionary process of humans actualizing their potentials to a future stage where man will have *"far transcended himself "*—so much so as to require a new name for our species. It's hard to imagine that we could evolve so far beyond our current state that it would require a renaming of our species, but that is precisely what Teilhard meant. Likewise, the butterfly may share similar feelings about being recognized and classified as merely an evolved caterpillar.

The big question posed by J. Krishnamurti and Dr. David Bohm is whether humanity can break free from the conditioning of who we have been to become who we have never been. We are limited in our ability to perceive beyond the boundaries of our previous conditioning the way a computer is limited to compute beyond its previous programing. Even though science is making great strides toward understanding bigger pieces of the *Great Mystery* of life, most of the mystery remains beyond human comprehension. In his book, *Across the Frontiers*, Nobel Prize laureate, Werner Heisenberg (known for his *Uncertainty Principle*), wrote: *Not only is the Universe stranger than we think, it is stranger than we <u>can</u> think.*

The term, *cognitive neuroscience*, was coined in the late 1970s by Harvard, Princeton and M.I.T. Professor George A. Miller and Michael Gazzaniga, professor of psychology at University of California, Santa Barbara. The field of Cognitive Neuroscience was the start of the modern scientific study of the mind, which extends far beyond the study of the brain to include abstract concepts of mind, intelligence and knowing. Even beyond the intricacies of the brain, are those of the mind. At least the brain is an organ that can be examined and analyzed; the mind, and its related consciousness, remains a mystery. It is through the portal of the mind, and the recognition of our consciousness, that we are able to gain access to the spiritual realm. On this journey into the discovery of the Soul, the greater part of who we are remains hidden, and for most of us, hidden throughout our entire lives. This is why we say that the spiritual journey begins as an investigation into what has already been discovered.

In his 1932 book, *Where is Science Going?* Max Planck wrote: *There can never be any real opposition between religion and science; for the one is the complement of the other. Every serious and reflective person realizes, I think, that the religious element in his nature must be recognized and culti-*

vated if all the powers of the human Soul are to act together in perfect balance and harmony. Fortunately, as religion became more institutionalized and compromised by the demands of becoming a large social, political and financial establishment, science picked up some of the slack by conducting its own investigations into the true nature of reality. Although science and religion have often found themselves at odds, we are now at a time when they will both need to recognize and respect the other. Our worldview is shaping into one that could be called *spiritual science.*

Opening of Part Two: In Search of the Soul

While Part One of this book explores the history and evolution of humanity's collective spiritualization (often viewed through the lens of religion, philosophy, psychology and science), Part Two focuses on our own personal spiritualization process. It is important to establish and trace who we have been collectively, before embarking on an individual quest to discover our personal, spiritual nature. Although the experience and teachings of others who have navigated the spiritual waters is invaluable, ultimately it is our direct, personal experience that brings us to Self-realization.

CHAPTER SEVEN: **Embarking on the Spiritual Journey**
According to the preeminent, Indian, spiritual master, Meher Baba (whose followers are estimated in the millions): *Most persons do not even suspect the real existence of God.* He adds: *There are others who, through the influence of tradition, belong to some faith or another and acquire the belief in the existence of God from their surroundings. Their faith is just strong enough to keep them bound to certain rituals,*

ceremonies, or beliefs... There are still others who are philosophically minded and have an inclination to believe in the existence of God... A true aspirant is not content with knowledge of spiritual realities based on hearsay, nor is he satisfied with pure inferential knowledge... [The] **True aspirant seeks direct knowledge of spiritual realities.**

When it comes to all things spiritual, we all share a common denominator: we are sorely lacking in our understanding and experience. And yet, even without profound understanding and previous experience of the spiritual, most of us have strongly held beliefs and well-established attitudes on the topic. Such long held attitudes, biases and beliefs leave little available space for something new and novel to emerge—the unknown (as well as the unknowable). This chapter begins with an attempt to assess the openness of our minds and the willingness of our hearts toward spiritual awakening.

After assessing the determination and openness of our hearts and minds, our spiritual quest begins by identifying its three key elements: the **spiritual pursuit** (including intention and volition), the **spiritual structure** and the **spiritual process.** Briefly, the **spiritual pursuit**, where we begin, is influenced by our sense of purpose and our will to pursue it. Unless one has clarity with respect to the purpose of his or her spiritual quest, it will be difficult to cultivate the motivation necessary to stay the course. Even if our initial purpose is just to discover that part of ourselves that is yet unknown, this initial intent is sufficient to commence. As the quest develops, so too, will the clarity of our purpose.

Souls exist within **the spiritual structure** that is not part of our surrounding physical reality (which is perceived through the physical senses). As Jesus taught: *The Kingdom* *of Heaven is amongst us.* It is here, although not perceptible—at least not in the same way that mountains and oceans are perceived. In order to fulfill our spiritual responsibility, we will need to *familiarize* ourselves with the spiritual dimension. This familiarizing approach is used to gain access to the spiritual domain—through understanding the spiritual structure we are able to perceive it. Once perceived, we have entered it.

After defining the spiritual quest and establishing the spiritual structure (where our quest will take place), the remainder of this book explores **the spiritual process** that leads to spiritualization, i.e., revealing our spiritual nature. This **spiritualization process** is both practical and mystical. In a practical manner, it is a straightforward formula: *gather greater knowledge* on this topic to *acquire greater understanding*, thereby *expanding our awareness* while *enhancing our perception*. Our ability to perceive the spiritual for ourselves is a key element in gaining absolute certainty of its existence. Mystically, this phase of the process is a major crescendo of many spiritual paths from various spiritual cultures—Self-realization. It is here that the human mind makes direct, cognizant contact with the Soul and receives it as its own. Simply stated, our spiritual purpose is to break through the obstacles of its concealment, connect to the spiritual *Light* and reflect it into the world.

The purpose of the spiritualization process is to achieve the *mystical experience* for ourselves—and to have it during the time we are still alive. In a *mystical experience*, one feels, firsthand, the true nature of reality—or, as Buddha put it, clarity and truth as to *the way things really are*. Unlike scientific truth or accurate historical reporting, this truth cannot be taught or even told to us by others; we must experience it for ourselves. This key spiritual tenet is echoed by many teachers. As stated by Aldous Huxley: *Truth cannot be given to you by somebody. You have to discover it; and to discover, there must be a state of mind in which there is direct perception.*

CHAPTER EIGHT: ***Recognizing the Spiritual Structure***
This chapter is intended to familiarize the reader with the spiritual structure—to make its acquaintance and to develop a working relationship. This is not an easy task as there are no legitimate definitions, descriptions, images or forms suitable for this purpose. All words and labels fall short of authenticity when it comes to the spiritual structure. As the Taoists have said for centuries, *if you can put it in words, it's not it.* As a matter of fact, the very term spiritual structure is an oxymoron—spiritual is the polar opposite of structure. However, this idiom is generic and vague enough to avoid the emotional tripwires embedded in centuries of the more traditional, religious terms. Of course, even the notion of entering the spiritual structure is misleading because we can't enter a space we already occupy. Thus, the phrase *entering the spiritual structure* is used metaphorically. A more precise statement would be: *recognizing the true nature of reality.*

Regarded as one of the world's most influential scholars and authors of religious studies, Professor Huston Smith makes a vital point in this discussion: from the materialist, scientific perspective, that which isn't observable and measurable simply does not exist. Although limited and biased by its own beliefs, science has dominated our perception of reality for centuries. Only recently has the "new" science begun to recognize the possibility of existence beyond what meets the eye. The spiritual structure is not covered by the natural laws of material science as it is neither physical nor material in form. It is not a part of time and space, or a measurable force. For those who hold an exclusively materialist worldview, the spiritual structure does not exist, and there is nothing available to satisfy their uninitiated request for proof. There are no numbers to add together that prove the existence of the spiritual structure, the presence of the Soul or God. Just as science speaks in numbers and religion speaks in words, the spiritual communicates its authenticity through direct, personal experience.

On the spiritual plane, the present moment of *now* is eternal—beginningless and endless. As we are accustomed to experiencing existence in momentary, fleeting sound bites, our first whiff of the infinite experience can be awesome and quite overwhelming, to say the least. This is why we often experience spiritual moments in the form of memories. Before we can even respond, these moments of awe are in our past. If truth be told, this is the same way in which we experience present time in our physical lives—through the rearview mirror. It is unfortunate how this rearview living leads to a life that is not fully experienced. This is a pattern that causes life to be experienced through memory rather than in real time.

Another important distinction between the material and the spiritual is the concept of limitations. The spiritual structure is neither limited nor limiting, whereas everything in our material world revolves around limitations. Time is limiting, as are space and matter—not to mention the overwhelming limitations generated by impermanence. Perhaps one of the most frustrating aspects of all things spiritual is that they cannot be given form (such as words and images) without losing their true meaning. The Buddha taught that man found it necessary to name everything he observed within his reality in order to refer back to it. However, when we label and define the spiritual, it is no longer spiritual; rather, it has become a concept or *thing* of material form such as *Soul, spirit, God*, even the word *spiritual*, which are all ineffable by design.

For the purpose of recognizing the spiritual structure, it is best to first understand that the typical impression of the spiritual realm consists primarily of traditional, age-old ideas. While these ideas may hold elements of truth, they are mostly based on opinions, myths and ancient folklore that became popular over time. Their popularity was the result of people needing something to satisfy their spiritual hunger or simple curiosity while having neither the time nor inclination to seek the truth for themselves. It best serves us to forego such limiting impressions of the spiritual in order to gain direct access to our own experience. The spiritual structure begins where words leave off—in silence. As a rule of thumb, to perceive the spiritual structure we must enter it; and to enter the spiritual chamber, we must first pass through the corridor of silence.

The spiritual quest, and its associated experience of spiritual awakening, leads us to gaining an expanded sense of self—including recognition of the Self (or Soul). Without recognition of the Soul, our mortal lives eventually become tedious, hopeless and even cruel. The tendency for our lives to be over before we actually understand them or the miraculous opportunities they hold, in and of itself, is inescapably depressing. It is the Soul that erases the scars and dries the tears of our superficial fears and limited perception. Even a brief glance through the lens of the Soul brings a warm and healing wash over our open sores and raw nerves. These initial flashes that come through the channel of the Soul cause us to recognize that we are not just a body with a mind, but a Soul that has *manifested* a body with a mind.

PART ONE

The Historic Development of the Spiritual

Hypothesis

From ancient Shamanistic cave drawings to modern-day, evidence-based, scientific theory, our species' quest to discover the truth of humanity's spiritual nature has been ceaseless and enduring. For many centuries, this exploration has been the source of debate and conflict between religion and science. Today we are fortunate to have been born into the unique era of a *scientific, spiritual worldview*. Part One of *The Epiphany* explores humanity's collective pursuit of our spiritual nature, while Part Two focuses this search on the individual discovery of our Soul. It is important to recognize where we have been as a people in order to identify where we must go as individuals.

We are not physical beings seeking a spiritual experience; we are spiritual beings having a physical experience."

— PIERRE TEILHARD DE CHARDIN

CHAPTER ONE

The Epiphany

Although Pierre Teilhard de Chardin, was a twentieth century French philosopher, scientist, and Jesuit priest, he echoes the idea taught by many great Saints and Sages, as well as the sacred scriptures of the ancient mystical traditions. When the Hasidic Master was asked by his students, *Rabbi, is it true that we have a Soul?* —his reply was an emphatic *no*. When the teacher saw the shocked expression on his students faces, he smiled and said, *it is true that your Soul has a body.* Regardless of how it is stated, or who is speaking, this basic spiritual tenet is supported throughout the spiritual world—the essence of the human is spirit; the essence of the mortal is immortal.

This is the epiphany referred to in the title of this book: ***To be human is to exist in two dimensions simultaneously—the physical and spiritual.*** We are both body and Soul; flesh and spirit; mortal and immortal. The purpose of this book is to bring the reader to the moment of this epiphany and the direct personal experience of its truth. The term epiphany comes from the ancient Greek word *epiphanea* (manifestation).

Epiphany is defined as: an experience of a sudden and

striking realization or insight; an illuminating discovery, awareness, or revelation; a sudden manifestation or perception of the essential nature or meaning of something. Additionally, an epiphany is generally the term used to describe a scientific breakthrough or a religious or philosophical discovery, but it can apply in any situation in which an enlightening realization allows a problem or situation to be understood from a new and deeper perspective.

In their 2015 book, *The Eureka Factor*, Dr. John Kounios, professor of psychology and director of Drexel University's doctoral program in Applied Cognitive and Brain Sciences, and Dr. Mark Beeman, professor of psychology at Northwestern University, explore how the latest research from cognitive neuroscience and psychology explains the phenomenon of insight/epiphany and how it works in the brain. In their words:

> *Insights have two key features. The first is that they pop into your awareness, seemingly out of nowhere. They don't feel like a product of your ongoing thoughts. In fact, you can't control them in the way you can control your deliberate, conscious thought. Insights are like cats. They can be coaxed but don't usually come when called. The other key feature of insights is that they yield, often literally, a different way of looking at things....*
>
> *The idea that insights are stepping-stones for personal development is not new. Many of the world's great religions have long taught that insights can offer the potential for profound transformation by offering a window onto transcendental and spiritual realms....*

The notion of sudden insight plays a special role in Zen Buddhism. The ultimate goal of Zen is "satori," which Japanese scholar D. T. Suzuki explained as "acquiring a new viewpoint for looking into the essence of things...."

"Satori is the sudden flashing into consciousness of a new truth hitherto undreamed of. It is sort of a mental catastrophe taking place all at once, after much piling up of matters intellectual and demonstrative. The piling has reached a limit of stability and the whole edifice has come tumbling to the ground, when, behold, a new heaven is open to full survey."

Professors Kounios and Beeman go on to reference a recent survey in the United States that documents the number of people who reported having personally experienced significant spiritual epiphanies is on the rise—up from 22 percent in 1962 to 49 percent in 2009.

This sudden and striking realization that is explored in the chapters ahead, is what the Eastern traditions call Self-realization; this is the grand moment when the mind makes contact with the Soul realizing its presence and nature.

Why is it that after centuries of inquiry we still have no certainty as to the truth of the aforementioned spiritual hypothesis? First, it's not a truth that can be taught to another; it can only be discovered on our own. Unlike science, math, medicine, and the like, spirituality cannot be transferred from the intellect of one person to another. Spiritual truths are recognized and experienced on the individual level, not collectively. Physical laws become universal truths. Even though it was initially highly contested, the truth that the earth revolves around the sun became a proven fact for all people to accept. Although teachers play an invaluable role in leading us to our spiritual awakening, it is the actual spiritual experience that brings us to spiritual realization. Each aspirant must assume the role of spiritual scientist and make his or her own discovery.

Second, it is a discovery that is not revealed at the beginning of the spiritual journey; it is an advanced spiritual crescendo. The discovery of spiritual reality, including the Soul, comes to those who have relentlessly pursued its path. Without the actual discovery, we are left with beliefs and trust alone. While these are advanced perspectives, they fall short of absolute certainty. There is a fine line that separates belief from certainty, but within that fine line, lies authentic spiritual realization.

Third, by its very nature, the spiritual is concealed from the physical. To perceive the spiritual, we must become spiritual. Similar to sight that we can only be experienced by seeing; the spiritual is only *seen* through the spiritual lens. Yet, while the spiritual is concealed, it is not imperceptible.

How is the spiritual perceived? —by removing that which obscures it. The purpose of this book is to provide the understanding, recognition, and eventual experience of the fundamental spiritual truth, referred to as "The Epiphany." Like removing the fish from the fishbowl so it can distinguish water, the book is designed to bring the reader to full recognition of the simple yet profound truth—we are living Souls having physical life in a material world—pure consciousness manifesting in physical form. Holding this idea as a belief can only be based upon speculation and opinion. The moment of truth is not one of logic or reason, but personal experience where certainty follows. Experience is the language of spirituality, the way that math is the language of science; as math proves science, experience proves the spiritual. While math is a universal language, experience can only be known on an individual basis.

How can an ordinary person, living an ordinary life, expect to have experiences akin to those of the great Prophets, Saints and Sages of religion? —it's the idea whose time has come. The spiritual geniuses of history were distinctively remarkable, paving the way for humanity to follow in their footsteps. Today, we have a tremendous advantage. We live on the brink of the spiritual tipping point. As Teilhard pointed out, in terms of consciousness, we are not born on square one. The collective consciousness is continually evolving and the higher it goes, the higher we are able to rise. Just as new scientific discovery is based on previous discovery, we benefit from the efforts of our ancestors. All previous spiritual progress is registered within the collective consciousness of our times. Once we familiarize ourselves with the experiences and conclusions of those who came before, we gain access to what they found. In this way we cultivate our own *Master within*. Our task is not to find the spiritual realm, but to recognize it, as it has been here all along. The uniquely human condition of existing in two dimensions simultaneously, physical and spiritual, provides the perfect setting for this tectonic shift.

Whatever the culture, in whichever century, the task before any human seeking the spiritual is the same—overcoming that which obscures it. As the Saint, Sri Ramakrishna, stated over a century ago, *it takes Chit to realize Sat*—meaning, it takes *Pure Intelligence* to realize *Eternal Existence*. Pure intelligence is that not tainted and distracted by the conditioned mind. Eternal existence is spiritual existence. If we are not seeking to view the spiritual through the lens of pure intelligence, then what we perceive is simply a reflection of our own conditioned thoughts and reactive feelings. We are unable to perceive eternal existence through the physical lens of rational thought—the very concept has no existence within the context of physical life. In the realm of time, space, and matter, it is apparent that all that has come into existence is passing out of existence. Thus, eternal existence is beyond the limiting scope of the scientific material worldview that has grown to dominance over the past five centuries. As a working definition for purposes of this book, worldview is a mental model of reality that serves as a framework of ideas and attitudes about the world, ourselves and life itself. It is a comprehensive system of beliefs that serves to provide answers to a wide range of life's questions. While not their intent, the science of Copernicus, Galileo, and Newton, has unfolded a picture of reality that does not include the spiritual.

Not until the emergence of quantum mechanics, did we recognize the possibility of science and religion sharing a similar view. For most of us, the spiritual quest goes against the grain of our contemporary materialist worldview. If this were not challenge enough, the spiritual quest also goes against the grain of our individual design principle. There is an intricate and overarching mechanism within the mind of each of us designed to obscure the spiritual. It is most often referred to as ego, identified as the seat of self-interest. Beyond the instinctual mechanism in all animals predisposing us towards self-preservation, the jurisdiction of the ego includes our drive toward sensory pleasures and gratification. As its primary function, the ego provides us our individuality and separateness. These are critical aspects of being human and should not be viewed as faults. However, the same ego-based view that makes us human, keeps us from recognizing our spirituality perceived through our sense of oneness and unity. So, when Ramakrishna teaches that we realize the eternal existence of spirit through pure, untainted intelligence, or consciousness, he is essentially teaching that we must overcome the limitations of our ego's version of reality.

This theme of the ego as an opposing force to the Soul is pervasive throughout the great religions and the teachings of the spiritual masters. Each generation makes its own contribution toward the evolution of human consciousness. While not necessarily linked to religion, these contributions are spiritual in nature. The spiritual quest is the quest for truth. It may come in the form of theology, philosophy or psychology as well as being the fruits of mathematics, science, or technology. It is expressed in the sequencing of the human genome, or in the cure for devastating diseases. The Buddha gave us a simple yet profound definition of Enlightenment—*to see things as they really are.* We must stand on the shoulders of ancestors to see beyond the apparent.

Will We Make Good Ancestors?

This is a fair and honest question for all generations carrying with it an extraordinary challenge of collective accountability. At first glance, one might think this question is directed to the earth's collective population. Will history judge our era favorably? From this macro perspective, it might seem easy for you and I to slip into the shadows and not be held accountable. Each of us constitutes a mere one out of over 8 billion people. However, the question becomes far more personal when applied directly to me. Will any part of this world be left better as a result of my birth? When I'm gone, will any part of my *footprint* still remain?

If you're thinking, *what difference does it make; I'll be gone?* —you are probably part of the majority. In truth, our times are marked by countless scenarios where we fail to make good partners, spouses, friends, neighbors, employers, employees, political leaders, religious leaders, teachers, coworkers, citizens, reporters, entertainers—the list is endless. For most of us, we wrestle daily with our responsibilities toward those closest to us, let alone anything so grand as those of future generations.

Consider this simple, but profound truth: To be a worthy ancestor to future generations, you are automatically of great benefit to your own generation. We are given a span of time in which to do something meaningful—a blank canvas to create living art and advance our spiritual purpose. If we pursue spiritual advancement in the same manner as we pursue material gain, our progress will be hampered. Material success is most often the result of a self-serving intent. Applying this same intent to our spiritual pursuit, the results will be compromised. We gain materially for ourselves; we advance spiritually for the benefit of all. This altruistic principle is taught by all the great religions of the world as well as the renowned spiritual Sages.

By focusing on becoming a good ancestor, we expand our intention beyond ourselves, beyond our immediate surroundings and the times in which we live to the vast *evolving collective consciousness* referred to by Teilhard. He conceived our collective consciousness as evolving toward the *Omega Point* where humanity will redeem itself and enter a new and enlightened era. Viewed from this vantage, every human who ever walked this earth, every Soul that descended into our world, left his or her unique imprint on this collective consciousness. It is here that our ultimate responsibility lies and it is here that we are held most accountable. So, when we are able to realize with pure intelligence, that we are indeed *spiritual beings having a physical experience*, not only have we elevated our own consciousness, but we have greatly contributed to the evolution of the collective consciousness.

From the historical perspective, every generation and every era has had a responsibility to *move the ball closer to the goal to which humanity has continually strived*. Every generation has had to stand up to the challenge or run from it. We all know which civilizations have lifted humanity to new levels of achievement and those that let us all slip deeper into our own demise. Any well-educated person of today can attest to the disgraceful and destructive lows to which humanity has previously descended. But who amongst us is willing to face up to the harsh scrutiny of our descendants?

Certainly, we have advanced impressively in the areas of science, medicine, industry, technology, and the like. Today, we travel further in a few hours than our ancestors did in a lifetime. There is no better historical period to have a life-threatening illness or injury than in our modern times. In developed countries, the standard of living and quality of public health and sanitation is at an all-time high.

All these categories share the common denominator of being rooted in the material world. As to our spiritual advancement, has our modern time successfully ended the continual threat of war and violence? Have those in power reached a level of peace and harmony where we can finally stop stockpiling armaments and weaponry? Have the strongest among us given up the need to exploit and victimize the weaker, taking on the role of supporting those less capable? At its most fundamental level, the question is precise and to the point. Are the spiritual priorities of our modern times higher than those of our predecessors? As Britain's first female Prime Minister, Margaret Thatcher, stated in the 1970s, we have an obligation "to make changes and sacrifices so **that we do not live at the expense of future generations.**"

Dr. Jonas Salk (1914-1995) is perhaps best known for the discovery and development of the first successful polio vaccine in 1955. The worst year of the polio epidemic in the US was 1952 with 58,000 new cases, making polio one of America's greatest fears—second only to the atomic bomb. Within two years, 100 million doses of the vaccine were distributed in this country. On January 27, 1956, President Eisenhower presented Salk with the Gold Medal and President Reagan honored him by declaring May 6th Jonas Salk Day. The title of this section is taken from a Salk quote published in *Learning from the Future: Competitive Foresight Scenarios* by Liam Fahey and Robert M. Randall: "Our greatest responsibility is to be good ancestors."

The most meaningful activity in which a human can be engaged is one that is directly related to human evolution. This is true because human beings now play an active and critical role not only in the process of their own evolution but in the survival and evolution of all living beings. Awareness of this places upon human beings a responsibility for their participation in and contribution to the process of evolution. If humankind would accept and acknowledge this responsibility and become creatively engaged in the process of metabiological evolution consciously, as well as unconsciously, a new reality would emerge, and a new age would be born.

—JONAS SALK

In his 1981 book, *World Population and Human Values: A New Reality,* Salk identifies two major epochs in human history which he called Epoch A and Epoch B. Epoch A is characterized by a Darwinian type survival of the fittest and competition involving win/lose relationships. Epoch B, in which "the welfare of the individual and the welfare of the species are inexorably bound", is characterized by cooperation involving win/win relationships.

In his 1973 book, *The Survival of the Wisest,* Salk asserts that nothing less than, *A complete inversion of values is necessary if man is to move from Darwinian era to the epoch of cooperation; the alternative is species suicide.*

Salk did not just *talk the talk;* he most definitely *walked the walk.* Along with Dr. Albert Bruce Sabin who developed the oral version of the polio vaccine, Salk nearly eradicated one of the Earth's most diabolical plagues that was paralyzing children throughout the world. Thanks to their dedicated work, the number of cases of polio worldwide today, has decreased by 99%, according to Global Polio Eradication Initiative. The vaccine has been provided to billions of children in over 200 countries with the assistance of millions of volunteers—at no charge to the recipient. Further, neither Salk nor Sabin were paid anything for their priceless discovery that saved so many lives. Further, there was no patent as their vaccines were *donated* as gifts to humanity.

While medical science has advanced dramatically since the discovery of the polio vaccine, it is doubtful that we have surpassed the ethics and morality of these distinguished humanitarians. For example, in 2013 an American research-based pharmaceutical company, developed *Sovaldi*, a drug critical to the treatment of Hepatitis C, the devastating disease that evolves to a chronic condition killing 350,000 people worldwide each year. Some 150 million people worldwide currently suffer from this long-term infection that is a leading cause in liver cancer. The World Health Organization (WHO) put Sovaldi, which claims to cure 99% of its hepatitis C patients, on its List of Essential Medicines, recognizing it as one of the most important medications in the health system.

Yet, according to media sources such as the New York Times and Daily Mail, the price quoted for a 6-month course of treatment is between $84,000 and $168,000 in the United States, while a course of treatment in other countries is adjusted to fit what the market will yield. According to CBS News, December 1, 2015, despite the fact that this cure was invented under the leadership of a celebrated doctor in the Department of Veterans Affairs, the VA cannot afford to save the lives of the 230,000 veterans infected with hepatitis C.

Unfortunately, this is not an isolated situation. It appears to be a growing trend in the pharmaceutical industry that once a drug is recognized as an essential component of a life-saving treatment, there is no limit to the amount they will charge.

The examples of Jonas Salk and Albert Sabin taken from the 1950s, in contrast to the modern pharmaceutical companies, represents a conflicting consciousness within science. It is not clear where the dust will settle regarding the cost of cures and the profits they generate. However, what is imperative is the need for ethical practices when it comes to preserving and saving human life.

A New Emerging Worldview
The new emerging worldview in which science and spirit are aligned is not all that new. It has its roots in the theories of quantum physics that date back to discoveries made

in quantum chemistry in the mid-1800s. In those fields it was recognized that there is an unseen force beyond the fundamental building blocks of matter that remains unpredictable and immeasurable. This alignment gained legs in the early 1900s with the work of Einstein, Max Planck, Werner Heisenberg, Max Born, Wolfgang Pauli, Niels Bohr, and Erwin Schrödinger, to mention only a few. Although quantum physics is over a century old, the scientific spiritual worldview remains in its infancy. Outside the scientific community, where people continue to argue about the age of the earth and the notions of big bang versus Divine design, the scientific spiritual worldview is hardly noticed by the average person. As science comes to terms with what might be called *consciousness*, religion must come to terms with a rational approach to the spiritual.

The philosophical debate over consciousness has been going on since ancient times with the voices of Plato, Descartes, and Spinoza joining into the discussion. Nobel Prize laureate Sir Dr. Francis Crick, a co-discoverer of the molecular structure of DNA, often spoke out against the dogma of religion. Crick became interested in neurobiology and the study of the brain. He devoted the last 15 years of his life to the study of consciousness. In his forward to Christof Koch's *The Quest for Consciousness: A Neurobiological Approach*, Crick wrote:

> *Solving the problem of consciousness will need the labors of many scientists, of many kinds, though it is always possible that there will be a few crucial insights and observations. ... A few years ago one could not use the word 'consciousness' in a paper, nor, say, Nature or Science, in a grant application.*

But thankfully, times are changing, and the subject is now ripe for intensive exploration.

In his own 1994 book, *The Astonishing Hypothesis: The Scientific Search for the Soul,* Crick claims: *Scientific study of the brain during the 20th century led to acceptance of consciousness, free will, and the human Soul as subjects for scientific investigation.*

A major premise of this book is that humanity has never been in a more advantageous position to gain breakthrough levels of spiritual advancement. It is not the tone or character of our times nor the progression of religious and ethical thought that is providing the fertile ground for the seeds of spirituality. Oddly, it is something utterly material in form—technology.

Recent advancement in technology, although not developed for spiritual awakening, have provided two key factors for that awakening: First, information, or knowledge as it is referred to by our Sages, is the driving force behind spiritual development. Second, connectivity, or unity as it has been called by our ancestors, is fundamental. The religious/spiritual community has always depended on both the knowledge imparted and received by their adherents, as well as the interrelatedness of its members.

If we measure the knowledge of today's individuals by what they hold in their minds as well as that contained in hand-held devices, their overall rating would far exceed that of the wisest of previous generations. Our modern men and women are able to give lengthy and comprehensive accounts on a vast range of topics if allowed the necessary *click to* an appropriate *link.*

This same technology has inadvertently touched on the

essence of spirituality—unity, or as it is called in our modern vernacular—connectivity. In ancient times, a person may have achieved a sense of being connected with his or her immediate family, village or even the nation or culture. However, communication—the external expression of our connection with others—was slow and cumbersome at best. It could take weeks if not years, for people in other parts of the world to learn of major events that occurred. If Jesus were to raise the dead son of a single mom today, as reported in Luke 7:11, the news would travel around the world before the funeral was over—complete with YouTube videos and a half million tweets.

While word of this great miracle spread from the town of Nain where it took place, throughout all of Syria, the speed of modern technology, bouncing signals off satellites, would have confounded the talebearer bringing word by camel caravan traveling through the desert.

Today's technology is giving an enormous boost to spirituality. In the past, a person seeking to learn from the great spiritual teachers would have to change the entire course of his or her life and travel the world to sit at their feet. Today, if we wish to have access to the teachings of the Dalai Lama, we need only click on *dalailama.com*. If you happen to be a member of Amazon Prime Now, his teachings can be delivered to your door within two hours with no additional shipping charge.

Extended Longevity gives Rise to Expanded Spirituality

Beyond the advancement of technology, there is a human side of this equation. Not only are we experiencing an information and communication revolution throughout the world, we are also experiencing a revolution in longevity. Due to advances made in medical science and public health, people are living longer lives. In turn, this allows for an extended *elderhood*—i.e., that fourth quadrant of life when career and family obligations are complete. At the beginning of the 20th century, life expectancy in developed countries was just under 50 years; death, not retirement, most often concluded one's career.

By the beginning of the 21st century, the average 65-year-old woman could expect to live past her 85th birthday. If she is conscientious about her medical care and continues to be physically active and nutritionally fit, these additional years can be quite vibrant. During this elderhood, the greatest potential exists for the spiritual perspective to gain roots. Aging is a process of decline and withdrawal; the word retire comes from the French word *retirer* which is translated *to withdraw.* Older adults recognize the withdrawal process, but are unclear as to where to retreat. Within this quandary, is a great opportunity for spiritual awakening as the physical structure diminishes. In this process one must actually prepare for a spiritual awakening. Without the proper perspective, the aging experience is all about physical withdrawal. With even a modicum of preparation, the spiritual counterpart can emerge and substantially nullify the ill effects our physical demise.

It is not uncommon for pursuit of the spiritual dimension to be deferred until the fourth quadrant of life (60 to 80+ years). Until this time people are typically involved in the demands of their *physical* existence. In elderhood, the physical commences to decline, making space for spiritual inquiry and pursuit. Of course, a younger person might be confronted with a crisis from the physical dimension such as a death, war, prison, addiction, divorce or bankruptcy, resulting in the earlier emergence of a spiritual pursuit. When our physical world becomes threatened, some of us may inadvertently stumble upon the spiritual. Otherwise, it is likely to remain dormant until we run out of other options for satisfying our physical and egoistic desires.

The other side of this picture relates to the unyielding allure of youth. Whether during the discovery stage of the first quadrant (ages 0-20) or the stage of development of independence in the second quadrant (ages 20-40), the various dimensions of experience in youth are quite intoxicating. Many of us become so addicted to our youth that we spend the better part of the third quadrant (ages 40-60) trying to recapture it. If such is the case, it is no surprise that we are overwhelmed by the *withdrawal* associated with the fourth quadrant.

In our modern materialist culture, the idea that something unprecedented and grand might emerge in our later years seems like the hollow content of a late-night infomercial. Yet this is precisely what is acknowledged by our spiritual Sages. While life holds many fulfilling and wondrous experiences along the path, it is all a preparation for what is to follow. Our time spent with the physical structure is meant to enhance our experience of the spiritual structure.

The challenges of a mass spiritual awakening are not caused by lack of know how or access. One simply can look to the teachings of the top dozen spiritual geniuses of history. Most of us today can make this inquiry without leaving our chairs. The collective knowledge we will encounter is more than sufficient to get the job done. Although the narratives may change, the messages are the same—while the Soul yet dwells within the body, discover your spiritual essence. While the knowledge is plentiful the problem has always been accessibility and intention. With access to information much greater than ever, people today lack spiritual intention and discipline. It is not that we are bad people, we are just hugely distracted. Over half the world's eight billion people live in poverty on less than $2.50 per day. According to UNICEF, a billion children are living in poverty and 22,000 of these children die each day of starvation. Living in a physical body within a material world, while facing poverty and starvation on a daily basis is more than a slight distraction from pursuing spiritual enlightenment.

Interestingly, our Sages teach that the opposite side of the spectrum is no less distracting. Those of us enjoying the so-called *good life* of our modern times are also plagued with incessant distractions. Spirituality does not distinguish between these two extremes. Distractions are distractions, regardless of the cause. On the material side of things, it is obviously much better to be distracted by the indulgent luxuries of the advantaged life rather than to be cursed by abject poverty, disease, and starvation. Spiritually speaking, however, there are some instances where the person suffering to survive is ranked above those wallowing in luxury, yet failing to develop proper character traits for advancement. While trite, it is often said that through life's greatest adversities one gains life's greatest achievement—character refinement.

From the spiritual perspective, it is not what you *obtained* in life, but what you *became*. This point is made by all the great Sages who echo the sentiments of the biblical quote: *For what shall it profit a man, if he shall gain the whole world, and lose his own Soul?* (Mark 8:36) This is not to say that a person is wrong to obtain a successful life. It is to say that if the process of material success caused us to forfeit our spiritual advancement—we missed the mark.

The purpose of our discussion is to provide a condensed and contemporized version of the ancient spiritual traditions without consideration of their diversity or religiosity. If the message prescribes a path to spiritual realization, it qualifies. All spiritual awakening begins with an increase of knowledge that in turn, leads to a heightened spiritual learning curve. Once the initial awakening is achieved, we are poised to elevate it until recognition blossoms into realization—Self-realization. A spiritually realized person is an expression of higher consciousness rather than one who is simply an expression of ego and self-interest. It is through the process of spiritual awakening and expression that we serve not only ourselves, but the whole of humanity—living, dead, and yet to be born. Regardless of whether current generations are recognized by future generations as good ancestors, we, as individuals, have the obligation to fill those shoes.

The Illusory Nature of Reality

The Buddha taught that what we think to be reality is actually not reality, but merely our *perception* of reality—and that is under the influence of previous conditioning. By analogy, imagine the mind as a movie projector, projecting a movie onto a large screen. We believe this is reality when in fact, it's only a movie projected onto a screen. The movie projects the film that runs through the projector; when the film is changed, so is the movie. The mind is like that projector and the film is analogous to the sum total of our impressions of previous experiences. Like the film, when these impressions are altered, we enter a new reality. If our impressions are altered by enhanced awareness of the truth, the new reality is more authentic than the one previously projected onto the screen. The Buddha taught that our greatest challenge is to grasp the reality that exists once the movie has stopped—that is, once the impressions of past experiences is silenced. What exists beyond the conditioned projections of the mind is the nature of things the way they really are. This view of things as they really are is often referred to as the *truth perspective*. Although it is a challenge, for most of us, this kind of truth is unapproachable. We have accumulated far too many *filters* that alter our perception. Every personal bias, opinion, and belief adds to our minds conditioning. Through developing the ability to isolate, concentrate, contemplate, and meditate, we are able to slow and eventually stop the mind from projecting its conditioned view of reality. Once free of these limiting *filters*, the mind is capable of glimpsing into the pure light of day—a reality where the physical and spiritual are in perfect harmony. According to the Buddha, this is the experience that precedes enlightenment and provides the gateway to Nirvana. What Nirvana provides that is different than our mundane holographic version of reality is clear perception, or as the Buddha taught, *"seeing things as they really are"*.

Most all great Saints and Sages bring the same message—beneath our conflicted and concocted version of reality awaits Ultimate Reality. Further, the only prerequisite to getting there is to clean the lens that we look through. With a clear perception of reality comes Self-realization. Here the nightmare ends and the dream begins. In the nightmare we imagine ourselves to be exclusively mortal with limited knowledge and unlimited ignorance, limited joy and an abundance of sorrow, limited time and much to achieve. Upon our first glimpse into our true Self comes the realization of our true identity and true reality. According to those who have had a glimpse of true Self, it is a moment unlike any other. Not only are there no words to describe this moment, but any attempt to define it through words diminishes the experience. It is utterly human to want to wrap this encounter into a clearly rational and explainable event. However, this will only serve as an interpretation of the ineffable—an analysis that is less about the actual event and more about the conditioning of the mind that is making the observation. For most of us born and raised under the domination of our modern worldview, our reaction upon hearing about this spiritual experience is shallow at best—considered to be illusory and the product of wishful thinking.

Monks and nuns enter into the cloistered life of the monastery while ascetics retreat into caves in an effort to get away from the influence of the modern materialist scientific worldview. Still, it penetrates the seclusion to uproot the possibility of a vibrant yet hidden spiritual dimension. Humanity has spent the better part of the last five hundred years painstakingly removing all traces of the spiritual from rational thought. Our greatest spiritual teachers are from centuries, if not millenniums gone by. This puts us at a significant disadvantage when it comes to breaking through to our spiritual core.

Honing the Instrument of Perception—The Mind

The idea that our entire and exclusive existence is that of a hunk of beef, thirteen major organ systems, some seventy trillion cells and a will to live out our 70–80-year life span, is truly naïve; and quite depressing. All of the great historic Sages have encouraged us with the same message—look beyond what is apparent; find for yourself that part of you that exists beyond the physical and psychological. Throughout human history there have been a variety of brilliant and influential contributions to this discussion. The content of this book is a sampling of many great spiritual teachings as well as those of teachers of science, philosophy, psychology, and the like. Humanity has been blessed with many great minds expressing the consciousness of highly evolved Souls.

In order to recognize the overarching influence of our modern materialist worldview, we must first recognize its rise to power. When Nobel Prize laureate, physicist Max Planck was asked during an interview, what is science's greatest contribution to humanity, his reply was, *it taught man how to think*. With so many innovations and discoveries that Planck had to choose from, it was the process of thinking itself that he selected. There is an art to thinking and like all art, it depends on cultivated skills. For example, effective thinking depends on the ability to gain and maintain complete focus. Once focused, the mind must become skilled at intense contemplation. An easily distracted mind is not capable of achieving the same results as a well-disciplined one. The Buddha taught, (Dhammapada 323): *Nirvana* [enlightenment/ultimate liberation] *is reached by that man* [or woman] *who wisely, heroically, trains himself* [herself].

Honing one's ability towards single pointed concentration is a critical element in the process of spiritual awakening. There is no quick fix for *monkey mind*—a Buddhist term used to describe a mind whose thoughts jump from one topic to the next, as a monkey jumps from limb to limb. In a time when attention-deficit/hyperactivity disorder (ADHD) is the most common neurobehavioral disorder of childhood, cultivating the age-old art of mindfulness can be quite challenging. To perceive that which is not readily apparent, it is essential to gain and sustain awareness, focus and concentration. This is particularly true when it comes to the formless, mystical tenets of spirituality.

If the body is not regularly fed it becomes malnourished and dies. The mind also has its appetites that require feeding; just as the body requires discipline to maintain health, so too the mind must be disciplined to gain perspective and achieve realization. One sacrifices much when the body loses its health; eventually all is sacrificed if the mind views through a faulty lens. The mind provides the bridge between the physical and the spiritual. For our spiritual journey to be a success, we must first make sure that the bridge will support our weight. Thus, disciplining and educating the mind is the beginning of the spiritual process.

Humanity's Endless Quest to Know vs. Our Ceaseless Resistance to Finding Out

According to ancient Hindu scriptures, the human quest to know is second only to the human quest to be. In other words, it is only our drive to maintain life that exceeds our drive to know *what* life is, *why* it is, and *how* we are meant to live it. We do not choose these driving impulses to live and to learn, rather these are a well-planned feature of our design principle—an integral part of our hard drive. If we are not fully engaged and committed to life, or striving towards greater understanding of its meaning and purpose, we are going against our nature. Ironically, it is within our nature to go against our nature—therein lies the struggle. Our lives are riddled with incidents and opinions that fight our natural inclination to sustain life and to grow intellectually.

Beyond honing the mind's skills of focus and concentration to cultivate the art of thinking, we must examine the learning process itself. Learning is made easier by first considering the *known* elements before taking on the *unknown* elements–the logical before the speculative–the physical before the metaphysical. Scientists begin with what has already been discovered before launching into areas yet to be discovered. It is the mental equivalent of taking a running start when attempting a challenging jump.

Our process follows this same model. It is our intention to take a quantum leap into the unknown element of spirituality in order to discover our hidden spiritual nature. At times we will utilize speculation and imagination, using intuition rather than logic. In order to prepare the mind for such a challenge, we will first examine what is already known—the thoughts of those who have experienced what we seek. The spiritual is often referred to as our experience of pure consciousness without the altering filters of the conditioned mind. Yet, once experienced, pure consciousness takes on form when communicated to others. Oneness of the spiritual plane takes on separation, individuation, and diversity on the physical plane. We will explore the discoveries and teachings of the experts—the great spiritual Sages of history and the thought leaders of science, religion, and philosophy.

To do this topic justice would require much more than the a single book—more like a library. From the earliest time there is evidence of the human quest for spiritual awareness—from the philosophies of Socrates, Plato, and Aristotle to the sacred scriptures of Moses, Jesus and Mohammed. History reflects a continuous exploration into the nature of spiritual reality—Hindu teachings found in the Upanishads, Bhagavad Gita, and Vedanta—the thousands of Buddhist sutras and scriptures and the ancient Hebrew Torah, the Gospels and the Koran.

In the next six chapters, we conduct a limited exploration into what Teilhard calls the *evolution of consciousness*. We are all unique expressions of individual consciousness the way humanity is an expression of collective consciousness. When a person raises his or her individual consciousness, he or she becomes more than before—an expanded version of a former self. In so doing each person automatically contributes to the collective consciousness of humanity. Our personal quest is like the overarching quest of humanity to come to terms with its essential spiritual nature.

These unprecedented modern times and our Western culture reflect centuries of focus on the physical nature of the universe and science's approach to natural laws. Our ancestors lived in different times, before the scientific revolution. A religious spiritual worldview shaped the hearts and minds of humanity. When religion was in charge, it did not recognize the validity of emerging scientific thought. In the early days of the scientific revolution, the church regarded most scientists as heretics doing the bidding of evil. When the great 15th century scientists Nicholas Copernicus and Galileo first recognized that it was the earth that revolved around the sun, as opposed to the then mistaken belief that the sun was in motion around a stationary earth, it did not fare well with religious authority. The church ordered Galileo to be burned at the stake for his heliocentric theories. Only after recanting his scientific findings did Galileo receive a reprieve and his life spared in favor of a sentence reduced to a life of incarceration.

It was not until October 31, 1992, after a 13-year investigation into the issue, that John Paul II admitted that the church was wrong for condemning Galileo in 1633—359 years after his incarceration. By this time, science had replaced religion as the dominant force in our worldview. It was now science that held the limelight taking aim at the "fantastical superstitions" of religion.

Eastern thought never lost sight of the spiritual world-view, while Western minds wrestled with the spiritual in a worldview rooted in science, or one that at least looked to be validated by scientific method and rational thought. This is not to condemn the progress of modern times or its scientific worldview. This is only to say that after so many fruitful years of scientific and technological achievement, humanity could now benefit by upgrading our ethical and moral software. This does not require us to dismantle our active scientific view, rather to expand it to include our dormant spiritual view. Science gave us the bomb, now it is up to the spiritual to protect us from it.

For those willing to try on its *garments* and look through the lens of the spiritual worldview, it will be helpful to review the groundwork that has come before. Innovative new thought leaders such as Emanuel Swedenborg, Emerson, and Thoreau contributed to the launch of the Transcendental Movement. The teachings of Phineas Quimby led to the rise of the New Thought Movement. Ernest Holms, author of *The Science of Mind*, founded the Religious Science Movement, which brought new definition to understanding the role of mind and spirit.

Mind and science ultimately converged in the birth of Human Psychology with schools of Psychoanalysis, Behaviorism, and Humanistic Psychology breaking new ground. Such great thinkers as William James, Freud, Jung, Adler, Frankl, Watson, and Skinner added unique dimensions to our understanding of human thought and behavior.

From the psychologist couch to the researcher's laboratory the mind was probed, expressed, and analyzed in hopes of finding new paths into fulfillment and the mitigation of frustration, anxiety, and anguish. As the field grew, so did the array of approaches. In the second half of the 20th century an awakening movement emerged toward actualizing the human potential. Contributors such as Carl Rogers, Abraham Maslow, Aldous Huxley, Timothy Leary and Richard Alpert brought new insights into this discussion. With this emergence came an entire generation with roots and branches delving deep into the psyche of the human entity. The quest for understanding went from the psychologist office and laboratory to the university classroom, to seminar rooms, mountain retreats and even the center stage of rock concerts. These are the tracks of what came to be called *unchurched spirituality*—a form of spirituality not tethered to the dogma, rituals, or interpretations of institutionalized religion.

In chapters Two through Six, we explore the progression of this quest. At times this search took some unconventional detours into philosophy, psychology, science, and even technology. As the author of this book, it is my belief that any authentic investigation into the *way things really are* is a spiritual quest. It is the process of viewing reality through the de-conditioned mind that leads to spiritual truth. This exploration may be viewed by some as a detour from a direct encounter with the spiritual structure. In fact, it is much more than a brief history lesson. It is a direct view of what shaped our current worldview—the perspective that influences the thoughts and identity of all who were born into it. It is a snapshot of how collectively we became who we are today. While it is humanity that shaped our worldview, it is also our worldview that shaped humanity.

Although beginning to change, our current worldview leans toward materialism, *i.e.*, the view that all that exists is ultimately physical. Those of us born and raised in the second half of the 20th century are inclined to perceive reality from this modern perspective. We are all under the influence of the times in which we live. The last 100 years represent the greatest advances in science and technology ever known. In order to embrace the spiritual and pursue Self-realization, it is necessary to expand our perception and core beliefs to include ideas that go against the grain of prevailing materialism. For the most part, spiritual awakening is a path of unlearning—distinguishing and stepping outside of the materialism of our current worldview that presents obstacles obscuring our ability to see through the spiritual lens.

The precepts, knowledge and experience of our spiritual nature are not easy to recognize. Our progress depends a great deal on the mind's willingness to grasp onto whatever piece it can without rejecting its otherworldly nature and formless composition. The first part of this book explores many spiritual principles from a perspective outside of the religions in which they might be imbedded. In this way, the mind can be introduced to these ideas and gain familiarity with them without being confronted by their religious pedigree. It is the learning process whereby one gains a rapport with already known and somewhat accepted information before confronting the unknown and speculative.

By going to such great lengths to set the context for the spiritual discussion, the mind is able to familiarize itself with what is utterly unfamiliar, and imagine that which is concealed. In this way we are able to extend our perspective into the esoteric nature of the ideas presented in second part of this book. Because our perspective is based on our beliefs and previous conditioning, it is inexorably linked to our identity. To alter our current perspective enough to gain spiritual awakening and Self-realization, requires a willingness to shift that identity.

Most of us tend to identify ourselves with the body and personality. In order to develop spiritual identity, we must first provide an unoccupied space within our psyche where it may take root. This space begins as a *spin free zone,* where ideas that are not aligned with ordinary thinking can be thought and expressed without prejudice. The Bible makes dozens of references to the importance of *good soil* for spiritual seeds to take root. The Books of Mathew, Mark, and Luke all speak of the parable of good seeds falling in fertile soil bearing fruit. This reference to *good soil* is a simile for the teachable heart. Sometimes the heart requires *tenderizing* to become teachable. This *tenderizing of the heart* is brought about through humility and unfortunately, often comes in the form of grieving and pain. If one has the ability to squelch the arrogant and self-protective protests of the ego when faced with spiritual teachings, he or she can avoid the need for this suffering. The process of *tenderizing the heart* through wisdom and love is far preferable to the alternative.

Whether Spiritual Learning be Individual or Institutional, the Responsibility for the Inquiry is Individual

In a strange and somewhat counterintuitive way, each individual is responsible for making his or her own inquiry, regardless of what is discovered. In other words, we are not held responsible for our results, rather only for our efforts. We do not determine the destination, only the path of our journey. Each life is overflowing with meaning and purpose. The simple fact that we are alive and human is a testament to the myriad trials and tribulations endured to reach our crowning position on the food chain. Even beyond the use of the thumb and the power to reason, the human is representative of higher consciousness in a physical form. Like lower animals, humans must provide themselves with food, shelter, and companionship to sustain and perpetuate life. Unlike lower animals, this is not the full extent of our responsibilities. Discovering of life's meaning and fulfilling our purpose are uniquely human responsibilities. Whether through formal education, religious study, or the school of hard knocks, it is our individual responsibility to discover life's meaning, awakening the sleeping giant within. Nobody else can refine our character or provide our Self-realization.

While institutionalized religion contains the elements of spiritual realization, they are sometimes obscured by the institutional agenda of self-preservation. This is not to say that religion is ill-suited for spirituality, only that religion has always had a perpetuation agenda that often distracts from the spiritual and, for some, may even be counterproductive. Religious institutions have obligations to their spiritual doctrines and objectives, but they must also attend to their worldly activities. They must follow business plans in the same manner as any other revenue collecting organization. They must be concerned with attendance and policies handed down by their boards as well as those of their larger political and social structures. These are often quite a diversion from direct spiritual interests.

Karen Armstrong (born 1944) is a former Roman Catholic nun who left the convent in 1969 to pursue a more mystical Christian faith. She has authored over two dozen books and is considered a leading authority in comparative religion. She is a fellow of the Royal Society of Literature founded in 1820 by King George IV, counting among its fellowship such noted authors as Samuel Taylor Coleridge, Thomas Hardy, George Bernard Shaw, Rudyard Kipling, William Butler Yeats, and the Bishop of Salisbury. In the preface to her 2000 book, *Islam: A Short History*, Armstrong states the matter as follows:

The external history of a religious tradition often seems divorced from the raison d'etre of faith. The spiritual quest is an interior journey; it is a psychic rather than a political drama. It is preoccupied with liturgy, doctrine, contemplative disciplines and an exploration of the heart, not with the clash of current events. Religions certainly have a life outside the soul. Their leaders have to contend with the state and affairs of the world, and often relish doing so. They fight with members of other faiths, who seem to challenge their claim to a monopoly of absolute truth; they also persecute their co-religionists for interpreting a tradition differently or for holding heterodox beliefs. Very often priests, rabbis, imams, and shamans are just as consumed by worldly ambitions as regular politicians. But all this is generally seen as an abuse of sacred ideal. These power struggles are not what religion is really about, but an unworthy distraction from the life of spirit, which is conducted far from the madding crowd, unseen, silent and unobtrusive. Indeed, in many faiths, monks and mystics lock themselves away from the world, since the clamor and strife of history is regarded as incompatible with a truly religious life. —Islam: A Short History

It is not our intent to disparage religion or even the antireligious. Religion has always made, and continues to make, huge contributions to the spiritual advancement of individuals and society. There are endless accounts of religion's contribution to the moral and ethical evolution of humanity. However, these are not central to the discussion of this book, which concerns itself with the *spiritual experience* and the *spiritual structure* that initiates it. Having a strong religious upbringing may facilitate one's ability to attain spiritual awakening. On the other hand, it might be an advantage to have no preconceived notions of the spiritual dimension. As the Buddha taught, our beliefs and convictions may serve to bring us to the distant shores of spiritual enlightenment; however, once we arrive, it becomes our challenge to become detached from all that brought us there. This is not to say that these teachings were false or deficient, only that they pale in comparison to the pure spiritual experience that we now find. This experience is not to be defined nor named—not even communicated. In scripture it is identified as *that which it is*. When you have reached it, you will know it to be true.

Following the Bread Crumbs Home...

For purposes of our discussion, we first provide an abbreviated description of the collective emergence of the spiritual structure within our history—how we collectively got to where we now find ourselves. Second, we provide a distilled and contemporized, yet authentic, method to engage the spiritual process that leads to individual spiritual realization. Once arriving on this *distant shore*, the reader no longer needs external teachings and guidance; all that is needed has awakened within. Whether we choose the metaphor of sleeping or concealment, whether the teachings are called seeds or sparks, they lead to Self-realization. This is the third and foremost element of our identity—that which exists beyond the physical and psychological, beyond body and mind.

To be human is to know reality through our five senses, our thoughts and our emotions. We experience our world as being physical and we react to it mentally and emotionally. From the beginning of time, people have also recognized something more. In the earliest cave drawings and the later writings of the shaman, in the wisdom of the Saints and Sages and the teachings of philosophy and theology, humanity has an expansive accounting of that which exists beyond the ordinary reality of the physical and psychological.

One might ask, "Isn't this the work of monks, nuns, and mystics?" Certainly, there are substantial examples of those who removed themselves "far from the madding crowd," such as Thoreau on Walden Pond, in order to discover what might be obscured by the "clamor and strife" of ordinary reality. Yet, the modern world is not always conducive to such extreme measures of isolation. We live in a time in history when seemingly ordinary people may be on the verge of spiritual awakening. There stimulus may be no more than listening to self-improvement lectures during their morning commute or volunteering as mentors to at-risk children.

As Zen Master D.T. Suzuki points out, *satori* (awakening) can often occur in a sudden instant during the most mundane setting. The mind can be accumulating and processing data from one's life during routine experiences of school, career, relationships, hobbies, etc. until reaching an obscured *tipping point* where everything snaps into place. There is no way to know how many years or lifetimes are involved with this mechanism, as it is occurring on the spiritual level. Then, like an incorporeal slot machine, without warning the lights flash, the bells ring, and our long overdue winnings surge forth.

It is our job to keep feeding the machine as every new coin enhances the opportunity to hit the jackpot. From the spiritual vantage, this is all there is to earthy life—feeding the mind until it is able to stand on its own. Once the mind has cleared the way to pure consciousness, it has achieved its highest calling. It no longer relies on faulty conditioning from the past to determine its true nature and the nature of all that surrounds it. It is no longer easily distracted by the selfish demands of the ego nor the cravings of the senses. The security of the familiar is released in order to access the wondrous adventure of the unknown. The Hindu Saint Ramakrishna expresses this sentiment to his disciples:

When the nest of the bird is destroyed, it betakes itself to the sky. Similarly, when all consciousness of the body and the outer world is effaced from the mind, the soul of man soars into the sky of the Supreme and merges itself in Samadhi. –Teachings Of Sri Ramakrishna

"Samadhi" is a Sanskrit term used in Hinduism and Buddhism describing the state of *superconsciousness* brought about through one-pointed focus and intense concentration, where the mind experiences its identity with ultimate reality. According to Patanjali, this state of pure clarity allows the mind to perceive the true nature of reality undistorted by previous conditioning. Many of the world's great religions espouse the notion of ultimate reality existing in the here and now. The challenge is not one of location or timing, rather it is one of perception. Until we are able to transcend the ordinary consciousness of our physical existence, ultimate reality remains concealed. As it turns out, the trail of crumbs leading us home is not a trail at all. Rather it is just one crumb and we are standing on it.

A Question of Perception

When Jesus was asked by the Pharisees for the time and location of ultimate reality, i.e., the Kingdom of God, he replied that it is not observable, nor can it be said that it is here or there, rather "The Kingdom of God is within you" (Luke 17:20-21). This spiritual tenet is supported through ancient Hindu scriptures, by the teachings of Buddha, the Abrahamic religions, and many of the great philosophers. It is a very important clue to understanding the spiritual puzzle. All roads lead us back home. Our search for Absolute Truth and Ultimate Reality begins and ends right here, right now. As frustrating as it might seem, the message throughout the ages is that we exist in a reality that is only partially revealed, but mostly concealed and the concealed portion far exceeds our wildest imagination. In the words of Werner Heisenberg:

"Not only is the Universe stranger than we think... It is stranger than we can think"

The spiritual is beyond sensory perception, beyond the mind's ability to visualize, beyond words and beyond thoughts. The only access is through experience. When one is blessed with the wondrous experience of spirit, it passes all too quickly and takes with it all evidence of its presence. We are left only with the intoxicating fragrance that lingers in our spiritual memory. The spiritual cannot be translated into the physical. Any attempt to personify the spiritual is both a distortion and a dilution. The spiritual encounter is expressed mainly through its impact upon the one expressing. The only trace left behind is the transformative effect on all that it touches. When one has had a spiritual experience, he or she can detect its footprints in the world and in others. This is the limited window through which we can perceive evidence of the spiritual having a physical presence.

Engaging the Spiritual Process to Achieve the Spiritual Experience

The design of this book is to present enough spiritual theory and technique from a variety of authentic sources, to lay a nondenominational path to the spiritual experience. Given that the underlying purpose of all religion is to bring the practitioner into Divine contact, religion should not be resistant toward this goal. The traditional sectarian approaches to spirituality should not be offended by our removal of religious packaging and dogma. Our approach should not be viewed as an invalidation of a traditional approach, rather this omission should be viewed as an alternative approach. It is not intended to conflict or compete with the traditional religious approach, rather to compliment and supplement it for those who find it difficult to operate under religion's strict rules of adherence. The essence of religion and the essence of spirituality are one and the same. However, organized religion is institutional, while spirituality is individual. The downside of unchurched spirituality is that the individual loses the support of the religious community. The downside of institutionalized religion is that many sense a loss of individuality and pressure to adhere to a prescribed mold or risk invalidation. As the ancient Hindu proverb suggests, the goal is the same for all:

> We must all eventually climb the spiritual mountain, and there are many paths all leading to the top; so it doesn't matter which path you take. The person running around the mountain telling everyone else that their path is wrong is the person not climbing.

Part Two of this book identifies the spiritual quest, describes the *structure* and prescribes the *method* necessary to navigate the spiritual journey to experience and transcend the dark and morbid destiny of our physical lives. Many people report that they are able to enjoy life without the need for spiritual intervention. This may seem like a life blessed with good fortune. Viewed through the spiritual lens, such fleeting satisfaction is the polar opposite of good fortune. It is precisely this fleeting satisfaction that causes one to miss the big picture. The physical is not permanent life. Setting up permanent residency in a burning building is destined to end badly. We are given a span of time within which to achieve an important mission. Treating this life as if it were permanent, is apt to mistake complacency for true contentment. A wise teacher put it this way: We are not yet in the life for which we were created; we are still standing in the corridor waiting entry. The reason this life is not permanent is to prevent us from indefinitely double-parking here.

An ancient mystical legend proclaims that the final request of the Soul before being imbedded into a physical body is that it not be put into a beautiful body nor be given a life of riches. There are no greater material distractions or physical attachments than beauty and wealth. Given that spiritual awakening and eventual Enlightenment depend upon our ability to overcome ego and transcend self-interest, great beauty and immense wealth significantly hamper our progress.

To live life for its own sake is a common mistake. The big questions of meaning and purpose are often left simmering on the back burner until they can no longer be in denial. The very purpose of disease and frailty in old age is to allow the vitality of the Soul to be recognized. Failing such recognition, aging becomes torture. Aging without spirituality is analogous to being ill without medicine. Unlike medicine, however, spirituality cannot be administered on an *as needed* basis. Without cultivating our spiritual nature in advance, it is not waiting for us when we need it.

Our intention is to spark enough spiritual interest to have the reader embark upon the spiritual journey. This moment of embarkation is not to be taken lightly—intention has been set in place—a decision has been made. By deciding to explore our spiritual nature, the road ahead splits and we begin to follow a new path. Initially the path may seem the same, but what lies ahead could never have been a part of the exclusively material path. Even though our spiritual perception may be in its infancy, its burgeoning new vision is gaining clarity with each new insight.

Setting intention begins the spiritual process—the flame is ignited. Like a campfire, the spiritual fire needs to be fed to keep us warm. How we feed it is a matter of personal choice. Of course, the test is whether the fire grows brighter or begins to smolder. Fire, flames, and sparks have always been metaphors for spiritual light, which in turn is a metaphor for higher consciousness. There is a sensation when turning knowledge into realization. Regardless of how latent the drive to know our spiritual nature, once accessed, passion soon emerges.

At the most fundamental level, the spiritual process has three parts: One is to draw in higher consciousness, second is to realize it as our own and third express it into the world. This process leads to the spiritual experience known as self-realization. Here we gain our first glimpse into our true nature—not merely body and mind, but the uniquely human form of body, mind and Soul simultaneously intertwined and existing in both spirit and form. Until we advance to the point where we can draw upon our own endless source of spiritual light, we are able to draw from the light of others—their knowledge becomes our knowledge. If their words are true and the teacher authentic, we are led to the experience that validates the effort.

Merging Science and Spirit: The Emergence of a New Worldview

The teachings referenced in this book are drawn from the world's great spiritual teachers. They are chosen for content without regard to religious affiliation or ethnicity. In some cases, the words are quoted directly, while in others their wisdom is distilled and contemporized for a modern audience. It is not our intention to endorse any particular religion, but rather to promote the spiritual experience that is the underlying goal of all religion. Neither teacher nor dogma relieves an individual of his or her obligation to discover. They only provide the means to navigate. In the words of the Buddha:

It is you that must make the effort. The Great of the past only show the way. Those who think and follow the path become free from the bondage of Mara. – Buddha, Dhammapada, Maggavagga: The Path

Mara is a term used in Buddhism to refer to that which tempts a person away from the spiritual path and obscures the spiritual structure. According to Buddhist legend, the Buddha was tempted to abandon his path toward Enlightenment by Mara as the Gospels similarly report that Jesus was tempted by Satan in the Judean Desert. Ancient writings provide narratives describing the events of Saints and Sages. These accounts are often poetic and beautiful, told in mystical language using parables and metaphors. For our purposes, their significance is found in the lessons they teach. In this instance the lesson is: The spiritual path can be turbulent, wrought with temptations designed to try the weak of heart.

One of the most common modern temptations is our conditioning toward rational interpretation and explanation. Remember the worldview that is currently dominant, particularly in Western cultures, is that of rational thought and material perception based on scientific evidence. This materialist scientific worldview represents centuries of diligent efforts and grand discoveries and is not to be discarded as inaccurate or obsolete. Just as it is not our intent to disparage the teachings of religion, it is not our intent to discredit the findings of science. It is our intent to present the new worldview that combines the best of both.

Our Sages would often say that to grasp the spiritual we must put faith above reason. Reason is a powerful force, especially in modern times. Faith was the dominant force in ancient times. Throughout the second half of the previous millennium, faith and reason have often been configured in opposition to one another. Today we have the opportunity to see the benefits of both. The physical world is governed by natural laws that pertain closely to rational thought. The language of science is mathematics—what could be more rational? The language of religion is words—what could be more malleable? The language of spirituality is purely experiential—what could be more ineffable?

Because the spiritual is indescribable and unexplainable, it is also incorruptible. Science leans in this direction as math is far less corruptible than words. If the numbers are correct, the results are indisputable. Unlike politics, science does not conduct opinion polls to determine truth. Like politics, religion has been accused of bending truth to gain popularity and achieve ulterior motives. Reducing scientific theory to its foundation, we find mathematics. Reducing spirituality to its foundation we find pure experience. When this experience is interpreted, we have entered the realm of religion and philosophy. Our purpose is to bring the reader to an *un-interpreted spiritual experience* so that he or she may decide independently where he or she stands and what is perceived.

It is not a requirement that one abandon the rational mind to find the Soul. One must, however, put faith above reason in order to access the spiritual domain. Interestingly, for many, faith is cultivated through exercising the rational mind. By expanding our knowledge of what the great Sages convey in their teachings, we will expand our faith. To *see* a thing that is not visible requires a greater understanding of the object than seeing something that is clearly visible. Knowledge can impact one's faith sufficiently to gain personal experience of the spiritual structure. When one reaches this pivotal point, he or she is well on the way. This is not to say that you will no longer encounter inner resistance–that is the nature of the endeavor. However, spiritual experience is quite intoxicating; once tasted, it takes on its own allure.

In the past, many transcended the material world to encounter the spiritual through faith alone. Certainly, there are those today who achieve this high level of faith. Given our modern scientific worldview, and its dominance over our perception, modern thinkers may find more effective an approach to spirituality through a more rational thought process. Our Sages characterized humans as being a unique blend of flesh and spirit–matter and consciousness. With this in mind we set out to explore the unchurched spiritual core underlying rational thought and methodical discovery.

When presented with all the examples in the chapters

ahead, from cave dwellers to space travelers, it will be difficult to dismiss the claim that humanity has been on an endless quest for truth, both spiritual and natural. Reviewing the inexhaustible investigation of humanity's most dedicated and brightest scholars, the rational mind will be coaxed into expanding its viewfinder to allow for what has traditionally been beyond its scope—the spirit.

Part One of this book is designed to do just that—supply the rational mind with the kind of firm foundation it requires in order to explore the ethereal path of the spiritual. It utilizes the "language" of documentation and historical examples in supporting the points made, while Part Two necessarily utilizes a more mystical tone so as to infer the path the reader is to follow in his or her own journey toward a spiritual experience. In the history of the spiritual, or more precisely stated, the evolution of consciousness, we are on the threshold of a new worldview merging discoveries of new science with the teachings of ancient mystics. Today, 2500 years after the Buddha spoke of the inherent *emptiness* associated with our physical world, we hear startling ideas from theoretical physicists reporting a similar phenomenon of emptiness and instability found at the quantum subatomic level. The following is taken from Chapter Six:

In 1975, Fritjof Capra (born 1939), an Austrian-born American physicist published his groundbreaking book, *The Tao of Physics: An Exploration of the Parallels Between Modern Physics and Eastern Mysticism,* where he drew a parallel between quantum physics and the teachings of Hindu, Buddhist, and Eastern philosophy. After its first edition the book has since been published in 43 editions in 23 languages. It was especially astonishing in the mid-70s, for a scientist such as Capra to boldly profess that modern science and ancient mysticism share a common denominator.

We shall see how the two foundations of twentieth-century physics—quantum theory and relativity theory—both force us to see the world very much in the way a Hindu, Buddhist, or Taoist sees it, and how this similarity strengthens when we look at the recent attempts to combine these two theories in order to describe the submicroscopic world... Here the parallels between modern physics and Eastern mysticism are most striking, and we shall encounter statements where it is almost impossible to say whether they have been made by physicists or by Eastern mystics. (Capra, *The Tao of Physics*, 1976)

Capra is not alone in recognizing that modern science resonates with the teachings of ancient mystics. In the chapters of Part One, we will delve into how the scientists of the 20th century struggled with their findings and how closely those findings correlate with ancient spiritual teachings. There is an increasingly popular assertion that the new worldview is one in which science and the spiritual have merged. Future generations will have the advantage of being born into such a remarkable worldview. They will not be burdened with inner stirrings that do not coincide with outward social norms.

Under this new *scientific spiritual* worldview, a person will be able to recognize the spiritual structure or acknowledge his or her own spiritual nature, without feeling he or she is going against the grain of the historic discoveries of science. This collective shift in perception is still in its infancy. In order to begin to experience our spiritual core, those of us born under the existing materialist scientific worldview, must not only confront modern perceptions, but must also overcome our own internalized materialist conditioning. Currently, in order to avoid the domination of our modern worldview, the religious ultra-orthodox have had to shun the technologies and luxuries of contemporary life and remain sheltered from their effects. Once these two pillars of life in the world, science and religion, have merged, a person will no longer feel compelled to betray one in order to embrace the other.

This book is intended to bring aspiring readers close enough to their spiritual nature so as to recognize the spiritual structure in the world. We will first separate the spiritual element from traditional religion in order to gain a clearer picture of its true nature. Once we have *unchurched* spirituality, our focus will shift to the various ways the spiritual has emerged (both within and outside of religion) and to the various modalities in which it has been expressed. We will review the turbulent journey humanity has traveled from cave drawings to the Worldwide Web, in order to gain insight into the vast untapped potential of our unique threefold nature—physical/psychological/spiritual. Once the historic macro view, of which we are all a product, has been established, we will shift focus to the current micro view—from the collective worldview to our individual perspective.

A Word about God...

The word *God* has been used by many individuals, cultures, religions, and scriptures throughout human history. It is a term that uplifts some, while oppressing others. It carries with it the very best and the very worst of the human experiment. It is a word providing many with the means to love one another, while providing others permission to hate. The word

God is perhaps the most familiar term in the human language, yet it refers to something that is, by design, unknown and unknowable. The Taoists taught a profound and illuminating riddle regarding the ultimate reality of *God*—those who speak of the Tao (ultimate reality) don't know the Tao; and those who know the Tao, do not speak of it.

It is not that there is no evidence or experience of the ultimate reality of *God* available for human perception; only that we are unable to interpret that which we experience; let alone communicate about it. And perhaps our worst blunder comes when we attempt to define that which is far too vast and grand for human comprehension based on a tiny flash of insight fleeting across our radar. In order to illustrate this point, imagine a person who has been deprived of all five of their senses throughout their life. This person has never known the experience of sight, sound, scent, taste, or touch. Suddenly and miraculously, on their fortieth birthday, for a few brief moments, all of their senses are restored. In this moment of sensory clarity, we hear this person say; *now I know what the world is all about.* Of course, it would be absurd to think a person would know the world based on a few brief moments of experiencing it. All the intricacies of life on our planet just aren't knowable from a fleeting experience—a spark of light in an otherwise darkened void. And so it is with the infinite notion of *God*. The great spiritual Sages teach that one must first achieve Self-realization before even approaching God-realization. Without the benefit of experiencing these high levels of consciousness, it is not possible to perceive or proclaim all that goes into our casual use of the infinite term referred to as God. Having said this, let's venture into what *is* available for us to consider...

In Summary...

Chapter One deals directly with the epiphany referred to in the title of this book. The spiritual hypothesis simply states: *to be human is to be more spirit than flesh—more Soul than body, more immortal than mortal.* This is the basic truth of the human condition; we are spiritual beings embedded in a physical creature. Eventually we must all decide for ourselves where we stand on this ancient hypothesis. Even though we are all challenged by this spiritual truth, for most it remains unexplored and, thus, unresolved.

The experience of this truth is nowhere to be found on the physical dimension. We must enter the spiritual realm to discover its whereabouts. Experience is the language of the spiritual the way math is the language of science. Our task is not to *find* the spiritual realm, our task is to *recognize* it, as it is already present—although masterfully concealed, the spiritual dimension has been here all along.

We begin by exploring the spiritual epiphany through the ancient teachings of the Hindu scriptures, the Buddha's Sutras, the mystical traditions of the Abrahamic religions and the sacred words of Saints and Sages, which all point toward a separate reality that remains hidden until we gain access to higher levels of awareness and perception.

The early teachings of *The Science of Mind* established the mind as the gateway to the Soul, paving the way for the birth of human psychology. Additionally, Chapter One introduces the astonishing parallel emerging between the teachings of ancient mystics and the discoveries of modern physics.

Because the spiritual dimension is beyond sensory perception, we become aware of its presence through direct personal experience. This is the topic and purpose of this book: to learn and engage the *Spiritualization Process* in order to achieve the spiritual experience.

CHAPTER TWO

Is Spirituality the New Religion?

The purpose of this chapter is to separate the subtle occurrence of spirituality from the well-known and highly communicated institution of religion. It is not being suggested that there is no place for spirituality in religion or vice versa. The separation is for illustrative purposes in order to gain an unbiased view of the phenomenon of *unchurched* spirituality, which is the topic of this book.

It is customary to blame secular science and anti-religious philosophy for the eclipse of religion in modern society. It would be more honest to blame religion for its own defeats. Religion declined not because it was refuted, but because it became irrelevant, dull, oppressive, insipid. When faith is completely replaced by creed, worship by discipline, love by habit; when the crisis of today is ignored because of the splendor of the past; when faith becomes an heirloom rather than a living fountain; when religion speaks only in

the name of authority rather than with the voice of compassion—its message becomes meaningless.
        —Abraham Joshua Heschel, *God in Search of Man*

Is spirituality the new religion? It's a trick question. Spirituality has always been the essence of religion. Religion is the container where spirituality has been kept. Religion is the outward expression of the inward spiritual plane found in this world. Religion is the history of the path that spirituality has taken in our world; its events and stories; its heroes and its villains. Throughout most of human history, the term spirituality and the term religion have been viewed as interchangeable; almost synonymous—this is no longer the case.

Over the last century, and certainly over the past few decades, there appears to have been a significant shift as people began to separate what they mean by spiritual apart from religion. Spirituality is far more intricate and obscure than religion; far more difficult to identify, describe, and detect. Where spirituality is most often a private affair reflecting personal experience, religion is far more public; a congregation of people adhering to common denominational doctrines and participating in common rituals. Religion is bent toward exclusivity while spirituality tends to be more inclusive.

Religion can be as basic as history; a collection of stories. The history of religion is often recognized as beginning around the same timeframe as when words were put into written form. Even before there were letters, humans would scratch out symbols and markings to convey some crucial message they felt the need to preserve. More often than not, these messages were of a religious/spiritual nature, dealing with the purpose of life, its meaning or ethical values.

For our purpose it will help to set a context for this question of spirituality and religion—as who we are today is inseparably connected to who our ancestors were in the past. Archeologists, historians, and scholars identify religious tendencies that date back even further than the time of Neanderthals. The earliest signs that humans have recorded religious thoughts have been related to the ceremonial rituals around the burial of the dead. Of course, these rituals may only signify the human response to grief and reverence around the death of loved ones.

Even in prehistoric times we find the use of grave markers that have been determined to be early deities, reflecting the genesis of recording religious thought and practice. In 2008, one of the oldest known relics of prehistoric art was discovered in Germany. The *Venus of Hohle Fels* was carved out of the tusk of a wooly mammoth. Researchers at one of Germany's oldest and most famous universities, University of Tubingen, estimate the figurine's age to be over 35,000 years.

During the Neolithic Era, when humans went from hunter/gatherers to farmers, there is evidence that their communities organized into early theocracies where governing was associated with religious beliefs. An archeological survey conducted by Istanbul University and the University of Chicago in 1963 discovered the ruins of Gobekli Tepe in Turkey and dated them at approximately 10,000 BCE. Although their early function has not yet been determined, it is believed that these ruins were most likely religious sanctuaries.

By the Bronze Age, when humans were well on their way towards recording events through a system called proto-writing, we find evidence of religious sacrificial rites conducted by the Proto-Indo-Europeans. From written language that became more prevalent some 5000 years ago, we can obtain a clearer picture of religious development. The earthly life of

Rama, an early God in Hinduism, is believed to have occurred around 5000 BCE. The writings that describe the beginnings of the religious development in Mesopotamia, Egypt, Ethiopia, and the Mediterranean, where the Abrahamic religions of today first began, were written some 3,500 years ago.

It is almost impossible to study the history of humankind without the inclusion of the history of religion. It seems that humanity has always had a fascination with all that religion encompasses. The stories and modern sermons would not be complete without the tales told by our ancestors gathered around their fires and within the walls of their sanctuaries.

Beyond its stories, religion takes on greater depth when these narratives are told with special emphasis placed on the moral implications. It was through this storytelling that the young were able to learn acceptable behavior from their elders; how communities and later societies established appropriate conduct which defined how people were to relate to one another. These moral implications evolved into a moral system of rules and laws; virtues and sins.

It should be noted that religion has always contained another component that goes beyond its link to morality, conduct, rules and laws. An unquantifiable factor has always accompanied religious practice and underlies religious meaning. It is a qualitative ingredient that lends itself to passion and wonder. Throughout history, religion has relied upon it to gain momentum and conformity.

This *other* component has come to be called spirituality. The primary focus of this book is on this other component—spirituality. In order to better illuminate the relationship between religion and spirituality, we will distinguish these lifelong friends and define them independently. Spirituality is to religion what electricity is to the light bulb; its source of power. Like the light bulb, religion can be seen, while its source of power remains invisible.

We can observe religion in many forms; the most common is its words. Most religions come with an operating manual, which we will call "its book." Another familiar way that we can observe religion is through the person representing its authority. In ancient times this person came with a book and particular garments; both representing authority. Along with the book and garb, religion acquired a collection of rituals and a whole cadre of followers to perform these rituals. In addition to the book, the person, the garb, the clergy and the followers, religion established the location of sacred activity—the *sanctuary*.

Through one of its most common rituals, the *holiday* or *holy day*, religion has not only been able to establish the sanctification of space, the *sanctuary*, but it has also sanctified time. In our inquiry, we ask, *"Why has humanity spent so much time and energy on religious involvement throughout all of human history?"* It seems that the great prophets, saints, sages, teachers, and scholars, agree that the pursuit of religion is, and has always been, about attaining the *sacred experience*—i.e., experiencing the spiritual while existing on the physical plane. Any idea, word or ritual that brings us closer to this revered experience is considered sacred and on the path to Enlightenment.

Although its books and garb are altered from one denomination to another, and the times of its various holidays are not all the same, the common thread throughout all religion is the *sacred experience*. In fact, most religions declare that their very purpose is to bring the *sacred experience* to their followers. In the words of the Sages, the whole purpose of life is for people to have this *sacred experience* while still amongst the living. In the mystical language of most scripture, the *sacred experience* is referred to as the key that unlocks the gates of heaven. Each assert that it is nothing less than a glimpse into the next dimension—the World to Come, the Kingdom of God, Nirvana, the Awakening, God Consciousness. Whatever the denomination, the meaning is the same, namely, that the *sacred experience* reveals that which we are all moving towards, whether in this world or the next.

This *sacred experience* is the primary focus of this book—what it is and how to have it. Unfortunately, one of the key characteristics of the *sacred experience* is that it is ineffable. Hence the challenge: to write a book about a topic that can't be described. The challenge from your perspective as the reader: to learn about a topic that can't be taught. If you are beginning to think this all has a very Zen flavor, you have just passed through the first gate. The *sacred experience* is what the Zen Grand Master, Lao Tzu, refers to in his famous work, *Tao Te Ching*, as the *path*. Although the *path* leads to *ultimate reality,* it cannot be perceived, at least not by the senses. As he states: *"The Tao which can be conceived is not the real Tao."* To my chagrin as your author, he goes on to say: *Those who know don't say, and those who say don't know.*

Of course, Lao Tzu provides us with his wisdom as a koan, a paradox to be contemplated, such as, *"the sound of one hand clapping."*

With all due respect to the Grand Master's warning, as it holds profound truth, we are fortunate that over the intervening millennia, many knowing teachers have found the right useful words to lead us where we want to go. Although the way of the Toa may be discovered without a single word being spoken, for many of us, language is fundamental for guidance.

In this book, my method will be to engage the reader in a variety of spiritual teachings, some spoken profoundly by the world's greatest Sages and others spoken inadvertently by minor teachers. We will not be exploring the various backgrounds, ethnicities or particular religions of which they speak. Rather our focus will be on the depth of their understanding and their commitment to truth (personal or universal, practical or sacred). It is not my intention to advocate any particular system or theology; rather to advocate all sources for the value they offer each of us in search of our own unique path, the path of our own distinctive Soul.

Three Potential Interferences

I recommend to you the same guide I use myself—*if the truth fits, wear it*. Resist the temptation to decide in advance if you believe it. Just try it on and see if it has value for you. The proof is always in the pudding, so to speak. If what you study brings you closer to the *sacred experience*, you're on the right track. If it does not, you may need to examine one or more of the following three adjustments. **First,** the message is sound, but our receptors may be dull. **Second**, the message is sound, but its transmission is unclear. **Third**, the message itself is flawed.

Of the three adjustments, the first is the most common—our receptors are out of whack. The reason for this is that all of us have receptors that are out of whack. In the words of many of the great Sages such as Saint Paul: ...*the lens through which we view reality is cloudy*. For now, we see through a glass, darkly; but then face to face: Now I know in part; but then shall I know even as I am known. —Saint Paul, 1 Corinthians 13:12

Our lenses are cloudy because they come that way from

the factory. We do not enter this life with absolute clarity. All of the great saints and teachers *achieved* their clarity. We note the exception of those religious figures that are purported to have been born into this world with perfect clarity and absolute truth. For the rest of us, we simply have *dirty windows.* By *dirty windows,* we mean that our ability to perceive truth/reality is altered by our own filters and biases—we all view the world differently. This difference stems from each of us having separate and distinct experiences and learning. The quote from 1 Corinthians makes us aware of a "now" and a "then" aspect of our clarity. Most commentaries on this passage suggest that the "dark glass" refers to our earthly clarity of "now" as opposed to the "face to face" heavenly clarity of "then."

There is no need to feel shame or regret over our imperfect perception, as it is characteristic of who we are. Yet one of the greatest challenges we can engage is the correction of this defect—to gain a clear perception. Be forewarned, however, this correction does not just happen without intention, focus, and effort. All that we have taken into our intellect first passed through our unique filters. These filters are the mind's mechanism of relating the objective external world to our subjective inner world.

Our brains automatically connect each new experience, the unknown, with that which is already known. Thus, every experience that we have had from our moment of birth impacts our beliefs and understanding of reality. It is as if our first impression coming into this world was our inner questioning; *"Where am I now?"* and *"What's going on?"* These questions never stop; they just recede deeper into our subconscious. The questioning may be modified a bit; *"Am I where I belong?"* and *"where am I heading?"* As we gain in wisdom, we face the biggest question of all— *"What does it all mean?"*

This process is simply a part of our endless inquiry into the nature of the reality we see before us. That reality is seen differently by each of us who gazes upon it. Further, what we each perceive as reality is not the same as the *collective reality* we all share. No two people experience the same object exactly the same. Each of us identifies what we encounter in present time with all that we have experienced in our individual past.

This is why so many of the great spiritual teachers begin their teaching by helping students become liberated from their past experiences. By this approach a student is able to experience truth outside of his or her personal biases and self-interest which alter perception.

The second possible interference with the message not resonating properly is more about transmission than reception. Whatever the message that is being shared, it is the response of another who has perceived spiritual truth and is attempting to pass his or her experience to us. The insights of the transmitter may have been gained over an extended period of time. As indicated previously, Taoists consider spiritual truth to be so ineffable, so beyond words, that any attempt to communicate it in words is faulty at best, if not futile.

Hence, if the effort to transmit a spiritual message does not initially resonate, it is to be expected. Like all spiritual messages, the information presented here is to be digested slowly. Once the reader has built a rapport with the material, a second reading is highly beneficial. It's astounding how much more can be absorbed by a second and third reading of spiritual teachings. Each reading brings new levels of understanding and reveals greater truth. This is particularly true when attempting to gain insight into the vast wisdom contained within the sacred writings.

We must also keep in mind that we are all human beings communicating to other human beings. This alone means the process is inherently flawed. It is difficult enough for a given group of friends in the same culture at the same time to communicate with one another. How much more difficult the task of gaining understanding from teachers who lived in different cultures centuries and even millennia before us. Somewhat consoling is the reminder that these teachings are providing a *map* to discover truth already present in the core of our being. It is a hidden *treasure.* If that treasure were gold and silver, surely, we would do our best to overcome the *static on the line.*

Finally, the third possible reason that may interfere with the reader properly receiving the message is the message itself. Humanity has been blessed with a handful of enlightened beings throughout our history. For the most part, the greatest spiritual teachers have been claimed by their various religions to be their exclusive source. From the perspective of religion, this is understandable, possibly even tolerable. After all, religions are exclusive organizations that often require membership. Although religions have half-heartedly accepted that they cannot claim an exclusive relationship with God, they do claim exclusive rights over their prophets.

It is when the pure message of a great Sage is adapted to the religion which claims ownership of that Sage that static is created in the clarity of the message. A spiritual message delivered by a great Sage is meant for all to hear and take in. This process may not fit the agenda of the exclusive religion claiming that Sage as its own. Accordingly, that religion may add context, subtext or interpretation that can become part of the message and thus filter or even obscure it.

For the purposes of our discussion, we will examine the spiritual teachings of the great Sages outside the context of the respective religions that adhere to their teachings. While holding these religions in the highest regard, we will minimize the connections between the great Sages themselves and the respective religions within which they taught. Hopefully, this will steer us clear of a multitude of digressions which might otherwise bog down our effort. Religion has preserved the spiritual teachings over the centuries and for this we should all be grateful. Yet, we can't deny that we have arrived at a time in history where people are seeking spiritual truth without religious context—without dogma, ritual, or even the religious community.

Tracing the History of "Unchurched Spirituality"

In order to view our spiritual aspect and to deepen our understanding of it, it will be useful to separate the discussion of spirituality from the religious practices and definitions in which it has become embedded. In no way do I intend to imply that spirituality has no place in religion. On the contrary, it is at the very heart of religion. This is simply an opportunity to view spirituality within our discussion as separate and distinct from religion. This will give us a better guide to understand the teachings of the Sages and great scholars on the subject, without the necessity of accepting or rejecting the religious practices in which the particular Sage or scholar is involved. This will also open our examination of the subject without the inquiry being seen as a challenge to the particular faith. This approach is referred to as "*unchurched spirituality.*"

From the vantage point of unchurched spirituality, we'll gain insight into the growing number of people who identify themselves as spiritual, and even believing in God, but not attending any particular church or holding an affiliation with an organized religion. There are others who feel that their spirituality and their religion are separate. In fact, they may attend religious services as a way of expressing their individual spirituality, even though they do not believe their religion gives them that spirituality or defines it for them.

Having addressed the "unchurched" half of the term *unchurched spirituality;* we will turn to the other ineffable half—the spirituality itself. While there is a vast assortment of definitions for *"spiritua*lity" that have been offered over the years, many are circular and bring us right back to religion. Case in point, Merriam-Webster's Ninth New Collegiate Dictionary: "1: Something that in ecclesiastical law belongs to the church or to a cleric as such 2: CLEREGY 3: sensitivity or attachment to religious values 4: the quality or state of being spiritual." As to the definition of "spiritual," among other similar circles we interestingly find: "concerned with religious values" and even "of or relating to supernatural beings or phenomena..." Hence the dictionary demonstrates perfectly that the term defies definition and as a result, it has accumulated too much definition. The dictionary is probably accurate in reflecting that common usage of the word spiritual includes, of or relating to the supernatural.

There have been so many words and images associated with the spiritual that some people are uncomfortable being linked to it at all. Some have undoubtedly avoided connection with it in conversation by relegating spirituality to the realm of the supernatural. In some ways, that is the equivalent of, "what cannot be defined, does not exist"—at least in the world of human experience. Perhaps, a better approach to its ineffable nature is offered by the Taoists who teach, the higher up the spiritual food chain we go, the less our words hold meaning until we reach the ultimate Tao where words cease to exist. It is useful, in some contexts, to work with spirituality in terms of how it might impact human experience. With that in mind, we might define it as a human dimension registering experience that is neither physical nor mental.

As discussed above, for centuries spirituality has been bound up with religion. When people sought the spiritual, they turned to religion to find its meaning and to search there for the *spiritual experience*. This is no longer the case. Today, spirituality can be found outside of the typical scope of religion. The *spiritual experience* can be found through philosophy, science, archeology, medicine, psychology, good health, honest politics, love, marriage, the environment, the arts, and even sports. Just about any thoughts or activity that leads to, or expresses the greater Truth, leads to the *spiritual experience*. One could say, spirituality has invaded every aspect of the non-spiritual, material world. More accurately, we might say that the spirituality that has always animated the material world is becoming increasingly recognized as a part of it.

Long ago, our Sages taught that all that exists on the worldly plane is a mere reflection of the spiritual—inseparable from it. In the Jewish Mystical Tradition, the Kabbalists refer to the "upper world" as being the source of the material world or "lower world." The spiritual domain is often described metaphorically as the roots of the Tree of Life, while the material domain is its branches.

Rabbi Adin Steinsaltz of Jerusalem, born 1937, has been hailed by Time Magazine as a "once-in-a-millennium scholar."

He has devoted his life to making the ancient wisdom of the Talmud more accessible to modern life. Rabbi Steinsaltz has studied mathematics, physics and chemistry at the Hebrew University and has a profound understanding of the physical and mystical nature of our reality. In his classic work, *The Thirteen Petalled Rose*, the Rabbi sheds new light on ancient mystical wisdom:

> *The physical world in which we live, the objectively observed universe around us, is only a part of an inconceivably vast system of worlds. Most of these worlds are spiritual in their essence; they are of a different order from our known world. Which does not necessarily mean that they exist somewhere else, but means rather that they exist in different dimensions of being. What is more, the various worlds interpenetrate and interact in such a way that they can be considered counterparts of one another, each reflecting or projecting itself on the one below or above it... It is the sum of this infinitely complex exchange of influence back and forth among different domains that comprises the specific world of reality we experience in our everyday life.*
>
> —Rabbi Adin Steinsaltz

Of course, this notion of the upper world existing within our space and the kingdom of heaven existing in our time-frame is not new. Perhaps the most famous quote referring to this spiritual concept is found in the teachings of Jesus when asked when the kingdom of God would come. Here Jesus replies,

The kingdom of God cometh not with observation: Neither

shall they say, Lo here! or, Lo there! for, behold, the kingdom of God is within you. {Luke 17:21}

The Prophet Muhammad (570-632) was born in Mecca and grew up to unite the entire Arab Empire under one religion; Islam. His message was aligned with that of Abraham, Moses, Jesus, and the Biblical Prophets. And his message spoke of this *other world* and of the Golden Rule: *You will not enter paradise until you have faith. And you will not complete your faith until you love one another.*

From the root of ancient mystical Judaism, Christianity, and Islam we move to the early days of America where these words are echoed by one of Native America's greatest warriors and holy men; Chief Crazy Horse, 1840-1877. The legendary account of this holy man's vision was captured by the Nebraskan poet John G. Neihardt while interviewing Crazy Horse's cousin, Black Elk, 1863-1950, on the Oglala Sioux reservation in 1930 for his book, *Black Elk Speaks*:

> *Crazy Horse dreamed and went into the world where there is nothing but the spirits of all things. That is the real world that is behind this one, and everything we see here is something like a shadow from that world.*
>
> —Black Elk

Unlikely as it may seem, there is even a somewhat obscure theory in quantum mechanics called the *many-worlds interpretation* that seems to echo, at least in part, the concepts mentioned above. This theory was first proposed in 1957 by physicist Hugh Everett III (1930-1982), who wrote of it in his doctoral dissertation titled *The Theory of the Universal Wave Function*. The theory remained somewhat hidden for over a decade until Harvard graduate and award-winning theoretical physicist Bryce Seligman DeWitt expanded and wrote about it. Admittedly, the many-worlds theory is far too complex for our discussion, but worth noting is this one sound bite from DeWitt's article in *Physics Today*, September 1970 titled *Quantum Mechanics and Reality*. According to the many-worlds interpretation (MWI), every event is a branch point ...every quantum transition taking place on every star, in every galaxy, in every remote corner of the universe is splitting our local world on earth into myriads of copies of itself.

Although these theories of other worlds and parallel universes are not critical to our discussion, they do offer a bridge to a theory that we must consider. Cognitive dissonance is a theory introduced in 1957 by psychologist Leon Festinger (1919-1989). This theory relates to the psychological conflict that occurs when individuals encounter new information that contradicts their currently held beliefs. In most cases this mental conflict is resolved by rejecting the new information while preserving one's current understanding. Often this whole process takes place as a spontaneous knee-jerk reaction while leaving the person with resentful feelings toward anything or anybody who is associated with the new conflicting information. In order to navigate our way through the turbulent waters of the spiritual journey, we must try our best to insulate ourselves from these defensive and protective mechanisms that are embedded in our psyche.

For our current purposes, it is not essential that we accept the concepts mentioned above, only that we do not fully reject them. The primary reason that we should not reject what is being said by Rabbi Steinsaltz, Jesus, Muhammad, Crazy Horse, and quantum physics, is that it is highly unlikely that any of us fully understand what is being said by them. The list of knowledgeable teachers and Sages who support some variation of the concept of existence beyond what is known and visible, is endless. They may use a variety of images and diverse languages, but the message remains the same—the existence that is known through our five senses and our contemporary mindset is but a small fraction of the greater existence that is available to us.

In the pages ahead we will explore what these spiritual teachers recognized and so graciously passed on to the rest of us. The Buddha will teach us what human hindrances we must overcome to gain access to a higher truth and greater reality. Jesus will guide us past our greatest barrier to gaining clarity into the higher kingdom that is amongst us in the here and now. The ancient Torah will make us aware of the twofold lens that is the source of our reality and how one lens carries the burden of falsehood and the other opens our mind to spiritual truth. The great Sufi masters will teach us how to open ourselves to our highest potential. Ancient Hindu swamis will explain how a simple adjustment in our priorities can align our lives with their intended purpose and bring us to higher levels of happiness.

Through this avalanche of spiritual wisdom, we will gain access to the greatest teacher of all—the teacher that resides within our essence; at our core. In the words of Tibet's famous Buddhist yogi, Jetsun Milarepa (1052-1135), *"In your heart and your mind, you have a monastery where all enlightened teachers unite."* As the Taoist masters said, until we are able to transcend words and have pure experience, we haven't yet arrived.

The method of this book is to provide the words of those who have attained this experience, and to provide them in modern contemporary language. But never lose sight of this fundamental spiritual notion; all words are simply a means to an end. Even the greatest wisdom of the most knowledgeable teachers is only an introduction to the teacher that resides within. Once you recognize and familiarize yourself with this inner source, the wick will have been lit and the fireworks will soon begin.

One additional caveat, it is a common error to reject the gift because the packaging is not to our liking. It is the nectar of the fruit that we are seeking. The words of the greatest Sages are still restricted in their universality by the limitations of language. In the case of spiritual messages, we are further encumbered by the very nature of mystical language. Like many of the world's most renowned writers, including Shakespeare and Chaucer, their language has both obvious and obscure meaning. So it is with mystical language; we must develop our ability to get past the communication barriers.

Because spirituality is all-pervasive, it belongs in the category with similar all-pervasive conditions found in the physical such as time and space. In the view of the Sages, however, time and space, the fundamental building blocks of physical reality, are subordinate to spirituality. While time and space are easily perceived, measured, and defined, spirituality remains inexpressible. Given this unusual challenge, let's try to move closer to a workable definition to assist us in our quest.

By removing spirituality from the lofty place where it cannot be held or defined, we're able to view it from a place where we can wrap our minds around it. The spiritual has always had an on-again, off-again relationship with science throughout history. Recently, science, and particularly medicine, has recognized spirituality as something real and functional.

In two key areas, doctors have found evidence of spirituality having both form and function. The first area is in working with the elderly who are facing terminal illness and death; and the second is in the treatment of patients who suffer from Post-Traumatic Stress Disorder which often leads to panic disorder, depression, substance abuse and feeling suicidal. In cases where the body or mind, or both, are in severe distress and the patient sees no sign of hope on the immediate horizon, some have been able to draw strength from a place outside the treatment protocols. The majority of these patients report that their benefit came from some form of spiritual connection.

Harold G. Koenig, M.D. is a Professor of Psychiatry & Behavioral Sciences at Duke University School of Medicine and Director of the Center for Spirituality, Theology and Health. His primary research is focused on the effects of spirituality and religion on health. Dr. Koenig has published over 550 scientific papers and scholarly professional journal articles, plus written nearly 100 chapters in professional books as well as 55 of his own books. He undertook the first systematic, evidence-based analysis on the connection between mental disorders and spirituality/religion.

Dr. Koenig's Center for Spirituality, Theology and Health compiled the research and findings of over 2400 studies regarding the corollary of spirituality on health and illness. The researchers conclude that there is good evidence that spiritual involvement is correlated with better physical and mental health in such areas as cardiovascular disease, cancer, depression, stress-related disorders and dementia.

One study conducted by Colombia University, published in the Journal of the American Medical Association Psychiatry in 2014, employed a functional MRI scan of the brains of patients suffering from major depression. These brain scans indicated that those with significant spiritual involvement had far less shrinkage of the cerebral cortex, which is responsible for the higher-level processes of the human brain, including language, memory, reasoning, thought, learning, decision-making, emotion, intelligence and personality. According to neuroscientist, Christof Koch, Chief Scientific Officer of the Allen Institute for Neuroscience, *the cerebral cortex gives rise to consciousness.*

Because spirituality provides greater meaning and purpose; hope and optimism (which lead to greater well-being and peace of mind), it has a positive impact on mental health. According to the field of psychoneuroimmunology, which studies the effect of the mind on health and resistance to disease, founded by Dr. Robert Ader, improved mental health is associated with an enhanced immune system, thereby improving physical health. In the words of Dr. Koenig: *One hundred percent of the time spirituality will be associated with and will predict better mental health.*

While much can be said about this experience, from a clinical perspective it is clear that patients who have a spiritual foundation are recognizably served by it. In many cases, those reporting a spiritual connection showed a profound and positive impact on the outcome of their condition.

Dr. Larry R. Decker, clinical psychologist and adjunct professor at University of California, provides us with a workable definition of spirituality from the clinical perspective. Spirituality is...

*...our search for **Purpose** & **Meaning** involving both **Transcendence** (the experience of existence beyond the physical/psychological) & **Immanence** (the discovery of the transcendent in the physical/ psychological).*

Simply stated, that which is spiritual is that which registers within the human experience beyond that which is physical and psychological. Thus, spirituality is purely defined as that which exists beyond the parameters of the fleshy matter of the body and the thoughts and feelings of the mind. It is the third leg of the *bodymind* stool. It is a dimension of being within the human being that is as present and applicable as the body and mind.

Dr. Decker's definition of spirituality provides us with both its form (rather its lack of form) and its function. Because the spiritual is formless it is never easy to define. The spiritual function is actually easier to define. Spirituality drives "our search for purpose and meaning." It is within the context of this search that we are able to transcend our physical limitations. There is more to being human than meets the eye.

If we peel back the spiritual onion even further than Dr. Decker's definition, we will find the words of the Buddha. *At our very core, all of humanity is on the same quest—the quest for Truth—Absolute Truth.* From the beginning of time to the present moment, humanity has been in constant pursuit of discovering the truth about our being and the reality in which we find ourselves. This was the Buddha's great message—*when we find Absolute Truth we will be in Ultimate Reality.*

In essence, it is the truth that we have discovered that determines the reality in which we live. Wise people live in a different reality than the foolish. Happy people live in a different reality than the depressed. And people who lie and cheat do not live in the same reality as those who are honest. It is our wisdom and virtue that determines our reality. And at the end of the spiritual journey is the eternal bliss of the Ultimate Reality—Nirvana.

Everything rides on this point. Our reality is changed by the truth we find. This has always been the foundation of the teachings of the world's spiritual leaders; i.e., it is through greater wisdom that a person is able to elevate themselves. Simply stated, as the mind expands its wisdom, the heart expands its love. In spiritual terms, both of these qualities merge into one word—Light. It is our wisdom that increases our Light and it is our love that reflects our Light to others. A truly wise person is always a loving person. If one is not a loving person, they may have great knowledge, but wisdom still eludes them. Therefore, it is the pursuit of Truth that is the spiritual path.

Once we remove spirituality from the context of religion, it is liberated from the agenda of religion. Without religion's agenda, spirituality has only one agenda of its own—Absolute Truth which provides Ultimate Reality. Within this definition, science becomes a spiritual quest, as well as mathematics, history, psychology, philosophy; even technology is related to the discovery of Truth in the form of how things work.

Electricity is a force found in nature; it wasn't invented, it was discovered. Long before Benjamin Franklin flew his celebrated kite into a thunderstorm, the Greeks discovered static electricity around 600 BCE. Archeologists discovered evidence in the 1930's near Bagdad that suggests ancient Persians may have used a rudimentary form of batteries. The discovery of electricity and making it a workable tool for humanity was a long and arduous pursuit of how our world works.

Within this definition of spirituality, the work of such venerated scientists as Jonas Sulk is viewed as a spiritual quest. Considering that there were nearly 58,000 cases of polio recorded in the US in 1952, and after Sulk's vaccinations began in 1955 that number dropped to 3,000 in 1960, it may easily be viewed as a grand discovery of truth that led to a higher reality. We can only imagine how grand our reality would become without the horrid plague of cancer stalking around every corner. Even the legend of St. George slaying the plague-bearing dragon in order to save the princess of Silene during the 4th century would pale by comparison to the contemporary hero that brings humanity to a reality free of cancer.

Beyond science, religion, and philosophy, the works of the great artists and musicians are also viewed through the spiritual lens. These are the geniuses who interpret our reality through art and music and bring us closer to Truth without ever having to utter a word. Who amongst us has not experienced the stirring of the Soul through works of great art and music? Is there any less wisdom being expressed in art and music than philosophy and science? And when we consider the universality of its appeal, the arts seem to run a close race with the sciences.

Influential Russian painter and groundbreaking art theorist, Wassily Kandinsky (1866-1944), closed the gap between art and spirituality with his 1911 book, *Concerning The Spiritual In Art*. Here Kandinsky portrays the artist akin to a prophet or visionary, while working in a different medium than mere words to convey the Soul's impression of spiritual truth.

Spiritual life, to which art belongs and of which it is one of its mightiest agents, is a complicated but definite and simplified uplifting movement. This movement is one of perception. It can take various forms, but basically it retains the same inner sense and purpose.

Veiled in obscurity are the causes moving us forward and upward by "the sweat of the brow," through suffering, evil, and pain.

—Wassily Kandinsky

He goes on to say how this movement "forward and upward" is not for the faint at heart. It is a path encumbered with "many grievous obstacles" that must be conquered only to find "an evil, unseeing hand" that tosses more obstacles along the way.

It is then that there unfailingly arises some human being, no different from the rest of humanity but for a secret power of "Vision" within him. He sees and points the way. Sometimes he would prefer to lay aside his power, as it is a heavy cross to bear; but he cannot do so. Though scorned and hated, he never lets go but drags the cartload of protesting humanity after him, ever forcing it forward and upward, over all obstacles in his way.

—Wassily Kandinsky

Clearly Kandinsky had a profound understanding of the plight of the artist as well as the prophet. And what makes the artist's gift to civilization even more distressing is that they are so seldom recognized during their lifetime.

Yet frequently, long after his disappearance from this earth, when no vestiges of his bodily "I" remain... they at last strive to honor... So it was with Beethoven, who at his highest peak also stood alone...

Each one of these artists, who can see beyond the limits of his present stage, in this segment of spiritual evolution is a prophet to those surrounding him and helps to move forward the ever-obstinate cartload of humanity.

—Wassily Kandinsky

In recognizing the many areas where the spiritual has long been in operation, we must not forget that religion has always played a key role in sustaining spirituality's place in the human experience. That role is in no way diminished by this expansion in our understanding of spirituality; it is however no longer entitled to an exclusive arrangement.

With this expanded understanding of the nature of spirituality, it is apparent that it is not merely a category of our lives, but the foundation of our lives—an innate component of our operating system with distinctive functions and capabilities. Through this book, we intend to provide people with greater access to this unique component and to enhance their ability to utilize their spirituality in their lives. Those as familiar with their spiritual function as they are with their mind and body, testify that it contributes more to their personal fulfillment and satisfaction than any other aspect of their lives.

Many who claim to have had a spiritual awakening report their previous insecurity and anxiety were superseded by an experience of permanence and equanimity. As the Buddha points out, the physical elements of life are rooted in suffering—we are born in suffering, we live in suffering; we age and ultimately die in suffering. Although there are myriads of pleasurable experiences along the way, nobody escapes the human suffering associated with earthly life. The escape route offered comes via the spiritual path—as the physical body degenerates and passes away; the spiritual component awakens and takes charge.

Distinguishing *spirituality* from its twin sister, religion, is difficult, since their connection goes back to the beginning of time. As indicated above, spirituality has always been wrapped in religion's packaging.

It tends to be characterized as the prize that one attains should he or she navigate successfully the rules and rituals of religious practice. In this book we aim to unwrap this sacred gift from its religious packaging in order to examine *spirituality* free of the typical biases and trappings that tend to limit and confine it. Religion has a spiritual core, but it has become focused on the material life, as well. It has a very *tangible* presence in the material world. It is the visible beacon upon which so many depend to find their way.

John Cleese, of Monty Python fame; delivers a profound insight concerning religion:

> *"Religion has had two functions throughout history— to bring the practitioner into direct contact with the Divine, and crowd control."*
>
> —John Cleese

I remember laughing when I first heard this as if it were a clever joke coming from a witty comedian. Over the years, however, I have found this notion to be quite profound. Especially in recent times, I am astounded by just how much "crowd control" and how little "Divine contact" our religions have brought to us.

I certainly do not mean to disparage organized religion as it has done extraordinarily good in the world. On the other hand, I can't help but recognize the disparity between the *control* aspect and the *spiritual* function. It is a mistake, however, to blame religion for our lack of spiritual connection, as true spiritual growth is ultimately the responsibility of the individual. Clearly, there are many throughout the world who would testify that it was their religion that brought them to the doorstep of their Divine connection.

History is replete with examples of unscrupulous characters that were attracted to the control aspect of religion and disguised their self-serving agenda beneath the robes of religious authority. In the end, the Crusades brought a great deal of shame and regret to the image of religion. In many cases, the misguided use of religion has left carnage and hypocrisy in its wake in proportions too large to ignore, and its followers bereft to fend for themselves.

By the 21st century, both the words *religion* and *spirituality* come with a truckload of *baggage*. To gain insight into the essence of the spiritual experience we must distinguish it from this baggage. By doing so, we will have the opportunity to view something new and unique. While religion tends to involve a group of likeminded companions, spirituality tends to focus on the experience of the individual on his or her inner journey, free of the biases, principles, and rituals of past beliefs. For those who may have felt stifled by the dogma and practices of their traditional religion, this inner journey could be quite liberating. What is being suggested is that by distinguishing the baggage from the spiritual experience, one will be able to see that the essence of religion is spirituality, yet the essence of spirituality is not necessarily religion.

As we glimpse at the historic timeline of the spiritual discussion, we should keep in mind that the intention is not to analyze or judge the various ideas and beliefs we encounter, but rather to view all contributions to the spiritual discussion from the vantage point of a neutral observer. The ideas and beliefs are the individual pieces to a vast and intricate puzzle. To engage in a comparison of ideas in order to assess which holds the greatest validity would be a distraction. Our purpose is to observe the various twists and turns that the spiritual journey has taken in its course to find us where we are today.

In Summary...
Chapter Two has attempted to separate spirituality from religion. The purpose of this separation is not to disparage religion as it has been an essential ingredient in humanity's historic quest for spirituality. Rather, our purpose is to examine the phenomenon of spirituality without the distraction of all the *baggage* religion has accumulated in its centuries old journey. This separation is for illustrative purposes in order to gain an unbiased view of *unchurched spirituality* without the additional distraction and confusion brought by the multifarious agendas of religious packaging.

Spirituality has always been the essence of religion. Religion is the container in which spirituality has been kept. Religion is the outward expression of the inward spiritual essence. Religion is also the his-

toric path that spirituality has taken in our world—its events and stories, its heroes and its villains.

Without the surrounding context of religion, spirituality is simply a mechanism that is a part of the human design principle. Like the mechanism of vision that allows us to see, or the mechanism of hearing that allows sound into our life, the mechanism of spirituality allows the mind to recognize its source. It is through this recognition of source, brought by overcoming the distraction of the incessant cravings of the senses and the needs of the ego, that the mind allows us the realization of our true spiritual nature.

CHAPTER THREE

The Influence of Our Modern Worldview on Spirituality

The purpose of this chapter is to understand the impact our current collective worldview is having on our ability to realize our own true spiritual nature. Although this influence varies through different cultures, families and individuals, our modern, scientific, materialist worldview has dominated the developed nations of the world for centuries. This is not to suggest that this particular view is wrong, but to recognize the limitations it puts on those who wish to explore their spirituality.

The wise expand their understanding to meet reality.
Fools reduce reality to meet their understanding.
— Rabbi Yosef Leib Bloch

One of the most significant aspects of tracking the historical perspective of spirituality is recognizing that spirituality is different in all the various societies because the worldview of each society is different. According to Professor Gary B. Palmer in *Toward a Theory of Cultural Linguistics*, the term *worldview* is being used as: *the fundamental cognitive orientation of an individual or society encompassing the entirety of the individual or society's knowledge and point of view.*

For our purposes, it is important to recognize that the operational mechanism of the worldview is twofold. **First,** we find the impact of the worldview reflected down on us as individuals. This could be referred to as the collective consciousness of our current world population including the major influences of past generations. Some might argue that it is not an equal representation of the total collective consciousness of all people. There are those who have a greater impact on our worldview than others. Certainly, those personalities that make up the great thinkers of any given era have had far more influence than the average person. This is especially true of those whose ideas have been amplified, published, and taught for years after their death.

Second, there is the view that we as individuals have projected up onto the macro-worldview. In this way, the worldview shapes us as we shape it. In other words, we are a product of our times and the times are a product of us.

Functionally the worldview is a double-edged sword. On the one hand it provides a context for the intellectual perspective of the individual, keeping members of a society in some semblance of like mindedness. In this way it becomes the very fabric of a society. However, a culture's, or subculture's worldview is a form of dogma which defines reality for those who adhere to it. In this way it becomes limiting and narrows one's experience of reality.

It is because of this limiting aspect of the function of worldview that it has become a part of our discussion. First, we examine how worldview forms and functions and then we explore the evolving worldview of our modern culture.

Finally, we illuminate how our modern worldview interferes with our ability to gain access to the spiritual experience. This is not to say that our modern worldview is wrong, only to point out how it narrows and limits our experience. It is up to each individual to determine when he or she must break away from the prevailing worldview to gain access to a new dimension of thought.

Going against the tide of the contemporary worldview has always been the challenge confronted by visionaries and innovators throughout history. Such was the case for Dr. Ignaz Semmelweis (1818-1865), a Hungarian physician who first recognized that doctors could drastically reduce mortality rates in medical procedures by washing their hands with antiseptic solutions. Even when mortality rates were dramatically reduced during childbirth for those doctors practicing antiseptic hand washing, the medical community continued to reject the practice. Semmelweis' theory simply went against the established worldview of that community. Semmelweis became the target of much ridicule by his colleagues even after demonstrating that antiseptic hand washing during child birth in his hospital reduced the death rate from 18% to just over 2%. It wasn't until the discovery of germ theory by Louis Pasteur (1822-1895), that Semmelweis' contribution was finally acknowledged, posthumously.

The mind is designed to protect what is already thought to be true. New ideas must break free of the old and endure the awkwardness of establishing something new.

This is the task where the human mind finds great difficulty: Relating familiar ideas to a new, completely unfamiliar time and place. We are dragged helplessly by the current of Time, mercilessly ripped from our

hold on the past that fathered us, forcibly confront-
ing a future with no chance to prepare. We are the
intimidated victims, servants and prisoners of Time,
forever bowing to the pressure of the moment.
    —Tzvi Freeman, *Bringing Heaven Down to Earth*

Great social movements begin with an idea that takes root. It becomes popular, gains momentum, and eventually reaches critical mass—the tipping point where it then becomes part of our worldview. At this point, people are not just influencing the view—the view is influencing people. In the words of the French novelist and poet Victor Hugo (1802-1885): **Nothing is stronger than an idea whose time has come.**

The Shifting Sands of New Worldviews

It is important to remember that the worldview is comprised of the reflections of collective consciousness at any given time—not a reflection of *pure* consciousness. The difference being that pure consciousness is a reflection of absolute truth, while collective consciousness can often be a reflection of falsehoods based on the perceived self-interest of the majority, or the *powerful elite*. Just the way laws can often become ordained by ignorant or corrupt lawmakers, collective thinking is subject to the same type of ignorance or self-serving motives. Even when the truth is known by the truly wise and preached by the Saints and Sages, it may take centuries to resonate with the masses and become the foundation of human belief and behavior.

For example, survival of the fittest has been a dominant worldview in the human species since the beginning of time. Found within this overarching worldview is the repugnant premise that condones the oppression, exploitation, and abuse of the weak by those who hold greater strength and power. Those in power have often justified their use of violence as a means of insuring a lasting peace. Of course, history, dating back to the earliest Mesopotamian wars, does not support this faulty hypothesis. Even our modern world wars were *marketed* as the wars to end all wars. As slowly as it seems to evolve, our collective consciousness eventually makes straight what was once crooked.

Another prime example of the evolving worldview that attempts to correct the oppression, exploitation, and abuse of women is reflected by the Feminist Movement. Feminism, as a movement, began in the later part of the 19th century when women became more vocal about their lack of political equality. Focusing initially on the right to vote and hold political office, the movement was identified as women's suffrage. From our modern worldview, a woman not having the right to vote seems preposterous. Yet the worldview held within our own culture in the beginning of the 20th century was quite different. Although only one century separates us now from then, we find vast imposed restrictions placed upon women's political rights. In the words of America's 22nd president, Grover Cleveland (1837-1909) quoted in the *Ladies Home Journal* (1905): *Sensible and responsible women do not want to vote. The relative positions to be assumed by man and woman in the working out of our civilization were assigned long ago by a higher intelligence than ours.*

This chauvinism was not unique to the American culture, nor was its opposing perspective. The earliest use of the term feminism was apparently by French philosopher Charles Fourier in 1837. The Oxford English Dictionary first included the word feminist in 1895. Feminist movements were well on their way in the Australian colonies and New Zealand by the turn of the century. In 1918, England granted women the right to vote. The torch was lit and in rapid succession women throughout the world formed feminist organizations with expanded agendas to include women's civil rights.

The 19th Century American woman had both a role in the house, and was the core of the family. Reflective of that role, was the worldview of the time that women would not vote in the affairs of politics, nor would they have jobs outside the home. The society worldview of the role of women shaped the worldview of the American woman, herself. Then came WWII. Because so many men were serving in the military, a national call was issued for women go to work in the factories to replace those men serving in the military.

More than 310,000 women worked in the U.S. aircraft industry in 1943, making up 65 percent of the industry's total workforce (compared to just 1 percent in the pre-war years). The munitions industry also heavily recruited women workers, as illustrated by the U.S. government's 'Rosie the Riveter' propaganda campaign. Based in small part on a real-life munitions worker, but primarily a fictitious character, the strong, bandanna-clad Rosie became one of the most successful recruitment tools in American history, and the most iconic image of working women in the World War II era.

— History.com Staff, *Rosie the Riveter*,
A&E Networks, 2010

With the rapid change in the role of women in America, when the war was over, the women no longer defined themselves as the *house matron* and *core of the family*. Their worldview of the role of women shifted. That shift affected how they would define their individual happiness, sense of worth, subservience, etc. They began following a path of self-discovery that would not be forced into a container dictated by the pre-war worldview of women.

Throughout the 20th century, the Feminist Movement influenced our worldview of women, and at the same time women influenced our worldview. Beginning as a political movement, Feminism shifted into a full blown social and economic revolution, including such issues as women's divorce rights, reproductive rights, domestic violence, sexual harassment, etc. Women faced varying issues from one culture to another. In one they dealt with female genital mutilation, while in another they fought against the corporate glass ceiling.

Clearly, the worldview has changed and continues to change regarding inequalities that women have faced for centuries. Once illuminated, examples of sexism and gender discrimination became apparent in every direction. Even after a century of focus and countless reforms, our modern worldview is still tarnished by the fact that half the world's population, the female half, remains under archaic oppression. One clear example is compensation for one's labor. According to the United Nations Human Development Report 2004, "Women perform 66 percent of the world's work, produce 50 percent of the food, but earn 10 percent of the income and own 1 percent of the property."

Virginia Satir (1916-1988) was an American author and social worker known as the "Mother of Family Therapy." Her contributions to family therapy and the development of relationship skills have had a profound influence throughout the world. She recognized the changing roles of women, particularly within the family structure, and the need for new guidelines.

> *As we moved into the 20th century, we arrived with a very clearly prescribed way that males and females in marriage were to behave with one another... The pattern of the relationship between husband and wife was that of the dominant male and submissive female ... A new era has since dawned ... the climate of relationships had changed, and women were no longer willing to be submissive ... The end of the dominant/submissive model in relationships was in sight. However, there was very little that had developed to replace the old pattern; couples floundered ... Retrospectively, one could have expected that there would be a lot of chaos and a lot of fall-out. The change from the dominant/submissive model to one of equality is a monumental shift. We are learning how a relationship based on genuine feelings of equality can operate practically.*
>
> —Virginia Satir

Beyond the political, social, and economic aspects of the Feminist Movement, there exists a feminist theological movement. It has impacted almost all of the major religions to reconsider the male dominance found in most religious traditions, practices, scriptures, theologies, and even the depiction of God as Father and referred to with the male pronoun in a Patriarchal religion. Today certain branches of Christianity allow women to be ordained as clergy, and in most denominations of Judaism, women are being ordained as rabbis and cantors.

The afternoon session of the Vancouver Peace Summit on Sunday September 27, 2009, included a program entitled ***Nobel Laureates in Dialogue: Connecting for Peace***. In this dialogue were four Nobel Peace Laureates including Jody Williams, Mairead Maguire, Betty Williams, and the Dalai Lama. During this panel discussion the Dalai Lama made his now famous statement, ***"The world will be saved by the Western woman."*** It seems as if this statement continues to hang in the air like the last cord of the last song on the Beatles' Sgt. Pepper's album—A Day in the Life—a cord that resonated for a full 40 seconds. From the moment the Dalai Lama uttered these long reverberating nine words, women, and men, throughout the world have pondered the depth of their prophetic meaning.

It is within the opening years of the 21st century that we are witnessing the crystallization of centuries of achievement towards a new worldview of women. Whether we are talking about Ala'a Hikmat, Iraq's sole female athlete in the 2004 Olympics or Mo'ne Davis, 13-year-old female Little League pitcher with a 70-mph fastball who landed on the cover of Sports Illustrated—these are modern young women benefiting from the extraordinary earlier achievements of their grandmothers who launched a changing worldview of women.

It is through worldview that individuals and culture interpret the world in which they exist. For example, as of 2010, over 15% of all new marriages in the U.S. include one spouse being of a different race than the other (Pew Research Report based on 2010 U.S. Census). More than one in three Americans (35%) have a family member who is married to someone of a different race (2008 Pew Survey). Prior to the 1967 Supreme Court decision, Loving v. Virginia, which deemed anti-miscegenation laws unconstitutional; many states held that it was illegal for people of different races to marry. In the 1950s, half of the U.S. states had such laws. This shift represents a significant change in the nation's worldview concerning race in general and interracial marriage in particular. Today the issue is no longer race or religion but same sex marriage.

These changing laws concerning marriage represent a changing worldview of our nation's collective reality. Laws are the most structured means for society to express its collective worldview. There are endless examples throughout history when laws were shaped by those who sought gain from their manipulation. Even something as immoral as slavery was supported by society's worldview and its laws as far back as the genesis of slavery in America in 1619. People unquestioningly believed they had the right to own other human beings the way they owned property, cattle, and furniture. Not only did they own other people, they had the right to do with them whatever they saw fit; including all forms of abuse. When asked what gave them such rights, they would refer to laws confirming the right to own slaves.

John Woolman (1720-1772) was a Quaker preacher during the colonial era. He preached against slavery throughout the frontiers of North America. Many of his journal entries indicate the conflicting feelings with which he and his contemporaries struggled:

Many good people in my church kept slaves but, despite their goodness, I became convinced of the evil of slavery. On one occasion a fellow-member, who purchased a slave, asked me to write a conveyance for him. I told him that I was unwilling to write it...

I explained my views. He replied that he too was uneasy about slavery; but his wife wanted a slave, he felt he had no choice but to provide her with one. In 1753 a man... asked that I write a will for his brother... leaving his slaves to his children. I told the man that keeping slaves is wrong; I was unable to collude with it by writing the will. He replied that many good Christians keep slaves.

—John Woolman's Journal

One might ask: *How was it possible for law to stray so far from truth? What is the force that makes so many blind to the obvious?* In posing such questions we might consider whether our prompts are coming from our own spiritual insights, or if we are simply mouthing the current societal worldview. When congress banned slavery in U.S. territories, the defenders of slavery turned to the Supreme Court. In the Dred Scott Decision (1857), the Court ruled that all blacks, free or slave, had no standing in the courts as citizens and had no legal rights—they were viewed as property and cited the U.S. Constitution to uphold the rights of slave-owners' to their property. **When law and truth are separated, evil abounds.**

We might think that the worldview of slavery in the 21st century has finally come to respect the right of all people to freedom. Sadly, this is not the case. According to the Walk Free Foundation, a worldwide organization committed to the end of modern-day slavery, there are 28.3 to 31.3 million people living in slavery, today! The Walk Free Foundation's report, The Global Slavery Index, which ranks 162 countries as to the prevalence of modern slavery by population, defines slavery as: *the condition of treating another person as if they were property – something to be bought, sold, traded or even destroyed.*

Clearly, such a prevalence of modern slavery suggests that the worldview has never really been resolved. Our world tolerates slavery the way it tolerates starvation, homelessness, pollution, genocide, and the sexual exploitation and abuse of those who cannot defend themselves. These are only a few of society's constraints preventing a spiritual worldview.

The societal worldview of spirituality has a profound impact on our individual spiritual perspective. Similar to the familiar failure to see the forest through the trees, it is not uncommon for us to be unaware of the contemporary spiritual consciousness into which we were born. If, however, we could be transported back into biblical times, it would become very apparent how much the spiritual worldview has changed. The most sweeping variance between our world and that of our ancestors is the reversal of the position of God and man. In ancient civilizations the worldview perceived humanity existing within God's universe. Today, it perceives God existing within man's universe.

By the time we reached the 21st century, we have all but eliminated the "prophetic" worldview once held by our ancestors. The worldview espoused by Abraham, Jesus, Muhammad, and the Hebrew prophets recognized our physical world to be subordinate and accountable to the spiritual realm. Both collectively and individually our ancestors recognized our human role in relation to God. Consequently, their thoughts, words, and deeds were a reflection of that relationship. Today, man defines God as well as the relationship that binds them.

Ancestral Worldview was Closer to Source

Of course, our ancestors were closer to Source. Some of them actually lived during the times of the great miracles and listened to the words of true prophets. We cannot overestimate the influence of living in times where the common denominator was a more mystical nature. These were times when people interpreted a plentiful harvest as coming directly from God, and gave thanks. And when the harvest was sparse, they prayed for forgiveness. Many of our ancestors witnessed miraculous events that by today's standards would find them committed for psychiatric evaluation.

Even those who did not witness first hand spiritual intervention were raised by those who did. Be careful, it's not being suggested that these ancient times of a God-centered worldview were superior to our times. The only point is that ancient times allowed for easier access to the spiritual. The process of spiritual awakening and the worldview of the time were in alignment. For us, in modern times, we must sort our way through handed down information that has been translated and adulterated for centuries. What remains is a message so foreign to the original that it is likened to the alteration of the original message in a child's game of telephone. (Aka Chinese whispers, grapevine, rumors, gossip, etc.) In the game, the last child speaks the message that has been whispered along the chain of a dozen other children. To anyone watching, it is immediately clear that humans have difficulty relaying a message through multiple minds and staying true to the original.

In 2012, the *International Games Day at Your Library* project engaged in a global game of Telephone joined by libraries around the world. The original phrase taken from Plato was "Life must be lived as play." It began at St. Kilda

Library in Melbourne, Australia and after 26 hours, seven languages, and six continents; it ended in Homer, Alaska. When all the rounds were completed and the final phrase was announced; Plato's "Life must be lived as play" came out "He bites snails."

The Present is Ripe for a Spiritual Rejuvenation

What has been handed down from our ancestors is *pure spiritual gold,* but it should not take the place of our own spiritual experience. We are not here to mimic the past, but to take from the past in order to transcend it. There has been no time in the past that brought about a global spiritual transformation. We know this because if it had we would not even be having this discussion—we would be basking in the dawn of a new era. Our historic past has been just that; the past. Although our history is rich in meaning and brimming with life experience, it lacks the immediacy of now. There has never been a time as right for spiritual awakening as this very moment. Even though contemporary life might appear to be spiritually lost, it is ripe with opportunity—hidden potential.

There has never been a time when craving for *more* was greater than now, nor was there ever a time when a better structure was in place to fulfill it; albeit our cravings may still be leaning toward material gain. Throughout human history, most ordinary people had little hope of having extraordinary lives. Today, access to *more* is our collective battle cry. Over one quarter of the earth's population is connected to one another and has access to more information than is contained in the total Library of Congress. This internet-based worldwide connectivity was originally designed for scientists and the military. It's now used by high school students to write their term papers and is carried in their hip pockets.

The only structure more impressive than that developed by modern technology is the underlying *spiritual structure* that brought it into being—the very same spiritual structure that brought us into being. What could be more fitting than the most scientifically advanced material society in history being the very culture to usher in the era of spiritual altruism?

With the mechanism ready, what we still lack is the motivation to shift the focus of our contemporary worldview from the material to the spiritual. When our collective desire for *more* no longer attaches itself to the biggest TV, fastest car, or the most elaborate wardrobe, but becomes a yearning for meaning and a sense of purpose, we will have turned a critical corner. The greatest treasures to be found are those that remain concealed from our material perspective.

Interestingly enough, two of the greatest Sages of humanity framed the same challenge over 2000 years ago in the following language:

Do not store up for yourselves treasures on earth, where moth and rust consume and where thieves break in and steal; but store up for yourselves treasures in heaven, where neither moth nor rust consumes and where thieves do not break in and steal.

—Jesus, Matthew 6:19

Let the wise man do righteousness: A treasure that others cannot share, which no thief can steal; a treasure which does not pass away.

—Buddha, Khuddakapatha 8:9

In order to accomplish this epic shift, humanity will have to overcome a series of fundamental hurtles. It is wired into our very human nature to act out of self-interest. While the ever-present egoistic drives might initiate our actions, they would eventually have to give way to our intentions bred by our evolving new altruistic nature. It is not practical to attempt such a spiritual feat with material motives—such an achievement requires a world of *givers* contributing to our collective betterment; not a world of *takers* in service of personal gain.

In the Mahayana Buddhist tradition, there are those extraordinary humans who achieve enlightenment and are able to reach *nirvana,* but instead they delay moving on in order to compassionately serve those suffering who remain lost. They refer to such saintly people as *bodhisattva.* One such person of great fame is Guan Yin who is credited for saying;

All things appear as they truly are to those who are not blinded by their own self-interest.

—Guan Yin

The blindness of self-interest almost always requires a *rude awakening* before we are shocked into a proper perception. Of course, the trouble with *rude awakenings* is that they are rude.

While our ancestors resembled us in form, they functioned in an entirely different reality; a reality that was determined by their particular worldview. It would be reasonable for us to assume that the physical structure of our ancestors was substantially similar to our own. Other than the variations brought on by phenotype (the interaction between genetic makeup and environment), educational, and developmental conditions, modern members of our species are closely related to our ancestors in our physical characteristics.

Taking an anthropologist's view, we find modern humans are perhaps more lightly built than our earliest ancestors with deviations in terms of skull and braincase anatomy as well as jaw and skeletal anatomy. These variations are minor compared to the one overarching difference between the techno savvy, well-travelled, fast-food consuming, urbanized citizen of the 21st century and our ancient grandparents—our perspective of reality. This difference is paramount. Even greater than our modes of learning and our advanced means of travel and communication, the difference in our worldview is definitive.

Shifting worldview is not a new phenomenon; its roots go as far back as the days of Babylon. Even though the people of Babylon worshipped stone idols—they worshipped. This is not to say that modern people do not worship; we worship from a different worldview. To our ancestors the world belonged to God and we were just visitors. Today, like the 1966 James Brown hit song proclaimed, *"This is a Man's World."*

Most modern people do not live their lives as if God were overseeing their every move. Those that do are the exception and stand out from the crowd. From a spiritual perspective, this shift of *ownership* from God to mankind has had a profound effect on our view of reality to the point where we no longer *experience* the spiritual domain. It's not that modern people do not *believe in* God, rather that even when we do worship God we do so from afar—at least as compared to our ancestors.

It is recorded that the *Children of Israel* were protected by a Divine cloud by day and illuminated by a pillar of fire by night as they wandered in the wilderness for forty years. This scenario would certainly make it much easier to perceive the presence of God in the physical world than the New York

Mets winning the 1969 World Series—both arguably being significant miracles.

This distancing of humanity from God is not a conscious choice; it is the result of centuries of conditioning. Even in the brief history of the United States we detect a radical shift from our founding principle that *unalienable rights come from God; not government.* Now, our national motto, *In God we Trust,* is continually under fire as being unconstitutional. The point here is not to judge this shift as good or bad or to vote one way or the other. Rather, it is mentioned only to support the premise that our modern world is spiritually removed from the God-ruled world of our ancestors. In his 2011 book, *Choice to Be,* the Jerusalem Rabbi Jeremy Kagan states that in our modern times we find ourselves...

> *...deeply entangled in a worldview that places us in the center of our world. Instead of subjugating ourselves to God, we strive for control of our surroundings, both conceptually and physically, usurping the place of God and blocking the recognition of His unitary Omnipotence.*

At first glance, this disparity in worldview doesn't really seem that significant. It would seem that our ancestors merely spent a lot more time referring and deferring to God. As it turns out, this simple variation is the origin of a completely opposite worldview and positions us in a completely different reality. If humans were primarily motivated by the desire to be attached to God and ultimately align their will with Divine will, then our view of reality would be highly impacted by this shift. Even those who consider themselves to be religious, seldom find God as instructing us through the minutia of our mundane life.

A question that continually recurs throughout the religious world is *why there are no modern-day prophets*. At least not the same kind of prophets that are referenced in the Bible and Koran. Did God stop talking to humanity? To some degree this question is approached by our Sages as being one-sided—it is not that God stopped talking to humanity, it's more like humanity stopped listening to God. Humans have progressively removed God from the center of our world and have placed ourselves in that central position.

There are many examples of how far society has wandered off the course of a God-centered universe. They demonstrate the pattern where the perpetrators show little concern for their sins before God, but are primarily concerned with hiding their actions from other humans. If our worldview was as our ancestors, our priority when we transgress would be to come clean knowing that God is omniscient. When humanity viewed reality as taking place on God's stage, we were all accountable to God; regardless of man's judgment against man. Today, even in the highest echelons of religion, government, and business, we witness people trying to hide the truth of their offenses to escape the worldly repercussions of their actions.

Consider the sexual abuse committed against children by members of the clergy. When the scandal began surfacing in the 1980s, there was an avalanche of victims coming forward. Initially the church attempted to hide the crimes to preserve the reputation of the institution rather than protecting the innocent victims. The U.S. military took the same errant approach when it discovered that thousands of service women were being sexually assaulted by fellow soldiers and officers. In both cases, the perpetrators were sheltered while the victims continued to be unprotected.

More recently, in the auto industry, we have learned that millions of cars were sold with known design flaws that could cause cars to crash, resulting in bodily injury or death. Those in authority chose to keep information hidden for over a decade until the number of crashes and deaths forced them to take action.

These examples of cover up reflect that even among religious leaders, their worldview is one of a human centered universe where man is the ultimate sovereignty. In a God-centered universe, no religious leader, general or titan of industry would compromise his or her standing before God by hiding child molesters, sexual abuse or product defects in order to avoid the earthly consequences, while allowing this abuse to continue. In a worldview where God rules, there is no hiding place; there is no carpet under which to sweep such debris.

The sin of concealing abuse demonstrates the priority to protect the institution, rather than the innocent victims. In other words, man being more concerned with the judgment of man than the judgment of God. This is a prime example of what is meant by the words of Rabbi Kagan; *"The natural perspective of modern man* [the worldview], *which excludes God's relevant involvement in events* [of this world] *results in a world that responds as if it were almost exclusively natural."*

This culture of crime and cover up has impacted almost every formal institution. The examples are endless—from industries willing to sell food additives that are carcinogenic, to politicians accepting financial favors to influence their votes.

Our purpose in referencing these scandals is not to bring further shame and judgment; although it is difficult not to cast judgment. Rather our purpose is to recognize the pervasiveness of the worldview of a man-centered universe. Man, continually shows himself to be exclusively accountable to man—not God. As long as he can manage his transgressions below the radar of man's laws and judgment, he does not concern himself with the judgment of God.

In a worldview that is exclusively *natural,* God has no real place. Although God is mentioned frequently, has top billing on our national motto, even stamped on our currency, God has little relevance in how we live our collective lives. While many individuals may have a God-centered worldview and experience living in the presence of God, collectively we have all been born into an overarching worldview in which man is at the center of our universe and God has been relegated to a prop on man's stage.

A *God-centered world* often appears in modern thought as something archaic and superstitious. This is especially the case if the *God-centered world* in question resembles the one perceived by our ancestors. Our purpose here is not to judge this phenomenon, but to simply recognize the shifts that have led to our current worldview of reality.

Of course, there are segments of our modern world that are still rooted in a *God centered world.* Such segments include Muslims who respond to the call to prayer five times a day, the Orthodox amongst the Jewish faith who adhere to ancient laws and customs such as donning tefillin daily and ceasing all work on the Sabbath, those Buddhists who meditate and chant mantras daily, and those devout Christians who are living a life in Christ, as well as the countless numbers who follow the teachings of the great teachers. Even though their numbers are enormous and their impact huge, the modern worldview is characterized more by the hand of man than the word of God; meaning our world is defined as being in the natural as opposed to being in the supernatural.

This is not to say whether this is a good thing or bad, or that the scales won't tilt back in the other direction, but rather to underscore that such a change would represent a major shift in the worldview that has been in place for centuries. It's not about making one worldview right and the other wrong. The point being made is that if aspirants wish to enhance their experience of the spiritual in modern times, they will need to break free of the dominant worldview currently in place.

Until we are able to view our world as being driven by compassion and altruism, without being ambushed by ego and self-interest, we do not share a collective God-centered reality. Bless all those who share the effort of establishing a compassionate humanity as they are our partners in this mission regardless of what logo they wear on their sneakers or what book sits on their nightstand.

The Concealment of Miracles in the Modern World

When one studies the ancient worldview and early scriptures from the perspective of modern times, we cannot help but wonder what happened to those astonishing *miracles* that occurred and were reported by our ancestors? What an enormous impact it would have on 21st century humanity to witness the raining down of manna from heaven to feed the starving masses or the splitting of the sea to protect the weak and devour the wicked. What might be the response of our Sages to this question of modern-day miracles?

Our Sages would respond by simply saying, "There are." There is no question that ancient Sages, as well as all of our ancestors, would recognize the miracles of modern times even though they are concealed from us. Perhaps this illustration will provide the reader with a new perspective on the nature of concealment.

Our Sages and ancestors would look to us from their ancient perspective and point out how people in their times were born, lived their entire lives, and finally died without traveling further than 25 miles from the place of their birth. In our times, an entire village of hundreds can enter the *silver tube* and travel half way around the world in the span of a day. Modern people can converse with people thousands of miles away just by speaking into a handheld device. Physicians routinely look into the human body to locate injury and disease and bring people back to life after they stop breathing. Our armies can burn and destroy entire cities without even leaving their ships.

Of course, we would respond to our ancient Sages that they do not quite understand modern technology. And they would reply to us that we do not understand the nature of *concealment.*

Our Sages would explain that our capabilities to fly, cure disease, wield mass destruction, and converse around the world existed in their times, but were concealed in the form of potential—not yet actualized. Even the great geniuses of their time could not have imagined such wonders. Through generations of discovery, potentiality actualized and became a part of our reality.

Our understanding of technology in modern times *is* the concealment of the miracle. We do not see the miracle in these wondrous activities because the miracle is concealed by our logical explanation of how they occur. Because the technology to actualize these miracles was discovered and implemented over time and with great effort, they are viewed as a natural progression rather than miraculous—manmade rather than the work of God.

To our ancient Sages, this current *misunderstanding* would be viewed as a testament to the immense power of the modern ego to obscure the hand of God. They might say to us: *We recognize this universal trait of the human ego as its origins date back to our times and before.* The first century historian, Josephus, recorded examples of man competing with God in an attempt to take credit for the manifestations of Divine Will. The Book of Genesis refers to this theme in the story of the Tower of Babel. Later the Greeks introduced the theme that was then adopted by the Romans. After the death of Alexander the Great, the Greeks entered a time of immense scientific and philosophic advancement. We saw a world dominated by Persian idol worshipping to the secular empiricism of Aristotle.

Through the eyes of the Sage this need in man to claim sole responsibility for his own glory and achievement has always been a common affliction. It seems to be echoed throughout history and to reach crescendos during the dominance of the great civilizations. From the spiritual perspective, this is the way of the ego. It allows us to maintain our illusion of independence from God and support our individuation.

On the other hand, the Sage sees this as yet another example of how the spiritual is able to remain concealed within the physical world. The sheer brilliance of concealment is that we can exist in a time of extraordinary miracles and yet construe them through ordinary perception as following the laws of nature; free of Divine influence.

One might surmise that the ego is synonymous with evil and the downfall of humanity. This is a logical conclusion based on what has been said. Our Sages take a different approach. We are reminded that the ego has a very important role in our spiritual development and is in no way our enemy. The vast achievements of the great civilizations such as Greece, Rome, and our modern Western Civilization are monuments to ego-based humanity. Most of the progress achieved since our species occupied caves and first discovered fire have been the result of the drives embedded in our ego. Far from being regarded as an enemy, our great Sages have referred to the ego in humankind as a *gift* from our Creator. It is through the drives of the ego that humanity has survived under such severe circumstances. We must keep in mind:

Concealment is central to achieving our spiritual mission, and it is the ego that affords us this concealment.

In the words of a modern-day Sage, the esteemed Lubavitcher Rebbe, Rabbi Menachem Mendel Schneerson:

There are open miracles that break the laws of nature... —miracles any fool can perceive. Then there are miracles that take some thought to realize, that, yes, something out of the ordinary occurred here. And then there are miracles so great, so wondrous, that no one but God Himself is cognizant of them. They are the miracles that occur continuously, at every moment...

The fact that you don't notice these miracles doesn't make them any less miraculous. On the contrary, their loftiness transcends your perception.

It seems that there have always been three key areas of inquiry that challenges humanity and demands the attention of the great geniuses. We seek to know more about God, about the universe, and about ourselves. This innate desire to know has given rise to our major areas of study. To know more about God, we study religion and philosophy. To know more about the universe, we study science and technology. And to know more about ourselves, we study psychology and medicine.

It is possible to merge the study of medicine, psychology and technology into the study of science. It is also feasible to merge religion and philosophy together; which then leaves us with two distinct channels of study to satisfy our inquiry into God, the workings of the universe, and the identity of ourselves.

We would suggest that these areas all share a common denominator—they are inquiries into Truth. As inquiries into Absolute Truth, they fit under the umbrella of spirituality; that is mankind's search for Absolute Truth. Whether we are searching the proper functioning of the kidneys, or determining whether humans have free will; whether we're designing and constructing electronic circuits or learning to meditate; or if we are simply observing our thought and behavior patterns in order to improve our relationships, we are on the spiritual journey. Call it what you will, at its core these endeavors share a common objective—separating that which is true from that which is false, and in so doing elevating the quality and purity of our experience.

At any given moment, our collective consensus as to what is truth reveals the worldview for that particular time. Although the worldview is in a constant state of flux, it reflects the evolving wisdom of humanity. The enlightenment of an individual is a painstakingly slow process, let alone the collective enlightenment of humanity. Certainly, there are, and have always been, those rare and extraordinary individuals who are able to move the masses to their next level of perception, but when looking through the long-range scope of history, they have been few and far between. In our next chapter, we will explore some of the significant contributions and the contributors who have shaped what has become our modern worldview.

In Summary...
History has been wrought with periods of false truths that shaped the collective consciousness of those who lived through them. With each new era, we benefit from what has been discovered by those who lived before us. Our descendants will benefit by our discoveries as well as by our mistakes. To explore and expand the boundaries of our spiritual

nature, we must recognize, that to a large degree, we are swimming against the tide. There are obstacles set in our path by the commonly held perspectives of our times. We are not able to get around such obstacles if we are unable to even recognize them.

This chapter explores the impact that the current, collective worldview is having on our ability to realize our own true spiritual nature. Since the sixteenth century, the *scientific materialist worldview* has dominated our species' understanding and perception of reality. For centuries, humanity has moved toward viewing reality from a materialistic understanding, thereby maintaining a materialistic perception and an exclusively physical experience of reality. This became the fundamental, cognitive orientation of society. Furthermore, it is the worldview that most of us entered at our time of birth.

This chapter identifies the spiritual hypothesis: *to be human is to be spirit formed into flesh*—consciousness manifesting as matter. The spiritualization process followed in this book is designed to generate our own experience of the spiritual hypothesis.

CHAPTER FOUR

The Historic Shaping of Our Modern Worldview

Our worldview, or collective consciousness, is not static; rather it is ever-evolving toward greater understanding. The purpose of Chapter Four is to provide the reader with an abbreviated overview of selected influential thought leaders throughout history that have left their indelible imprint on our current worldview. Beyond our individual heritage, education, and genetic DNA, the overarching worldview we were born into shapes our perspective on matters of the flesh and of the spirit.

A worldview is a commitment, a fundamental orientation of the heart, that can be expressed as a story or in a set of presuppositions (assumptions which may be true, partially true or entirely false) which we hold (consciously or subconsciously, consistently or inconsistently) about the basic constitution of reality, and that provides the foundations on which we live and more and have our being.

—Dr. James W. Sire

Our worldview is useful in educating ourselves regarding the common beliefs recognized by society at large. It provides a necessary commonality for people to relate to one another. It is often a key underpinning of the culture that defines us. However, the worldview can also be counterproductive. It tends to limit thinking and can actually cause individuals with intuitive curiosity to feel out of place, even becoming ostracized by those who share a contrasting perception of reality. Throughout history many great thinkers, as well as many of the prophets and visionaries, have experienced such alienation first hand.

Imagine worldview as an immense ceiling over the world. Think of it as being similar to the 16th Century, world famous ceiling of the Sistine Chapel by Michelangelo. Unlike the Chapel, instead of one artist, imagine a multitude of artists over time all contributing their versions of truth upon the world's ceiling. We are about to explore that expanded ceiling with the contributions of the world's great thinkers and visionaries depicted.

Keep in mind that as we explore the *big ideas* that have shaped our worldview, it is not our purpose to analyze and evaluate their validity. We are not presenting these ideas as the suggested paths to follow. Rather they are the established ideas that have led us to where we currently find ourselves. Whether you choose to dig deeper into a particular idea or not is up to you. Our focus here is to set the *lay of the land* that we all recognize as our collective familiar ground, i.e., our present worldview.

A complete depiction of the ideas that have brought about our modern scientific/rational worldview would require nothing less than the entire library of human history. As fascinating as such an endeavor might be, it is clearly beyond the scope of this book, and probably not your reason for reading it. It is presented to establish the context for the spiritual discussion which follows. Having said this, we take an enormous step back in time to gain a running jump into the future.

Ancient Greek Philosophers

Setting aside the great spiritual Sages that shape our later discussion, we begin our time travel around the 6th century BCE. One of the most influential characters of his time was Pythagoras of Samos (570-495 BCE). Not only was he a pre-Socratic Greek philosopher and mathematician, but also the founder of the religious movement that carries his name—Pythagoreanism. In fact, he is likely the first philosopher to be called a philosopher, although many of his followers believed him to be divine with supernatural powers. His passion for wisdom and living the virtuous life impacted Plato and later philosophers, ultimately influencing all of Western philosophy.

There was a great deal of secrecy around the teachings of Pythagoras with very little written. His followers, called Pythagoreans, memorized his teachings in order to pass them on. Women played an integral role in Pythagoreanism. Themistoclea, the Greek priestess of the 6th century BCE, is considered to be the teacher who taught Pythagoras the moral doctrines fundamental to his religious teachings. A number of his disciples were also women, including his mother, his wife, and sisters. The Pythagorean women are considered to be the first female philosophers.

Another highly influential, but mysterious Ancient Greek philosopher is Socrates (468-399 BCE). Because he did not commit his beliefs to writing, our understanding of Socrates is based upon secondary sources, the most significant of whom being Plato (427-347 BCE), who wrote his dialogues with Socrates in order to teach his beliefs.

Prior to Socrates, philosophy focused on the grand explanations of the physical world. Socrates shifted the discourse to the path of virtue. For him, virtue was a skill that one must cultivate and practice; and there is no greater virtue than wisdom. Without the pursuit of wisdom, he teaches that one's life is worthless; worse yet, it is ignorance that leads humanity into evil; and ignorance is most evil in those who govern.

His outspoken contempt for politicians who lacked virtue may have ultimately led to his trial and death sentence at age 70. Socrates held firm to his beliefs and refused to acknowledge the gods of Athens. For this crime the judges ordered him executed. Socrates is considered one of the founders of Western Philosophy; albeit through those who were his disciples.

Socrates' passion was contagious and attracted followers as well as enemies. The young Plato was captured by the spell of Socrates and subsequently crushed by his execution. Plato put the teachings of Socrates into writing and set the world on the course of Western culture. Like Socrates, Plato saw his world being governed by rulers who were ignorant and lacking in virtue. He established the Academy in 387 BC to train and educate politicians in wisdom and ethics. To Plato, politicians were too often guided by self-interest and their unrestrained senses, driving them towards injustice and corruption.

While Plato is credited with vast contributions to Western philosophy, for our discussion, it is his theory of Forms (or theory of ideas) that is of special interest. He declares that the non-material world, beyond time and space, is the highest reality and not the ever-changing material world recognized by us through sensory perception. In distinguishing the material from the spiritual, Plato provides the seeds for the worldview that we will later explore.

In Plato's dialogue, Timaeus, he distinguishes between our physical world which is impermanent and subject to change, and the eternal world which is unchanging and everlasting. Plato also introduces, or expands upon, the idea of consciousness being at the center of all that exists. The psychological dimension, or consciousness that is characteristic of humans is to some degree applied to lesser animals, plants, and all forms of matter. This early notion of *universal mind* is the foundation of one of the oldest philosophical theories known as panpsychism later ascribed by such philosophers as Spinoza, Leibniz, and William James, as well as the teachings of Taoism, the Vedanta, and Buddhism. This notion is supported by a number of modern quantum physicists such as David Bohm who stated, *"Even the electron is informed with a certain level of mind."*

The term panpsychism was coined in the sixteenth century by Italian philosopher Francesco Patrizi, and is derived from the Greek term *pan* meaning *all, everything, whole*; and *psyche*, meaning *mind* or *Soul*. This notion that everything in the universe has the mental component or consciousness has had resurgence with the discovery of the subatomic level of existence which reflects the possibility that even electrons have consciousness.

At the age of 18, Aristotle (384-322 BC), moved to Athens and joined Plato's Academy. He remained there until he was thirty-seven, when Plato died. Not only was he Plato's most renowned student, recognized as the third of the three great Ancient Greek philosophers, Aristotle is also referred to as the world's first scientist. It was Aristotle that brought method and logic to the philosophical understanding of reality. Unlike his teacher, Aristotle believed that human knowledge is ultimately based on perception, shifting from Plato's view to empiricism.

Where Plato recognized a domain of essence or Forms, a spiritual dimension (if you will) that gives rise to the physical world, Aristotle believed that the world we see and touch is the only reality. Therefore, careful observation of the physical world is the path to Truth. Reality exists to serve an ultimate purpose; to reach its goal or potential. Aristotle saw humanity as a work in progress needing to advance towards greater understanding and wisdom. For him, this process began with self-reflection. In his words, "Knowing yourself is the beginning of all wisdom."

The teachings of Aristotle influenced the theological writings of Judaism, Christianity and Islam. For most of history, philosophy and theology were as if Siamese twins. The link between philosophy and religion was not distinguished until the philosophers of the 18th century. It is important for our discussion to recognize this connection and be aware of how it dominated our worldview.

Fast Forward

Emerging into modern times we see how philosophy takes on its own identity, as do science and psychology. We'll unravel the threads that bind these paths together and ultimately even separate the overarching theme of spirituality from the traditional view that kept it tethered to religion.

In his illuminating book, *Spiritual, But Not Religious*, Dr. Robert C. Fuller provides a comprehensive exploration into the *historical and cultural context of unchurched spirituality*. As an internationally recognized authority in the fields of religion and psychological studies, Dr. Fuller has a keen understanding of this ongoing dance between the spiritual and religious. He indicates that within the history of America, we see evidence of a growing trend towards *unchurched* spirituality, traceable to the Pilgrims where some estimate less than one in three colonists belonged to a church. According to Roger Finke and Rodney Stark in *The Churching of America,* by the time of the American Revolution, only 15% of Americans belonged to a church, yet most people held strong belief in God.

From the time of the Ancient Greek philosophers through the Enlightenment, we find the emergence of man needing to overcome ignorance through reason as opposed to needing redemption from God. In the theological writings of the 17th and 18th centuries, we find a trend towards what was to become known as Deism. Here, in true Aristotelian fashion, it is reason rather than revelation that leads man to God. The followers of Deism are encouraged to follow evidence rather than faith.

This *nonreligious yet spiritual belief* is amplified in the writings of the political activist Thomas Paine (1737-1809) who was a proponent of Deism and a key activist for the colonist declaring independence from England:

> *I believe in one God, and no more; and I hope for happiness beyond this life... I do not believe in the creed professed by the Jewish church, by the Roman church, by the Greek church, by the Turkish church, by the Protestant church, nor by any church that I know of. My own mind is my own church... The World is my country, all mankind are my brethren, and to do good is my religion.*
>
> —Thomas Paine, *Age of Reason*

The founding fathers and those who fought for America's independence were not just rebelling against the political tyranny of the crown; they were also rebelling against the religious tyranny of the church. There seemed to be a cry for a government that was *by the people and for the people* as well as a religion that operated in a similar way; i.e., one that addressed a *personal* experience and inspired one's *personal* potential. It seems that whenever we find the equanimity of humanity disturbed by religion's agenda of crowd control, spirituality is forced out of the picture—as was the case with George Fox.

George Fox

George Fox (1624-1691), born in England, and traveled to America in 1671. He was the founder of the Quaker movement within Christianity and was often rejected by the established clergy for such unconventional beliefs as: *Women have Souls* and *rituals can safely be ignored as long as one experiences a true spiritual conversion.* Fox would often preach publicly that *"God dwelleth in the hearts of his obedient people."* He felt so strongly on this point that he refused to call the "steeple-house" a church as it detracted from the true dwelling place of the Lord. He would go so far as to say that people are worshipping the building with its steeple rather than the God within—clearly a form of idolatry.

George Fox believed and preached that all people have access to Divine contact and that we should all pursue this path with passion. His avant-garde preaching went against the grain of the contemporary clergy's attempt at *crowd control.* Fox felt compelled to follow the *inner voice* that directed him into challenging situations as demonstrated in the following excerpt from his journal (Entry 1652):

I had entered the church in Ulverston, and spoken against idolatry; some members of the congregation rushed toward me, and attacked me with their fists and books: and when they had pushed me to the ground, they trampled on me... Then an officer cried out 'Give him to me!' He handed me over to four constables, and ordered them to take me out of the town and whip me. People friendly to me followed, and the constables hit them over the heads with truncheons; I saw blood running down many faces. Many of those who had attacked me in the church had gathered round; and, after whipping me, the constables handed me over to them. They hit me with their walking sticks on the head, arms and shoulders, until I was unconscious.

George Fox was not a violent man. He believed wholeheartedly in the Christian faith, albeit a somewhat atypical approach for his time. He believed that Christians should shun life's extravagances, luxuries, and indulgence in strong drink. In place, he urged instead a simple life dedicated to prayer and spiritual pursuit. In return, he was often beaten, humiliated, and even imprisoned by those very same people who righteously stood their place in their "steeple-houses" to pray for *"Peace on earth and good-will to men."* Christmas Bells—Henry Wadsworth Longfellow

The behavior perpetrated against George Fox was not only tolerated, but possibly even promoted by the religious and political leaders of the offenders. On the other hand, spiritually elevated people could never have behaved in such fashion—what the law may allow the Light forbids.

Here we find one of many examples in which religion has

led to behavior that spirituality would not tolerate. There are many rules in religion often repeated by various teachers. These rules have been handed down throughout human history. As demonstrated in the children's game of *telephone*, where a message is told from one child to the next until it is revealed by the last in the chain—people are not trustworthy to get the original message right. Most religious scholars studying the process of religion for its accuracy and authenticity find the fingerprints of man all over the facts. For centuries, in the name of *crowd control,* religious leaders have often taken great license in *shaping* the truth to achieve their objectives.

The complexity of being human is exacerbated by possessing both a physical nature and a spiritual nature, which more often than not are in conflict. Adding to the challenge, is the hidden nature of our spiritual portion, we have just defined the central struggle of the exigent human condition. Once this twin nature is recognized and further addressed, we have taken a quantum leap towards their harmony and spiritual escalation; a glimpse into the *spiritual experience.*

> *We shall come closer to finding inner happiness and steadiness if we do not think of our spiritual life and our practical life as existing without connection. These two realms, the practical and the spiritual, are intercommunicating rooms in the house of Life. The door must be kept open between them.*
>
> —Thomas Cole, Standing Up To Life

Transcendental Movement
This passion was echoed in the words of Swedish scientist, mathematician, philosopher and theologian, Emanuel Swe-

denborg (1688-1772). A source quoted often by American Transcendentalists like Emerson, Swedenborg is considered a *universal genius* who became a Christian mystic in his mid-50's, claiming to have had a spiritual awakening that allowed him to see into what he called the *afterlife*. He asserted a sort of *near*-death *experience* that lasted almost 30 years. During this period, he began his magnum opus, *Secrets of Heaven*— an eight volume, seven-year work laying out his spiritual interpretation or the inner meaning of the Bible. Swedenborg states that one should not take the Bible literally, pointing out parts of the Bible make no sense when taken literally. He explains that every word of the Bible has profound inner spiritual meaning, a "correspondence" between the spiritual world and the physical world, *i.e.*, the interactions between the Soul and the body.

Over the next twenty-five years Swedenborg added fourteen more spiritual works to his credit. Throughout his life, Swedenborg published over 14,000 pages leaving another 28,000 pages in manuscript. He taught that all causal power emanates directly from God into the physical world. An individual need not depend on any organized institution to benefit from Divine Spirit. One need only apply oneself through diligent study and enhanced spiritual awareness to gain access to these "higher powers."

In his most popular book, *Heaven and Hell*, Swedenborg describes what it's like to die. He characterizes death as a wondrous experience that is far more peaceful than frightening—more beautiful than ever imagined. Like many of the great Sages, he claims that after this life we enter the spiritual domain which we immediately recognize as the more *real* existence, and understand the physical world to be illusive and dreamlike by comparison. We find ourselves in a world dominated by love and it is the love within us that determines our positioning in the spiritual world. He explains that if a person dies young in the physical world they will mature in the spiritual world and those who die old grow younger—all people arrive at the peak of maturity before any aging diminishes their youth and beauty.

Swedenborg cautions that very few of us have a true understanding of love. In his book, *Divine Love and Wisdom*, he states in the first few sentences, *"Love is the life of man. Man knows that there is such a thing as love, but he does not know what love is."* He goes on to say that without a profound understanding of love, *"life is nothing but perceiving with the senses..."* Like many of the great Sages, Swedenborg recognized that the light of God includes the ultimate state of love, as well as wisdom. It is through our cultivation of wisdom and love that we are able to awaken our spiritual nature:

THE DIVINE ESSENCE ITSELF IS LOVE AND WIS-DOM. Sum up all things you know and submit them to careful inspection, and in some elevation of spirit search for the universal of all things, and you cannot conclude otherwise than that it is Love and Wisdom. For these are the two essentials of all things of man's life; everything of that life, civil, moral, and spiritual, hinges upon these two, and apart from these two is nothing... Love together with wisdom in its very essence is in God.
—Swedenborg, *Divine Love and Wisdom*

Swedenborg goes on to further explain that only through wisdom is one able to recognize God's love throughout our world of good and evil. When we are unable to see the loving intention behind suffering in our world, it is because of our limited understanding and our shortsighted perception. There is no suffering on Earth that is not destined to blossom into goodness. In his book *Divine Providence,* Swedenborg emphasizes the theme that God is always acting to benefit humanity, even when we are unable to discern the greater purpose. In that purpose, it is our mission to correct our inner nature.

In His final book, *True Christianity,* Swedenborg shines a light on the human divisive inclination, condemning the violent practices of Europe's organized religion of his time. He explains how the Bible supports a different form of religion—one that moves humanity toward its ultimate salvation. Although the tone of this book is quite confrontational, at the same time it is uplifting and optimistic.

Swedenborg is said to have been way ahead of his time in understanding science and technology, as well as spirituality. Because he was a respected scientist, he was able to bring together the esoteric knowledge of spiritual matters and empirical science—all within the framework of his Christian beliefs. As science and rational thought were progressing in the colonies, Swedenborg's message resonated well with the American colonists.

In the preface to the book *Emanuel Swedenborg: The Universal Human and Soul-Body Interaction* translated by George F. Dole, Paulist Press, 1984, Robert H. Kirven writes:

Swedenborg's interests and experiences, as well as his methodology, led him to a profound respect for physical reality. Therefore, his awakening perceptions of spiritual reality did not bring him to a radical subordination of matter, nor even a dualistic construct, but

rather produced a vastly enlarged whole of reality...
a comprehensive view of reality as whole—reality in
which the distinctions between matter and spirit are
never blurred, but in which the inherent and consis-
tent interconnections that unite them are never for-
gotten.

Emerson and Thoreau

The mystical spiritualism of Emanuel Swedenborg was a key influence on what followed—Transcendentalism; a movement based on intuition and thought rather than the empirical. Led by American author and lecturer, Ralph Waldo Emerson, the Transcendentalist movement originated in the Northeast region of the United States in the 1830's as a protest against the "corruption" of the inherent goodness of people brought about by organized religion, politics, the intellectualism of the times, and the promising of religion that moves humanity toward its ultimate salvation. Transcendentalists proclaimed that people are their best when they are allowed to be "self-reliant and independent;" free of oppressive authority and guilt inflicting dogma.

The Transcendentalist movement maintained that the most important aspect of a person's life is his relationship with God, and nature is the expression of God that surrounds us. Emerson used the term *nature*, in its common form as well as in a philosophical form, suggesting that through nature man has the ability to experience God—the universe, i.e., nature, is made of matter and spirit. To Emerson, the most grievous mistake a person can make is to forego the experience of God that is available in present time to look into the traditions of past experience.

The foregoing generations beheld God and Nature face to face; we—through their eyes. Why should not we also enjoy an original relation to the universe?

—Emerson

In 1837, Emerson was invited to speak at Cambridge regarding his legendary essay, *Nature*, a defining text in the Transcendentalist movement. He called his speech *The American Scholar*. Emerson closed his remarks by calling for a revolution in human consciousness born out of this new *idealist* philosophy:

So shall we come to look at the world with new eyes. It shall answer the endless inquiry of the intellect, — What is truth? and of the affections, — What is good? by yielding itself passive to the educated Will. ...Build, therefore, your own world. As fast as you conform your life to the pure idea in your mind, that will unfold its great proportions. A correspondent revolution in things will attend the influx of the spirit.

In his audience was a young Harvard graduate deeply moved by Emerson's words—Henry David Thoreau. In his book, *My Friend, My Friend: Story of Thoreau's Relationship with Emerson,* author Harmon Smith writes regarding Emerson's book *Nature:*

Nature was a serious attempt on Emerson's part to come to grips with the meaning of existence... The lesson that he had carried to the world in his book was that man is an independent being who must find understanding and a correct path for action within himself rather than 'impotently relying upon a dead past... man may discover his own divine attributes in the mirror held up to him by nature.

Although Thoreau's family lived only ten minutes from the Emerson's, the two had not met until Thoreau's sister, Sophia, and Emerson's sister-in-law, Lucy Brown, attended one of Emerson's lectures together. Sophia recognized a close similarity between Emerson's lecture and a paper written by her brother, Henry, who was in his final year at Harvard. Sophia found the manuscript after the lecture and gave it to Lucy to read. Within no time it was being read by Emerson who was impressed and suggested that the two meet.

On Sunday April 9, 1837, the two great American thought leaders met face to face. Although Emerson was fourteen years older than Thoreau, and certainly coming from a far more distinguished background, the two hit it off at once. Emerson used his influence to secure Thoreau's position at Harvard through graduation. It was at Henry's graduation that Emerson delivered his celebrated *"American Scholar"* address, where he proposed a *new calling* where success was *"identical with self-realization."* This had a profound and lasting effect on young Thoreau.

Emerson had a passion for the scriptures of ancient Hinduism and in turn ignited this passion in Thoreau. By the 1840's, Thoreau had developed a ravenous appetite for Indian philosophy and had read almost everything available in the Harvard University Library on the topic. Later, his friend Thomas Cholmondeley made a gift to him of 44 Oriental spiritual books, including the Upanishads, the Bhagavata Gita, the Vishnu Puranas, Rig Veda Samhita, and the like.

Whenever I have read any part of the Vedas, I have felt that some unearthly and unknown light illuminated me. In the great teaching of the Vedas, there is no touch of sectarianism. It is of all ages, climes and nationalities and is the royal road for the attainment of the Great Knowledge. When I am at it, I feel that I am under the spangled heavens of a summer night.

—Henry D. Thoreau

Both Emerson and Thoreau espoused the value of nature and solitude as it leads into the *inner journey*. The nature of which they speak is more than the rocks and plants, the sky and waters; it is the connection between humanity and divinity. Through nature, God speaks to humanity in a language that defies words. In nature, it is through pure experience that a person becomes aware of all that we are and how we fit into a vast scheme that reaches far beyond our physical limitations. It's as if the Creator knew that by putting humankind within the context of nature we would be constantly reminded of our true essence.

This point is reminiscent of the words of the Buddha (Udana 6:9). The story refers to a night where the Buddha and his monks are out in the open air. The Buddha is teaching his monks of the Way, when they notice how the night moths and insects continually fly into the flame of their fire. The Buddha said to his monks:

Those insects see the flame and misunderstand it. They imagine that it offers them life and happiness; but in truth it means misery and death. In the same way human beings see bright flames: the bright flame of wealth; the bright flame of power; the bright flame of honor and fame. They rush towards those flames, thinking they will offer life and happiness—only to find that they bring misery and death. So turn away from what you see and hear outside yourselves; and turn inwards to your own mind and soul.

There is however an additional component to this equation—solitude. It is only when the noise and distractions of society are muffled that the sounds of nature and our inner being begin to be realized. This seems to be a reoccurring theme through many generations and various faiths—turning down the outward volume allows us to *hear* our inner voice.

Emerson recognized that over indulgence in the world has two key detrimental effects. First, it is the world (i.e., society) that distracts a person from recognizing their inner journey and keeps them outside of nature. Second, society molds a person into its own version of a social being. Of course, this is not entirely a bad thing, as people play critical roles within society. The problem arises when the person is so consumed with becoming a reflection of society that he or she no longer reflects their true nature which includes spirit.

Discovering the essence of self is the first step. *Self-realization* requires the courage to explore one's true identity aside from the clamor of society. Once realized, it leads to true *self- expression* — the self-acting out of its essence, free of the judgments and pressure of others. In the words of Emerson: *"To be yourself in a world that is constantly trying to make you something else is the greatest accomplishment."*

Through solitude, particularly solitude within the sacred space of nature, a person is able to connect with their *inner being* and with the divine. Both Emerson and Thoreau advocated solitude in nature as an elemental *source of self-reali- zation and spiritual experience*. It is within nature that one can feel essence and become familiar with his or her Soul. This journey into self and the spiritual experience, along with the consequent expression of our unique voice into the world, may very well be the top priority during the time we have in this life. If we have been created with a purpose in mind; what is that purpose?

To face these questions and to pursue their answers would seem like the most obvious path for all who walk this earth. Yet, as our Sages have warned, it is the rare person who looks beyond the apparent and scratches below the surface. Most often these *pioneers of consciousness* must endure the end- less taunts and ridicule that comes from so many who do not understand their unique approach to life, and may even feel threatened by it. As Emerson points out, to be amongst the misunderstood, is to be in good company:

> *Is it so bad, then, to be misunderstood? Pythagoras was misunderstood, and Socrates, and Jesus, and Luther, and Copernicus, and Galileo, and Newton, and every pure and wise spirit that ever took flesh. To be great is to be misunderstood.*

In keeping with the premise of solitude, Thoreau ventured on his experimental journey into a *life in the woods*. For a period of two years, two months, and two days, Thoreau left the material world behind and burrowed into his personal sanctuary on Walden Pond. He lived in a cabin that he built himself on land owned by his close friend and mentor, Emer- son. His purpose in taking on this quest:

I wanted to live deep and suck out all the marrow of life, to live so sturdily and Spartan-like as to put to rout all that was not life, to cut a broad swath and shave close, to drive life into a corner, and reduce it to its lowest terms, and, if it proved to be mean, why then to get the whole and genuine meanness of it, and publish its meanness to the world; or if it were sublime, to know it by experience, and be able to give a true account of it in my next excursion.

—Henry David Thoreau

In his epic work, *Walden*, Thoreau makes clear the choice each of us faces between a life that has been described to us by others and a life that is revealed to us through our own ability to "see" that which surrounds us and resides within us waiting to be released. By "seeing" we also understand that life is a bounty of continual streaming insight that can only be addressed by those who have turned down the volume of all that distracts the mind into a hypnotic trance of society's self-imposed priorities. Thoreau refers to the words that can only be heard in silence under the soft blanket of solitude where man can come to know his maker.

Most of the luxuries and many of the so-called comforts of life are not only not indispensable, but positive hindrances to the elevation of mankind... If a man does not keep pace with his companions, perhaps it is because he hears a different drummer. Let him step to the music which he hears, however measured or far away.

—Henry David Thoreau

Tracking the Evolving Exploration of the Mind

The journey towards spiritual discovery is navigated through the corridors of the mind. The mind that will eventually recognize spirit is one that has been painfully cultivated in the proficiency of focus and concentration. To such a person, the mind becomes a finely tuned instrument that is capable of great compositions. The endeavor to understand the workings of the mind has been a long and arduous undertaking. Within the collective voice of this historic venture, are the contributions of many. In Part Two of this book, we'll explore the cultivation of one's individual mind in order to recognize the spiritual. In Part One we are surveying the enormous collective effort that has led to where we currently find ourselves. The macro and the micro are intertwined and working in sync; each impacting the other. It is not our mission at this time to judge or draw conclusions from the insights of previous thinkers, only to observe the earlier path that has led to now.

From the beginning of recorded history, there have been great thinkers who've pondered some variation of the theme of *who are we* and *what's going* on—the mind and the surrounding reality. During the 18th and 19th century, we find a refocusing of attention from the vast external world to the inner domain of the human mind—from looking outward to looking inward. Fascination with the functioning and capabilities of the mind was emerging throughout the Western world that would continue to blossom into the 20th and 21st century. Unlike the lesser animals, humans are more than physical creatures with keen instinct; the rational, analytical, and imaginative dimensions of the human mind gradually emerged onto center stage. Although not yet a true science, questions of how the mind works and how its workings might be enhanced, were no longer exclusive to the traditions of the East.

Beyond the influence of Swedenborg, Emerson, and Thoreau, there were others who added their contribution to the psychological/spiritual movement, always navigating cautiously around the definitive boundaries of the established institutions of religion. One such voice was that of Franz Anton Mesmer (1734-1815), a German physician who developed a theory that came to be called *mesmerism*, where natural forces within the body could be harnessed and utilized to achieve the healing of oneself and of others; a sort of *healing hands*. Being a physician, Mesmer wanted recognition for his theory amongst the scientific community, but this proved to be quite a challenge. There was no doubt that many people experienced *healing* during their sessions with Dr. Mesmer, but science was not ready to accept his theory into the practice of medicine. This was especially true of Mesmer's notion that there is only one disease and only one cure, and that had to do with an energy or *fluid* within the human body that was referred to as *animal magnetism*. When the system is deficient in this substance, we are sick and when it is replenished, we are healed.

Although science was not ready to accept the theories of Mesmer, the world at large was fascinated by them. And what was most fascinating was that Mesmer was getting results with his unorthodox practices. In 1784, the King of France, Louis XVI, assembled a commission from the Faculty of Medicine and the Royal Academy of Sciences to investigate this notion of *animal magnetism* that determines whether a person is ill or well. The commission, led by Benjamin Franklin, did not, however, investigate whether Mesmer's treatments healed people, this was somewhat apparent; rather they concerned themselves with the existence of *animal magnetism*. And so, the commission concluded that there is no evidence of the substance *animal magnetism* within the human body, and whatever healing came from Mesmer's treatments was attributed to *imagination* (or perhaps what would one day be called consciousness). Because the commission could not find a physical substance at the root of Mesmer's impressive results, he was deemed a charlatan—clearly making Mesmer a victim of the old adage *"that's all very well in practice, but does it work in theory?"*

After the conclusions of the commission were made public, Mesmer left Paris, and for the remaining two decades of his life he was not heard from again. Mesmer's theories contributed to the worldview and continued to fascinate people, gaining popularity for well over a century. One such person was Abbé Faria (1756-1819), a Catholic monk who added to Mesmer's view by establishing that it was not so much the person conducting the treatment, as the subject themselves that determined the outcome. And, like the commission had concluded, the *healing* takes place in the subject's *imagination*. Perhaps the most significant outcome of the investigation was the discovery of the power of one's *imagination* (or, as it was destined to become referred to—*autosuggestion*).

It was Émile Coué (1857-1926), a French psychologist and pharmacist who expanded the work of Mesmer by introducing the method of psychotherapy based on *autosuggestion*. Coué observed the noticeable improvements enjoyed by patients who were *convinced* that they were improving. In his studies, he would use positive reinforcement with some patients, while not with others, as they received their medication. He soon discovered that he could improve the efficacy of a medication with the suggestion that the patient was improving. This later became known as the *placebo effect* in medicine.

Like a snowball rolling down a mountain, the theories that Dr. Mesmer put into motion in Europe, were about to hit America with a punch. After some constructive adjustments, *mesmerism* would make its debut across the Atlantic Ocean. In the 19th century, *Mesmerism* was having an impact in America—an impact that was destined to link two unlikely comrades; science and religion.

Mental Healing Launches the New Thought Movement

This work that was originated by Franz Mesmer had contributed a new piece to the worldview of medicine in Europe and then made its way to America where it would take on a spiritual component. In 1838, Phineas P. Quimby (1802-1866), a clockmaker from Maine, attended a demonstration of mesmerism where subjects with various maladies were put into a sleeplike state and awoke with the experience of being cured. Quimby was immediately impressed by what he had witnessed and began his own investigation. He discovered that he actually had a *gift* for being able to gain people's confidence, allowing them to enter this *mesmeric trance*. This would begin Quimby's work as a mesmerist and plant the seeds of a new movement of mind and spirit into the worldview.

Quimby realized that he played only a small role in this seemingly miraculous cure; the real *healer* was the subject's own beliefs—they expected to be healed. He also concluded that it was their beliefs, or more precisely their erroneous beliefs, that caused their disease originally. According to Quimby, it was a person's mind, the sum of their beliefs, which determined their state of health. When these beliefs are rooted in ignorance they result in illness; and when the patient opens their mind to the wisdom of God, they are restored. In retrospect, what Quimby had stumbled on would ultimately become known as the theory of psychosomatic illness. In *the Quimby Manuscripts* he states: *...that a man's happiness is in his belief, and his misery is the effect of his belief... Establish this and man rises to a higher state of wisdom, not of this world, but of the World of Science... the Wisdom of Science is Life eternal.*

Quimby was able to echo the metaphysical message of Swedenborg and Emerson in a way that resonated with a new audience and had relevant practicality. His message was not just for those drawn to philosophy and theology. People were clearly benefiting from what Quimby was promoting—right beliefs act as a conduit to health and happiness. What's more, those who benefited from Quimby's treatment were not just cured of their condition; they now possessed the means to cultivate their own receptivity to the *influx of spirit* into their unconscious mind. This was believed to be the key to enhanced personal power.

Quimby's patients often became his students and some advanced to becoming his disciples. It wasn't long before the teachings of Quimby had launched an entire movement—the New Thought movement. This movement which began in the first half of the 19th century continues to influence groups today. One of the most notable groups is Religious Science, founded by Ernest Holms (1887-1960), who wrote *The Science of Mind*, in 1926 that suggests a *science* which establishes a new relationship between humans and God. Another is the Unity Church, a movement that began within the New Thought movement as a positive spiritual healing ministry founded by Charles Fillmore (1845-1931) in 1889. The Unity Church is still active today and its popular publication, *The Daily Word,* is a monthly magazine that has been in print for over 80 years and has a circulation of 600,000. There is also the Church of Divine Science, founded by Malinda Cramer (1844-1906) in the 1880s that was born out of the New Thought movement. Cramer was a healer who taught of a "limitless God" who manifests in Creation, yet transcends Creation, and whose presence can be found in all humans.

Another student of Quimby and the New Thought movement destined to make a contribution to our worldview was Mary Baker Eddy (1821-1910). Mary suffered from debilitating physical maladies and severe depression. She initially reported that she was cured by Quimby's treatment. Then, in 1866, when Eddy experienced a significant physical healing while reading her bible, she realized that the ultimate healer is God. Quimby provided the channel for the patient to make Divine contact.

This profound experience caused Eddy to conduct her personal investigation into how the mind and spirit work to heal the body. This was the genesis of what would ultimately be called *Christian Science.* In 1875, Eddy published her groundbreaking work, *Science and Health with Key to the Scriptures,* which posits a metaphysical view of Christianity. Subsequently, she founded the *Church of Christ, Scientist* in 1879.

The *Church of Christ, Scientist* has lasted over a century and still has over 1000 congregations and a membership of about 85,000 worldwide. It is perhaps most known for its popular weekly publication *The Christian Science Monitor,* which at its peak in 1970 claimed a circulation of nearly a quarter of a million. Regardless of the basic tenets of the church, Mary Baker Eddy made a significant contribution to our worldview and the evolving story of *mind-body-spirit*, particularly in the area of healing.

By the close of the 19th century, the New Thought movement was well on its way. Although it continued to keep a close proximity to religion, and particularly Christianity, it maintained a defining distance from the traditional approach—often taking the scriptures of the Bible into new applications. These applications varied to some degree but tended towards self-improvement, prosperity, and enhanced health.

The idea that seemed to be the catalyst, and fundamental to most New Thought leaders, was the notion that the human mind has far greater power over the realm of cause than previously determined. By gaining in wisdom and self-understanding, a person could renew themselves into a greater expression of their true potential. But the mind was not alone in this endeavor; it was linked to the spirit and thus ultimately to the Divine. One great advantage shared by this new spiritual approach was a sort of freedom from traditional religious guilt; rather than bearing the guilt of innocent and pure humans falling from grace, the new perspective portrayed humans in a far more favorable light; i.e., flawed beings aspiring to achieve their God-given potential.

Today the teachings of the New Thought movement and found throughout modern religion and philosophy. Its seeds are traced through the contemporary concepts of creative visualization, positive thinking, spiritual healing, personal power, metaphysical meditation, the law of attraction, and a wide range of self-help books.

New Thought Authors such as James Allen
The New Thought movement produced hundreds, if not thousands, of authors who *painted* their unique version of this

new worldview. One of the many great authors of the New Thought movement was British philosophical writer and

poet, James Allen (1864-1912). His most well-known work, *"As a Man Thinketh,"* has inspired millions of readers over the past 100 years. Allen took his title from the Book of Proverbs, chapter 23, verse 7; *"As a man thinketh in his heart, so is he."*

In the forward to Allen's book, which is a classic example of the *responsibility assumption* espoused by the New Thought authors of his time, he writes:

This little volume (the result of meditation and experience) is not intended as an exhaustive treatise on the much-written upon subject of the power of thought. It is suggestive rather than explanatory, its object being to stimulate men and women to the discovery and perception of the truth that— 'They themselves are makers of themselves' by virtue of the thoughts which they choose and encourage; that mind is the master weaver, both of the inner garment of character and the outer garment of circumstance, and that, as they may have hitherto woven in ignorance and pain they may now weave in enlightenment and happiness.

The skills that Allen speaks of are cultivated in the hearts and minds of those who are motivated to rise above the limitations set by the boundaries of their beliefs. His insight and expression of this old metaphysical law is as relevant today as when he first published them in 1902. All of those who venture down the path that Allen cleared for us, come away with a greater awareness of the system in which we live and the method of self-mastery.

The 19th century began the philosophy of evolution, which brought with it the notion of *gradual development*. In the words of New Thought leader Horatio W. Dresser (1866-1954), *we realized that evolutionism was simply a new form of materialism... we had to work our way back to divine providence.... Spiritualism is a protest against the materialism of the 19th century.*

The new age began in part as a reaction against authority in favor of individualism and the right to test belief by personal experience. By acquiring the right to think for himself in religious matters, man also gained freedom to live according to his convictions. Inner experience came into its own as the means of testing even the most exclusive teachings of the Church... The Emersonian idea of self-reliance is an expression of this faith in the light which shines for the individual within the sanctuary of the soul... This emphasis on inner experience is a sign of our age, but it took us a long while to read the signs.

—Horatio W. Dresser

Dr. William Henry Holcombe (1825-1893) was the first doctor in the mental-science period to use the term "New Thought" in describing the mental healing movement. In his pamphlet, *Condensed Thoughts About Christian Sci-*

ence, he states that, *New Thought always excites combat in the mind with old thought, which refuses to retire.* From the time that Dr. Holcombe used this term, it caught on in America. England, however, initially preferred the term *Higher-Thought.* After 1890, New Thought was used in place of *mental-healing, Divine Science,* and *Christian Science.* Regardless of the term used, the idea that was taking hold focused on the role of the mind in both the cause and cure of human malady while proposing the benefits of the inward journey. In Dr. Holcombe's words;

> *When one has grasped the idea that by creative laws mind (thought) is dormant in all things of the body... many things before incomprehensible become clear.*
>
> *From the standpoint of this grand truth we see how emotions (which are produced by thought) determine the most rapid changes in the secretions of the body; how fright turns the hair gray; how terror poisons the mother's milk; how great mental excitements or the slow torture of mental anxiety write their baneful effects upon the tissues of the brain...*
>
> *Of the idealistic theory, which is the basis of mind cure, physical appearances are only the external forms or natural embodiments of spiritual causes (human wills) which are the real motor powers. Effects are produced not by the apparent external means, but by internal and corresponding spiritual means.*
>
> *It is therefore the maxim of the metaphysician that the cause and cure of disease is always mental.*
>
> *The part which the mind has always played in the cure has been ignored, or not recognized, because of the prevalent and dominant spirit of materialism.*

The notion of the healing power of belief and faith is spoken of throughout the Gospels; such as Matthew 9:22; *Jesus turned and saw her. 'Take heart, daughter,' he said, 'your faith has healed you.' And the woman was healed at that moment.* One of the earliest known references to the ongoing *mind over matter* debate dates back some two thousand years ago, 19 BC, when the ancient Roman poet called Virgil (70 BC-19 BC) coined the phrase *"the mind drives the mass"* in his epic poem *Aeneid.* Virgil is considered to be one of Rome's greatest poets and his twelve-book poem, Aeneid, is considered ancient Rome's national epic.

These were the teachings of P.P. Quimby; *What we believe, that we create,* and that it was essential to believe that all causality was in the realm of the mind. Many of the New Thought leaders set out to gain the endorsement of the scientific community for their therapeutic ideas concerning *mind-over-matter* and *mental-healing.* But the results tended to be similar to those of Dr. Mesmer's claim as to the existence of *animal magnetism*; rejection. There were more attempts at gaining the acceptance of science regarding the notion that physical properties are subordinate to mental properties.

The Science of the Mind; Psychology

Although the study of the mind, with its impact on the body and a person's behavior, dates back to the ancient Greeks and Egyptians, psychology, as an academic applied discipline of science, was not recognized as a field separate from biology and philosophy until the 19th century. Wilhelm Wundt (1832-1920), often referred to as one of the founders of modern psychology, published the first psychology textbook, *The Principles of Physiological Psychology*, in 1874, and established the first laboratory for psychological research at the University of Leipzig in 1879. Then, in 1886, John Dewey published the first American textbook on psychology, titled *Psychology*, and Sigmund Freud began his private practice in Vienna.

William James the Father of American Psychology

The world we see that seems so insane is the result of a belief system that is not working. To perceive the world differently, we must be willing to change our belief system, let the past slip away, expand our sense of now, and dissolve the fear in our minds.

—William James

One of a number of key figures credited with the launch of the "new" science of psychology in America was William James (1842-1910), American psychologist, physician, and philosopher. James, Harvard professor for over 30 years, is often called the *Father of American Psychology*, and his books, including *Varieties of Religious Experience* and *Principles of Psychology,* have always been recognized as key influencers in the whole spiritual/scientific discussion. James is recognized as one of the first academics to bridge the new emerging science of psychology with the spiritual. Along with his studies in psychology, James was educated in religion, mysticism, and metaphysics. He differentiates the two areas as shown in this quote from Newsday: *There are minds, argued James, and there is the world; psychology is the study of the interaction between them. Speculation about the deeper meaning of our thoughts belongs to metaphysics.*

William James is an early example of a venerated man of science who recognizes and accepts the spiritual worldview. In his book, *The Varieties of Religious Experience,* James makes the distinction between the psychology of religious experience and religious institutions. He states that religion is the *experience* that an individual has in relation to whatever they consider the divine; and that human consciousness has an awareness of reality beyond the senses. He felt strongly that the study of religion should be wholly focused on this *experience* rather than religious institutions, since they are merely the social descendent of this experience.

James eased the discussion of spirituality into the direction of science and philosophy. As a physician and a respected psychologist, James established a unique entry to the mind-body-spirit discussion. He posits that beyond the philosophy and customs of religion, there lays a core experience that defies definition. It is this experience that is the common denominator in all religion; only the approach is altered by the various denominations. The nature of the experience is mystical, making it unlike our common experiences in life; i.e., the physical.

By drawing this distinction between our common, natural state of mind and the unconscious underlying mystical core that ultimately guides us, James adds his piece to the evolving spiritual puzzle—a piece that recognizes two parts to the whole; the psychological and the spiritual. In *The Varieties of Religious Experience*, James also suggests that these two states of being are in conflict with one another; always vying for our attention and focus: *There are two lives, the natural and the spiritual, and we must lose the one before we can participate in the other.*

With James's perspective, we can distinguish a somewhat new path of unchurched spirituality emerging. William James was a key figure in orchestrating a spiritual path that blended psychology, philosophy, and the mystical. He had a unique focus that adhered to scientific study, yet at the same time veered in the psychic direction.

It was the case however, that not only were men of science moving toward the spiritual, but the believers in religion were now adhering to the tenets of science. One such theory, in particular, was that of evolution. James singles out this premise in the focus of his fourth lecture on natural religion delivered at Edinburgh in 1901-1902, titled The Religion of Healthy-Mindedness where he states:

> ...that "theory of evolution" which, gathering momentum for a century, has within the past twenty-five years swept so rapidly over Europe and America, we see the ground laid for a new sort of religion of Nature, which has entirely displaced Christianity from the thought of a large part of our generation. The idea of a universal evolution lends itself to a doctrine of general meliorism and progress which fits the religious needs of the healthy-minded so well that it seems almost as if it might have been created for their use. Accordingly we find "evolutionism" interpreted thus optimistically and embraced as a substitute for the religion they were born in, by a multitude of our contemporaries who have either been trained scientifically, or been fond of reading popular science, and who had already begun to be inwardly dissatisfied with what seemed to them the harshness and irrationality of the orthodox Christian scheme.
> —William James, The Varieties of Religious Experience

In James' third lecture titled The Reality of the Unseen, he provides testimony of a variety of reliable, though anonymous, individuals who experienced something beyond their sensual perception that generated strong feelings of spiritual clarity and delight. Such instances lead James to the conclusion that there is within human consciousness a sense of reality, or feeling of *objective presence* which triggers the *perception of something more*. This perception is characterized as being deeper and more general than any of the *particular 'senses' by which current psychology supposes existent realities to be originally revealed*. Although these experiences are profoundly *real* for those involved, they tend to be short-lived and after passing, one is left with its residue but no ability to describe it.

Along with William James' interest in the psychic worldview, he was deeply rooted in science, psychology, and philosophy. Through it all, this evolving notion of the spiritual dimension existing within the psyche of humans played out. Many voices have echoed this reoccurring premise; i.e., that humans are a part of a living system of organisms inhabiting a material world, while simultaneously existing within a more subtle dimension of thought and ultimately spirit.

Emerson expanded on this mystical theme of *inner Divine presence* within humankind and the capacity to increase the spiritual flow that one receives. However, the harmony between human psychology and spirituality was to be shattered with the work of one of the field's most celebrated names; Sigmund Freud.

Sigmund Freud

Sigmund Freud (1856-1939), and his psychoanalytic system of psychology, became the dominant influence in the field of psychology during the early part of the 20th century. His work was greatly influenced by his colleague and friend Josef Breuer

(1842-1925), who Freud credits with the development of psychoanalysis (the *talking cure*). It was Breuer's discovery of the correlation between the patient's past traumas and their current neurosis that pointed Freud in the direction employing his method of psychoanalysis. Inspired by Breuer, Freud proposed that the neuroses being expressed by patients were rooted in traumas occurring in their past that have become hidden within their unconscious. By bringing past traumatic experiences into the patient's consciousness and allowing the patient to confront them, the therapist might cause the patient to overcome his or her symptoms. In 1895, Freud and Breuer published their theories in *Studies in Hysteria*.

Freud's psychoanalytic theory of personality—structural theory, is one of the most recognized contributions to the worldview. Freud asserts the structure of the mind in three distinct arenas; the id, ego, and superego. The id operates on the pleasure principle and contains deep and hidden desires that are often socially unacceptable. The superego operates on the morality principle and provides a moral compass to counteract the unbridled desires of the unconscious id. The ego mediates between the two to provide a compromised version of the outward personality; it operates on the reality principle. To Freud, most of the mind functions unconsciously where the three basic structures remain in constant conflict.

While there are volumes written about Freud's various theories and methods, for purposes of our discussion, we will focus on Freud's beliefs concerning religion and their contribution to the worldview. This inquiry into Freud's spiritual theories is not from a judgmental perspective as to their validity; rather from the standpoint of their impact (right or wrong) on the worldview under which we were born. Each of the great thinkers of history, especially at the level of Freud, has had a lasting impact on our collective view—each illuminated their own particular piece of the puzzle.

Freud asserted that God is an *illusion* created by humans to fulfill their "patently infantile" need for an all-powerful father figure. He did tolerate religious belief as he felt that it provides a necessary function in society. Freud claimed that due to the nature of their unconscious desires, humans are prone to all forms of decadence and violence. He found that religious beliefs play an intervening role, preventing people from expressing their violent tendencies. For this reason, he found religion to have merit. In his 1927 book, *The Future of an Illusion,* Freud states: *Religion is a system of wishful illusions together with a disavowal of reality, such as we find nowhere else but in a state of blissful hallucinatory confusion. Religion's eleventh commandment is "Thou shalt not question."*

He goes on to say that by their very nature, *illusions* are rooted in wishful thinking. A person will reject reality when it does not appear to be heading toward the fulfillment of his or her wishes. In its place, the person will construct an *illusion* better suited to serving his or her desires. An *illusion* may even become a reality, i.e., a wish may come true—while unlikely, it is nonetheless possible.

Freud claims: *The instinctual unconscious desires within the human psyche incline heavily toward lust, murder, and destruction. It is only through the influence of individuals who can set an example and whom masses recognize as their leaders that they can be induced to perform the work and undergo the renunciations on which the existence of civilization depends.*

It's in this backhanded way that Freud admits the value of

religion—its critical ability to get between a person's unconscious cravings toward death and destruction and the appropriate social behavior required to exist in a civilized world. He points out, however, that this *illusion* of religion also interferes with one's ability to employ his or her own logic and reason to establish guidelines for appropriate behavior, thus tethering the person to psychological immaturity.

In *Civilization and Its Discontents,* Freud elaborates on some key themes from his previous work, *The Future of an Illusion.* He details the source of conflict between the collective whole and the individual, namely, the individual's need to attain freedom by expressing unconscious desires and society's need for individuals to repress their primary desires and conform to what society deems appropriate. This elaborate dance plays out throughout civilization— the instinctual desire for unobstructed personal pleasure versus the communal requirement to conform to social and cultural boundaries.

For centuries, religion has been able to suppress human drives when governments have fallen woefully short. Curious about this phenomenon, Freud personally had not discovered any form of religious experience that would motivate him towards or away from particular actions. He had no personal experience of religion functioning in this way. For the most part, he was suspicious of those who claimed that they were being directed by this *illusion.*

In *Civilization and Its Discontents,* Freud acknowledges a letter written to him by his friend and Nobel laureate, Romain Rolland (1866-1944). Rolland, a French novelist, essayist, mystic, and student of Eastern philosophy, attempts to expand Freud's understanding of the sacred religious experience beyond what he calls an *illusion.* Freud reports:

I had sent him my small book that treats religion as an illusion, and he answered that he entirely agreed with my judgment upon religion, but that he was sorry I had not properly appreciated the true source of religious sentiments. This, he says, consists in a peculiar feeling, which he himself is never without, which he finds confirmed by many others, and which he may suppose is present in millions of people. It is a feeling which he would like to call a sensation of 'eternity', a feeling as of something limitless, unbounded—as it were, 'oceanic'... it is the source of the religious energy which is seized upon by the various Churches and religious systems.... One may, he thinks, rightly call oneself religious on the ground of this oceanic feeling alone, even if one rejects every belief and every illusion.

After considering the words of Rolland, Freud went on to reflect:

The views expressed by the friend whom I so much honour, and who himself once praised the magic of illusion in a poem caused me no small difficulty.... From my own experience I could not convince myself of the primary nature of such a feeling. But this gives me no right to deny that it does in fact occur in other people. The only question is whether it is being correctly interpreted and whether it ought to be regarded as the fons et origo [source and origin] of the whole need for religion.

It is not an everyday occurrence that Sigmund Freud would rebuke himself for stating his contempt for what he called the *illusion* of the spiritual; let alone to do so in print. Certainly, it appears to be the result of his high regard for Rolland, yet on other similar occasions when confronted by other scholarly colleagues, Freud was not quick to question his right to deny others their spiritual experience. For purposes of our discussion, it is noteworthy that the question of the spiritual experience had a timely place in the birth of modern psychology.

Each of the ***three Viennese schools of psychotherapy*** is headed by one of the great minds of human psychology. Each approach has its own techniques and its own perspective on what it is that drives the human will. The ***first of these is Freud's Psychoanalysis***. He determined that the human will is driven by the *will to pleasure*, and primarily *sexual drives*. It is this desire for pleasure and the avoidance of pain that motivates humans to endure their existence; this is the key driver that humans engage to satisfy our physical and psychological needs.

As Freud worked with more and more patients, he became increasingly convinced that the primary pleasure that all people desire is sexual. Regardless of the symptom, it could be traced back to sexual experiences. He states: *Whatever case and whatever symptom we take as our starting-point, in the end we infallibly come to the realm of sexual experience.* His friend and colleague Josef Breuer was somewhat dismayed by Freud's sweeping theme of sexuality as the root of patient neurosis obscuring all other desires. This difference between them ultimately ended their collaboration as well as their friendship.

Alfred W. Adler
Alfred W. Adler (1870-1937), Austrian physician and psychotherapist, is the founder of the ***second Viennese school***

of psychotherapy— *Individual Psychology*. The name is taken from the Latin individuum meaning undivided. Where Freud's approach to the human personality viewed the mind as having *conflicting* factions leading to neurosis, Adler's approach viewed the mind as an integrated whole. Although Adler's approach was quite different from his, Freud invited Adler to join the Vienna Psychoanalytic Society; which he accepted and later became its president.

In 1912, Adler broke with Freud over issues related to the Oedipus complex and founded the Society for Individual Psychology. In that same year, Adler organized government sponsored child counseling clinics in Vienna. In these clinics, he introduced what would later be called group therapy.

His emphasis was on the conscious mind and the patient's current standing within a family and social structure. Freud's focus was on the unconscious mind with its repressed early traumas having the greatest influence. Where Freud emphasized the role of sexual desire, Adler minimized its role. Adler did, however, recognize the importance of early childhood which he saw as the root of universal inferiority feelings. These feelings of inferiority, which are the normal condition of all people, are brought about by being a child in an adult's world.

Inferiority feelings become the driving force as the child strives to feel superior, thus providing the very roots of motivation. Even amongst the most damaged childhoods, *self-mastery and self-overcoming in the service of social interest* (Gemeinschaftsgefühl), *the opposite of egotism* (Ichgebundenheit), can provide the context and drive to overcome personality disorders. If one has courage, understanding, and the proper training, the individual can overcome the early damage. If inferiority feelings are not overcome, one tends to overcompensate; resulting in what Adler called the inferiority complex.

In contrast to Freud's **will to pleasure**, Adler determined that it is the **will to power** that is the primary driving force in human behavior. Echoing the notion of Friedrich Nietzsche (1844-1900) and Arthur Schopenhauer (1788-1860) that everything must have reason or cause at its root, Adler, like his predecessors, claimed the primary cause behind all human endeavors is the *will to power*. He states that desire to strive beyond one's limitations, striving for perfection in order to achieve one's ideal self, is the common motivating force in all people.

Viktor Frankl

The **third Viennese school of psychotherapy** founded by Viktor Frankl (1905-1997) is given the name *Logotherapy*. Frankl was a rare human being. An Austrian neurologist and psychiatrist, who survived the Nazi death camps, turned his abominable experience into a valuable contribution for all humanity. During his time as a prisoner in the concentration camp, Frankl had a profound insight—all of life, even the most despicable events, holds deep meaning that must be uncovered and understood. It was his quest for meaning under the most deplorable of situations that gave Frankl the cause he needed to continue living. This deeply personal experience was the genesis of Frankl's contribution to the field of *humanistic psychology*.

We who lived in concentration camps can remember the men who walked through the huts comforting others, giving away their last piece of bread. They may have been few in number, but they offer sufficient proof that everything can be taken from a man but one thing: the last of the human freedoms — to choose one's attitude in any given set of circumstances, to choose one's own way.

And there were always choices to make. Every day, every hour, offered the opportunity to make a decision, a decision which determined whether you would or would not submit to those powers which threatened to rob you of your very self, your inner freedom; which determined whether or not you would become the plaything of circumstance, renouncing freedom and dignity to become molded into the form of the typical inmate.

Fundamentally, therefore, any man can, even under such circumstances, decide what shall become of him—mentally and spiritually. He may retain his human dignity even in a concentration camp. Dostoevsky said once, "There is only one thing I dread: not to be worthy of my sufferings." These words frequently came to my mind after I became acquainted with those martyrs whose behavior in camp, whose suffering and death, bore witness to the fact that the last inner freedom cannot be lost. It can be said that they were worthy of their sufferings; the way they bore their suffering was a genuine inner achievement. It is this spiritual freedom—which cannot be taken away—that makes life meaningful and purposeful.

—Viktor E. Frankl, *Man's Search for Meaning*

As Freud espoused the **will to pleasure**, and Adler the **will to power**, Frankl distinguished the principal force that motivates humanity as the **will to meaning**. The innate desire in humans towards purpose and meaning is a far more sophisticated drive than that of the instinctual need of pleasure and the ego gratification from power. In spiritual terms, the pursuit of physical pleasure and the thrust to gain power over others, are part of man's lesser construct. These traits are found in young children and ignorant adults.

When a person feels the need for meaning, he or she has clearly entered a higher stage of maturity. This driving force is recognized in the wise, but is often lost among the foolish. Although the drive for meaning is embedded in our hard drive, it does not become operational unless we access it. Unlike pleasure and power, meaning and purpose are not involuntary responses. Nobody has to teach a child to crave pleasure or to exert power over others; it all comes naturally. Imagine a child who asks for clarity as to the meaning of his or her life, or questions the purpose he or she is here to fulfill. This would be an extraordinary child of epic proportions.

As to epic proportion, of the millions of victims who were forced into the Nazi genocide machine, what an extraordinary human being it took to find a *golden ticket* into the sacred world of meaning in the midst of such decadent profanity. The life of Victor Frankl is a testament to the emergence of a new era of enlightenment. Not just the man, but his story reflects the artistry of the Creator—*out of the ashes arises the phoenix.*

Frankl asserts that as long as a life reflects itself as being on course of its meaning, the external circumstances are secondary. In the midst of such palpable hatred, he was able to cultivate an inner experience of genuine love by focusing on the image of his wife. Our Sages taught that the outer world is the subordinate reality; it is the stage on which the action takes place. All that is real, meaningful, and lasting takes place internally, within the person. As we shall discuss later in the material, our purpose is more about the process than the product of life. We exist to fulfill something far more profound than how we arrange our time and decorate our space.

From his experiences, Frankl added his groundbreaking insight to the field of psychology. Recognizing the role that *meaning* plays in our quest for wholeness and stability, Frankl demonstrated a new source for human neurosis—that brought on by a personal sense of *meaninglessness*. As Freud shifted the flow of theoretical psychology away from anything resembling the spiritual, Frankl shifted it back again. Logotherapy, which could be called *meaning-centered* psychotherapy, ultimately seeks to connect the unconscious spiritual and the conscious personality components.

There are many pieces to the human puzzle. Each of the great scientists discussed above form another pane through which to observe the worldview. Although the puzzle remains incomplete, there is an image emerging through the mist. The spiritual Sages of long ago each recognized fundamental truths that resonate in the theories of Freud, Adler, and Frankl. The ancient mystical tradition of Kabbalah teaches wisdom that is included in all three of their schools of psychology. To the Kabbalist, it is not an *either/or* situation that determines the driving motivation behind human behavior. It is based on a continuum. The lowest level of human behavior is, as Freud states, motivated by sense desires. The need for food, shelter, and the desire for pleasure, especially sex, drives our motivation. As we mature and gain knowledge and awareness, we graduate from the basic drives of the body to those more sophisticated drives of the human ego. Beyond the pleasures of the senses, humans crave ego gratification. As Adler stated, it is power and ambition that drives behavior. The need for status, recognition, wealth and power feeds these elevated cravings.

Finally, as Frankl stated, beyond the body and the ego, there is a craving for something far grander—meaning and purpose. Unlike our need for food and shelter, power and wealth, our human need for meaning and purpose is not involuntary. It is a craving that must be cultivated. Although there are numerous *triggers* pointing to what lies below the surface, to awaken our passion for meaning requires concerted effort. Nobody stumbles upon Enlightenment.

Initially, the human will is under complete domination by incessant cravings for pleasure. As our tastes begin to sophisticate and mature, pleasure expands into the realm of power. It is not enough to experience pleasure through our senses, we crave gratification through the intellect; the ego's need for power—to be right and have control over others. These are both stages of spiritual *endarkenment* and physical dominance. Although there are a variety of intervening moments throughout one's lifetime when communion with spirituality flares up and even breaks through the hypnotic trance of the material life, people often spend the entirety of their lives under the influence of the driving force towards pleasures and the driving force towards power.

When the bright light of consciousness focuses beyond our lust for pleasure and power and awakens an inner yearning for meaning, we have reached a pivotal point in our personal evolution. Just as Frankl points out, in the pursuit of meaning, we are able to neutralize even the most un-pleasurable and powerless circumstances. Viewed through the spiritual lens, the pursuit of meaning far exceeds the puny rewards of fleeting sensory pleasures or imagined power and control. Nonetheless, it is a rare individual that sees through the façade of pleasure and power; let alone breaks free from its charms.

Carl Jung

Carl Gustav Jung (1875-1961) was a Swiss born psychiatrist and psychotherapist who added dramatically to our collective consciousness. Jung is the founder of *analytical psychology,* which distinguishes itself from his close colleague and friend—Sigmund Freud's *psychoanalytic* psychology. Freud, nearly twenty years his senior, often referred to Jung as his "adopted son and his successor." They had a close relationship and initially saw things eye to eye. However, as to their views on spirituality, there was a huge chasm between them. According to Jung, Freud was an atheist who saw religion and spirituality as fantasy and illusion, often using his psychoanalytic theories to discredit religious beliefs and rituals, while Jung saw humans as being related to the *infinite* through our spiritual and religious nature:

> *The decisive question for man is: Is he related to something infinite or not? That is the telling question of his life. Only if we know that the thing which truly matters is the infinite can we avoid fixing our interest upon futilities, and upon all kinds of goals which are not of real importance... The more a man lays stress on false possessions, and the less sensitivity he has for what is essential, the less satisfying is his life. ... If we understand and feel that here in this life we already have a link with the infinite, desires and attitudes change. In the final analysis, we count for something*

*only because of the essential we embody, and if we do
not embody that, life is wasted...*
   —Carl Jung, 1965 *Memories, Dreams, Reflections*

As a physician, psychiatrist, and practicing psychoanalyst, Jung was a man of science, yet often viewed as leaning heavily towards religion, Eastern philosophy, and the mystical. He was a key influence in bringing spirituality into the scope of modern psychology. In 1952 Jung wrote; "It must gradually be dawning on any responsible doctor what a tremendously important role the spiritual element plays in the psychic economy." He took the meaning of his profession as a psychiatrist literally; i.e., Greek *psyche* + *iatros* = *physician of the Soul*. He saw his work and that of others in his profession as the service of those who heal the Soul. This is not an easy task. In Jung's words, **people will do anything, no matter how absurd [or destructive] to avoid facing their own Souls.** This resistance to recognizing our Divine nature is at the core of our internal conflict. Further, both the resistance and the conflict intensify as we age into the second half of life. Jung saw the modern worldview of 1964 as one that has *stripped all things of mystery and numinosity; nothing is holy any longer.* For Jung, it is the separation of the human psyche from its relationship with the spiritual that is the root of the *widespread social, cultural, economic, and political malaise that marks contemporary reality.*

Jung believed that psychology must take into account the biological, cultural, and spiritual aspects of the patient's personality. He advocated self-awareness, transformation, and self-actualization to achieve a *meaningful* life; with a particular emphasis on development during the second half of life. According to Jung, the first half of a person's life is dedicated to individuation; becoming a unique individual. In the attempt to forge our own identity, we tend to become self-absorbed, expressing only self-interest in our behavior. This can become extreme in some rebellious young men who express anger and exhibit destructive behavior.

Somewhere between the ages of thirty-five and forty, Jung proposes that people move into what he called a *second puberty*; one not centered on sexuality, but rather focused on spirituality. At this stage, a person's self-serving nature shifts into being more community-centered and empathetic; individuation gives way to being a part of the collective whole. The obsessive focus on materialism and sexuality is overshadowed by fascination with spirituality, contribution, and finding a "religious outlook."

> *...Among all my patients in the second half of life—that is to say, over thirty-five—there has not been one whose problem in the last resort was not that of finding a religious outlook on life. It is safe to say that every one of them fell ill because he had lost what the living religions of every age have given their followers, and none of them has been really healed who did not regain his religious outlook. This of course has nothing whatever to do with a particular creed or membership of a church.*
>
> —Jung

Here, as was often the case, Jung made a clear distinction between religious experience and the creed of organized religion. According to Jung, religion was the resulting attitude from a changed consciousness through experiencing the mystical, or as he often referred to it—the *numinosum*. In his essay *Psychology and Religion*, Jung provides a definition of *numinosum*:

> ... *a dynamic agency or effect not caused by an arbitrary act of will.... The numinosum—whatever its cause may be—is an experience of the subject independent of his will.... The numinosum is either a quality belonging to a visible object or the influence of an invisible presence that causes a peculiar alteration of consciousness....*

He goes on to state that the elements of organized religion, particularly creed and dogma, create more of a hindrance than a help in achieving the numinous experience.

> ... *dogma is the very thing that precludes immediate experience... Dogma is like a dream, reflecting the spontaneous and autonomous activity of the objective psyche, the unconscious. Such an expression of the unconscious is a much more efficient means of defense against further immediate experiences than any scientific theory.*
>
> —Jung

Jung is also credited with recognizing the trait of *extroversion/introversion* in the human personality. He defined the extrovert as being outgoing, energetic, and communicative, while the introvert tends toward being more reserved and preferring solitude. He also asserts that all people fall somewhere on the extrovert/introvert continuum. Jung identified how these two personality traits manifest in a person's approach to life. The introverted type tends toward inward activity and development, gaining satisfaction from mental stability and psychological progress. By contrast, the extroverted type has an interest in all that is external, finding gratification from what is outside the self. Spiritually speaking, we would do well to cultivate both introversion and extroversion within our personality. The spiritual process is one that requires us to seek the light of higher consciousness by going inward, and to express this light out into the world. If what we express in the world is not rooted and sourced by what we have discovered within, it is not a spiritual expression but rather an expression that is rooted in self-interest. It may just be that the spiritual requirements of solitude and inward focus are genetically predisposed to those who lean towards introversion. Even though the wondrous starlit sky and the fiery sunrise at dawn may inspire and stir the Soul, communion takes place inward.

Jung also distinguished the *personal unconscious* (that Freud defined as unique to each individual's life experience that is forgotten or repressed) from *collective unconscious*, which does not develop individually, but has innate content common to all people. Some have argued that this *collective unconscious* was Jung's method of bringing God into modern psychology. Embedding God into the human *collective unconscious*, Jung developed his spiritual psychological theory:

It had become clear to me, in a flash of illumination, that for me the only possible goal was psychiatry. Here alone the two currents of my interest could flow together and in a united stream dig their own bed. Here was the empirical field common to biological and spiritual facts, which I had everywhere sought

and nowhere found. Here at last was the place where the collision of nature and spirit became a reality.
                    —Jung, *Memories, Dreams, and Reflections*

A common symbol of the way life has its conscious and unconscious side—its physical and spiritual aspects—is depicted by trees. Even though we can see the branches of the tree, its leaves, flowers, and sometimes fruit, in the ground beneath it all, is an elaborate system of roots that supports the life that is manifest above the surface.

It may be that Jung saw even more spiritual implications within his notion of *collective unconscious*. Like the great Sages and mystical teachers asserted in previous centuries, Jung not only suggests a connection with God, but also an elaborate system that connects all humanity with one another along with our past and future:

Life has always seemed to me like a plant that lives on its rhizome. Its true life is invisible, hidden in the rhizome. The part that appears above ground lasts only a single summer. Then it withers away – an ephemeral apparition. When we think of the unending growth and decay of life and civilizations, we cannot escape the impression of absolute nullity. Yet I have never lost a sense of something that lives and endures underneath the eternal flux. What we see is the blossom, which passes. The rhizome remains.
                    —Jung, ibid.

By the end of his career, Jung was recognized as a major force in bringing psychology and spirituality together.

Behaviorism

In the chaotic and divergent atmosphere set in play by Freud and his two most eminent students, Adler and Jung, yet another system of psychology emerged to muddy the psycho-spiritual waters. Skeptical of the Viennese schools of psychology and their analysis of the mind through introspection, the new school of psychology was based on the science of behavior which focused on the *mechanics* of life and viewed past *conditioning* to be the horse that led the cart.

This new approach rejected Freud's focus on sexuality as the driving source behind human motivation, Adler's *Individual Psychology* which identified man's struggle for power, and even the religious inclination of Jung. Not even Frankl's will toward meaning resonated with this new school of psychology as the driver of human behavior.

In 1913 John B. Watson (1878-1958), delivered his famous address at Colombia University, *Psychology as the Behaviorist Views It,* calling for a shift in the focus of the field of psychology. This new philosophy of psychology, called *behaviorism*, was a response to psychoanalytic subjectivism. It focuses entirely on objective experimentation to predict and control animal and human behavior. It postulates that only what is observable is appropriate for scientific psychological study. According to the behaviorist, consciousness is neither a definite or usable concept. Any belief in it is relegated to man's archaic superstition and magic, not sufficient for the psychologist.

In the late 1800s, Wilhelm Wundt asserted that psychology should relinquish the human mind and inner personality. Wundt asserted that man is devoid of spirit and self-determinism. He set out to prove that man is the summation of his experiences, of the stimuli which intrude upon his consciousness and unconsciousness.

From psychoanalytical study on the therapist couch to experimentation in the laboratory, the orientation of psychology was moving in a direction away from human spirituality and the sacred realm and even away from the mind itself. This is particularly evident in the contribution of B.F. Skinner (1904-1990), Professor of Psychology at Harvard University, who established his own variation of *behaviorism* called *radical behaviorism*. Skinner claimed all human activity is behavior, including such private activity as thoughts and feelings.

Skinner developed the *theory of operant conditioning*, which expanded his influence in the field. He theorized that all behavior is determined by its consequences, regardless of whether those consequences are reinforcements or punishments, *i.e.*, the attraction towards pleasure or the avoidance of pain. These consequences of one's behavior, good or bad, determine the likelihood of whether the behavior will occur again. Thus, it is the nature of the consequence or stimuli that modifies a person's tendency to repeat his or her behavior or to avoid it. Through continuous reinforcement, it is possible to shape behavior in the laboratory in ways that are not likely in ordinary life. The therapy technique known as *behavior modification* resulted from Skinner's work.

Skinner put forward that behavior is *determined* rather than the result of *free will*. To Skinner, *free will* is an illusion; behavior is the result of conditioning, classical or operant, and any internal process is irrelevant. Skinner applied his approach to the specific behavior known as sin, stating:

> *To say that a man is sinful because he sins is to give an operational definition of sin. To say that he sins*

because he is sinful is to trace his behavior to a sup-
posed inner trait. But whether or not a person engages
in the kind of behavior called sinful depends upon cir-
cumstances which are not mentioned in either ques-
tion. The sin assigned as an inner possession (the sin
a person "knows") is to be found in a history of rein-
forcement.

—B.F. Skinner

Although Skinner was hailed as the most influential American psychologist of his time, according to *Time* magazine (September 20, 1971), *second only to Freud as the most important psychologist of all time,* not everyone shared this enthusiasm. In her book, *Philosophy: Who Needs It,* Ayn Rand (1905-1982), Russian-American award-winning novelist, philosopher, and playwright, critiques Skinner's *Beyond Freedom and Dignity* by saying;

Autonomous Man" is the term used by Mr. Skinner to denote man's consciousness in all those aspects which distinguish it from the sensory level of an animal's consciousness—specifically: reason, mind, values, concepts, thought, judgment, volition, purpose, memory, independence, self-esteem. These, he asserts, do not exist; they are an illusion, a myth, a "pre-scientific" superstition. His term may be taken to include everything we call "man's inner world," except that Mr. Skinner would never allow such an expression; whenever he has to refer to man's inner world, he says: "Inside your skin."

"Inside his skin," man is totally determined by his environment (and by his genetic endowment, which

was determined by his ancestors' environment), Mr. Skinner asserts, and totally malleable. By controlling the environment, "behavioral technologists" could— and should—control men inside out. If people were brought to give up individual autonomy and to join Mr. Skinner... the behavioral technologists would create a new species and a perfect world. This is the book's thesis.

What kind of a world would this be? Rand asks. To answer this fair question, we look to Skinner's own words.

. . . it should be possible to design a world in which behavior likely to be punished seldom or never occurs. We try to design such a world for those who cannot solve the problem of punishment for themselves, such as babies, retardates, or psychotics, and if it could be done for everyone, much time and energy would be saved.

—Skinner, *Beyond Freedom and Dignity*

Rand was not alone in her criticism of Skinner. Another voice was added to this discussion by Silvano Arieti (1914-1981), a psychiatrist and professor of clinical psychiatry at the New York Medical College, recognized as the world's foremost authority on schizophrenia. In his 1976 book, *Creativity: The Magic Synthesis*, Arieti takes issue with Skinner in his book regarding the behaviorist approach to human psychology. Although he credits Skinner in part, he maintains the independence of free will and particularly the expression of creativity.

People like B.F. Skinner have characterized man as being molded, conditioned, and programmed by the environment in rigid, almost inescapable ways. Skinner should be appreciated for having shown the extent to which man can be affected in this manner; but...we must stress man's ability to escape his fate. Creativity is one of the major means by which the human being liberates himself from the fetters not only of his conditioned responses, but also of his usual choices.

—Arieti, *Creativity: The Magic Synthesis*

Another key figure to take issue with the behaviorist theory was George Ivanovich Gurdjieff (1872-1949), a Russian born, Greek-Armenian mystic who traveled extensively in his search for ancient wisdom and practical truth. As one of the 20th century's prominent spiritual teachers, he developed his own "method of self-work" designed to awaken the practitioner out of the *hypnotic trance* of everyday life and to elevate one's consciousness into becoming that which he or she *ought to be*. His system employed the mystical side of religion, particularly Christianity, Eastern philosophy, psychology and science.

One of Gurdjieff's most noted pupils was Peter D. Ouspensky (1878-1947), a Russian mathematician who studied under him and taught his "System" for twenty-five years throughout the United States and England. Under the direct supervision of Gurdjieff for ten years, Ouspensky attempted to master such complex practices as *self-remembering*. This technique requires that a person divide focus and attention between the circumstances happening in the outer world and what is going on within. While this intense self-observation is taking place, the practitioner is also engaged in a third aspect—the non-expression of negative emotions. (P.D. Ouspensky, *Conscience*)

In *The Psychology of Man's Possible Evolution*, Ouspensky expresses his own and Gurdjieff's response to the notion of man's *machinelike* nature theorized by the behaviorists such as Watson and Skinner:

> *Man is a machine, but a very peculiar machine. He is a machine which, in right circumstances, and with right treatment, can know that he is a machine, and, having fully realized this, he may find the ways to cease to be a machine.*
>
> — P. D. Ouspensky,
> *The Psychology of Man's Possible Evolution*

We find the same basic ideas in the ancient scriptures of the east—the Vedanta. Ironically, the mystic teacher Swami Vivekananda uses the same analogy of the *machine* when describing man without awareness of his higher self. He recognizes that humans can live out a lesser life programmed by their conditioning. Unlike the behaviorist psychologist, however, Vivekananda teaches that it is our mission in this life to rise above rote conditioning to achieve liberation. He is quoted as often asking his students with great passion: *What are you but mere machines until you are free?*

Again, we see another example where the great minds of science and the great teachers of spirituality speak with one voice. One might well ask: *What is this freedom that is being discussed? Where will this liberation deliver us?* These questions were asked of all the ancient Sages who prescribe seeking liberation. It is not surprising that this very same discussion emerged in modern science—not by revelation of the Soul, but through investigation in the laboratory.

Many have debated whether Skinner should be commended or condemned for his premise of man's *machine-like* nature and his recommendation to implement a universal system by which to program humanity towards appropriate behavior. In the words of Arieti, *Skinner should be appreciated for having shown the extent to which man can be affected in this manner.* What a crucial piece of the puzzle discovered and verified by the likes of Watson, Pavlov and Skinner. We are all in fact imprisoned by the restraints of our prior conditioning—enchained by self-imposed limitations.

The Sages all say that the world we witness around us is not the *promised land*—not the intention of our creation. Although the lessons of this world are essential and lead to our destined future home, they can at the same time be all consuming and in the words of the Buddha, *entangling.*

If there were no freedom, beings could never disentangle themselves from the world. But since there is freedom to transcend the world, beings are able to become disentangled.
—Buddha, *Anguttara Nikaya*

This lesson is one of the most fundamental principles that the Buddha provided for all humanity. The world we perceive is characterized by impermanence, sorrow, aging, immense suffering and death. In our ignorance, we cling to this life believing that it is all there is other than endless, dreamless sleep—non-existence. By attaining higher wisdom, one is able to recognize the folly of this belief and eventually fully recognize the grandeur hidden behind the shadows of life around us. Such recognition is the liberation we seek—to be free of illusion brought by our conditioning and of the fears rooted in our ignorance.

While such transition has been a part of the spiritual teachings for thousands of years, only recently has it been accepted by science as a plausible system of psychology. This seems only logical since science has always been bound by its own chains—accepting only that which is apparent, empirical, quantifiable, and rational. In the words of the great Hindu mystic, saint, and teacher of Vivekananda, Sri Ramakrishna (1836-1886):

> *People do not see that science deals only with conditional knowledge. It brings no message from the Land of the Unconditioned. Such message has been brought by holy men, who have seen and realized God, like the Rishis* (a seer of Truth to whom the wisdom of the Vedas was revealed) of old. It is they alone that are competent to say, "God is of this nature."*
> —Ramakrishna, *The Gospel of Sri Ramakrishna*

The twentieth century was about to write a new chapter in the science of the mind. Perhaps it was the rigid boundaries of the behaviorists that pulled the taut string of psychology's bow far enough to launch its arrow into uncharted territory—uncharted by science, but familiar ground to the mystical Sages of religion.

Humanistic Psychology
In response to the *dehumanizing* implications of the behaviorist, a new voice emerged in the science of psychology. Humanistic psychology is often referred to as the *Third Force*

in psychology. The *First Force* is Freud's psychoanalysis. The *Second* is behaviorism. Humanistic psychologists see personality developing out of the individual's personal experience and values—a more holistic approach including a person's health, creativity, free will, and his or her potential. It also includes the spirituality of a person—his or her beliefs and aspirations. Comparatively speaking, this approach is characterized by the positive outlook that humanity employs—i.e., self-analysis and free-will to overcome the conditioning of one's traumatic past experiences—to gain self-improvement toward becoming the best version of oneself.

It's this notion of free-will that distinguishes humanism from behaviorism and from Freud's psychoanalytic approach. Humanists theorize that one's free-will facilitates a person's actualizing his or her full potential. Behaviorists posit that behavior is the result of external conditioning and environment, while Freud's approach also rejects the role of free-will, claiming it is unconscious desires that ultimately determine one's behavior.

Otto Rank

Freud's teachings attracted many brilliant students, some as disciples, while causing many others to strike out on their own with conflicting theories. Such was the case with one of Freud's closest disciples and colleagues—Otto (Rosenfeld) Rank (1884-1939). Rank began working with Freud as Secretary of the Vienna Psychoanalytic Society at age 21. He completed his Ph.D. at the University of Vienna by age 28. His association with Freud remained intact for some twenty years, witnessing the difficult parting of others like Adler and Jung. Finally, at age 40, Rank too began to question the Freudian psychoanalytic approach. He was drawn more to the conscious mind than to the unconscious; to present, here-and-now, relationships rather than to those of the past, and his approach also focused on the human will.

His interests also included the arts and philosophy. In 1926 he broke away from Freud and moved to Paris where he met feminist and artist, Anais Nin and became her therapist. She held a modern version of the Buddha's view in her writing: *We don't see things as they are, we see them as we are.* And challenged the French novelist Marcel Proust: *If what Proust says is true, that happiness is the absence of fever, then I will never know happiness. For I am possessed by a fever for knowledge, experience, and creation.*

In his book, *Wrestling with the Prophets*, Matthew Fox refers to Otto Rank as "one of the great spiritual giants of the twentieth century, a genius as a psychologist and a saint as a human being."

In Rank's 1941 book, *Psychology and Social Change*, he acknowledges the inherent conflict that individuals always face by the worldview into which we are born:

In the history of mankind we see two alternating principles of change in operation, which seem to present an eternal dilemma: the question as to whether a change in the people themselves or a change in their system of living is the better method for improving human conditions. In our own era of social distress, where the two principles of change seem actually to overlap, we are becoming increasingly aware of the two dynamic forces inherent in this human conflict of the individual striving against the social impact of the civilization into which he happens to have been born.

Rank had significant but indirect influence on the development of humanistic psychology. His influence was felt by such early sources as Carl Rogers, Rollo May, Irvin Yalom, and others. Dr. Judd Marmor (1910-2003), the internationally renowned American psychiatrist who played a critical role in removing homosexuality from the American Psychiatric Association *Diagnostic and Statistical Manual of Mental Disorders,* recognized the influence of Otto Rank:

> *In some ways Otto Rank may well be the most important forerunner of the brief dynamic psychotherapy movement... [He] laid the groundwork for the subsequent recognition of the predominant importance in personality development of the pre-oedipal years... It is unfortunate that the issue of disloyalty to Freud has cast a heavy shadow over the value of Rank's achievements... We can now perceive that Rank was the prime theoretical precursor of these developments [including the concept of separation and individuation].*
>
> —E. James Lieberman,
> *Acts of Will: The Life and Work of Otto Rank*

Rank was also the first to recognize therapy as learning and *unlearning* experience. He emphasized the need to replace or unlearn neurotic patterns stemming from unresolved past experiences with creative patterns of thinking. Rank compared this new creative thought process to that of an artist creating art. In his 1932 book, *Art and Artist: Creative Urge and Personality Development*, he refers to this *reframing* as the process of *"stepping out of the frame of the prevailing ideology."* In a 1938 lecture, Rank said:

Life in itself is a mere succession of separations. Beginning with birth, going through several weaning periods and the development of the individual personality, and finally culminating in death – which represents the final separation.

At birth, the individual experiences the first shock of separation, which throughout his life he strives to overcome. In the process of adaptation, man persistently separates from his old self, or at least from those segments off his old self that are now outlived. Like a child who has outgrown a toy, he discards the old parts of himself for which he has no further use ....

The ego continually breaks away from its worn-out parts, which were of value in the past but have no value in the present. The neurotic [who cannot unlearn, and, therefore, lacks creativity] is unable to accomplish this normal detachment process ... Owing to fear and guilt generated in the assertion of his own autonomy, he is unable to free himself, and instead remains suspended upon some primitive level of his evolution.

The idea of *self-concept* is fundamental to humanistic psychology. This notion of *unlearning* represents a separation from one's self-concept—one's unique individuality. As we will explore in a later chapter, the process of separation and individuation is what led us to our physical aspect in a material world. It is what provides us with our ego-identity and is at the root of our self-interest. The process of spiritual awakening is a journey away from that of separation and individuation.

Many humanistic psychologists have preferred varying

descriptions of the self-concept. Each adds another dimension to the idea. Self-concept not only refers to *the individual's belief about himself or herself, [it also includes] the person's attributes and who and what the self is,* according to Dr. Roy F. Baumeister, social psychologist, known for his work on the concepts of self. The humanistic psychologist must view human behavior not only through the eyes of the observer, but also through the eyes, or self-concept, of the person behaving.

Dr. Michael Lewis (born 1937) is Professor of Pediatrics and Psychiatry and Director of the Institute for the Study of Child Development at Rutgers Robert Wood Johnson Medical School. He suggests that development of the self-concept has two aspects. First, is the *Existential Self*—the basic aspect of the self-concept that provides the sense of separation from others and the awareness of the constancy of the self. Second, is the *Categorical Self*—that places the self into various categories such as gender, age, height, weight, race, cultural distinctions, etc. As any other object existing in the world, the self has properties which define it. When a person is a child, these properties are usually of an apparent nature, but as the child matures, these properties become more complex and include internal personality traits as well as comparative evaluations of one self.

Carl Rogers (1902-1987) is an early source of ideas for humanistic psychology. Rogers theorized the developed self-concept as having three distinct components. The first being the *self-image* as the component that views and establishes the image of one's self. This self-image includes such properties as physical description, social roles, and personal traits like responsible, gregarious, and charitable—plus that aspect of the self-image dealing with *existential statements* regarding one's morality and spirituality.

Rogers' second component is *self-esteem*. It is here that we find how much value we put on ourselves and to what degree we approve of ourselves. High self-esteem lends itself to confidence in our abilities and allows us to feel free of repression by the judgments of others. It also promotes an attitude of optimism towards life. Conversely, low self-esteem often breeds envy and a lack of confidence. It leads us to obsessive concern about the judgments of others and can spiral into an all-around pessimistic attitude.

In the third component, Rogers refers to the *ideal self*. It is here that one constructs the image of who one wishes to be—his or her ideal. When a person's self-image is not in alignment with the ideal self, it is likely to affect self-esteem and how much one values him or herself. In the third component, we see how Rogers' self-concept is interrelated with the other two. When a person's actual life experience falls short of the ideal self, the person finds him or herself in a state of incongruence. When the actual experience and the ideal self are consistent, we have a state of *congruence*. Rogers believed there must be a state of congruence for a person to achieve *self-actualization*.

Rollo May

For the purpose of our discussion, it is important to recognize the complexity and the enormous investment each of us has in our individual identity of self. To a large extent it holds a significant influence on how we experience our lives and how others experience us. This theme is expanded by another of the distinguished co-founders of the Humanistic Psychology movement—existential psychotherapist Rollo May

(1909-1994). May was largely responsible for integrating the humanistic and existential traditions. He posited that human nature cannot be understood without recognizing a person's subjective experience of life. He believed that it is the anxiety one experiences that triggers the inner exploration, thus making anxiety the key to selfhood.

In an interview with Dr. Jeffrey Mishlove, psychotherapist and television host, Rollo May elaborated on his view of anxiety as *a gateway for exploration to the meaning of life:*

> *Existential psychology was just what was needed as the medical model had turned out to be a dead end... I think that anxiety [not viewed as a symptom] is associated with creativity. When you are in a situation of anxiety you can certainly run away from it... take a pill for it... but this does not lead to creativity. What anxiety means... is that you need to create something—you need to do something... For people who have found their own heart; their own soul; it is a stimulus towards creativity.*

May goes on to say that anxiety is the healthy response to being conscious of the human dilemma; i.e., conscious of our own self and our tasks, and the knowledge that we are going to die. Humans are the only creatures who can be aware of their death.

> *Out of that comes normal anxiety. When I let myself feel that, I apply myself to new ideas... I communicate more honestly. It is this knowledge of our death that gives us normal anxiety and says to us, make the most of these years that you are alive.*

Creativity is not merely the innocent spontaneity of our youth and childhood; it must also be married to the passion of the adult human being, which is a passion to live beyond one's death.

—Rollo May

According to May, it is free will and our freedom to choose responsibly that leads to creativity and the discovery of our authentic self. It's the evil in man that is reflected in our culture's evil, as it is the evil in our culture that is reflected in man. Freedom from evil is not achieved by avoiding evil, but by confronting it. May warned that by avoiding this confrontation with evil, both in ourselves and in our world, we fail on a grand scale. In this regard, May states, *"Life to me, is not a requirement to live out a preordained pattern of goodness, but a challenge coming down through the centuries out of the fact that each of us can throw the lever toward good or toward evil."*

It is the responsibility of each of us to mold ourselves to our essential being. For May, this was a key issue; too much emphasis on doing and not enough on being. Each of us must have a clear experience of our being, our very existence, for true and lasting change to occur. This experience May called the "I am experience" which puts a person in touch with the full impact of his or her authentic existence and can occur during meditative states of relaxation and contentment, or during times when one is at odds with life—experiencing states of anxiety and fear. According to May, this is the path toward self-exploration necessary for a person to live out his or her own potential rather than merely following the norm. It's within this approach of holistic change that May views the role of the psychotherapist; as opposed to working through particular symptoms.

In an interview with Dr. Kirk J. Schneider, leading spokesperson for contemporary humanistic psychology and the editor of the Journal of Humanistic Psychology, Rollo May stated:

> *It was not the purpose of the forefathers of psychology, Freud, Jung, Adler, etc., to treat single symptoms of single patients. Their purpose is to make the unconscious, conscious... The therapy that is important, as I see it, is the therapy that enlarges the person, makes the unconscious conscious. It enlarges our view, it enlarges our experience, makes us more sensitive... it enlarges our intellectual capacities... This is what Freud was setting out to do... this is what Jung was trying to do... They were not interested in curing symptoms; they were interested in making a new person.*

This notion of *making a new person* is aligned with that of the spiritual makeover taught by the ancient Saints and Sages. The Buddha and the great Yoga Masters also weighed in on the complexity and entanglement of the human psyche that must be recognized and reorganized before we transcend our lower states of consciousness. The psychologists discussed above became co-founders of the new, burgeoning science of psychology, each bringing a unique perspective with roots dating back to the time of Socrates. Carl Rogers worked to ensure that the developmental processes of humanistic psychology led to a healthier more creative personality—one emphasizing free will, self-exploration, and actualizing human potential. Rogers coined the term *actualizing tendency* which eventually led Abraham Maslow (1908-1970), another co-founder of humanistic psychology, to study self-actualization as one of the human needs.

Throughout the 1950s, multiple meetings were convened at which prominent psychologists of the day discussed the possibility of moving in a new direction. In 1954, Abraham Maslow published his book, *Motivation and Personality* based on his earlier 1943 publication, "A Theory of Human Motivation" and his 1950 paper, "Self-actualizing People: A Study of Psychological Health." In his writings, Maslow identifies 13 traits of self-actualized people. In doing so, Maslow was proposing a more holistic theory of human psychology, incorporating many aspects of personality. It was in his 1950 paper that Maslow first used the term "self-actualization."

> *This term, first coined by Kurt Goldstein, is being used in this paper in a much more specific and limited fashion. It refers to the desire for self-fulfillment, namely, to the tendency for him to become actualized in what he is potentially. This tendency might be phrased as the desire to become more and more what one is, to become everything that one is capable of becoming.*
> —Abraham Maslow, *Theory of Human Motivation*

In 1957 and 1958, psychologists interested in founding a professional association for those committed to the humanistic vision, attended meetings in Detroit, Michigan organized by Maslow and Clark Moustakas. The vision included principles such as self-actualization, creativity, individuality, the intrinsic nature of being human, the human potential, and others, all within the context of meaning. In 1961, with the sponsorship of Brandeis University, the movement was launched as the American Association for Humanistic Psychology (AAHP).

On November 28, 1964 the AAHP held its first professional conference in Old Saybrook, Connecticut to determine the depth and character of this new psychology. Maslow, Rogers, May and Moustakas were among the participants in this first meeting to establish the humanistic tenet of self-actualization, health, creativity, intrinsic nature, being, becoming, individuality and meaning.

In his 1964 article, *Five Basic Postulates of Humanistic Psychology*, appearing in the Journal of Humanistic Psychology, James Bugental articulated the Five Basic Postulates of Humanistic Psychology:

1. Human beings, as human, supersede the sum of their parts. They cannot be reduced to components.
2. Human beings have their existence in a uniquely human context, as well as in a cosmic ecology.
3. Human beings are aware and aware of being aware — i.e., they are conscious. Human consciousness always includes an awareness of oneself in the context of other people.
4. Human beings have some choice and, with that, responsibility.
5. Human beings are intentional, aim at goals, are aware that they cause future events, and seek meaning, value, and creativity.

There are a number of fundamental spiritual tenets within these postulates of humanistic psychology. The notion of the human as a synergistic unit that can reach beyond its limitations, and our responsibility to do so, is purely spiritual in nature. Also we find the recognition of our consciousness as being a key component towards attaining our potential and our responsibility both to ourselves and to the cosmos. Embedded in these postulates are found traces of the spiritual tenets that point towards our free will and the karmic causes in determining our future—all within the context of meaning. Humanistic Psychology was an offshoot of many of the teachings of existentialism and phenomenology and was influenced by the Ancient Greeks, Eastern philosophy, and psychology. It also embraces certain spiritual overtones as it is concerned with the nature of human existence and consciousness.

Carl Rogers and Abraham Maslow

Of all the co-founding contributors, the two names most associated with the field of *humanistic psychology* are Abraham Maslow and Carl Rogers. Both believed the highest state of attainment for humans is self-actualization. A self-actualized person fulfills his or her potential. Both also advocated the idea that psychology should recognize and reinforce the positive aspects of human personality rather than obsess over apparent harmful symptoms. By reinforcement of a patient's positive traits and behaviors, he or she is able to advance toward the ultimate goal of self-actualization.

Humanistic Psychology was an offshoot of many of the teachings of existentialism and phenomenology and was influenced by the Ancient Greeks, Eastern philosophy, and psychology. It also embraces certain religious overtones as it is concerned with the nature of human existence and consciousness.

Rodgers was a proponent of the personality theories of

Donald Snygg and Arthur Combs. They asserted that we all exist in a separate world unto ourselves— *phenomenology*. Rogers's theory holds that people experience reality not based on what *it* is, but rather based on *who* we are. Since who we are, is always different from who somebody else is, so too our reality is always different. Simply stated, humans live in a *subjective reality*.

In *subjective reality*, things exist the way we perceive them to exist. Our perception is tuned into our beliefs, including our desires and fears. Over a lifetime, the *subjective reality* in which each of us exists continually alters to match new experiences and new beliefs. Key to our reality is the position each of us holds in our own world. A person will go to great lengths to protect his or her identity within *subjective reality*. This means that we all spend an inordinate amount of time and energy protecting ourselves from anything that poses a threat. To remain alert to self-protection, each of us must constantly evaluate and judge our interactions with others. One can only imagine the impact such a mechanism has on our ability to relate to others, especially when each of the others is similarly engaged in his or her own self-protective responses, based on his or her *subjective reality*.

Rogers asserted that a person could overcome this limiting process of continually evaluating and molding reality to fit self-imposed standards. Once relieved of this burden, a person gains the ability to live in the moment as it is, rather than always working to reshape it. By letting go of the burden of judging and evaluating in order to re-frame all encounters, a person gains access to an enhanced experience of life undistorted by the need to protect and defend. Without being tethered to this relentless hidden agenda, a person gains greater freedom of choice and is able to actualize more of his or her potential. Freed up from the burden, a person may also serve others through empathy and concern. Such a person is able to enter the *subjective reality* of another without the need to rearrange for his or her own personal gain:

> *Being empathic means: To be with another in this way means that for the time being you lay aside the views and values you hold for yourself in order to enter another's world without prejudice. In some sense it means that you lay aside your self and this can only be done by a person who is secure enough in himself that he knows he will not get lost in what may turn out to be the strange or bizarre world of the other, and can comfortably return to his own world when he wishes. Perhaps this description makes clear that being empathic is a complex, demanding, strong yet subtle and gentle way of being.*
>
> —Carl Rogers

In alignment with Rogers's theories, Abraham Maslow studied those "exemplary" people who actually reach their potential and make up the top percent of humanity. He focused attention on how they are different from others and how more people might achieve such status. Maslow is perhaps most well-known for his psychological theory of human motivation, *Maslow's Hierarchy of Needs.* In his 1943 paper, *A Theory of Human Motivation,* published in Psychological Review, Maslow first expressed his now famous theory and the needs that drive it. According to Maslow, humans are motivated and active when they experience themselves as deficient in what they believe they need. He divided and categorized these needs into five (later extended to eight) groupings. Not surprising, the lower the category on the hierarchy, the larger the percentage of people engaged.

Thus, the hierarchy is usually depicted as a pyramid, with each category decreasing in size as one ascends to the top. Maslow suggests that as few as 1%-2% of all people operate at the highest level, attaining satisfaction at the top of the pyramid. However, he also claims that all people are capable of operating at the top level. He named the top or fifth level, the *being needs,* and later he extended them to three additional groupings. These are the higher needs that humans develop through growth and higher consciousness. These needs involve a person *being* his or her full potential.

He named the first four levels the *deficiency needs.* Being deficient in any of these needs, a person will spring into action.

The lowest and largest category is that of *physiological needs*, including the physical requirements for our physical survival. We share these needs with all animals—food, water, air, sleep, and the need to procreate. Maslow estimates that 85% of Americans are fulfilling the *physiological needs*. A big part of being a human in a physical life is to be motivated and engaged in the process of fulfilling these basic needs.

Once the basic needs are satisfied, a person focuses on the needs grouped in the next category—*safety needs.* These include shelter and protection, order and stability, and even safety from fear and anxiety. The need to feel safe and protected is frequently a major influence on how we live our life and the behavior we express. Some people cannot satisfy the need to feel safe, despite all of the effort put into fulfilling it.

Some cannot seem to feel secure in terms of financial security, health maintenance, or physical danger. There are those who stay stuck in a bad career or relationship situation only because it provides some semblance of security and stability. For many, familiarity alone can be experienced as security. Maslow estimated that about 75% of people are enmeshed in fulfilling their *safety needs.*

Once we have satisfied our needs regarding survival and safety, we are free to focus on the next level of our *deficiency needs—our social needs.* It is at this level that one experiences the need to belong in the group, whether it is a family, friendship, romance, congregation, community, or work group. Along with *belongingness* at this level, are our emotional needs for *love* and *affection.* At this level, we fulfill our need to be connected, interacting and communicating. Maslow put the number of people feeling fulfilled in social needs to be 50%.

Closely related to social needs, and the last of the basic *deficiency needs,* are those under the heading *needs of esteem.* These very real human needs involve both inward self-esteem, and outward esteem derived from others; *i.e.,* what we think about ourselves and what others think about us. In this category are acknowledgement, compliments, self-respect, recognition and reputation, status, expertise, achievement, and the like. Maslow estimated some 40% of Americans are satisfying their *esteem needs.* These basic four levels of needs Maslow called *coping behavior.* Behavior at this level is primarily merely coping with life.

During the 1960s and the 1970s, Maslow's five level hierarchy was expanded to a seven and, later, eight level hierarchy. The additional three levels are regarded as a part of the original fifth level; Self-Actualization. Some feel the additional levels help clarify what is included in the concept of self-actualization.

The first expanded level comes into the hierarchy at the

fifth spot following the basic four *deficiency needs*. This revised fifth level in the *being needs* is that of *cognitive needs* or the need for *knowledge* and *meaning*. Although *meaning and knowledge* are both implied in the level of self-actualization, they are separated into a level of their own. This fifth level begins the higher *being needs* that culminate in our ultimate need to reach our full potential. It is the need for *knowing* that the ancient Hindus put as being second only to the human need of *being*, or our need to exist. Maslow recognized that even humans reflecting on their own desires can be confused while chasing after illusive satisfaction: *It isn't normal to know what we want. It is a rare and difficult psychological achievement.*

In the expanded version of Maslow's Hierarchy of Human Needs, the sixth level is that of *aesthetic needs*. This level embraces the human need for beauty, balance and form. As was the case with Emerson, nature plays a key role at this level of the hierarchy by offering satisfaction to the human need for beauty. It's possible that one could embrace the notion of self-actualization, yet not recognize the role of aesthetics. Here we must recognize that creation is as much an expression of beauty and artistry as it is an expression of science and logic.

The seventh level is the original fifth and final level that Maslow first identified. It embodies all four of the higher levels of need. This is the rarely fulfilled human *need for self-actualization* which is the response to the age-old question, *"what is the meaning of my life?"* It is here that all other human needs culminate and provide support. According to Maslow, *"what a man can be, he must be."* Self-actualization is not just a design option for this life; it is the very purpose of this life. When a person has satisfied, if not mastered, the basic needs of the body's survival and the ego's gratification, it's time to focus attention and concentration on the higher need of actualizing one's full potential.

Interestingly, there is also the need to adhere to a code of morality that is embedded at this level. It is here that a person with compromised morals might attempt to cheat, lie, steal, or worse, in an attempt to actualize his or her potential. This, of course, would not be representative of the self-actualized individual. Maslow determined that as few as 1%-2% of people are fully satisfying their need for self-actualization, and perhaps as many as 10% are satisfying a portion of this higher need. He also stated that his study of college students revealed that only 1/10th of 1% of students were satisfying their *self-actualization need.*

In the revised and extended version of the hierarchy there is the eighth and final level; the *transcendence need.* It is here that a person actualizes beyond his or her personal need. Attainment here may very well be the level referred to by the ancient Sages, whereby a person transcends self-interest and expresses behavior rooted in altruism. After a person attains full self-actualization, he or she moves on to facilitate the actualization of others. This is the basis for higher human virtues such as empathy and compassion. Maslow theorized that a person reaches this level of virtuous living only after all of the lower needs have been met. Of course, some people become *enslaved* by self-interest and continually experience more needs for pleasure and ego gratification thus never moving on to fulfill the higher needs.

American born Tibetan Buddhist, Lama Surya Das, b.1950, has spent decades closing the gap between East and West. In his book, *Awakening the Buddha Within,* he acknowledges this struggle: *Just as a caterpillar must shed its familiar cocoon in order to become a butterfly... you must be willing to change and shed the hard armor of self-centered egotism... it can be difficult because it brings you face to face with reality... face to face with who you really are.*

It's more common than not to become stuck in the various stages of our growth. It is characteristic of our nature to

adhere to the familiar while resisting the urge to move into undiscovered territory. So many of us endure the hidden pressure to morph into the greater version of ourselves, but resist, clinging to our past and its cherished memories.

Life is a process of becoming, a combination of states we have to go through. Where people fail is that they wish to elect a state and remain in it. This is a kind of death. And the day came when the risk to remain tight in a bud was more painful than the risk it took to blossom.

—Anais Nin

In this final *transcendence need* of Maslow's hierarchy we see similarities to the Buddha's high level of enlightenment, or the Abrahamic religions' notion of altruistic living in which it is better to give than to receive. Similar to the other philosophies and religions, Maslow's transcendence stage is one that literally transcends the human nature of self-interest and the *"me first mentality"* that accompanies ego.

As Oliver Wendell Holmes Jr. referenced in his address to the Harvard Law Association in 1913, perhaps humanity has "cosmic destinies" of which we ourselves remain unaware and unable to understand. Like the caterpillar, we go about our effort in preparation for a destiny that is unknown at the prior stage of our lives.

> *I think it not improbable that man, like the grub that prepares a chamber for the winged thing it never has seen but is to be—that man may have cosmic destinies he does not understand. And so beyond the vision of battling races and an impoverished earth, I catch a dreaming glimpse of peace.*
>
> —Oliver W. Holmes

One might surmise that Maslow would ask: Are we, like the caterpillar, programmed to weave our cocoon of solitude in order to emerge a grander version of ourselves? Are we destined to transcend the sluggish mobility of the grub in order to take flight? Are we indeed destined to shed our heavily encumbered human suffering, to become free of regrets and resentments; pain and sorrow? If so, why is it that we, unlike the caterpillar, have the option to resist and procrastinate our metamorphosis? Why do we not prepare for our transformation even before understanding what is about to occur? These are the sentiments reflected in the words of Prague-born poet Rainer Maria Rilke (1875-1926), when he encourages us not to be thwarted by our questions, but to live our lives forward into a time when the answers will unfold.

> *Be patient toward all that is unsolved in your heart,*
> *And try to love the questions themselves.*

Do not seek the answers that cannot be given you
because you would not be able to live them.
And the point is to live everything.
Live the questions now.
Perhaps you will then gradually, without noticing it,
live along some distant day into the answer.
— Rilke, *Letters to a Young Poet*

Could it be that like Rilke's letter, we too are being directed not to wait for evidence that we contain a hidden butterfly, but to construct our spiritual cocoon in a more or less "if you build it he will come" fashion? Could nature be illuminating a significant spiritual lesson for humanity in its portrayal of metamorphosis through the caterpillar and the butterfly? Is there something of great beauty and capable of flight existing within our earthbound mortal existence longing to emerge? And, if so, what is expected of us to move this transformation along? In the words of America's most celebrated evangelical preacher of the early 20th century, Billy Sunday: *Faith is the beginning of something of which you can't see the end but in which you believe.*

In Summary...
This chapter is a continuation of the formation and influence of our worldview. While the previous chapter explored how our collective worldview impacts humanity, this chapter explores how humanity shapes our worldview; both aspects influence the other concurrently. Spiritually speaking, individual consciousness impacts collective consciousness while, at the same time, collective consciousness is impacting the individual. This chapter is a study of

the big ideas of some of history's great thought leaders, from the Greek philosophers and Christian Mystics to the Transcendental Movement and the Science of Mind; from Freud and Jung to Carl Rogers and Abraham Maslow.

First and foremost, the spiritual quest is a striving for truth—Absolute Truth. This truth, the Buddha called Enlightenment, or *seeing the way things really are.* Long before we reach the summit of Absolute Truth, we must climb through endless passages of relative truth—truth that points us in the right direction but does not necessarily get us to our ultimate destination.

CHAPTER FIVE

Actualizing the Human Potential

The long and winding road that explores the mysteries of the mind led to a key universal message for all who navigate this life—there is untapped power and unbounded delight hidden within us. These treasures of a greater version of ourselves are hidden in the form of human potential—yet to be discovered, and yet to be actualized. The mind is the instrument designed to discover and actualize this hidden potential. It's able to drill through learning and insight—the discovery is made through experience and realization.

We fear to know the fearsome and unsavory aspects of ourselves, but we fear even more to know the god-like in ourselves.

—Abraham Maslow

There are things known and there are things unknown, and in between are the doors of perception.

—Aldous Huxley

There is no deficit in human resources; the deficit is in human will.

—Martin Luther King Jr.

From Mesmer to Maslow the science of mind worked its way into our modern worldview. While religion continued to repeat and reinforce the ancient teachings of scripture, science strived to gain practical understanding and updated applications for humanity's *motherboard*—the mind. It is not that religion had it wrong; only that its audience was shrinking and its message, for many, was not breaking through. Scientific thought and empirical investigation are not tethered to their founders; rather they are inspired by them. While religious inquiry is threatened by modernizing perspectives, science encourages them. In fairness to the religious founders and sacred scripture, all that is necessary for spiritual awakening is contained within their teachings. It is the seeker who often needs a contemporized version to gain the necessary insights—a new path to an old destination.

About two decades after Maslow first published his *Theory of Human Motivation* proposing the *Hierarchy of Needs*—and the launch of humanistic psychology—a profound shift emerged in the field of psychology; particularly in the approach to therapy. Traditionally, treatment had been confined to those plagued by psychological disorders—the mentally ill. In the early 1960s, a particular approach began to shift focus from those whose ability to produce results had been stunted, to those recognized as high achievers. Humanistic psychology espoused the notion of hidden potential just waiting to be tapped, and the power of human will to overcome one's limitations. Similarly, Maslow's study focused on the self-actualized human being. These developments unleashed a revolution of new thought and new possibilities.

Aldous Huxley

Aldous Huxley (1894-1963), the English author, professor and philosopher relocated to California in 1937. Huxley was a key player in this *new thought* revolution zeroing in on our untapped hidden potential. In his speech delivered at U.C. Berkeley on March 20, 1962, Huxley pointed out that past revolutions have always been aimed at changing human behavior through changing the system or environment, i.e., political revolution, economic revolution, even religious revolution. In the early 1960s, we witnessed a revolution aimed directly at the mind of humanity.

In his speech, *The Ultimate Revolution,* Huxley described a number of worrisome scenarios of the future. In particular was the idea that humanity would need to guard against an elite and powerful oligarchy governing the masses while answering only to the interests of those who would finance their authority. In Huxley's future world, the elite ruling class would gain the trust of the masses who would become their *servants.* One method by which the ruling class would gain the acceptance of the masses to their role of servitude was through a powerful pharmaceutical industry that would keep people under the influence of drugs that relieved such feelings as anxiety and depression.

Interestingly, a 2009 Mayo Clinic study found that nearly 70 percent of Americans are taking at least one prescribed medication daily, and topping the list are antibiotics, antidepressants, and opioids (class of drugs known for their ability to produce a euphoric high and extremely addictive). Combine these numbers to the 23.9 million people who the

National Institute on Drug Abuse says are using illicit drugs, and we see that Huxley's vision of an addicted society, complacent to their powerless position and mediocrity, was not too far off the mark. Huxley proclaimed:

> *Anatomically and physiologically, man has changed very little during the last twenty or thirty thousand years. The native or genetic capabilities of today's bright city child are no better than the native capabilities of a bright child born into a family of Upper Paleolithic cave-dwellers. But whereas the contemporary bright baby may grow up to become almost anything... the Paleolithic baby could not possibly have grown into anything except a hunter or food-gatherer, using the crudest of stone tools and thinking about his narrow world of trees and swamps in terms of some hazy system of magic. Ancient and modern, the two babies are indistinguishable. Each of them contains all the potentialities of the particular breed of human being to which he or she happens to belong. But the adult into whom the babies will grow are profoundly dissimilar; and they are dissimilar because in one of them very few, and in the other a good many, of the baby's inborn potentialities have been actualized.*
>
> – Aldous Huxley, *Human Potentialities*

This simple yet astounding observation by Huxley paled by comparison to the profound questions he then posed:

> *The Paleolithic baby was as richly endowed with human potentialities as is the baby of today. How, in the course of history, were so many of those potential-*

ities actualized? And what should be done now and in the immediate future to actualize the many and great potentialities which in most individuals still remain latent?

These questions would catch the attention of a generation and bring about what some have called a revolution in the pursuit of the potentialities of modern humanity. It certainly caught the attention of his audience at the University of California, San Francisco Medical Center in 1960. Huxley spoke about all that is hidden within each of us, waiting to surface under the proper conditions. This he called *Human Potentialities* and challenged his audience to develop the necessary mechanisms and techniques that would provide for people the conditions in which their latent potential might become actualized.

Richard Price and Michael Murphy

Two Stanford graduates, Richard Price and Michael Murphy, were in attendance and took this challenge very seriously. They reached out to meet with Huxley at his Hollywood Hills home, but, as fate would have it, he was not available. Instead, Huxley encouraged them to meet with his close friend Gerald Heard (1889-1971) who lived in Santa Monica. Heard, also English, graduated with honors from Cambridge where he studied history and theology and later developed a strong interest in the sciences. After meeting Swami Prabhavananda (1883-1976), Heard became an initiate of Vedanta, one of the six orthodox schools of Hindu philosophy. Prabhavananda was an East Indian philosopher and monk of the Ramakrishna Order, a monastic organization founded by the Bengali saint Sri Ramakrishna and his leading disciple

Swami Vivekananda. Today there are nearly 170 Ramakrishna monastic centers worldwide.

After meeting with Heard and being introduced to his Hindu philosophy, Price and Murphy became committed to assisting people in tapping into their hidden potential. They decided to develop an ideal setting in which to pursue this worthy objective. As it turned out in 1910, Michael Murphy's grandfather, Dr. Henry Murphy, a California physician, had purchased a 120-acre parcel perched along the mountainous Pacific coast in Big Sur, California. It had once been the home of a Native American tribe known as the Esalen. The location was thought to have healing powers and Dr. Murphy intended to turn it into a health spa. In 1962, Michael Murphy along with Richard Price, co-founded the Esalen Institute on his grandfather's scenic 120 acres where the Santa Lucia Mountains rise up from the California Pacific Ocean. It is ideally located between San Francisco to the north and Los Angeles to the south.

Michael Murphy and Richard Price gathered such influential supporters as Aldous Huxley, his close friend, Gerald Heard, Stanford professor Frederic Spiegelberg, noted British-born author and Eastern philosopher Allan Watts, and English anthropologist and social scientist Gregory Bateson. Esalen became the nexus for an already thriving movement, albeit a movement without a name. In 1962, the eminent humanistic psychologist Abraham Maslow found his way into the Esalen family. He was followed by German-born distinguished psychiatrist and psychotherapist Frederick (Fritz) Salomon Perls (1893-1970) who coined the term *Gestalt Therapy*. Perls actually lived on site at Esalen from 1964-1969 where he delivered his Gestalt therapy seminars. In the introduction of his book, *Ego, Hunger and Aggression*, Perls describes Esalen: *What the Bauhaus was in Germany for the creation of a new style in architecture and the arts, Esalen is as a practical center of the third wave of humanistic psychology.*

In this same time frame, another key player, George Leonard (1923-2010), joined the mix. Leonard was a senior editor for Look magazine from 1953 to 1970. In the 1960s, he was doing research for Look throughout the United States regarding human potential. In fact, Newsweek once referred to him as "the granddaddy of the consciousness movement." On February 2, 1965, George Leonard met Michael Murphy and they talked through the entire night. When the sun came up the *movement* had its name and Leonard was an integral part of the Esalen team. Aldous Huxley had provided the gist of the name from his speech entitled *Human Potentialities*. Leonard and Murphy simply added the final word to coin the *Human Potential Movement*.

Today, after Esalen has been in operation for over a half century, it has served over three quarters of a million people from all over the world, all under the banner of "spiritual, but not religious." Its list of teachers is a virtual who's-who in the areas of human psychology, philosophy, science, the arts, and even some very distinguished rock stars. Beyond those already mentioned, a host of additional honored names have taught at Esalen: Psychologist and co-founder of the humanistic approach, Carl Rogers, Nobel laureate Linus Pauling, famed author and designer Buckminster Fuller, Harvard professors Richard Alpert and Timothy Leary, American psychologist, inventor, social philosopher, pioneer of modern behaviorism and recipient of the National Medal of Science, B.F. Skinner.

Great religious scholars have also taught at Esalen, including American mythologist and author, Joseph Campbell (1904-1987). Campbell shared his concept of *mono-myth,* a term borrowed from novelist James Joyce. Campbell claims that all of the great mythic narratives of mankind are but variations of one single story. The story often includes a single hero existing within ordinary reality who is *called* into a non-ordinary state of perception. From this expanded vantage point, our hero *sees* what others have missed. Returning to the ordinary reality of the common perspective, the hero is able to elevate the whole of humanity based upon his now expanded view.

Huston Smith

Huston Smith (1919-2016) also spoke at Esalen. Smith was an eminent religious studies scholar, author of fourteen books, the Thomas J. Watson Professor of Religion and Distinguished Adjunct Professor of Philosophy, Emeritus at Syracuse University. Awarded twelve honorary degrees, his book *The Religions of Man,* has sold over two and a half million copies, was translated into twelve languages, and is still one of the most widely used college textbooks on comparative religions. As chairman of the philosophy department at MIT for fifteen years, Smith met up with professors Timothy Leary and Richard Alpert, both of whom taught at Esalen. Although a Christian, Smith developed an appetite for mysticism and was influenced by two other proponents of Esalen, Aldous Huxley and Gerald Heard. Huxley directed Smith toward the teachings of Swami Vivekananda and Ramakrishna, and the practice of meditation.

In 1996, Bill Moyers broadcast a 5-part PBS special, *The Wisdom of Faith with Huston Smith,* devoted to his life and work. In 2012, noted psychologist and gerontologist Dr. Ken Dychtwald, interviewed Smith, who was then 93 years old.

Dr. Dychtwald and his wife Maddy, founded the company *Age Wave*, an international think tank, providing to millions of the world's thought leaders a greater understanding of the global implications of aging. Ken, himself a frequent Esalen teacher, released this interview on DVD in 2012, *The Arc of Life: Huston Smith on Life, Death & Beyond*. This fascinating interview is a statement to the human potential. Well into his ninth decade, Huston Smith continued to teach and lead humanity toward a greater understanding of its past and the potential of its future. Perhaps most apropos for today's youth obsessed culture is Smith's response to Dychtwald's probing question: *Do you ever wish you could be young again?* To which Smith replied an unequivocal, *No. That was fine then, and it took a lot of energy... but I have no wish to repeat it.* With regard to aging, Smith resolutely affirms *the body descends while the mind and spirit ascend.* This notion of the simultaneous *descending body with the ascending spirit* is a fundamental tenet of spirituality that illuminates the purpose and meaning of physical aging and death. We explore this concept in Part Two of this book.

Carlos Castaneda

Another well-known speaker at Esalen was the American author and anthropologist, Carlos Castaneda (1925-1998), whose 12 books sold over 28 million copies in 17 languages. From the time Castaneda stepped into the limelight in 1968 with his first book *The Teachings of Don Juan*, until he withdrew from public view in 1973, his persona was marked by controversy and mystery. *Teachings of Don Juan* was Castaneda's master's thesis in anthropology and was published by the University of California Press. It documents the apprenticeship experiences that Castaneda himself had from 1960-

1965 while working under Yaqui Indian Sorcerer, don Juan Matus. Castaneda describes a *specialized* version of the ancient Toltec culture where one who is chosen can learn the ways of knowledge and be introduced into a *separate reality.*

With the use of "power plants," such as peyote, one alters his or her perception and allows for higher levels of awareness. While critics debated whether Castaneda's books were an accurate account of authentic Mexican Indian culture, the 60s generation could not get enough of what he had to say. Nearly 30 million readers worldwide were much less interested in the authenticity of his facts, but focused on the impact of his words. Suddenly suburban college students were sitting in vacant lots contemplating the precise moment when the day comes to an end and the night is about to begin or staring endlessly at the spaces between the leaves of the trees in an attempt to "stop the world" as it appears. As don Juan explained, what we view to be the world is merely a description of the world—a consensually created reality that we have cultivated since our earliest childhood. Only through suspending ordinary perception, is one able to see the truth that it conceals. Not only is our world limited by our ordinary perception of it, don Juan taught Carlos that we also suffer from a limiting perception of ourselves. We are a daily continuous replica of who we have been in our past. It is only through "erasing our personal history," that we gain the freedom to become someone new and a more authentic representation of our current knowledge.

The world that don Juan saw was far beyond that of ordinary reality, it was magical yet pragmatic with infinite possibilities. To live in this *non-ordinary reality,* one must break free of ordinary perception and learn the *art of seeing.* A warrior, as don Juan called those who have advanced, chooses his or her state of mind and defies external circumstances. These were the words that resonated with a generation of readers whose awareness seemed to expand with each new page.

For the generation coming of age during the 1960s, the chrome was beginning to peel off the old established order of things. Hypocrisy and corruption, along with violence and assassination, left a stench that needed to be washed away through a new worldview. Castaneda had just enough insight and understanding to fill an ever-widening gap between what had been and what was beginning to emerge. These were big ideas that found their way into the hearts and minds of his worldwide audience.

He described the role played by what he called one's *internal dialogue*. Don Juan taught that this voice in our mind not only defines us, but it defines the world in which we live. Again, we find a somewhat contemporized idea of an ancient spiritual teaching; *to think is to create.*

> *We talk to ourselves incessantly about our surrounding world. In fact, we maintain our world with our internal talk... Not only that, but we also choose our paths as we talk to ourselves. Thus, we repeat the same choices over and over until the day we die, because we keep on repeating the same internal talk over and over until the day we die. A warrior is aware of this and strives to stop his internal talk.*
>
> —Castaneda, *Separate Reality*

> *The internal dialogue is what grounds people in the daily world. The world is such and such or so and so, only because we talk to ourselves about its being such and such and so and so. The passageway into*

the world of shamans opens up after the warrior has learned to shut off his internal dialogue.
                                    —Carlos Castaneda, *Tales of Power*

Like many great Sages and mystics for centuries before him, Castaneda cautioned his readers to keep the mystery a mystery.

The world is incomprehensible. We won't ever understand it; we won't ever unravel its secrets. Thus, we must treat the world as it is: a sheer mystery.
                                    —Castaneda, *Separate Reality*

While infinitely mysterious, the world also has order and great purpose underlying the apparent confusion and chaos. Each of us is continuously challenged by what we encounter. The way we meet these challenges determines everything. Our greatest asset in overcoming the endless challenges of life is what don Juan called *personal power*.

It doesn't matter how one was brought up. What determines the way one does anything is personal power...

The trick is in what one emphasizes. We either make ourselves miserable, or we make ourselves strong. The amount of work is the same.

[Concerning the world] *We're not talking about the same thing, don Juan said. For you the world is weird because if you are not bored with it, you're at odds with it. For me the world is weird because it is stupendous, awesome, mysterious, unfathomable; my interest has been to convince you that you must assume responsi-*

bility for being here, in this marvelous world... in this marvelous time... to make every act count, since you are going to be here for only a short while... too short for witnessing all the marvels of it.

—Castaneda, *Journey to Ixtlan*

Castaneda spoke of an unfamiliar culture often overlooked by most people. At first these concepts seemed foreign, subsequently we're recognized as sharing the same root system as many of our great spiritual teachers. For his many readers who carried *the books* with them throughout their daily routines, and who cherished moments when they could *stop the world* and enter their own *separate reality,* it was irrelevant whether Castaneda followed formal protocol in his investigations or if his recollections were flawed. It was not the historical or the anthropological accuracy that kept the millions enthralled. Rather authenticity was found within the hearts and the minds of the reader.

Many have associated the adventures of Castaneda with the role of psychotropic plants and the use of hallucinogenic drugs. The plant most often referenced in his books is what he called *Sacred Datura,* or as it is called in the desert southwest—*jimsonweed.* Originally used for its medicinal properties, this herb is also known as a powerful hallucinogen. However, the tropane alkaloids in jimsonweed can be extremely toxic and, if taken in excess, can be fatal.

Use of mind-altering substance in order to open one's perception and raise consciousness is nothing new. According to Dr. David Lewis-Williams (born 1934), Professor of Cognitive Archeology at the University of Witwatersrand in Johannesburg, the cave drawings of Upper Paleolithic Europe were produced by *shamans* whose consciousness had been altered by hallucinogenic plants. Williams is the founder of the Rock Art Research Institute and has been designated as a "leading international researcher" having an A-1 rating by the National Research Foundation. His specialty is the theoretical perspective that determined how ancient cultures thought and expressed themselves.

Evidence of *Shamanism* and the mystical experience of the *Shaman* has been traced throughout the prehistoric world, including sites in Africa, Australia, Europe, and Asia. The word *shaman* is believed to have come from the Siberian Tungus and can be translated as "one who knows." Basically, *Shamanism* refers to the beliefs held by a particular group similar to modern religion. An article in the November, 2008, National Geographic entitled *Oldest Shaman Grave Found,* reports archaeologists in northern Israel discovered the remains of the world's oldest known shaman. The 12,000-year-old grave contains the cadaver of a female shaman of the Natufian culture. Archeologists determined that the woman held the distinct shaman position in the ancient society by the manner in which she was buried and the status of the grave.

Robert Gordon Wasson (1898-1986) an expert in ethnomycology (study of the historical uses and sociological impact of fungi) theorized that religion had its early origins rooted in the ingestion of hallucinogenic mushrooms. His work was echoed by Terrence McKenna (1946-2000) who studied Shamanism and the altered states of consciousness achieved by Shamans; both through natural methods of meditation, dancing, fasting, drumming, and the ingestion of plant-based entheogens such as psilocybin mushrooms—often called "Holy Children" by shamans. Once the shamans entered the altered state of consciousness, they were able to see beyond three-dimensional reality. The visions and knowledge attained through this mystical experience were the earliest forms of religion.

The use of entheogenic plants and chemicals goes back to society's earliest cultures. Carlos Castaneda was not the only Sixties icon who ingested them to gain spiritual insight. Oddly, our modern world began using the same methods of inducing the mystical experience as did our ancient ancestors. The key difference between the early cultures' view and our modern worldview of the mystical experience is the educated lens of the advanced science of psychology through which we observe and report findings.

The Harvard Psilocybin Project

Perhaps the most famous explorers of drug-based spiritual awakening were the Harvard professors Timothy Leary (1920-1996) and Richard Alpert (born 1931); both were teachers at Esalen. Leary, whose recommendation to a generation became the sixties battle cry: *Think for yourself and Question Authority*. He had his first encounter with psychedelic substance in 1960 when he took psilocybin mushrooms. It was just before his 40th birthday, and coaxed by his colleague and fellow Esalen teacher, Frank Barron (1922-2002), who was an internationally recognized psychologist and UC Berkeley scholar, Leary took his first psychedelic trip. Afterwards, Leary made his now famous statement: *I learned more about psychology in the five hours after taking these mushrooms than in the preceding 15 years of studying and doing research in psychology.*

Shortly after his experience with psilocybin, Leary had his first LSD trip. From these experiences, he organized *The Harvard Psilocybin Project* that included experiments in psychology conducted by Leary and his colleague Richard Alpert. The founding board of the project included Aldous Huxley and John Spiegel, who became president of the American Psychiatric Association. The project lasted about two years and resulted in Harvard terminating both Leary and Alpert from their faculty.

The drug experience had a huge impact on those qualified to recognize what it was and who attempted to define their personal experiences. Huston Smith asserts in his book:

> *Cleansing the Doors of Perception: The Religious Significance of Entheogenic Plants and Chemicals: ... there is no such thing as 'the drug experience.' All are conditioned by what students of the subject call 'set and setting.' By 'set' they mean the personality and personal history of the person ingesting; by 'setting', the circumstances under which the ingestion occurs.*

Smith defines entheogens as psychoactive plants or chemicals that, under some circumstances with some people, have the power to facilitate mystical experiences of a very extraordinary order. Clearly the well-educated minds of psychologists ingesting chemicals would have a far more profound experience than that of over stimulated college students at a fraternity party.

Entheogen experiences, whether taking place within the context of psychological research, religious realization, or to add to the profundity of a rock concert, have been credited with causing spiritual elevation and providing profound insights. Aldous Huxley, who Smith says was his guru for 15 years, compared the experience of mescaline to the blissful state of happiness known by the saints whose Souls connect with God—*i.e.,* heavenly.

The mescaline experience is, without any question, the most extraordinary and significant experience

available to human beings this side of the Beatific Vision. To be shaken out of the ruts of ordinary perception, to be shown for a few timeless hours the outer and inner worlds, not as they appear to an animal obsessed with survival or to a human being obsessed with words and notions, but as they are apprehended, directly and unconditionally, by Mind at Large - this is an experience of inestimable value to anyone.

—Aldous Huxley

William James

Many qualified professionals attempted to illuminate and quantify the mystical experience, whether brought about through meditating or ingesting. Such people include the American psychologist, philosopher, and physician, William James who provided his version of the mystical experience in the eminent collection of his lectures published in 1902 as *Varieties of Religious Experience, A Study in Human Nature.* In the chapter on "Mysticism" James offers *"four marks which, when an experience has them, may justify us calling it mystical."*

The first of these *four marks* which characterize the mystical experience is echoed by many of the great Sages—***Ineffability***. Numerous sources commenting on the mystical experience repeatedly state that it defies expression, or as James states:

> *No adequate report of its contents can be given in words. It follows from this that its quality must be directly experienced; it cannot be imparted or transferred to others. In this peculiarity mystical states are more like states of feeling than like states of intellect. No one can make clear to another who has never had a certain feeling, in what the quality or worth of it consists.*

The second mark is **Noetic Quality.** Here James recognizes that not only is the mystical experience expressed through one's feelings, it is also linked to the intellect:

> *Although so similar to states of feeling, mystical states seem to those who experience them to be also states of knowledge. They are states of insight into depths of truth unplumbed by the discursive intellect. They are illuminations, revelations, full of significance and importance, all inarticulate though they remain; and as a rule, they carry with them a curious sense of authority for after-time.*

This description coincides with many conclusions drawn over a half century later by those researchers at Harvard who studied the effects of entheogenic plants and chemicals. Often after such experiences, subjects testified to having greater insight and clarity—new understanding about the nature of things. James recognized early on that the mystical experience not only engaged the feelings but also the mind.

James distinguished the first two marks from the remaining two as being the more significant. If the experience opens the mind to new realization and insights into the nature of reality, while leaving the mouth unable to communicate it, the state is most likely of a mystical nature. The two remaining items are *"less sharply marked, but are usually found."*

The third mark that James distinguished he called **Transiency.**

Mystical states cannot be sustained for long. Except in rare instances, half an hour, or at most an hour or two, seems to be the limit beyond which they fade into the light of common day. Often, when faded, their quality can but imperfectly be reproduced in memory; but when they recur it is recognized; and from one recurrence to another it is susceptible of continuous development in what is felt as inner richness and importance.

This notion of mystical states being difficult to sustain is observed by many spiritual teachers, particularly when the experience is brought about by natural means such as meditation. For the beginner, especially, the slightest flash of spiritual awakening causes thoughts to distract the mind into losing focus and concentration. Even the quick internal thought of "this is it" will cause "it" to vanish.

Conversely, if the mystical state is brought on by plants or chemicals, the experience is often more stable and less likely to evaporate spontaneously. In some cases, the drug-induced mystical state can become overwhelming and the person struggles to get free of it. Needless to say, this can become an extremely dangerous situation and should be avoided.

The final mark distinguishes the loss of control over one's will—***Passivity***

> *Although the oncoming of mystical states may be facilitated by preliminary voluntary operations... when the characteristic sort of consciousness once has set in, the mystic feels as if his own will were in abeyance, and indeed sometimes as if he were grasped and held by a superior power...When these latter conditions are well pronounced there may be no recollection whatever of the phenomenon... Some memory of their content always remains, and a profound sense of their importance. They modify the inner life of the subject between the times of their recurrence.*

Professor Walter T. Stace

Jumping forward to the 1960s, Professor Walter T. Stace (1886-1967) joins the conversation. Stace was English born and a professor of philosophy at Princeton University, well recognized as a leading authority on the subject of the mystical experience. He is most well-known for his two books on the topic—the academic work, *Mysticism and Philosophy*, and for more popular consumption, *The Teachings of the Mystics*. Stace would often say that a mystic is simply a person who has had the mystical experience, thus eliminating those people who advocate mysticism, study it, or have powerful dreams or hear voices. Although these people may be on the path, Stace reserved the *label* mystic for those who actually had the mystical experience. He characterized the event as being *a non-sensuous and non-intellectual union* fully transcending our normal human sensory-intellectual consciousness and bringing us into the awesome wonder of Oneness that is the core of all spiritual experience, dating back to the earliest scriptures, i.e., the Vedanta and the Torah.

> *The most important, the central characteristic in which all fully developed mystical experiences agree, and which in the last analysis is definitive of them and serves to mark them off from other kinds of experiences, is that they involve the apprehension of an ultimate nonsensuous unity in all things, a oneness or a One to which neither the senses nor the reason can penetrate. In other words, it entirely transcends our sensory-intellectual consciousness.*
> —Walter Stace, *The Teachings of Mystics*

It entirely transcends our sensory-intellectual consciousness. This is not an easy concept to grasp. How can anything register without passing through the human filters of the senses and the intellect? For most of us, this includes the entire mechanism of our perception. Our mind is not designed to register experience beyond the intellect and our five senses. Or so it would seem. According to our ancient mystical Sages, there exists another mechanism of perception beyond the apparent; one that is rooted in our intuition and is experience based, defying reason and logic. It's astonishing that the mystical experiences that date back thousands of years to ancient shamans, and the experiments of modern psychologists, run a parallel course.

The Phenomena of the Mystical Experience—
Dr. Walter N. Pahnke

Each new attempt to gain scientific conclusions about the mystical experience brings us closer to solving one of history's oldest mysteries—the spiritual realm. Such is the case with Dr. Walter N. Pahnke (1931-1971) who was awarded his MD from Harvard Medical School, his MDvi from Harvard Divinity School, and his PhD from Harvard Graduate School of Arts and Sciences. Both Harvard professors, Timothy Leary and Richard Alpert, were Pahnke's PhD thesis advisors when he conducted his experiments to determine whether entheogenic plants and chemicals facilitate the mystical religious experience. Participating in his study were professor Leary and MIT professor Huston Smith. One group was given a 30 mg dose of psilocybin, while the control group was given an active placebo of vitamin B. The results overwhelmingly confirmed the ingestion of psilocybin facilitated the mystical experience.

In 1967, Dr. Pahnke, then a physician, psychiatrist, and minister, joined the team at the Maryland Psychiatric Research Center conducting research on the impact of psychedelics on terminal cancer patients and those suffering from severe neurosis. He published a paper entitled *Drugs and Mysticism* in The International Journal of Parapsychology (Vol. VIII, No. 2, Spring 1966) where he credits the pioneering work of William James (1935) and W.T. Stace (1960) in assisting him in compiling a typology of nine categories defining *the universal phenomena of the mystical experience*. Although drug induced, these conditions are present during the mystical experience:

Category I: Unity is considered the most important characteristic of the mystical experience. As did Stace, Pahnke divides the experience of unity or Oneness into an internal and external variation. Internal unity is experienced as a loss of one's usual sense impressions and self, where one's individuality is not perceived as being separate but rather fades or "*melts away while consciousness remains... pure awareness beyond empirical content, with no external or internal distinctions.*" External unity is perceived outwardly with the physical senses. Although the observer recognizes the usual separation between himself and the external objects, on another level there is "*a sense of underlying oneness is felt behind the empirical multiplicity... Another way of expressing this same phenomenon is that the essences of objects are experienced intuitively and felt to be the same at the deepest level.*"

Category II: Transcendence of Time and Space tends to be a common phenomenon whenever one has an encounter with the spiritual. Here Pahnke describes it as;

> This category refers to loss of the usual sense of time and space. This means clock time but may also be one's personal sense of his past, present, and future. Transcendence of space means that a person loses his usual orientation as to where he is during the experience in terms of the usual three-dimensional perception of his environment. Experiences of *timelessness* and *spacelessness* may also be described as experiences of *eternity* or *infinity*.

Category III: Deeply Felt Positive Mood is often what is being sought when people take up the practice of meditation or engage in unsupervised, nonclinical drug use.

> The most universal elements (and, therefore, the ones that are most essential to the definition of this category) are joy, blessedness, and peace. The unique character of these feelings in relation to the mystical experience is the intensity that elevates them to the highest levels of human experience, and they are highly valued by the experiencers. Tears may be associated with any of these elements because of the overpowering nature of the experience. Such feelings may occur either at the peak of the experience or during the "ecstatic afterglow," when the peak has passed but while its effects and memory are still quite vivid and intense. Love may also be an element of deeply felt positive mood, but it does not have the same universality as joy, blessedness, and peace.

Category IV: Sense of Sacredness accounts for the experience some people report of having *seen or felt God*.

> This category refers to the sense of sacredness that is evoked by the mystical experience. The sacred is here broadly defined as that which a person feels to be of special value and capable of being profaned. The basic characteristic of sacredness is a non-rational, intuitive, hushed, palpitant response of awe and wonder in the presence of inspiring realities. No religious "beliefs" or traditional theological terminology need necessarily be involved, even though there may be a sense of rev-

erence or a feeling that what is experienced is holy or divine.

Category V: Objectivity and Reality is a characteristic that is difficult to describe or defend in logical terms. It is a sort of awareness of truth that is accepted without the normal path of reason; truth revealed rather than decided. It carries with it an authoritative quality that defies explanation.

This category has two interrelated elements: (1) insightful knowledge or illumination felt at an intuitive, non-rational level and gained by direct experience; and (2) the authoritative nature of the experience, or the certainty that such knowledge is truly real, in contrast to the feeling that the experience is a subjective delusion.

These two elements are connected, because the knowledge through experience of ultimate reality (in the sense of being able to "know" and "see" what is really *real*) carries its own sense of certainty. The experience of "ultimate" reality is an awareness of another dimension unlike the "ordinary" reality (the reality of usual, everyday consciousness); yet the knowledge of "ultimate" reality is quite real to the experiencer.

Such insightful knowledge does not necessarily mean an increase in facts, but rather in intuitive illumination. What becomes "known" (rather than merely intellectually assented to) is intuitively felt to be authoritative, requires no proof at a rational level, and produces an inward feeling of objective truth.

The content of this knowledge may be divided into two main types: (a) insights into being and existence in general, and (b) insights into one's personal, finite self.

Category VI: Paradoxicality echoes the teachings of many of the Sages. It also embraces the notion that opposing conditions exist simultaneously as one unit; i.e., both hot and cold are made of the same essence; you cannot know cold without knowing hot—or, without ugly there can be no beauty. The Buddha taught that the experience of complete fullness is recognized as complete emptiness. Of course, the Buddha was not referring to drug induced enlightenment.

Accurate descriptions and even rational interpretations of the mystical experience tend to be logically contradictory when strictly analyzed. For example, in the experience of internal unity there is a loss of all empirical content in an *empty* unity which is at the same time *full* and complete. This loss includes the loss of the sense of self and the dissolution of individuality; yet something of the individual entity remains to experience the unity. The "I" both exists and does not exist. Another example is the separateness from, and at the same time unity with, objects in the experience of external unity (essentially a paradoxical transcendence of space).

Category VII: Alleged Ineffability is a characteristic referred to by the great Sages and the mystics. It is not so much that the words that describe the mystical experience cannot be spoken, it is that once spoken they are not adequate to communicate the experience. It is most often taught that the path to understanding the spiritual realm is through personal experience. Although words can be useful to bring a person to the experience, only through the actual experience will a person feel the fulfillment of true knowledge. As Pahnke wrote;

> In spite of attempts to relate or write about the mystical experience, mystics insist either that words fail to describe it adequately or that the experience is beyond words. Perhaps the reason is an embarrassment with language because of the paradoxical nature of the essential phenomena.

Category VIII: Transiency is a quality characteristic of the mystical experience that is brought on by entheogenic plants or chemicals. For the most part, when the effects of the substance ingested wears off, simultaneously much of the experience wears off with it.

> Transiency refers to duration, and means the temporary nature of the mystical experience in contrast to the relative permanence of the level of usual experience. There is a transient appearance of the special and unusual levels or dimensions of consciousness as defined by our typology, their eventual disappearance, and a return to the more usual. The characteristic of transiency indicates that the mystical state of consciousness is not sustained indefinitely.

Category IX: Persisting Positive Changes in Attitude and Behavior refers to the lasting imprint of the mystical experience. Regardless of whether the experience was brought about through spiritual practice or ingested substance, if insights came as a result of expanded consciousness there will be lasting benefits. Some Sages refer to the lasting effects of one's encounter with the mystical as a *residue* left behind.

Because our typology is of a healthful, life-enhancing mysticism, this category describes the positive, lasting effects of the experience and the resulting changes in attitude. These changes are divided into four groups: (1) toward self, (2) toward others, (3) toward life, and (4) toward the mystical experience itself.

(1) **Increased integration of personality** is the basic inward change in the personal self. Undesirable traits may be faced in such a way that they may be dealt with and finally reduced or eliminated. As a result of personal integration, one's sense of inner authority may be strengthened, and the vigor and dynamic quality of a person's life may be increased. Creativity and greater efficiency of achievement may be released. An inner optimistic tone may result, with a consequent increase in feelings of happiness, joy, and peace.

(2) **Changes in attitude and behavior toward others** include more sensitivity, more tolerance, more real love, and more authenticity as a person by virtue of being more open and more one's true self with others.

(3) **Changes toward life in a positive direction** include philosophy of life, sense of values, sense of meaning and purpose, vocational commitment, need for service to others, and new appreciation

of life and the whole of creation. Life may seem richer. The sense of reverence may be increased, and more time may be spent in devotional life and meditation.

(4) **Positive change in attitude toward the mystical experience** itself means that it is regarded as valuable and that what has been learned is thought to be useful. The experience is remembered as a high point, and an attempt is made to recapture it or, if possible, to gain new experiences as a source of growth and strength. The mystical experiences of others are more readily appreciated and understood.

Satori; The Mystical Experience—Zen Master D.T. Suzuki

It is fascinating to recognize that the above characteristics compiled by modern science regarding the mystical experience brought about by the ingestion of entheogenic plants and chemicals, and those identified by Zen Master D.T. Suzuki (1870-1966) regarding *satori*, mystical experience of sudden enlightenment, are so closely related. As we will see, Suzuki adds his Zen Buddhist definition to what psychologists James, Stace, and Pahnke have discovered through their research.

Suzuki begins by saying that *Satori* is an "intuitive grasp of reality beyond forms" which alters one's complete worldview and that most often arises from contemplation or through imagery as in meditation. Satori is akin to the term enlightenment used by the followers of Buddha in India. He is aligned with the teaching of Stace when he says:

Satori may be defined as an intuitive looking into the nature of things in contradistinction to the analytical or logical understanding of it. Practically, it means the unfolding of a new world hitherto unperceived in the confusion of a dualistically-trained mind.

Or we may say that with Satori our entire surroundings are viewed from quite an unexpected angle of perception.

Whatever this is, the world for those who have gained a Satori is no more the old world as it used to be... it is never the same one again... all its opposites and contradictions are united and harmonized into a consistent organic whole...

Satori can thus be had only through our once personally experiencing it. For what Zen proposes to do is the revolution, and the revaluation as well, of oneself as a spiritual unity... the opening of Satori is the re-making of life itself.

—Suzuki, *Selected Works of D.T. Suzuki*

In his book, *Zen Buddhism: Selected Writings of D.T, Suzuki*, Suzuki refers to characteristics present in Satori, the spiritual awakening experience. According to Suzuki, the entire aim of Zen is the achievement of satori. Here Suzuki provides a list of:

8 Characteristics to Illuminate the Mystical Experience of Satori:

1 **Irrationality:** Satori is not reached by reason or rational thought; it is not a conclusion found through the intellect. *"Those who have experienced it are*

always at a loss to explain it coherently or logically," says Suzuki.

2 **Intuitive Insight:** There is noetic quality in the mystical experience; however, it is more intuitive than rational. Another name for satori is Kensho which means *to see essence or nature.* As Suzuki puts it, *"Without this noetic quality Satori will lose all its pungency, for it is really the reason of Satori itself."*

3 **Authoritativeness:** There is knowledge that is realized by Satori which defies any sort of logical debate. The mind may attempt to interpret Satori or even explain it, but *"Satori is thus a form of perception, an inner perception, which takes place in the most interior part of consciousness,"* says Suzuki.

4 **Affirmation:** Satori is life affirming and cannot be negative. It holds *"an affirmative attitude towards all things that exist; it accepts them as they come along regardless of their moral values."*

5 **Sense of the Beyond:** This quality is perhaps the most referred to by those who experience even the slightest depth in their meditation or by those who experience the effects of entheogenic plants or chemicals. This may be akin to the *"oceanic feeling"* that Romain Rolland refers to in his letter to Freud describing the religious experience.

In Satori there is always what we may call a sense of the Beyond; the experience indeed is my own but I feel it to be rooted elsewhere. The individual shell in which my personality is so solidly encased explodes at the moment of satori. Not, necessarily, that I get unified with a being greater than myself or absorbed in it, but that my individuality, which I found rigidly held together and definitely kept separate from other individual existences, becomes loosened somehow from its tightening grip and melts away into something indescribable, something which is of quite a different order from what I am accustomed to. The feeling that follows is that of complete release or a complete rest—the feeling that one has arrived finally at the destination.

6 **Impersonal Tone**: This sixth characteristic of Satori that Suzuki describes is somewhat alien to Western culture and religion. This is very Zen in nature and similar to the cultures of India, China, and Japan. Satori is an experience that defies any human reference; it defies individuation. Although it is happening to you, it is not about you; or at least not the familiar *you,* the individual you that you recognize. Even the setting and conditions which appear to trigger Satori are often of a mundane nature.

Not only Satori itself is such a prosaic and non-glorious event, but the occasion that inspires it also seems to be unromantic and altogether lacking in super-sensuality. Satori is experienced in connection with any ordinary occurrence in one's daily life. It does not appear to be an extraordinary phenomenon... Someone takes hold of you... or brings you a cup of tea, or makes some most commonplace remark, or recites some passage from a sutra or from a book of poetry, and when your mind is ripe for its outburst, you come at once to Satori.

7 *Feeling of Exaltation:* How can one experience such feelings of joy and grandeur without it being personal? Many describe this aspect of spiritual awakening as tantamount to the discovery of buried treasure; you have just found what you have always desired. However, as Suzuki explains, Satori is not just the finding of something; it is also associated with losing something.

That this feeling inevitably accompanies Satori is due to the fact that it is the breaking-up of the restriction imposed on one as an individual being, and this breaking-up is not a mere negative incident but quite a positive one fraught with signification because it means an infinite expansion of the individual... To be released of this [general feeling of restriction and dependence], therefore, must make one feel above all things intensely exalted.

8 *Momentariness*: In Suzuki's words, *"Satori comes upon one abruptly and is a momentary experience. In fact, if it is not abrupt and momentary, it is not Satori."* Where this becomes somewhat complicated is that satori is a mystical experience; and, like all mystical experiences, it is bridged between physical reality and the spiritual realm. Thus, we are talking about a moment that is not in time; or more precisely, Satori is in time without duration—in the words of Suzuki, *"when time emerges into eternity."*

Although we have introduced this notion of a two-dimensional reality, both physical and spiritual, the full exploration of this concept is reserved for part two of this book. However, we cannot separate the mystical discussions of William James, W.T. Stace, W.N. Pahnke, and D.T. Suzuki from the two-tier reality that characterizes them. The mystical experience is, after all, the gateway into the spiritual domain.

Huxley's Perennial Philosophy impacts Alexander Everett

Aldous Huxley played an integral role in the research of Richard Alpert and Timothy Leary, as well as the genesis of Esalen by Dick Price and Michael Murphy. They were not the only visionaries who were moved by Aldous Huxley's words and who germinated the seeds of the Human Potential Movement. Another Englishman, Alexander Everett (1921-2005), was inspired by Huxley as well, especially after reading *The Perennial Philosophy*. Perennial philosophy is a term originally coined in its Latin form *philosophia perennis* by Agostino Steuco (1497-1548), refers to a perspective of religious philosophy which views all of the world's great religions as having the same universal truth at the foundation of all religious knowledge—the unity of religion.

It is a term that was used by the Transcendentalists of the 19th century, such as Emerson, the Hindu mystics Sri Ramakrishna and Swami Vivekananda, and later popularized by the founders of the Theosophical Society, H.P. Blavatsky and Annie Besant. The unifying essence varies in description from that of the Soul and Divine love to the term *religious experience* coined by William James. Regardless of the terminology, it is the direct experience that provides true understanding of the spiritual—and it is the recognition and cultivation of this experience that is the purpose of this book.

In 1945, Huxley published his classic book, The *Peren-*

nial Philosophy, borrowing the term from Gottfried Wilhelm Leibniz (1646-1716) which illuminated and expanded on the term's previous impact. The book's dust jacket of the British first edition states:

> *The Perennial Philosophy is an attempt to present this Highest Common Factor of all theologies by assembling passages from the writings of those saints and prophets who have approached spiritual knowledge of the Divine.*

In the opening paragraph of Huxley's introduction, he identifies this notion of *perennial philosophy* that permeates the words of the Sages:

> *Philosophia Perennis—the phrase was coined by Leibniz; but the thing—the metaphysic that recognizes a divine Reality substantial to the world of things and lives and minds; the psychology that finds in the soul something similar to, or even identical with divine Reality; the ethic that places man's final end in the knowledge of the immanent and transcendent Ground of all being—the thing is immemorial and universal. Rudiments of the Perennial Philosophy may be found among the traditional lore of primitive peoples in every region of the world, and in its fully developed forms it has a place in every one of the higher religions. A version of this Highest Common Factor in all preceding and subsequent theologies was first committed to writing more than twenty-five centuries ago, and since that time the inexhaustible theme has*

been treated again and again, from the standpoint of every religious tradition...

Knowledge is a function of being. When there is a change in the being of the knower, there is a corresponding change in the nature and amount of knowing.

—Huxley, *The Perennial Philosophy*

By the same token, when there is a change in the nature and amount of what a person knows—an expansion and elevation of their knowledge—there is a change in their being. Here again is a message that has played down through the ages; we are the sum total of our mind's awareness, understanding, and perception. But where does this leave the average person? The vast majority of people do not experience a quantum leap into greater knowledge and enhanced awareness while left on their own. It does happen; but it is not the norm. Often people, who have endured and survived extreme situations, report that the whole experience made them stronger and wiser. But who would be willing to put their life on the line and bear extreme torment and suffering in order to gain greater insight? To this utterly human question, Huxley would reply:

If one is not oneself a sage or saint, the best thing one can do, in the field of metaphysics, is to study the words of those who were, and who, because they had modified their merely human mode of being, were capable of more than merely human kind and amount of knowledge.

He goes on to say that it is the responsibility of every human being to discover for ourselves the truth of who we truly are at our most fundamental core—to know the spiritual ground of things within us and outside of us.

These are the words that burned their way into the mind of Alexander Everett and sent him on a spiritual quest visiting Greece, India, and Egypt. He was involved with Christian Science and later studied Theosophy with Rudolf Steiner (1861-1925), who founded a spiritual movement called *anthroposophy* in the beginning of the twentieth century. It was Steiner's intention to expand the boundaries of natural science into the phenomena of the human Soul and spiritual experience. In this way, Steiner hoped to free the individual's spiritual quest from the precarious dependency of external authority.

Large Group Awareness Training (LGAT)

In 1962, Everett moved to the United States where he worked for the Unity Church, founded in Kansas City, Missouri in 1889 by Charles and Myrtle Fillmore, and continues today under the direction of their children and grandchildren. In 1963, he moved to Texas where he helped establish a preparatory school and worked as an instructor. It was during this time in Texas that Everett met another key character, José Silva (1914-1999). Silva, parapsychologist and author, developed the self-help program called The Silva Method, aka Silva Mind Control, which teaches its participants specialized techniques intended to reprogram subconscious negative thought patterns in order to tap into their hidden potential and actualize their goals. Today their seminars are offered in over 130 countries worldwide.

Everett studied these techniques taught by Silva in mind control, meditation, and self-hypnosis to develop his own course called Mind Dynamics in 1968. Mind Dynamics became the beginnings of another channel of the Human Potential Movement—self-awareness seminars, or as psychologists came to call them, Large Group Awareness Training (LGAT).

Although Everett acquired the name "Father of the Human Potential Movement" a second key character emerged with another similar program about the same time—William Penn Patrick. Around 1967, Patrick started an executive training for *self-improvement* and *personal development* call Leadership Dynamics, or LDI, Leadership Dynamics Institute. Originally LDI was a training program for the distributors and management staff of the Holiday Magic cosmetics company, a multi-level marketing organization that Patrick founded in 1964. In 1970, Patrick bought the Mind Dynamics course which stated it provided "a means of achieving personal success through the conscious use of the subconscious mind."

Whereas Mind Dynamics used non-confrontational techniques and teachings learned during Everett's time with Silva, The Theosophy Society, Unity, and the work of Edgar Cayce, LDI employed hard hitting confrontational group encounter techniques. What resulted was a blend of both styles.

But there was a third component added to the two delivery styles—the business plan. The Holiday Magic empire was based on a multi-level marketing structure that was later characterized by the Office of the State Attorney General in Maine as a *pyramid scheme*. Although Mind Dynamics was a separate company, some of the marketing mechanisms of Holiday Magic seem to have been absorbed into propagating the seminar business. This confrontational style of "enrolling" people into the training both supported and haunted the growth of the Large Group Awareness Training arm of the

Human Potential Movement. The spiritual notion of one who gains *awakening* has a responsibility to serve others in their pursuit of *awakening*, became somewhat corrupted when applied to the business practice of badgering customers to do the company's prospecting. For many, this practice of pressuring those who already *graduated* from the course, into filling the next training was not a spiritual process. Critics called this scheme both self-serving and exploitive.

By 1974, both Holiday Magic and Mind Dynamic were defunct companies in the United States. However, the Large Group Awareness Trainings were about to make history. In Dr. Neal Vahle's 2002 book, *The Unity Movement: Its Evolution and Spiritual Teachings*, nine Mind Dynamic instructors went on to start their own LGAT companies. The largest of these companies was founded by Werner Erhard, EST, in 1971. EST trainings continued through 1985 when the name was changed to The Forum. Six years later, in 1991 The Forum was sold to Werner's brother Harry Rosenberg and the employees when it became known as Landmark.

Another distributor of Holiday Magic and the Mind Dynamics instructor who trained Erhard, Charlene Afremow, worked with three other Mind Dynamics instructors, Bob White, Randy Revell, and founder John Hanley, to launch Lifespring in 1974. Later, White left Lifespring to travel to Japan and start Life Dynamics. Stewart Emery was the first CEO of EST and in 1975, along with another EST employee, Carol Augustus, co-founded Actualizations, a term borrowed from Abraham Maslow's hierarchy of needs. In 1973, another Mind Dynamics instructor, Thomas Willhite, along with his wife Jane, co-founded PSI World Seminars. PSI is considered to be the oldest continuously-operating LGAT company in the U.S. with over a half million graduates.

Although having many of its roots in England, this distinctly American version of accelerated, albeit *drive-thru enlightenment* had its fair share of critics, both on the intellectual side, Esalen, and on its more commercial side, the LGAT. To list those denigrations and those who have written endless articles and even a number of books would be counterproductive to our discussion. For the purpose of this book, it is relevant to observe the emergence of yet another example of *unchurched spirituality* in a new form with new faces and new perceptions.

And, like the work of Carlos Castaneda, those hundreds of thousands of people who benefited from their experience at Esalen or the millions who achieved positive results from the trainings of EST, Actualizations, Lifespring, PSI, and so many others, the proof of the pudding is in the eating. The commendable intent of greasing the grand wheel of attaining human potential may have fallen a bit short on the level of humanity at large, but clearly there are numerous people who attest to their own individual potential having moved and their personal consciousness having been raised by their experience.

One Man's Story...
An example of such a person was a middle-aged man who attended the EST training in its early days; we'll call him Frank (not his real name). Frank was a survivor of the Nazi death camps during World War II. Of all his family, he was a lone survivor. Although Frank now lived in Northern California's wine country, the bigger part of him had never left Auschwitz, as he suffered from severe survivor's guilt.

Like so many of the participants in the training, Frank had a *story*. And like many of his fellow participants, it was his story that justified his unhappy, limiting existence. Of course, Frank's story was far from ordinary. When Frank finally chose to share his story, there was not a dry eye amongst the 250+ people who listened. With respect for Frank, I will not detail what he said that evening, but I will say that what Frank endured as a young boy is a statement of how inhumane the human animal can become without boundaries to hold its insane cruelty in check. The mildest way to express it is to say that Frank witnessed the brutal murdering of every one of his loved ones. The words that he spoke that evening had not been spoken aloud by him before and certainly not in the presence of so many strangers.

Frank recalls the trainer asking two assistants to stand on either side of him to provide physical support during his bouts of relentless wailing and weeping. When he had finished telling his story in graphic detail, he looked at the trainer and asked "Why? Why was I spared?" To which the trainer replied, "Your right, you should have died." Not a person in the room could believe their ears. There was a collective groan. After cautioning the room to keep still, he continued. "The bigger part of you did die in the camp. Now you must endure living as a corpse. It's time to let go Frank. The war is over... we won. You are not in Germany and this room is not filled with Nazis. You're in America and every Soul in this room loves you. It's time for you to make the best of the one life in your family that was spared... live the life that would make them all proud." Frank looked at his group and said the words that so many others said before him... "You know, *I get it.*" It was at this point that the trainer himself could no longer hold back his tears.

When Frank came back for his follow-up session, he was wearing jeans, a flannel shirt, and cowboy boots. He was now an American and his new friends could not stop hugging him. To hear Frank tell the story, he was born again. It would be hard, in front of Frank, to criticize the process that brought him to his realization. Even though the system is imperfect, and the business may seem exploitive, it had its moments of grandeur—Frank's was one of those moments.

Certainly, it was neither the company nor the trainer that produced the experience that impacted Frank so deeply. They simply facilitated the experience by setting up the conditions that led to it. They developed the mechanism and injected the intention for what followed. They utilized the group dynamic structure which allowed people to be themselves—albeit a truer sense of themselves than they tend to be under normal circumstances.

At the pinnacle of Frank's experience, his identity was revealed to the group. He was no longer a crotchety old Jewish man with a scowl frozen on his face. In place of this unfriendly curmudgeon emerged a character that was larger than life; a character worthy of being found in a Hemmingway novel. Here was a man who faced one of the most ferocious dragons in human history, and he emerged a survivor. He witnessed tragedy that most of us would shudder to encounter even within the context of fiction. But Frank is true and so is his story. He is the lone survivor of a family who had fallen victim to insanity reigning terror.

Frank did not escape unscathed. He was deeply damaged beyond the powers of medicine or even traditional therapy. He carried his pain and his scars for over a quarter century prior to the night in question. But on that evening, he trusted people enough to let it out; not just the words, but the tears, the cries, and the shrieks of injustice that he carried inside. And when he was done, he had emerged an even greater victor.

However, that is only half of what took place during his 45 minutes of catharsis. That's what he let go in order to allow an opening for something new. After endless hours of drilling into the essence of each participant, the training process had opened the cavern of compassion that all people have inside. Two hundred and fifty people fell in love with Frank that night—and not in a small way. In his raw and vulnerable state, Frank could not deflect nor deny the impact of such compassion all focused on him. It was this collective outpouring that healed one of the Holocausts' survivors that night in a large hotel ballroom in a small northern California town. Those who were there to watch Frank *get it*, understood something extraordinary about the human potential.

Seminar leaders and training facilitators would converse behind the scenes about the nature of their work. Often, they would say that after working in this business for years and seeing thousands of people come through their programs, everyone has their story. Some stories are more creatively crafted, while some are more accurate in their delivery, but they share a common thread. Each story is a justification for why the teller is a victim. It is as if they are saying, "I cannot reach my potential of a happy, fulfilled human being, because this or that happened to me." It is this justification that keeps a person tethered to a lesser life.

As trainers, we are there to facilitate an experience that will allow the participant to recognize the folly of holding onto and protecting their role as victim in their own story. And, like Frank, once they are liberated from their self-imposed burden, their life has the potential to become easier and more joyful. The Buddha taught that our liberation was through letting go of our attachments—the attachment to our role as victim and its accompanying suffering often seems stronger than our attachment to sense-pleasure and ego-gratification. What a strange and wondrous moment it is when a person finally recognizes how committed their attachment is to their own suffering.

Not all LGAT programs used the confrontational style to get the job done. When Stewart Emery and Carol Augustus left EST and started their own company in 1975, Actualizations, it was partially with the intent to innovate a new transformation mechanism that brought the participant to a heightened awareness within a loving environment. According to their graduates, they were able to achieve the necessary results without the use of encounter group tactics.

Brian Klemmer (1950-2011), a West Point graduate, mentored by the co-founder of PSI World Seminars, Tom Willhite, founded his own company with his wife Roma, Klemmer and Associates. Klemmer, a devout Christian, was able to bring the element of religion into the traditionally secular setting of the LGAT. Although the Klemmer seminars contain many of the same principles and techniques of their predecessors, Brian recognized the importance of focusing in on the role of intention, even over mechanism, when generating results. His techniques proved to be a powerful modification for both spiritual and professional enhancement.

Klemmer coined the term *compassionate samurai* in his book of the same name:

> As long as you allow your past to haunt you, you'll never be free to pursue your future. You won't even be able to focus on your present.
> — Brian Klemmer, *The Compassionate Samurai: Being Extraordinary in an Ordinary World*

It is difficult to estimate the number of people who have been through the vast array of programs offered by the various groups. Some estimates range well into the millions. It is certainly not our purpose to endorse or denigrate these programs or those who founded them. For the purpose of our discussion, it is relevant to observe the Human Potential Movement as being a part of larger modern worldview and its role in *unchurched spirituality*. This continuous theme of deeper reservoirs of human spirituality that are not tethered to any form of organized religion, yet certainly contained within the teachings and sanctity of all religions, is where our focus takes us.

Unlikely Bedfellows: East meets West

For many, the quest for spiritual awakening took an unlikely twist during our formative years in the 1960s. Although we didn't see it coming, an entire youth culture was swallowed up by the sounds and ideas of Eastern spirituality as it merged with that of the 1960s *pop culture*. How did ancient Hindu Traditions, meditation, and the *Woodstock Generation* find common ground? In a word—Beatles.

A seemingly random event took place in the mid-1960s that brought the East and West into a new and inseparable union. And if the implausible union of such diverse components were not strange enough, the circumstances which lead to this merger have all the makings of a Hollywood (or Bollywood) Fiasco.

In the summer of 1966, the Beatles were completing a long tour with two concerts in Manila. Somehow there was a misunderstanding about a palace meeting with the Philippines' First Lady, Imelda Marcos, and her three children.

For some unknown reason, this meeting was not put onto the band's schedule. The Beatles' absence was viewed by the Manila press and the public as an insult to the First Family. The hostile feelings went from TV newscasters to an angry mob at the airport where many in the Beatles group were physically attacked including Ringo Starr who was punched to the ground and a roadie who sustained broken ribs.

When their flight bound for London made a stop in New Delhi, the stewardess insisted that the four Beatles deplane as the airline had sold their seats to London. It was here that the Beatles experienced India for the first time—a meeting that was destined to link the mysticism of the East to an entire generation of Western youth.

George Harrison was perhaps the most spiritually inclined of the group. His fascination with India continued as he stud-

ied sitar with Ravi Shankar and later met Maharishi Mahesh Yogi who instilled in him the desire for meditation—along with millions of the Beatles' fans. Harrison became immersed in the teachings of Hinduism, Eastern philosophy, and Indian music. Although still in his 20's, he recognized that "Everything else can wait, but the search for God cannot..."

From the Hindu point of view each soul is divine. All religions are branches of one big tree. It doesn't matter what you call Him (God) just as long as you call.
— George Harrison

From their first trip to India, the tone and lyrics of the Beatles' music changed. There was now an underlying theme of the Spiritual. In 1970, George Harrison wrote and sang the song "I Me Mine." Its title and content reflect the dominance of the ego over human life. It was taken from ancient Hindu scripture:

A person who has given up all desires for sense gratification, who lives free from desires, who has given up all sense of proprietorship and is devoid of false ego — he alone can attain real peace.
—Bhagavad-Gita 2:71

And so it was stated in the lyrics of Harrison's groundbreaking song:

All through the day
I me mine, I me mine, I me mine
All through the night
I me mine, I me mine, I me mine

Now they're frightened of leaving it
Everyone's weaving it
Coming on strong all the time
All through the day I me mine

All I can hear
I me mine, I me mine, I me mine
Even those tears
I me mine, I me mine, I me mine

No one's frightened of playing it
Everyone's saying it
Flowing more freely than wine
All through the day I me mine

When Harrison was asked about the lyrics in a TV documentary that aired in November of 1995, he linked the set of pronouns in the song's title to the Hindu text referring to the ego.

I Me Mine is the ego problem. There are two 'I's: the little 'i'... and the big "I" ... There is nothing that isn't part of the complete whole. When the little 'i' merges into the big 'I' then you are really smiling!
— George Harrison

For millions, a new and unlikely bond had been formed between Eastern Spirituality and Western rock 'n' roll. What was the catalyst that set this match in motion? —Interest. Certainly, from the Hindu perspective, the Beatles represented an enormous PR campaign. Clearly, nobody on staff at the ashram could generate so much interest in uncharted waters as the Beatles. And from the perspective of the Beatles, this opening to the Spiritual was able to fill a void that their extreme material success had generated.

Even John Lennon, often recognized as the most rebellious and anti-establishment of the group, added to the discussion of religion and spirituality:

> *I believe in God, but not as one thing, not as an old man in the sky. I believe that what people call God is something in all of us. I believe that what Jesus and Mohammed and Buddha and all the rest said was right. It's just that the translations have gone wrong.*
> —John Lennon

Although spirituality permeated the music industry and could be detected in many of the lyrics of the times, the genre of music did not lend itself to the educational format of Esalen and the LGAT. Like its less artistic second cousin, drugs, music was able to produce a version of the spiritual experience but without offering any explanation of how and why. People who attended the large-scale rock concerts and music festivals of the 60s and 70s, of which Woodstock was the most noted, often commented on the sense of *oneness* and *universal love* that they experienced. Whether these spiritual overtones were attributed to the music, the camaraderie, or the preponderance of intoxicants, it became a defining feature of these events and a new *pane* in our worldview.

Through the turbulence of the times, and the controversy of the various venues, the spiritual message was finding its way from the core to the surface of humanity. Whether it was being written and published, lectured in seminars, preached in the hallowed sermons of religion throughout its temples, ashrams, churches, synagogues, and mosques; or amplified through Vox amps and accompanied by Fender electric guitars, the sound and the experience of spirituality was bubbling to the surface.

Television Talk Show Venue

It was also around this same time that another *branch* of the spiritual tree was sprouting out. Even though it would be decades before this innovation would define itself in spiritual terms, the seeds were planted early in the 1950s for a new media channel. The new medium was television which would provide the pipeline into many homes; and the genre was the *talk show*.

The first talk show was a broadcast in 1951 hosted by radio personality Joe Franklin. A few years later, in 1954, the longest running talk show got its start—The Tonight Show, hosted by another radio personality, Steve Allen. Allen established the format of late-night talk shows with an opening monologue, celebrity guests, along with new musical and comedy acts. He was later succeeded as host by Jack Paar, and later followed by The Tonight Shows longest host, Johnny Carson who held the position for thirty years (1962-1992).

Another pioneer in the talk show genre was celebrated journalist and war correspondent Edward R. Murrow who first hosted *Now You See It*, and later, *Person to Person*, and *Small World*, during the 1950s. Murrow is credited with beginning a new slant towards the political talk show and educational television.

By the end of the 1960s, a subgenre of the talk show was emerging; the *tabloid talk show*. These shows were less about education, politics, and celebrity interviews, and more about controversy and confrontation. Hosts such as Joe Pyne and Les Crane would book guests who were clearly on opposite sides of a controversial and provocative topic and let the fireworks fly; often involving the audience. In 1967, Phil Donahue created and hosted the Phil Donahue Show, a show that lasted nearly 30 years on national television. Although Donahue was known for pitting opposing points of view against each other and having the audience serve as an integral part of the formula, his shock journalism style at least suggested the objective of some resolution. He was also recognized for adding audience participation into the talk show formula; paving the way for future shows such as Maury Povich and Jerry Springer, both airing in 1991.

So, what was it about such a chaotic, and at times sordid TV genre that impacted the fading Human Potential Movement? How did an industry that lives off its ratings and must often appeal to a low spot in human nature, gain a spiritual perspective? Within such darkened and murky waters, where was the proverbial lotus that reflected a rebirth of spiritual awakening? In a word—Oprah.

Although it was not apparent in the beginning, Oprah Winfrey would be the connective tissue to link Maslow and Huxley, Esalen and EST, to a modern new audience of spiritual seekers by providing the platform for contemporary spiritual teachers. No other talk show host has had the courage or the power to take such a bold step towards raising human consciousness on the grand scale—to put the glitz and tinsel aside in the name of that which is authentic and elevating—to risk the superficial in the name of what is profound. Oprah was willing to dismiss people's need for gossip and mockery in the name of education and elevation. To use this powerful medium, television, for purposes of education and potentially, for some, at the cost of entertainment, is the mark of a *warrior who follows her heart.*

Today, if you look to one source as your well of spiritual teachings that is both readily accessible and wholly abundant, that source is likely to be Oprah's Super Soul Sunday. While Esalen may reach a few hundred attendees, and Landmark worldwide may see a few thousand participants on any given Sunday, Oprah will draw from over 22 million loyal viewers to be enriched by some of the world's most adept teachers. These are the kind of numbers that don't just transform the individual; they impact the whole of humanity and shift our worldview.

Eckhart Tolle (born 1948), considered to be one the most spiritually influential teachers in the world by Watkins Review, published his first book, *The Power of Now*, in 1997; there were only 3000 copies in the first edition. In early 2000, Oprah recommended his book and by August of that same year *The Power of Now* had reached the New York Times Best Seller list. In 2002 it was number one on the list. Of course, Oprah's recommendation wouldn't have brought such success if the work itself were not so worthy. Tolle is worthy of his recognition. His contemporary style and his all-inclusive spiritual approach reflect the teachings of the great Sages, while his impact is the result of personal experience. His overarching spiritual message in his first book is one that is echoed from the ancients while being relevant to a modern audience—the power of now.

> *Realize deeply that the present moment is all you have. Make the NOW the primary focus of your life... Time isn't precious at all, because it is an illusion. What you perceive as precious is not time but the one point that is out of time: the Now. That is precious indeed. The more you are focused on time—past and future—the more you miss the Now, the most precious thing there is.*
>
> —Eckhart Tolle, *The Power of Now*

Tolle's work is a master synthesis of Buddhism, Christianity, Hinduism, Taoism, Hasidism, Sufism, Kabbalah, and so much more. Through his text he makes another important overarching point—ultimately all religion is amplifying the same truth.

Like don Juan Matus in the Carlos Castaneda series, Tolle makes it clear that the mind is not our true identity; rather it obscures our true identity. As the Buddha taught, enlightenment is the end of suffering, and our point of entry begins with gaining control over our mind—stopping the internal dialogue. The unenlightened voice of the mind is made up of the words of the ego. Egoistic words that reflect the incessant noise of our desires always seeking sensual pleasures. Tolle echoes the Buddha again when he suggests the process for gaining control over compulsive thinking of the mind begins with *mindfulness* or observation—watching the mind in action and seeing its motivations. Tolle points out that just the recognition that you and your mind are two distinct entities puts you well ahead of the game. You cannot gain control over your mind if you are not cognizant of this distinction. He recommends that you take your focus away from your racing thoughts and place it on your body; i.e., think of the energy flowing through your hands, your arms, your feet, legs, etc. In this way you have used the "inner body" as an "anchor for the state of presence" to ground your thoughts. When you are really in the body, the mind will have slowed its thought process. It is also important to recognize that thoughts arise in the mind but they are not real; they are reflections of things that took place or may take place, but not happening in present time.

Tolle focuses in on a particular group of thoughts that can be devastating; those thoughts cause us to feel guilt. This is usually due to something we did or failed to do. He points out that nobody can perform beyond the level of their own consciousness. At the time, you acted in accordance with your state of consciousness, and the fact that you see wrong in that action suggests that you are at a higher level of consciousness now. For this you should feel grateful. This new insight into your past blunder takes back the control over your emotions and relieves your sense of guilt. If we do not give our thoughts control over our emotions they must evaporate. This alone is the beginning of control. Eventually we will recognize that the observer is our true identity; not the storm of thoughts generated by a frenzied undisciplined mind.

Another spiritual author whose teachings have been amplified by Oprah is Gary Zukav (born 1942). Zukav, author of four bestselling books, has appeared on Oprah's shows over 30 times since 1998. Like other contemporary spiritual teachers, he is able to bring new attention and understanding to the ancient traditions. Zukav is particularly focused on the notion of dividing the human psyche into that which is impermanent and worldly, the personality, or as others have called it the ego; and the Soul, which is eternal. He recognizes that which is spiritual as one's source of *authentic power*.

> *When you choose the energy of your soul—when you choose to create with intentions of love, forgiveness, humbleness and clarity—you gain power... It is the health of the soul that is the true purpose of the human experience.*
>
> —Gary Zukav, *The Seat of the Soul*

This is the message that has resounded through the ages; the human entity is a composite of opposites; corporeal and spiritual, ego and Soul, falsehood and truth, temporal and eternal; darkness and light. And, as Zukav masterfully points out, true power, not mere force and manipulation, is achieved when one is able to distinguish the choice before us, and allow the Soul to be our guiding light.

Almost one year to the day before her death, the legendary Dr. Maya Angelou (1928-2014) made her final appearance on Oprah's Super Soul Sunday. Her public life spanned over a half century and her work will live on forever. Dr. Angelou held over 50 honorary degrees, wrote seven autobiographies, three books of essays, and several books of poetry. Her story is like an entire shelf of American history. Like her dear friend Oprah, she rose high above adversity to set new standards in the human potential. Many of the world's great leaders have learned a lesson or two from Maya Angelou; and many of those who struggle to survive were comforted knowing that she was ever vigilant of their plight. It is no coincidence that the word *angel* is found in her name.

> *I have great respect for the past. If you don't know where you've come from, you don't know where you're going. I have respect for the past, but I'm a person of the moment. I'm here, and I do my best to be com-pletely centered at the place I'm at, then I go forward to the next place.*
>
> —Dr. Maya Angelou

Along with Dr. Angelou, another peace and human rights activist and colleague of Dr. Martin Luther King is the renowned Zen master and contemporary spiritual teacher, Thích Nhất Hanh (born 1926). Thầy, as he is called, felt his spiritual *calling* at age seven and at the age of sixteen he entered the monastery where he would be ordained a Buddhist monk in 1949. In 1960, he traveled to the United States to study at Princeton University and later began lecturing on Buddhism at Columbia University. Today, in his 90s, Thầy has been in exile from his homeland for nearly four decades for opposing the Vietnam War. He authored over 100 books, and is considered one of the most influential spiritual teachers of our time.

In May of 2012, Thầy was interviewed by Oprah on Super Soul Sunday. She began her interview by commenting on the sense of peace that seemed to radiate from the exiled monk. To this he replied that this is what he practices; living entirely in the moment in a state of complete peace. He then spoke of a 45-minute conversation that he had with Dr. Martin Luther King in June of 1966, prior to King's press conference. He explained to Dr. King why Buddhist monks were burning themselves alive in protest to the war, and that it was not an act of suicide brought on by despair. He said that their self-imposed death was an act of love and compassion comparable to the death of Jesus. It is the role of the *Bodhisattva*, enlightened beings, to work towards peace and the betterment of humanity. He noted that Dr. King also made the ultimate sacrifice in the name of peace and gaining human rights.

Another important topic in this brief interview was that of *deep or compassionate listening*. Thầy defined this particular form of listening as one that allows the speaker to *empty their heart and Soul* in order to relieve their suffering. He went on to say that even if you recognize the source of the suffering to be a misconception that is confusing their thinking, it is not the time to make corrections and give advice. It is the compassionate listening that provides their therapy at this particular time—not guidance and instructions.

Oprah, recognizing the value and application this lesson could provide her viewing audience, encouraged Thầy to say more. He said that a person needs to let out their fear, anger, and despair before they are able to take in advice, as these are the emotions that bear wrong perceptions. These wrong perceptions about ourselves and others are the foundation of all violence and war. Human conflicts are served by compassionate listening to determine the cause of another's suffering. He went on to say that people use anger to motivate actions, but when you are angry you are not lucid which leads to mistakes. It is always better to use compassion rather than anger as the motivation for action. Our suffering is there for us to learn—*In the ash of suffering, a phoenix can be born.*

It is here that the monk referred to an overarching theme in Buddhism—mindfulness. We can only recognize this mechanism through the attribute of mindfulness. Through vigilant mindfulness we are able to respond appropriately to life's events rather than through mindless reactions.

When Oprah asked Thầy about his book, *Living Buddha, Living Christ*, he boldly stated that "Jesus Christ is the Buddha of the West." To a Buddhist monk there could be no greater compliment. He went on to say that both enlightened teachers taught the virtues of understanding and compassion, as well as the importance of living in the moment. In the Gospel According to Matthew, Jesus said "Don't worry about tomorrow, tomorrow will take care of itself." (Matthew 6:34) Thầy further explained that by taking care of the present moment you will not have to worry about the future; joy in the moment brings joy in the future.

Then Thầy echoed the great wisdom of the Tao's yin and yang. He explained that we are in a world of opposing forces which at first appear to be separate but exist as one. It is the dance of opposites that provides the energy that moves us. Although happiness and suffering are experienced as opposites, they are in fact two sides of the same coin; they "inter-are" said Thầy. Here he is referring to a fundamental concept in Buddhism; "all phenomena are interdependent...endlessly interwoven." Nhất Hanh calls this principle *interbeing*. This principle adheres to the notion that all individuation and separation is illusory; all objects, events, and experiences are interwoven with other components connecting endlessly into infinite Oneness. These connections are relationships—patterns of Interaction. Nothing exists by itself. There can be no right without a left; no cold without hot.

> *In every one of us, there are good seeds and there are bad seeds... You need the mud to grow the lotus. Suffering is the kind of mud that we must be able to use in order to grow the flower of understanding and love.*
>
> —Nhất Hanh

In the closing moments of the interview, Thầy provided the viewers with a profound lesson in human relationships. First, to give those you love the gift of your total presence, not a distracted version of yourself that is absent in the present moment. Secondly, to let them know that you are aware of their presence as well. And in your awareness of their presence, you are truly happy to be with them—body, mind, and Soul. *"To be loved means to be recognized as existing."*

Finally, in times of suffering, it is particularly crucial to communicate that you are completely there for them. The presence of a loved one in times of suffering can bring relief. This can be particularly complicated when it is you that is suffering, and the cause of your suffering is the person you love. Your instinct is to withdraw and be alone; you may even crave revenge. It is here that you must overcome these feelings, communicate your pain, and ask for their assistance in overcoming your suffering. The experience of your suffering is linked to them, as is the experience of joy that can replace the suffering. All that exists is interwoven relationships in a process of endless change.

This concept of interwoven relationships is delved into by another significant contemporary spiritual teacher and guest on Super Soul Sunday—Marianne Williamson (born 1952). "Your greatest power to change the world... is your power to change your mind about the world—and all minds are joined." This is the point that Williamson makes regarding those who have harmed us. If we hold contempt for these people, we are expanding the very same energy that harmed us. However, when we pray for those who have harmed us, we overcome the anger, toxicity, and bitterness. As hard as it is to pray for our offenders, it is harder to carry such poison in our hearts. She goes on to say that the universe is self-correcting, and to hold onto negativity puts us at odds with this overarching healing process. Williamson calls this process the *Principle of Divine Compensation*. Namely, when something is taken from us in the form of being harmed, the universe is already working to restore us. But when our hearts are closed, we are not available to receive these new possibilities. In short, our potential is put on hold by our own doing. Our fully actualized state of being is already in the works, it is through our actions that we either accelerate or slow down the process. "The file is there; we just need to download it." Here we see the true cost of our relentless attachment to negativity—we sacrifice our blessings to play out the role of victim.

Williamson takes this conversation from the micro to the macro perspective. It is not only the actualization of the individual potential that is at stake, but the survival of humanity. It is no secret to the post World War II generation, that our world is at risk. Many of us grew up in the 50s and 60s with the nightmare of *nuclear winter* terrorizing our thoughts. Today we add the threat of *global warming* to the grim image of *nuclear winter*. As Williamson puts it: *We are on the Titanic heading for the iceberg.*

This cloud is not without its silver lining. It is often fear of losing what is dear to us that promote the greatest efforts. She sees two simultaneous phenomena going on; one clearly threatening destruction while the other offers immense hope. At the same time that the world faces its most threatening conditions, there is this "burgeoning spiritual understanding. Enlightenment has become a mainstream impulse." It is not just for ourselves that we must move beyond limiting perspectives; we have a responsibility to the whole that we are a part. As Williamson puts it "We must turn the Titanic around." She goes on to say that we have done well in the information gathering phase, now we must become the embodiment of the information.

An important distinction is made in this conversation regarding our individual awakening and our collective awakening. Williamson states that it will not be a majority that brings the world to its enlightened next phase of development, but an elite minority who will be responsible for reaching that *tipping point*. It has always been this way. Every great social and political change has been the result of a few leaders. Williamson emphasizes this by adding that the majority did not free the slaves or give women the right to vote. It has always been a small group viewed as radicals during their time that have brought great change. "If you know what changes the heart, you know what changes the world."

Deepak

The Indian-American author and physician, Deepak Chopra (born 1947), has written 75 books with 21 of them making the *New York Times Bestseller list*. After publishing *Ageless Body, Timeless Mind* in 1993, he appeared on Oprah's show; the book sold over 400,000 copies by the end of the week. Since his initial interview with Oprah, he has appeared on her network many times. He is a strong proponent of alternative medicine and teaches transcendental meditation. Chopra is considered an expert in the area of metaphysics and Vedanta philosophy. He spoke on Super Soul Sunday about the "acceleration" currently happening towards a more peaceful, just, healthier, sustainable, happier world. Chopra recognizes the magnitude of the spiritual movement operating towards this ultimate objective and promotes the spiritual perspective even in the case of modern medicine. He encourages physicians to "look into the Soul not only the body." His particular perspective tends toward a blend of modern physics and ancient Hinduism.

> *There is no fixed physical reality, no single perception of the world, just numerous ways of interpreting world views as dictated by one's nervous system and the specific environment of our planetary existence...*
>
> *The world sometimes feels like an insane asylum. You can decide whether you want to be an inmate or pick up your visitor's badge. You can be in the world but not engage in the melodrama of it; you can*

become a spiritual being having a human experience thoroughly and fully.

—Deepak Chopra

These are just a sample of the abundant stream of knowl-

edgeable teachers that have used Oprah's venue to spread modern spiritual light over the airwaves. Although Oprah has accumulated her own vast library of knowledge and experience, she remains the provider, the catalyst, and the hub of a modern spiritual wheel.

Like the contribution to our collective spiritual awakening made by Richard Price and Michael Murphy and those who developed the group awareness trainings, Oprah provided a context for the spiritual experience to be accessed. Had the Buddha only been concerned with his own Enlightenment and not taught thousands of monks and nuns the Way, we would probably not have access to his teachings today. Had Jesus been content to have his own personal relationship with God, and not passed his teachings on to his disciples and those who came to hear him speak, there would be no Christianity today. Had Muhammad learned from God without writing his book to pass on to humanity, his message would have been lost centuries ago. The wisdom and experience of spirituality needs a context to serve others, and these others are needed to serve spirituality.

As crass as it may sound, it's a numbers game, and the

spiritual puzzle has many pieces. The only place where the individual is the central concern is within the ego of the individual. Other than within that small, insignificant context of human ego, spirituality is served at its highest level within the context of interdependence where individuals recognize their most worthy purpose is in serving the whole of humanity. For the vast majority of us, we have benefited greatly from the extraordinary spiritual advancements made by the spiritual elite. It has been their thoughts and insights, even beyond our own, that have guided us most in our awakening.

In Summary...
The underlying message regarding human potential is focused on the untapped power and unbounded delight that is concealed within us all. These resources of a greater version of ourselves are hidden in the form of potential and are yet to be discovered and actualized. This chapter explores the notion of our hidden potential and those who have contributed to its discovery.

Two key change agents who revolutionized the approach toward actualizing our human potential were Abraham Maslow and Aldous Huxley. Maslow provided a significant insight into our limitations: *We fear to know the fearsome and unsavory aspects of ourselves, but we fear even more to know the godlike in ourselves.* **And Huxley asked the all-important question:** *What should be done now and in the immediate future to actualize the many and great potentialities which in most individuals still remain latent?*

From Abraham Maslow's *Theory of Human Moti-*

vation to Aldous Huxley's *Perennial Philosophy;* from the Harvard Psilocybin Project to the Beatle's chance encounter with the ancient mystical traditions of the East; and from Large Group Awareness Trainings to Oprah's Super Soul Sunday, our evolving spiritual awakening, with its *Human Potential Movement,* was conceptualized and launched into our modern era.

CHAPTER SIX

The Noosphere and the New Worldview

Chapter Six is a continuation of the previous two chapters; as a developmental exploration of the worldview in which we find ourselves. While the previous chapters focus on the evolving science of mind, chapter six also focuses on evolving physical science. From the early days of Aristotle, through the great era of the scientific revolution, to the beginnings of quantum physics in the early part of the 20th century, we find an emerging theme that holds wondrous discoveries of *how things really are*.

Although science and religion have traditionally viewed the world through their own separate lens, they have focused on the same reality. Perhaps one of the most significant coalescences of modern time is that of science and the spiritual; the physical and the mystical; matter and consciousness. Here we explore the link, or interdependence, of these two grand movements in forming a new and unprecedented worldview.

Chapter Six introduces us to a new concept, the

noosphere, referring to the evolutionary development of humanity's collective consciousness. There is a reciprocal relationship between individual consciousness and humanity's collective consciousness. As each individual is impacting collective consciousness, this noosphere of collective consciousness is, simultaneously, impacting each individual.

The two key aspects of the noosphere explored in this chapter are its concept and its content. Of the two, content is more accessible and understandable, as it is essentially a history lesson. The content of our current noosphere, or collective consciousness, is made up of the events and ideas; fears and dreams; joys and sorrows of our past. Whereas the concept of the noosphere is far more complex and challenging; esoteric and mysterious. For this reason, we explore the content of our noosphere first and then take on the fascinating concept itself—from both scientific and spiritual perspectives.

Caution: The Means May Obscure the End

> *The most beautiful and profound emotion we can experience is the sensation of the mystical. He to whom this emotion is a stranger, who can no longer wonder and stand rapt in awe, is as good as dead. To know that what is impenetrable to us really exists, manifesting itself as the highest wisdom and the most radiant beauty, which our dull faculties can comprehend only in their primitive forms—this knowledge, this feeling, is at the center of true religiousness.*
> —Albert Einstein

While Part One of this book (first six chapters) sets a chronological context, the ultimate objective of this book is to provide a *launching pad* for the reader's own spiritual journey. The epiphany, referenced in the title, is the full recognition and experience that we, as humans, consist of more than our physical nature. Each of us contains a component that is neither aging nor dying, not vulnerable to disease or suffering, nor is it at the effect of sadness or pain. Our physical presence is only an actor on the stage of mortality.

The epiphany occurs when the full depth of this idea of who we are is fully realized. As a prelude to grasping this truth and experiencing the epiphany, it is helpful to recognize that we are not alone in this quest. As previously shown, there are fundamental ideas that have been contemplated, taught, yearned for and realized by fellow spiritual travelers throughout human history. In every era, in every culture and religion, in every genre and under a variety of doctrines and dogmas, great minds have pondered the very same questions of who we are and the meaning of our existence.

In the beginning of Part One, we distinguished spirituality from religion. We did not do this because spirituality and religion do not belong together, but rather to illuminate spirituality independent of organized religion. Our purpose is to provide guidance to the reader in achieving his or her own personal spiritual experience. To accomplish this goal, it is best to diminish all preconceived notions, as well as the dogma that has been introduced by organized institutions. While one of the functions of religion is to bring the practitioner into the spiritual fold, all organized religions must also fulfill the necessary functions of perpetuating the organization. Such secondary functions can often serve as a distraction from achieving the primary purpose—spiritual awakening. Once a person is grounded in his or her own spiritual experience, that person may reengage whatever religion he or she deems appropriate.

The Buddha taught the lesson that having too much emphasis on the means causes us to lose sight of the end. Buddha's Raft Parable begins with a man travelling along the shore of a large body of water, mired on a path of thorny vegetation and rough terrain. The man recognizes that he is surrounded by danger and is afraid and feeling vulnerable. Contemplating the peril of his situation, he notices that the shore across the water is serene and peaceful—the very sight of it brings him joy and tranquility.

He decides to abandon his present path, and focuses on getting to the distant shore. Since there is no bridge or ferryboat, he decides his only option is to build a raft. With great ingenuity and effort, the man gathered what materials he could find and constructed a raft which he launched. Paddling feverishly through turbulent waters, he finally reaches the distant shore. Overcome with joy, he pulled his makeshift raft onto the beach. He loved the raft as it had served him well—but what now? Should he lift the raft over his head and carry it with him as he explores the beautiful new shore? The raft had served its function, but the man remained attached to it. Perhaps his handiwork would serve another if he left it on the shore.

Here the Buddha draws the analogy between the raft and his teachings. All teachings, no matter how great, are meant to be like a raft in order to reach our destination. They are not meant to become a burden and hinder us from moving forward.

The Buddha teaches that Absolute Truth is found by removing the layers of partial truth and falsehood from our perception. We actually obscure the truth with our theories and beliefs which according to Buddha, lead to *dense jungles and arid deserts, (causing) anger, delusion, and argument and do not bring about peace, knowledge, or wisdom leading to enlightenment (Digha Nikaya).* The Buddha further states in the *Diamond Sutra: If you are caught up in ideas, then you are caught up in the self. That's why we should not get attached to the belief that things either exist or do not exist. This is the hidden meaning when I say that my teachings are a raft to be abandoned when you see true being.*

In previous chapters, we made an abbreviated and simplified exploration of our current worldview as it pertains to the topic of unchurched spirituality. Spirituality is the key component of religion. So when we speak of unchurched spirituality, it is not unrelated to what we recognize as religion. It is religion without the cumulative effects of centuries of civilization, interpretations and dogma. It is the experience of religion without words—the corn without the husk. Spontaneous spirituality can only occur in the present moment. It is not attached to any past or future thought. The moment we bring in thoughts outside of the present, this spontaneous spiritual experience is diminished—fortunately however, it does leave a *residue*—more about this residue at the appropriate time.

Grand Scientific Shifts in Worldview

Religious condition of the Greeks in the fourth century before Christ. —Their invasion of the Persian Empire brings them in contact with new aspects of Nature, and familiarizes them with new religious systems. — The military engineering, and scientific activity, stimulated by the Macedonian campaigns, leads to the establishment in Alexandria of an institute, the Museum, for the cultivation of knowledge by experiment, observation, and mathematical discussion. —it is the origin of Science.

—John William Draper MD,
History of the Conflict Between Religion and Science

Neither spirituality nor religion has dominated our modern current worldview. Today's worldview mostly reflects the advancement and achievements of science. This is especially true when we include the innovations of technology. Science began impacting the worldview of humanity as far back as the ancient Sumerians and Greeks. Thales of Miletus, a pre-Socratic philosopher who is recognized as the first mathematician, used geometry in the design of the pyramids. Aristotle (384-322 BC), is recognized as the first true scientist. His works focus on such subjects as physics, biology, and logic. His perspective on physical science shaped the future for centuries.

Aristotle influenced diverse groups of philosophers such as the Iraqi Muslim mathematician, known as the father of Islamic philosophy, Al-Kindi (801-873) and the preeminent Torah scholar, physician, and Jewish philosopher, Moses Maimonides (1135-1204). The Aristotelian perspective separated humanity from the plants and animals, and placed Earth in the center of the universe, and God at the pinnacle of absolute knowledge and ultimate authority. Aristotle brought metaphysics into the question of what exists and the one substance that exists and causes all things to exist.

Shift: The Scientific Revolution
Nicolaus Copernicus (1473-1543), a Polish mathematician and astronomer, triggered a major shift in the worldview by

formulating a new model of the heliocentric universe, challenging the Aristotelian model that places Earth at the center of the universe. Copernicus was a church administrator in the bishopric of Lukas Watzenrode, his uncle, in northern Poland. Beyond his duties of supervising church finances, he occupied his time trying to resolve the problem of accurately predicting the equinoxes and solstices with an outdated calendar system. Without revision, it was not possible to accurately predict the occurrence of holy days such as Christmas and Easter. It was this work, echoing assertions made by the ancient Greek astronomer Aristarchus of Samos (310 BC-230 BC), that eventually led to the Copernican Revolution.

This shift in worldview, begun by Copernicus, would eventually lead to the Scientific Revolution in mathematics, physics, astronomy, biology, and chemistry—overhauling our entire view of society and nature. The Copernican model of the universe was expanded by German astronomer and mathematician, Johannes Kepler (1571-1630) who added the orbits of the planets. The sun-centered model was also corroborated by the observations made by Italian astronomer and physicist, Galileo Galilei (1564-1642), using a telescope. Galileo, known as the father of modern physics, found himself at odds with the Roman Inquisition, in 1615, due to his advocacy of heliocentrism, the theory that puts the sun in the center of the solar system as opposed to Earth, as it appeared to conflict with scripture.

The Inquisition had harassed Galileo for his observations previously, and on April l2, 1633, the chief inquisitor, Father Vincenzo Maculano da Firenzuola, appointed by Pope Urban VIII, ordered Galileo to turn himself over to the Holy Office to be imprisoned and stand trial. Galileo was charged with heresy for holding the belief that Earth revolves around the sun as opposed to the Catholic Church's belief that the sun revolves around the stationary Earth. On June 22, 1633, the Church handed down its verdict:

We pronounce, judge, and declare, that you, the said Galileo... have rendered yourself vehemently suspected by this Holy Office of heresy, that is, of having believed and held the doctrine (which is false and contrary to the Holy and Divine Scriptures) that the sun is the center of the world, and that it does not move from east to west, and that the earth does move, and is not the center of the world.

Galileo's publications were banned and he was sentenced to be burned at the stake. His life was spared when he conceded to recant his scientific findings as *abjured, cursed and detested*. He was then sentenced to spend the rest of his life in prison before the Church later showed some compassion by allowing Galileo to spend his remaining years on house arrest.

Interestingly, when Galileo first began experiencing criticism and hostility from his discoveries, he wrote a letter to the Grand Duchess Christina of Tuscany in 1615. In his letter, he addressed the issue of his discoveries overturning what was then commonly believed by science and the Church. Galileo wrote: *They seemed to forget that the increase of known truths stimulates the investigation, establishment, and growth of the arts; not their diminution or destruction.* Galileo went on to make a comment that holds as true today as during the beginning of the 17th century: *Showing a greater fondness for their own opinions than for truth they sought to deny and disprove the new things which, if they had cared to look for themselves, their own senses would have demonstrated to them.* After addressing the criticism from his fellow scientists and colleagues, Galileo focused on the Church by quoting St. Augustine:

> *If anyone shall set the authority of Holy Writ against clear and manifest reason, he who does this knows not what he has undertaken; for he opposes to the truth not the meaning of the Bible, which is beyond his comprehension, but rather his own interpretation, not what is in the Bible, but what he has found in himself and imagines to be there.*

The clash between the Church and one of history's great scientists is recognized as a prime example of the ongoing conflict between reason and dogma—the evidence of science and the authority of religion. To put this into a contemporary perspective, imagine a religious governing board taking offense to theoretical physicist Stephen Hawking's views that heaven is a myth and that the universe is governed by laws of science. Imagine this board having the authority to have him arrested for his views and sentencing him to be burned alive.

The abuse of power in the name of religion has been wielded over scientists throughout history. Even after scientific claims have been proven correct, religion has dragged its feet to admit its errors. It took the Vatican over 350 years to acknowledge the inaccuracy and the injustice perpetrated upon Galileo. Pope John Paul II, in October of 1992, after a 13-year investigation into the Church's condemnation of Galileo, formally acknowledged the wrongdoing.

Regardless of whether the scientific perspective was being challenged as heresy or revolutionary, there is little doubt that empirically tested theories and practical knowledge were replacing traditional explanations and beliefs about the natural world. Astronomy, physics, mathematics, chemistry, biology, and anatomy were shaping and transforming the worldview ushering in a whole new era of rational thinking

The Scientific Revolution impacted the worldview in ways that would be felt for centuries. Sir Isaac Newton (1642-1726), an English physicist, mathematician, and philosopher, not only advanced the scientific revolution, he impacted the Age of Enlightenment. In 1684, Newton formulated the mass and distance laws of gravity. Three years later, in 1687, he formulated the three laws of motion which laid the foundation for classical mechanics in physics. Along with Gottfried Leibniz, Newton developed what is today modern calculus—the mathematical study of change used in science, as well as engineering and economics. To Newton, his great scientific discoveries were further evidence of the majesty of God. Although Newton was a devout Christian, his journals reveal that he held unorthodox religious views that might have caused the Church of England to deem him a heretic, had they become public while he was alive.

The dance between science and religion was one of a love/hate relationship; both searched for knowledge of the universe but used different methodologies to arrive at truth. While religion looks to revelation and dogma, science is repelled by them. For centuries science has employed the scientific method to approach knowledge and gain new discoveries. In addition to Newton, Francis Bacon (1561-1626), an English scientist and philosopher, was a key proponent of the scientific method. He is often referred to as the father of empiricism, establishing inductive methods for scientific inquiry.

In the scientific revolution, science stood against the authority of the Church, stating that reason trumped dogma in determining the nature of reality. Where ideas and beliefs were once rooted in theology, religion, fears, superstition, and ironfisted authority, they were replaced by scientific evidence, experimentation, mathematics, and knowledge. The idea of a *changing* truth was revolutionary—what is true today, through science may be proven false tomorrow.

The shifting worldview during the Age of Reason was characterized by the continuing face-off between the theories of science and the beliefs of religion. This ongoing dispute marked the 19th century. Such concepts as "transmutation of the species" and "transformism" were the topic of many debates. Perhaps the most famous was the one which took place at the Oxford University on June 30, 1860— just seven months after the publication of Charles Darwin's epic work, *On the Origin of the Species*. It was during this debate that Bishop Samuel Wilberforce is reported to have asked biologist Thomas Henry Huxley which of his grandparents were monkeys. Huxley supposedly replied that he would have no shame in having a monkey for his ancestor. Although both sides claimed victory, the debate has always been recognized as significant in the advancement of Darwinism.

The 19th century *Conflict Thesis* proposed an inherent intellectual conflict between science and religion. The two leading proponents of the thesis were Dr. John William Draper (1811-1882), physician, scientist, historian, philosopher and author of *History of the Conflict between Religion and Science* (1874) and Andrew Dickson White (1832-1918), writer, historian and co-founder with Ezra Cornell of Cornell University. When the university opened in 1865, White proclaimed that Cornell would be *an asylum for science—where truth shall be sought for truth's sake, not stretched or cut exactly to fit Revealed Religion.*

In the introduction of his two-volume epic work, *A History of the Warfare of Science with Theology in Christendom,* White states:

> *In all modern history, interference with science in the supposed interest of religion, no matter how conscientious such interference may have been, has resulted in the direst evils both to religion and to science—and invariably. And, on the other hand, all untrammeled scientific investigation, no matter how dangerous to religion some of its stages may have seemed, for the time, to be, has invariably resulted in the highest good of religion and of science.*
>
> —Andrew Dickson White

In his book, *History of the Conflict Between Religion and Science,* Draper supports this notion:

> *The history of Science is not a mere record of isolated discoveries; it is a narrative of the conflict of two contending powers, the expansive force of the human intellect on one side, and the compression arising from traditionary faith and human interests on the other.*

Although there was a basis for such a thesis reflecting the somewhat strained relationship between science and religion of the 19th century, many 21st century historians question the validity of the conflict model. While the famous examples used to depict the conflict, (i.e., Galileo and Charles Darwin),

Professor Colin A. Russell, in his article, *Science and Religion: Conflict or Complexity,* suggests that perhaps the word *conflict* may be too strong. He suggests rather it is a *complex* relationship that at *different phases of their history, science and religion were not so much at war as largely independent, mutually encouraging, or even symbiotic.* Professor Gary B. Ferngren, in the introduction of his book *Science & Religion: A Historical Introduction,* writes: *The conflict thesis, at least in its simple form, is now widely perceived as a wholly inadequate intellectual framework within which to construct a sensible and realistic historiography of Western science.*

Shift: The Enlightenment (1650s-1780s)

This scientific revolution was now poised. Sir Isaac Newton was not only a leader of the scientific revolution; he was a key influence in the Enlightenment. As one of history's greatest scientists, Newton also had a passion for religion and searched the bible incessantly, looking for clues that suggest deeper meaning. Other key figures in the scientific revolution were also devout in their religion—Copernicus, Kepler, Galileo, Bacon, Descartes. However, it was mathematics, physics, chemistry, biology, and astronomy that were the foundation of the *new philosophy.*

The debate continued to rage on—was it the senses of the human entity or our capacity of reason that initiates all knowledge? Was it the empiricist or rationalist perspective that would prevail?

The Scientific Revolution ushered in another grand shift in worldview—the Enlightenment, or Age of Reason. Following on the heels of the Renaissance, the Enlightenment was not as much of a unified movement. It emerged in the 17th

century and peaked during the 18th century. The Enlightenment was a time of challenge to all forms of authority—especially religious authority. It emphasized individualism and
egalitarianism rather than the traditional authority of institutions. Reason and analysis were valued over dogma and
revelation.

Not only was authority being challenged, the approach
to knowledge was shifting to a more organized and scientific
methodology. Sir Francis Bacon (1561-1626) summed up the
tone of the times when he stated *"Truth can never be reached
by just listening to the voice of an authority."* Considered one
of the key founders of the Enlightenment, he is often referred
to as the father of modern science. Bacon's science was more
than exploring the great mysteries; it was pragmatically
rooted in alleviating man's suffering. In the 18th century, his
non-metaphysical approach to science became more preva-
lent than the dualism of Descartes.

Bacon and Newton, along with other key Enlightenment figures, believed in the unity of knowledge, individual
human rights, and natural law. Newton's three volume *Prin-
cipia,* published in 1687, is often viewed as one of the most
significant scientific works forming the foundation of classical physics. The ideas of the Enlightenment philosophers
would emerge as the philosophy of science, determining how
research would be conducted.

In his *Personal History of Lord Bacon* (1861), biographer
and historian William Hepworth Dixon writes:

*The obligations of the world to Francis Bacon are of
a kind that cannot be overlooked. Every man who
rides in a train, who sends a telegram, who follows a
steam plough, who sits in an easy chair, who crosses*

the channel or the Atlantic, who eats a good dinner, who enjoys a beautiful garden, or undergoes a painless surgical operation, owes him something.

Perhaps the biggest shift brought by the Enlightenment was the notion of *reason*, itself. In fact, the Enlightenment is often referred to as the Age of Reason. Simply put, reason, the idea of using one's intellect and logic as the basis of knowledge, was being proclaimed as superior to the previous path of tradition, authority, or even emotions to determine what is right and true. People were discovering that they had the ability to think for themselves, rather than needing to be told how to think. This new idea of reason led to another Enlightenment belief that all people are, in principle, equal and should enjoy equal rights and opportunities.

This new *Enlightenment Worldview* was, of course, threatening to both crown and church. People no longer accepted the authority of the nobility or the truth of the priests. They began to question the special rights and privileges granted to them. The crown and the church regarded such questioning as treacherous, to be avoided at all costs. It's not surprising that a number of Enlightenment philosophers were exiled or imprisoned.

It was not long before the revolutionary ideas of the Enlightenment were expressed by bullets and cannonballs. Newton's Laws of Nature were applied to politics and government. John Locke (1632-1704) and Thomas Paine (1737-1808) influenced Thomas Jefferson, Benjamin Franklin and America's Founding Fathers; Voltaire's (1694-1778) opposition to the inequality of Louis XIV and the Church, and Rousseau's (1712-1778) political ideologies influenced both the American and French Revolutions.

The American Revolution provided the opportunity for the ideas of the Enlightenment philosophers to be put into practice in a new society based on reason rather than the traditions of royalty and clergy. It promised a good life for the common man with inalienable rights of *life, liberty and the pursuit of happiness.*

In the latter part of the 18th Century, 80% of France's population was working the land and was barely able to feed their hungry families. Nevertheless, the Crown expected them to pay high taxes to the extravagant nobility and the Church expected them to tithe another portion to the rich and powerful Church. Revolution was imminent and the French followed the Americans in short order with their own Revolution intending a cultural and social shift away from the authority of King and Church, and the emergence of a *middle class* made up of commoners aspiring to gain political equality with the aristocracy.

There were other revolutions during the 18th century. In his book, *The Age of Democratic Revolution: A Political History of Europe and America, 1760-1800,* Dr. Robert Roswell Palmer (1909-2002), professor at Princeton and Yale, describes the emergence and collision of two competing forces. On the one hand, the ideas of democracy and equality were sweeping through the hearts and minds of ordinary people, while at the same time the aristocracies were gaining in power. However, not all of the democratic movements of the time were as successful as that in America and France. Dr. Palmer points out the often-overlooked failed attempts in Geneva, Poland, Ireland, Sweden, Belgium, the Netherlands, England, Italy, and Hungary.

Nevertheless, the revolutionary wave continued into the 20th century with revolutions occurring in Russia, Argentina,

Persia (now Iran), Turkey, Monaco, Greece, Portugal, Mexico, and China. These all occurred before World War I. Then, after that war, came the next Russian Revolution, German Revolution, and the continuing Indian independence movement that lasted 90 years from 1857-1947. And the list goes on. In the opening of *The Age of Democratic Revolution*, Palmer quotes G. K. van Hogendorp (1762-1834), the Dutch statesman:

> *Two great parties are forming in all nations... For one, there is the right of government, to be exercised by one or several persons over the mass of the people, of divine origin and to be supported by the church, which is protected by it. These principles are expressed in the formula, Church and State. To this is opposed the new system, which admits no right of government except that arising from the free consent of those who submit to it, and which maintains that all persons who take part in government are accountable for their actions. These principles go under the formula, Sovereignty of the People, or Democracy.*

The great ideals of the Enlightenment—freedom and equality with government by the people and for the people—were not to come, however, without significant bloodshed. Unfortunately, the new Enlightenment view was both polarizing and frustrating. People were now *aware* that a better life was conceivable, but it also had to be *achievable*. For the masses struggling in poverty, they saw their biggest obstacle as those who were living the better life they sought, but who were holding them down.

Unlike the philosophical Enlightenment taught by the

Buddha and other spiritual Sages, this new political Enlightenment was being expressed in hatred and bloodshed. People were waging revolutionary wars against their oppressors and civil war against their neighbors—all justifying a dastardly machine of death and destruction.

Shift, Crisis in Worldview—Acceptable Atrocities

From the perspective of the noosphere, we now consider what has been fed into our collective consciousness by the events of the last century. On July 28, 1914, the world launched into the worst, most unprecedented bloodbath in human history—World War I. After all of the explanations history has provided for such hell on earth, it boils down to the same

root causes that have plagued mankind since the beginning—man's conflicted psychology expressed in ego-driven violence, hatred, intolerance, greed and the incessant desire for more than we have in order to feel superior and to control others.

Newly developed war technology added to the capacity of the killing power. Machine guns provided strong advantage to fighting in trenches. Armored vehicles and tanks, flamethrowers and poisonous gas added to the equation. Airplanes had only been around a short time before the war broke out, but they offered obvious advantages for combat. War planes were soon equipped with machine guns and bombs and began being launched from moving aircraft carriers. The violence lasted for four years and three months. When it was over, there were 38 million casualties—17 million dead, including 7 million civilians, and over 20 million severely wounded. With science and technology playing an ever-increasing role in the global balance of power, it was no longer merely greater scientific understanding driving the exploration of our physical reality, now science was at the center of global warfare.

In the closing decades of the 19th century and the beginning decades of the 20th century, while the science of mind was emerging into modern psychology, the philosophy of nature and natural phenomenon was emerging into the science of modern physics as well. Although it may not have been apparent at the time, this new science would lead to a revolution in warfare and the merging of science and spirit.

World War I, the Great War, drew in all of the major economic powers. When it was over, the world had a new map; new nations appeared while some great empires ceased to exist. Estimates cited by H.E. Fisk, *The Inter-Allied Debts (1924)* show that the world spent about $208 billion (US 1913 dollars) to put on this four-year massacre—$147 billion by the Allied Forces and $61 billion by the Central Powers. In today's dollars that would amount to nearly $5 trillion.

The victors were determined that the world would never have to endure such horror again. However, the underlying conditions were left unresolved. The hatred, intolerance, and greed that led to war were still alive and actively involved in the terms of the negotiated peace. As is often the case, violence seldom resolves violence. According to many historians, "the war to end all wars" never really ended; it simply was left simmering on the back burner. A decade later, Japan seized Manchuria from China in 1931. Italy invaded Ethiopia in 1935, and Adolf Hitler escalated re-militarization of Germany's Rhineland. The next year saw the start of the Spanish Civil War.

The world appeared only to have taken a brief intermission—just long enough to catch its breath and make significant upgrades in its military arsenals. On July 7, 1937, war broke out between Japan and China and on September 1, 1939 Germany invaded Poland. WWII was underway, again using violence to make the world a better place. While 32 countries were involved with WWI, 61 countries were involved with WWII. Estimates of how many people lost their lives during WWII range between 50-60 million and when war-related deaths from disease and starvation are factored in, that number jumps to 80 million—civilian deaths amounting to nearly double the military death toll.

It was no longer military and economic power that determined success on the battlefield. Science became a key determinant of who would have the upper hand. Hence, the famous statement by Sir Ian Jacob, the military secretary of Winston Churchill, regarding the enormous influx of refugee scientists (including 19 Nobel Prize laureates): *The Allies won the war because our German scientists were better than their German scientists.*

Even though the Treaty of Versailles which ended WWI, imposed severe restrictions upon German military research and development, Germany continued to advance combat technology in secret.

New fighters and bombers, as well as ballistic missiles, were developed. New aircraft carriers, tanks, submarines, torpedoes, machine guns, mortars, artillery, and other improvements were devised to increase the killing power in the new war. Scientific advances were also made in chemical warfare producing nerve agents that would disrupt the ability of nerves to transfer messages to the organs. Napalm, a highly flammable gelling agent put into bombs and flamethrowers, was developed at Harvard University.

Yet all this development pales by comparison to science's greatest contribution to the potential total annihilation of human life—the Atomic Bomb. In the words of President Truman's Secretary of State James F. Byrnes, in an attempt to shorten the war and, put the U.S. in a dominant position to determine the course of the postwar world, the U.S. dropped the first nuclear bomb ever used in warfare on the Japanese city of Hiroshima. On August 6, 1945, this 9,000-pound bomb called *Little Boy* exploded 2,000 feet above the city, with the power of 15,000 tons of TNT. It formed a fireball over 900 feet in diameter and sent a mushroom cloud soaring nearly 60,000 feet into the sky. The blast was felt as far as 37 miles away, two-thirds of the city's buildings were demolished, and the firestorm incinerated everything within a 4.5-mile radius of the blast. The second use came three days later on August 9th when an even larger 10,000-pound nuclear bomb named *Fat Man* delivered a 22-kiloton blast (equivalent to 22,000 tons of TNT) on the city of Nagasaki. The estimates range as high as a quarter of a million deaths from both bombings—mostly civilians. However, this number does not come close to describing the devastation brought by the effects of radiation and the intense psychological damage to those who survived, or those who witnessed their loved ones endure the effects of such a torturous death. The A-bombs produced the military objective; Japan surrendered. Politically, the U.S. was now a superpower with all the burdens of responsibility.

In terms of military weaponry, the world had entered a new era of nuclear warfare. Certainly, the world had previously engaged in *arms races* to determine military superiority. Just prior to WW I the major countries in Europe were competing feverously to gain naval superiority. After the bombing of Hiroshima and Nagasaki, the world's military powers had found a new god. The atomic bomb had set a new gold standard for death and destruction—and every kid on the block wanted one. And the kid who wanted one the most was Russia, or rather the Soviet Union (USSR).

The relationship between the U.S. and the Soviet Union had been strained throughout the war—two enemies forming a bond to beat a common enemy. Although the *Hot War* had ended, a new war emerged—the *Cold War*. The arms race of the past was now a nuclear arms race which would threaten the future of the planet and all its inhabitants.

On August 29, 1949, the USSR exploded its first atomic bomb; a 22-kiloton implosion type nuclear bomb very similar to the Nagasaki bomb dropped by the U.S. Although the Soviets had intended to keep their progress hidden to prevent the U.S. from accelerating their atomic program, the U.S. Air Force detected the radioactive fallout from the blast. On September 24, 1951, the USSR exploded a larger, 38.8 kiloton atomic bomb, followed by an even larger 41.2 kiloton bomb on October 18, 1951.

With the Soviets well on their way in the nuclear arms race, the U.S. would need something far more powerful to maintain its lead. This began the serious discussion of bringing into existence a greater monster with more firepower. Scientists were at odds with each other on what was being suggested— the development of a hydrogen bomb. Most of the scientists of the Los Alamos laboratory involved with the development of nuclear weapons refused to work on the development of the hydrogen bomb and left the lab.

Theoretical physicist, Edward Teller (1908-2003) was a

key H-bomb proponent and became known as *the father of the hydrogen bomb*. He was opposed by one of his foremost colleagues and a founding father of the school of theoretical physics, J. Robert Oppenheimer (1904-1967). Oppenheimer felt similar to the two Nobel Prize laureates Enrico Fermi (1901-1954) and Isidor Isaac Rabi (1898-1988), who wrote in their report to the General Advisory Committee convention of the Atomic Energy Commission, "Since no limit exists to the destructiveness of this weapon, its existence and knowledge of its construction is a danger to humanity as a whole."

Despite all the global risks, unknown consequences, and scientific warnings against it, President Truman favored the position that the U.S. had to stay ahead of the Soviets. On November 1, 1952 the U.S. detonated the first hydrogen bomb that the world had ever known. It was a 10.4-megaton hydrogen device weighing far less than the atomic bomb dropped on Hiroshima yet carrying 1000 times the firepower. Detonated on an island in the Pacific, the explosion vaporized the island and destroyed all life on the surrounding islands. Its mushroom cloud expanded for 100 miles and soared 25 miles into the sky. Fourteen months later the U.S dropped a second hydrogen bomb on Bikini Atoll with a yield of 14.8 megatons, making it the largest U.S. nuclear test ever. Its 3-mile fireball sent several million tons of radioactive debris into the air and contaminated local fishermen and inhabitants of neighboring islands up to 300 miles away.

The USSR detonated its first hydrogen bomb at the Semipalatinsk test site in northeast Kazakhstan as the first of 456 nuclear tests at this site between 1949 and 1989. According to the records released by Russian government in 1991, the Soviets tested a total of 969 nuclear devices during those four decades. Between 1957 and 1992 there were an estimated 1,352 underground nuclear test explosions and since 1993 there have been another 520 atmospheric nuclear test explosions yielding a total of 545 megatons.

As of 2014, the *Bulletin of the Atomic Scientist* estimates the world nuclear arsenal consists of approximately 16,300 nuclear weapons located at 98 sites in 14 countries. According to studies conducted by the United Nations, that number could be over 26,000. 93% of these weapons are owned by the U.S. and Russia and the majority of these bombs are stored within their respective countries, with 1,800 of their weapons on high-alert status—ready to be launched within minutes.

Today, nine countries have nuclear weapons; United States, Russia, China, France, United Kingdom, India, Israel, Pakistan, and North Korea—which means there are nine participants who hold the keys to a process that has the potential of ending the world as we know currently know it.

In his book, *The Odyssey of Science, Culture, and Consciousness,* Dr. Kishore Gandhi takes a peek into the devastation of the nuclear engagement that awaits a complacent world.

In a recent study brought out by the World Health Organization, it is estimated that any future major exchange of nuclear war will straightaway extinguish 1.1 billion people by blast, prompt radiation, and fires. An additional 1.1 billion people would suffer fatal injuries and probably be exterminated within a few weeks or months. Obviously, over a half of the human population of our planet would be eliminated by the direct effects of a nuclear war. The indirect implica-

*tions of the ecosystems and biological life would be
quite staggering.*
— Kishore Gandhi, *The Odyssey of Science,
Culture, and Consciousness*

World War II left other scars on the collective Soul of
humanity. This was not just a political and economic war,
it was a war to determine human superiority, masters and
slaves, illustrating the depth of Man's brutality. The Nazi
invasion of Russia in 1941 was the beginning of genocidal
conflict in human history. It is now estimated that as many
as 30 million inhabitants of the Soviet Union died during the
war—this includes more than three million who were the victims of intentional starvation in prison of war camps.

This blatant inhumanity was not only directed against
enemy combatants, it was perpetrated upon women and girls
as well. On the Russian side, Stalin's police chief, Lavrenty
Beria, was a serial rapist. (In 2003, Beria's case files in the
Soviet archives were opened. They recorded that he had committed "dozens" of sexual assaults during the years he was
NKVD chief. British journalist Simon Sebag-Montefiore, a
biographer of Stalin, concluded that the information "reveals
a sexual predator who used his power to indulge himself in
obsessive depravity.") According to historian Laurence Rees
in *World War Two: Behind Closed Doors*, along with Beria,
his commanders literally encouraged soldiers to rape the
women of the villages as a form of reward for their valiant
efforts. In many towns, every female from age 10 to 80 was
raped, often left for dead.

Some estimates indicate as many as 2 million German
women were raped by Soviet soldiers. The rapes of WWII were
not just committed by the Red Army. It appears that armies

of all nations were implicated—German, British, French, Japanese, and American. In his book, *Taken by Force: Rape and American GIs in Europe in World War II,* J. Robert Lilly, a Northern Kentucky University professor of sociology and criminology, explores the incidents of rape committed by U.S. servicemen during WW II. Lilly draws from court records, newspaper articles and trial transcripts covering 14,000 rapes occurring in England, France, and Germany by U.S. soldiers. His work has been highly acclaimed and recognized as being "extensively researched and referenced." Concurring, British historian, Antony J. Beevor (born 1946) claims, the time of WWII was the "greatest phenomenon of mass rape in history" including 1.4 million women raped in East Prussia.

The women were not just abused by enemy soldiers, but in many instances were raped by their liberators. Such rapes cannot be considered as motivated by revenge. Beevor finds that sexual violence during war is an "inherent feature of military culture," especially when condoned or encouraged by those in command. Women surviving this victimization were left permanently traumatized. The German women of this generation still refer to the Red Army War Memorial in Berlin as the "Tomb of the Unknown Rapist."

Through a series of trials and discoveries, and research by Historian Yoshiaki Yoshimi published in his book, *Comfort Women* and the Asian Women's Fund, the Japanese Imperial Army was found to have kidnapped as many as 200,000 women and girls to serve as *comfort women* for their troops. Kidnapped from China, Korea, the Philippines, Burma, Thailand, Vietnam, Malaysia, Indonesia, and in some cases, the Netherlands and Australia, these women were forced into sexual slavery for the Japanese army. While this horrific human rights violation has remained somewhat silent since the war, some brave victims have spoken out.

One such woman, 92-year-old Dutch Australian human rights activist, Jan Ruff- O'Herne, was kidnapped one month after her 21st birthday and forced into a military brothel. Fifty years later she decided to speak out and demand a formal apology from the Japanese government. In her personal memoir, *Fifty Years of Silence,* she documents her nightmare. On February 15, 2007, O'Herne appeared before the United States House of Representatives as a part of the congressional hearing on "Protecting the Human Rights of Comfort Women." This is a portion of her statement:

*Many stories have been told about the horrors, brutalities, suffering and starvation of Dutch women in Japanese prison camps. But one story was never told, the most shameful story of the worst human rights abuse committed by the Japanese during World War II: The story of the "Comfort Women", the **jugun ianfu**, and how these women were forcibly seized against their will, to provide sexual services for the Japanese Imperial Army...*

...I have forgiven the Japanese for what they did to me, but I can never forget. For fifty years, the "Comfort Women" maintained silence; they lived with a terrible shame, of feeling soiled and dirty. It has taken 50 years for these women's ruined lives to become a human rights issue.

The total number of women who were actually victims of sexual violence during World War II is still unknown, but the number most often cited in studies since the war is 2,000,000.

The cruelty that man is capable of inflicting on his brethren reached a shocking extreme during World War II. The incidents of torture, sexual abuse, prisoners being buried alive, medical experimentation on POWs and civilians, biological and chemical warfare, the use of nuclear weapons of mass destruction, as well as the systematic, state-sponsored genocide of six million Jews by Germany's Nazi regime is well documented and only too familiar.

Unfortunately, genocide is not limited to the Nazis in WWII. Ethnic genocide has been documented for the Turkish slaughter of 1,000,000 Armenians, the Holodomor or manmade famine of the Stalinist regime resulting in an estimated 2.6 million deaths in the Ukraine, the elimination of an estimated one million people in the killing fields of Cambodia by the Khmer Rouge regime, the killing of an estimated 1,000,000 Tutsis in Rwanda, the starvation of an estimated one million Somalians by that country's elongated civil war and the list goes on.

Take a good look at these atrocities of the 20th Century; familiarize yourself with every aspect; know their true cause and ultimate effect. This is organized and sanctioned violence—war. It is man's *go-to* solution for not having the peace and loving-kindness that we dream of in our hearts. Although it is not my custom to show gender bias in my use of pronouns, I use the male form here intentionally. Let's face it guys, if women would have been in possession of the remote control all these years, do we really think that the Death and Destruction Channel would have been their top pick? Would the female of our species have used the greatest scientific breakthroughs in history to create the deadliest bombs in history—bombs that have the potential to eliminate all advanced life forms from the face of the Earth in the course of a day?

Would the female of the species, the gender that bore the world's population, be willing to replace it with a world dominated by ants, cockroaches, and scorpions? Although we have always blamed Eve for our original sin; I can't see a way of blaming her descendants for our ultimate demise.

Surely, this is not the global transformation that our Enlightenment philosophers had in mind. It is not the freedom that our forefathers gave their lives to provide for us. Certainly, our Creator had a different path in mind in providing for our existence.

Can We Save Us from Ourselves?

We have met the enemy, and he is us.

–POGO

At the time of the 17th century Enlightenment, there was a surge in human consciousness. Unlike previous periods of higher consciousness, it was not just the philosophers and scholars who were awakening to this higher consciousness—it had trickled down to the masses as well. Unfortunately, our collective consciousness of the time was dominated by strong feelings of resentment, anger, and hatred that people felt for their desperate lives. Without the proper channels to counterbalance such extreme emotion, this mass awakening erupted into violence.

Today, there's not a thinking person alive that hasn't at least considered the possibility of a World War III. WWI and WWII both ended with unresolved hostility and continuing violence. Nations did not stop building military arsenals and training millions for combat. We've not yet *beat our swords into plowshares and our spears into pruning hooks.*

On January 17, 1961, U.S. President and former five-star general, Dwight D. Eisenhower, in his Farewell Address, warned America and the world about the potential perils of the emerging unleashed war machine:

A vital element in keeping the peace is our military establishment. Our arms must be mighty, ready for instant action, so that no potential aggressor may be tempted to risk his own destruction...

*This conjunction of an immense military establishment and a large arms industry is new in the American experience. The total influence — economic, political, even spiritual — is felt in every city, every statehouse, every office of the federal government. We recognize the imperative need for this development. Yet we must not fail to comprehend its grave implications. Our toil, resources and livelihood are all involved; so is the very structure of our society. In the councils of government, **we must guard against the acquisition of unwarranted influence, whether sought or unsought, by the military–industrial complex**. The potential for the disastrous rise of misplaced power exists, and will persist. We must never let the weight of this combination endanger our liberties or democratic processes. We should take nothing for granted. Only an alert and knowledgeable citizenry can compel the proper meshing of the huge industrial and military machinery of defense with our peaceful methods and goals so that security and liberty may prosper together.*

The *military-industrial complex*, or as it is often called, the *military-industrial-congressional complex*, refers to the financial and policy relationships between the armed forces who fight wars, the arms industry that sells the implements of war, and the legislators who award contracts for armaments and commit the nation to the wars. With the unique vantage point of the new war machine, Eisenhower, who led the Allied forces to victory and was elected twice as the president of the U.S. superpower, by his own admission, was not comfortable with, and warned people about, what he saw emerging—a military-industrial-congressional dragon that was fed by war.

This monster has grown exponentially since WWII, along with the vast array of rationales for going to war. At the same time, there is an emerging consciousness, inner and outer—individual and social. As one becomes more self-realized, his or her individual reality becomes enhanced—lives improve. With greater consciousness of the surrounding universe, our collective reality gets better. On the other hand, the world, as a whole, will not get better until we elevate our collective consciousness.

Although *Homo sapiens* are evolving toward higher consciousness, there is the threat of *too little too late*. Our collective taste for death and destruction has significantly diminished over the years, but in the most developed and powerful countries, less people and fewer weapons are required to wreak massive damage. A serious nuclear holocaust could occur, leaving our once green planet in ruins before the average person ever sees it coming. In the prophetic words of Marianne Williamson: *We are on the Titanic, heading for the iceberg.*

What is it in our inherent design that would cause us to turn our world into a living hell? More importantly, is it possible to recalculate this hateful violent mechanism into one that promotes compassion, tolerance, and peace? If so, what will it take to change the course of human events to prevent our future demise—our own self-destruction? What is the colossal shift that will be required in the collective consciousness of the noosphere to change our predictable path?

We now stand at a very dangerous crossroads. Many wise minds, especially those of science, recognize what is ultimately at stake should the world decide to once again engage in world war. We do not need the predictions and revelations of ancient mystics to know the catastrophic results. Our great scientific thinkers should have recognized that putting power equivalent to what is unleashed by the sun into the hands of our world leaders was tantamount to putting a loaded gun in the hands of a reckless child.

This is where we sit 3300-3500 years after receiving the Torah and Hindu Scriptures, 2500 years after the teachings of Buddha, 2000 years after the proclamations of Jesus, and 1500 years after the words of the Prophet Muhammad. Are we on the brink of salvation? Have we achieved peace on Earth? It is highly doubtful with 50,000 nuclear warheads in our collective arsenal, each having 1000 times the strength of the atomic bomb dropped on Hiroshima. Even if we could say with certainty that those who hold the authority to unleash such dreadful carnage are trustworthy, can we actually say the same about the technology that holds these weapons at bay? Who amongst us has not experienced, firsthand, technology being less than perfect? In the words of the Dalai Lama:

History shows us that violence only engenders more violence and rarely solves problems. On the other hand, it certainly creates unfathomable suffering. It is also apparent that even when war seems wise and logical as a means to end conflict, we can never know for sure whether by putting out a fire we are not in fact lighting a furnace.

It is up to everyone to bring an end to war. We can of course identify those who have incited conflict, but we cannot pretend that they sprung up out of nowhere or that they acted in isolation. They were members of a society of which we are all members too, and for which each one of us carries a share of responsibility. If we want to bring about peace in the world, let us start by creating it in ourselves.

It is important to recognize that this is not someone else's crisis; the buck cannot be passed. We are the generation of the living who still have the opportunity to create the future and validate our past. It is within our power to take astute and expedient action. Or, we can be blinded by our own self-interest and fail to see what is unfolding before our eyes. It is during our watch that the global chess game escalated to one of such high stakes as to leave nothing for another day. It is also during our watch that we have allowed the effects of human life to threaten the very ecosystem that sustains life. We no longer have the luxury of remaining unaware while waiting for someone else to fix things. It is up to each of us to take a stand for a new course that is founded on repair and avoidance—the repair of what needs correction and the avoidance of what must not take place.

How can one person repair and save a world? This is an age-old question that has an age-old answer—we begin by fixing ourselves. The design of the human and the design of the planet share a common mechanism: until we cease to exist, we are always fixable. The repair work is done on two levels, physical and spiritual—matter and consciousness. The same course of action will repair both levels simultaneously. Just as we need to repair our bodies to avoid the ravages of disease, we must elevate our collective consciousness to avoid the ravages of violence and war.

Throughout the 20th century, science and technology were playing an ever-increasing role in the global balance of power. It was no longer merely greater scientific understanding driving the exploration of our physical reality; now science was at the center of global warfare.

In the closing decades of the 19th century and the beginning decades of the 20th century, while the science of mind was emerging into modern psychology, so too the philosophy of nature and natural phenomenon was emerging into the science of modern physics. Although it may have not been apparent at the time, this new science would lead to a revolution in warfare and the merging of science and spirit.

In 1900, the fundamental ideas of quantum mechanics (the theory of atoms and subatomic systems) began being introduced by Max Planck (1858-1947), a German theoretical physicist who won the Nobel Prize in Physics in 1918. Planck's quantum theory revolutionized human understanding of the atomic and subatomic world the way Einstein's theory of relativity revolutionized our understanding of time and space. Both of these great men of science acknowledged the significance of the spiritual. In the words of Max Planck:

There can never be any real opposition between religion and science; for the one is the complement of the other. Every serious and reflective person realizes, I think, that the religious element in his nature must be recognized and cultivated if all the powers of the human soul are to act together in perfect balance and harmony. And indeed it was not by accident that the greatest thinkers of all ages were deeply religious souls.

—Max Planck, *Where is Science Going?*

Albert Einstein *dittoed* Planck's view of religion and science in harmony, and further added art to the mix: *In my view, it is the most important function of art and science to awaken this religious feeling and keep it alive in those who are receptive to it.*

In the beginning years of modern physics, the International Solvay Institutes for Physics and Chemistry was founded by Ernest Solvay in Brussels (in 1912). Every few years, the institute would hold a conference for the preeminent scientists in the fields of physics and chemistry. The most legendary of these conferences was the Fifth Solvay International Conference on Electrons and Photons, held in October of 1927. Here the world's most renowned physicists convened to focus on the newly formulated *quantum theory*. Of the 29 scientists assembled at the conference, 17 were (or would become) Nobel Prize laureates, including Marie Curie (1867-1934), the only female attendee and the only person to win two Nobel Prizes in two different sciences—physics and chemistry.

With the greatest minds in science present at this conference, it is interesting how often the topics of spirituality, mysticism, religion and God surfaced. Perhaps the most famous quote came from Einstein in response to Werner Heisenberg's Uncertainty Principle, which states that the observation of a particle's position will alter the particle's speed, and vice versa. In a moment of frustration with the apparent randomness being implied, Einstein responded by saying: *God does not play dice with the universe.* To which Nobel laureate Niels Bohr replied: *Einstein, stop telling God what to do.*

In his book, *Physics and Beyond*, Heisenberg recalls a moment of banter between the Solvay attendees regarding the religious views of Planck and Einstein. Wolfgang Pauli, Heisenberg, and Paul Dirac were the main characters in the discussion. Dirac was somewhat heated in his criticism of the *political manipulation* of religion and said:

> *I cannot understand why we idle discussing religion. If we are honest—and as scientists, honesty is our precise duty—we cannot help but admit that any religion is a pack of false statements, deprived of any real foundation. The very idea of God is a product of human imagination... I do not recognize any religious myth, at least because they contradict one another.*

Pauli kept silent. But when he was finally asked for his opinion, jokingly he responded: *Well, I'd say that also our friend Dirac has got a religion and the first commandment of this religion is God does not exist and Paul Dirac is his prophet.* Everyone burst into laughter, including Dirac.

Their lighthearted tone hardened somewhat when Einstein accused Niels Bohr of introducing an element of "ancient mysticism" through elements of quantum mechanics that was incompatible with science. Bohr denied this accusation, blaming it on a misunderstanding concerning his comment about ancient wisdom, *that when searching for harmony in life one must never forget that in the drama of existence, we are ourselves both actors and spectators.* Bohr later commented in his book, *Discussions with Einstein on Epistemological Problems in Atomic Physics,* that: *Utterances of this kind would naturally in many minds evoke the impression of an underlying mysticism foreign to the spirit of science.*

Concern over whether the mystical would taint pure science was not the focus for many years. The geniuses of science were about to face their greatest challenge regarding the threat of war and the need for military superiority.

According to the Sages, one key element that would lead us into another world war, or prevent it, is our collective consciousness. It is consciousness, they teach, that is behind all of our earthly events—both individually and socially. This is no longer just a tenet of spirituality or mysticism; it's also emerging in modern scientific theory.

The bad news is that we are on course for disaster; the good news is that we have the time and the means to avert it. All we truly need is the *intention* to do what's required. In Part II of this book, we will explore three key elements of elevating consciousness: *intention* that fuels the journey, *structure* that serves as the ship, and *process* that leads to accomplishment. In the next chapter, we take note of the power of intention—without it, we just go through the motions. Honing our intention may be the greatest method ever for enhancing personal power. Without proper intention we are destined to fail; with it, we can overcome all obstacles.

All the great Saints and Sages taught a similar version of this fundamental, spiritual truth—when your intention is to give rather than to receive, your personal power thrives. Simply put, when you put effort into improving this world for the benefit of others, without the motivation of personal gain, you flourish. As the Buddha taught: *Do good things, not for your own sake, but for all the beings in the universe.* This widely respected spiritual trait is the result of *clear perception* and a *compassionate heart*. Such a person asks *how might I contribute to the solution,* rather than, *what might I gain from this situation.*

The lesson is, that to move forward in the process of elevating consciousness, intention is the critical factor, and the best intention is that of serving others through raising the collective consciousness. We are social beings; what happens to us as individuals, happens to all of us. Work on what we can control—individual consciousness with a goal of raising collective consciousness. To be complacent, is to hit the iceberg.

It is this collective consciousness, along with natural laws, that forms our reality. In this way, we are most connected to all of humanity and to all of nature. If our world appears to be overly committed to evolving through recurring violence, we have only ourselves to blame. We are a people who have always had a history of violence.

Over the previous few centuries, many scientists have believed that the fate of humanity is cast and that we are living out our determined existence. Science was always the study of what can be observed and proven—our material world made of matter. The modern science of physics has changed that view. Physics has discovered that the very building blocks of life, atoms, are not as we once thought. Atoms are not the solid impenetrable material that provides the foundation of our universe along with time and space. For the first time, science is bringing the nonmaterial aspect of our reality into the equation—consciousness. In the words of Nobel Prize laureate Max Planck, who revolutionized human understanding of our atomic and subatomic world:

I regard consciousness as fundamental. I regard matter as derivative from consciousness. We cannot get behind consciousness. Everything that we talk about, everything that we regard as existing, postulates consciousness.

—*The Observer*, January 25, 1931

This puts that indefinable and untouchable phenomenon of human consciousness at the forefront of creating our reality. Matter is no longer the foundation of our reality. It is merely an expression of the consciousness behind it. Viewing history through this new lens brings clarity to the mystery of how periods of extreme violence have ambushed our world and how they reduced us to a species more ignorant and cruel than the lesser animals.

Many of the great spiritual teachers, such as Moses Maimonides (1135-1204), philosopher, astronomer, physician and eminent Torah scholar, recognized the evil in man as simply the absence of goodness. He would teach that the Soul is so susceptible to evil that even the witnessing of evil, let alone being the source of it, will cause the Soul to become sick and unhealthy. Once the Soul is sick, evil no longer appears as evil and can actually be perceived as good and pleasurable. It is in this way that evil gains legs and can overrun entire populations. One can only imagine the widespread sickness our collective Souls must endure from all that has taken place through man's hostility and violence. It's a rare and saintly being who could witness such violence without succumbing to such feelings from within.

Each new day, while most of us face the struggles of earning a living, caring for our families and educating our children, there are still those who continue to scheme and maneuver for the world to move backwards toward the sheer horror of combat with newer technology just itching to be used. Could it be that here in the 21st century, with so much wisdom and history in our collective intellect, we are still undecided as to whether our species will flourish and thrive or self-destruct? If the emerging new science and ancient religion are correct, the answer lies in our collective consciousness—the part of us that maintains our oneness, while itself remains a mystery. A few brilliant scientists of the previous century recognized this overarching sheath of human thought and consciousness and gave it a name—the Noosphere.

The Noosphere

Vladimir Ivanovich Vernadsky (1863-1945), Ukrainian scientist, is considered one of the founders of geochemistry and a key figure responsible for expanding the current view of the biosphere—the second stage in the earth's development after the geosphere. The geosphere is made up of the inanimate matter of the earth—the rock. The biosphere is made up of animate biological life—the plants and animals.

Vernadsky discusses yet another sphere that envelopes the earth and plays a dramatic role in what we are and the reality that surrounds us. Vernadsky's theory refers to this other sphere as the *noosphere*. The noosphere is far more subtle than the geosphere or the biosphere, as it is made up of human thought or consciousness. It is the sphere of human brain activity shaped by the collective thinking of our past and current time. Ironically, it reciprocally impacts the thinking of the time. It works both ways—a receiver and a transmitter. Our thinking is both a product of history while, at the same time, influencing the future.

Two French philosophers had heard Vernadsky speak at

the University of Paris and further developed this theory of the sphere of human thought. Edouard Le Roy (1870-1954) was the student and close follower of Nobel Prize laureate and eminent French philosopher, Henri-Louis Bergson (1859-1941). Bergson professed that experience and intuition trumped rationalism and science in our attempt at understanding the absolute reality that surrounds us. He was an empiricist who claimed that the big truths, the absolute truths, could never be revealed through the process of analysis, but rather only through experience and intuition. To Bergson, when all is said and done, analysis simply reduces an object to its fundamental elements, which are already known. Through intuition we are able to *become one with an object* and discover for ourselves that which is unique and inexpressible in it.

Bergson's notion that intuitive wisdom is superior to rational analysis echoes the teachings of the Hindu Swami Vivekananda. In his *Complete Works of Vivekananda*, the author makes it clear that to gain Enlightenment one must first learn to *"feel from the heart."* He then draws a comparison between heartfelt understanding and that of the intellect: *What is the intellect, or reason? It goes a few steps and there it stops. But through the heart comes inspiration. Love opens the most impossible gates. Love is the gate to all the secrets of the universe.*

French scientist and priest, Pierre Teilhard de Chardin, was a third key figure with Le Roy and Vernadsky in popularizing the theory of the noosphere. Of the three, Teilhard is most often credited with coining the term noosphere and giving it definition. In Sir Julian Huxley's introduction to Teilhard's 1955 book, *The Phenomenon of Man*, he states:

In 1925 he [Teilhard] coined the term noosphere to denote the sphere of mind, as opposed to, or rather superposed on, the biosphere or sphere of life, and acting as a transforming agency promoting hominisation (or as I would put it, progressive psychosocial evolution).

Huxley explains this term, *hominisation*, to denote the process by which the original proto-human stock became (and is still becoming) more truly human, the process by which potential man realized more of his possibilities. Teilhard extends this evolutionary process of humans actualizing their potentials to a future stage where man will have *far transcended himself* —so much so as to require a new name for our species. Huxley further explains:

The different branches of science combine to demonstrate that the universe in its entirety must be regarded as one gigantic process, a process of becoming, of attaining new levels of existence and organization, which can properly be called a genesis or an evolution.

Because Teilhard was forbidden by the Church to publish his writings about evolution, his masterwork, *The Phenomenon of Man,* could not be published until after his death. Many of his scientific colleagues urged him to resign from the Jesuit order; however, he remained faithful and submitted to their requirements. Recently the Catholic Church resigned itself to the theory of evolution. On October 22, 1996, in his message to the Pontifical Academy of Sciences on evolution, Pope John Paul II stated:

Today... some new findings lead us toward the recognition of evolution as more than a hypothesis. In fact it is remarkable that this theory has had progressively greater influence on the spirit of researchers, following a series of discoveries in different scholarly disciplines. The convergence in the results of these independent studies—which was neither planned nor sought—constitutes in itself a significant argument in favor of the theory.

Teilhard, as did others, distinguishes between two types of substance—thinking substance and extended substance. Extended substance being that which occupies the material world, has volume and takes up space. Thinking substance is the substance of the mind. Teilhard's view of consciousness and matter is similar to that of Spinoza who states that *the thinking substance and the extended substance are one and the same substance... but expressed in two ways.* Spinoza goes on to say that *the mind and the body are one and the same thing.*

Teilhard viewed human existence as having both an Outside aspect and an Inside aspect and expressed frustration because science is concerned exclusively with the Outside aspect (physical reality) and essentially ignores the Inside aspect (consciousness). He proposed his theory, The Law of Complexity-Consciousness, in his book, *The Phenomenon of Man*, where he posits that matter becomes more complex as it becomes more conscious. In this way, all matter, including humankind, evolves. The evolution of consciousness is leading all of humanity to its highest threshold of complexity and socialization—the merging of the physical and the spiritual—human with the Divine. According to Teilhard, the conscious sheath that encircles the Earth, the noosphere, is a sort of collective *evolving* Soul. Asserting that all of humanity is moving toward a state of unanimity and oneness brought about by an increase in complexity and greater consciousness, he claims this is what drives the evolution of humans and the universe toward what he called the *Omega Point*. His *Omega Point* is where the material and the spiritual come together—humanity's ultimate consciousness. It may be compared to the Messianic Era, the Redemption, or Nirvana—the ultimate convergence points of human with Divine.

The evolutionary process of self-consciousness began the first time a living creature perceived itself as living, life reflecting on life, the first conscious awareness of self. As Teilhard states:

It is generally accepted that what distinguishes man psychologically from other living creatures is the power acquired by his consciousness of turning in upon itself. The animal knows... but only man, among animals, knows that he knows.
—Teilhard, *The Future of Man*

When for the first time in a living creature instinct perceived itself in its own mirror, the whole world took a pace forward.
—Teilhard, *The Phenomenon of Man*

This ability of the individual to reflect back upon itself leads to the whole human species collectively to reflect back upon itself. At this level of self-awareness and collective reflection, the human species finds itself, in Teilhard's words, *in possession of the super-organism we have been seeking, of whose existence we were intuitively aware.*

Is this highly complex network of thought and socialization already taking form? One could make the case that the modern internet (and World Wide Web) is, in fact, the material expression of the organized web of thought that encircles the Earth as hypothesized by Teilhard some fifty years earlier. Of course, these early twentieth century visionaries were not describing a technological innovation. They were describing the nonmaterial concept of the noosphere. The new technological connectivity that has emerged out of the digital revolution and the internet is merely an outward expression of the noosphere. It is the most comprehensive innovation in human history and points to the Oneness that is at the core of all spiritual teachings.

Our Sages have always taught that we are accountable for every thought, word, and deed of our existence. The noosphere simply puts a face on this concept. If we are offended by the violence and lack of compassion in our world, look no further than what we hold in our hearts. The world reflects us and we reflect our world. It is a cycle that is not easily broken. But there are those who apply effort and persistence to what they know to be spiritually correct, and they alone are making our world more right in the process.

In 1997, Princeton University launched an international project to study the phenomena of collective consciousness. From 1980 until his retirement, Roger D. Nelson, holding degrees in experimental cognitive psychology, with a background in physics and statistical methods, was the director of the Global Consciousness Project (GCP). The project uses technology to study the effects of major world events on global consciousness, such as the death of Princess Diana and the terrorist attacks of 9/11/01.

The Global Consciousness Project maintains a network of random number generators (RNGs) interfacing with computers in 70 locations worldwide collecting data and forwarding it to a server at Princeton University. The program is designed to explore whether the construct of interconnected consciousness can be scientifically validated through objective measurement. The project has been running for over two decades and is not without challenges or critics. The GCP has concluded that: *The experimental results clearly show that a broader examination of this phenomenon is warranted.*

For our purposes, the project represents a true attempt by science to observe and quantify the existence and fluctuations of collective consciousness—a subject that was not a part of the scientific agenda until the last century. It is this intention alone, to bridge consciousness and science, that is to be celebrated as science has never settled for itself the issue of consciousness. For many scientists, consciousness does not exist. Others recognize consciousness as random brain events—a sort of hologram. English biologist and champion of Darwin's theory of evolution, Thomas Huxley, once said that consciousness was *as completely without power of modifying the workings [of the brain] as the steam whistle that accompanies the working of a locomotive engine is without influence upon its machinery.*

The worldview that has dominated our era, and the eras that came before us, has progressively become more science based than religious. Just as Copernicus, Kepler, and Galileo recognized the need to put the sun in the center of our solar system in place of Earth, science is showing the initial signs of coming full circle in recognizing consciousness as the foundation of our material world. Spiritually speaking, this is the only way that we can break free of our limited, rational perspective of reality and gain the vision necessary to behold the Divine.

Although our ancestors had a spiritual worldview, our newly emerging modern, scientific, spiritual worldview is not exactly the same. Whereas the ancient, spiritual worldview was driven by religion; our modern, spiritual worldview will be backed by science. It is important not to make the mistake of thinking science is replacing religion in this new worldview; rather it is merging with it—and the common ingredient in both is spirituality. At the end of this emerging process, both science and spirituality will share the limelight of a new worldview. Simply put, the truth of religion will be supported by the truth of science. In order for this epic merger to take place, both institutions will need to concede to the validity of the other. In the words of Albert Einstein: *Science without religion is lame, religion without science is blind.*

Teilhard was clearly moving in the direction of another convergence besides that of mind and matter—that of religion and science. This should not come as a surprise since the merging of science and religion was a part of Teilhard himself being both a Jesuit priest as well as a brilliant geologist and celebrated paleontologist. He believed in evolution and participated in numerous excavations to discover human fossils. He was part of the team that discovered Peking Man, a group of fossil specimens discovered between 1923-1927, near Beijing. In 2009, these fossils were dated to be approximately 750,000 years old.

Years later, Heisenberg asked Bohr about the argument in favor of extending quantum theory to accommodate human consciousness. Bohr replied:

This argument looks highly convincing at first sight. We can admittedly find nothing in physics or chemistry that has even a remote bearing on consciousness. Yet all of us know that there is such a thing as consciousness, simply because we have it ourselves. Hence consciousness must be part of nature, or, more generally, of reality, which means that, quite apart from the laws of physics and chemistry, as laid down in quantum theory, we must also consider laws of quite a different kind.

—Heisenberg, *Physics and Beyond: Encounters and Conversations*

Bohr recognized the validity of the notion of consciousness, but chose to distance himself from it, labeling it as mysticism and relegating it to the science of psychology and spiritual teachers such as Buddha and Lao Tzu.

In his book, *Across the Frontiers*, Heisenberg arrives at the profound conclusion: *Not only is the Universe stranger than we think, it is stranger than we can think.* Clearly these physicists were seeing reality through a new scientific lens—one that was at least open to the spiritual aspect. Even those who began their investigation as atheists often concluded with the possibility of God. This point is made apparent by the following words of Werner Heisenberg: *The first gulp from the glass of natural sciences will turn you into an atheist, but at the bottom of the glass God is waiting for you.* Heisenberg further states:

In the history of science, ever since the famous trial of Galileo, it has repeatedly been claimed that scientific truth cannot be reconciled with the religious inter-

pretation of the world. Although I am now convinced that scientific truth is unassailable in its own field, I have never found it possible to dismiss the content of religious thinking as simply part of an outmoded phase in the consciousness of mankind, a part we shall have to give up from now on. Thus, in the course of my life I have repeatedly been compelled to ponder on the relationship of these two regions of thought, for I have never been able to doubt the reality of that to which they point.

In an article published in the May 2009 issue of the European Journal of Physics titled *Mysticism in Quantum Physics: The Forgotten Controversy*, Harvard historian Juan Miguel Marin does an in-depth analysis of the key players attending the 1927 Solvay Congress regarding where they stood on the issue of mysticism in quantum physics. Marin identifies a significant difference in the tone of the ongoing science vs. religion debate over the past century: *Science vs. religion is a very recent forced choice that the founders of quantum mechanics would have never recognized, much less accepted.*

One of the key players at the 1927 Solvay Congress was Nobel Prize laureate Wolfgang Pauli (1900-1958), a theoretical physicist and one of the early pioneers of quantum mechanics. Pauli worked closely with Swiss psychiatrist and psychoanalyst Carl Jung in an attempt to unravel such questions as the role of consciousness in quantum theory. He was also greatly influenced, as were a number of his distinguished colleagues, by German philosopher Arthur Schopenhauer (1788-1860) who wrote in his famous work *The World as Will and Representation: Physics is unable to stand on its own feet, but needs a metaphysics on which to support itself, whatever fine airs it may assume towards the latter.* Schopenhauer held a similar belief as the Buddha and Eastern mysticism in that all human suffering finds its origins in one's attachment to desires.

In his book, *Across the Frontiers,* Heisenberg called Pauli's philosophy one of *lucid Platonic mysticism... which involved a synthesis embracing both rational understanding and the mystical experience of unity.* Pauli responded to this saying: *I do not believe in the possible future of mysticism in the old form. However, I do believe that the natural sciences will out of themselves bring forth a counter pole in their adherents, which connects to the old mystic elements.*

We often think of physics and psychology as being unrelated; however, they became related in the last century through these two gifted scientists—Wolfgang Pauli and Carl Jung. Not only would these two men close the gap between their respective fields, they would also narrow the age-old gap between mind and matter. Similar to Spinoza's *dual-aspect monism,* Jung and Pauli viewed the mental and the physical as two aspects of one underlying reality. In fact, in similar fashion as the ancient teachings of Hinduism, Buddhism, and Taoism, Western science would begin to see the validity of a reality whose essence knows no gaps—no separations—Oneness.

In their 2014 book of essays, *The Pauli-Jung Conjecture and Its Impact Today,* compiled by Harald Atmanspacher and Christopher A. Fuchs, David A. Laveman opens his essay titled *Business Leadership, Synchronicity, and Psychophysical Reality,* by saying:

In the second half of the mid-20th century, boundaries between traditionally separate domains of physical, psychological and cultural inquiry were breaking down at an accelerated pace. Established disciplines such as the natural sciences, anthropology, sociology, and religion were beginning to notice connecting patterns of behavior and thought across cultural domains. Their findings raised significant epistemological questions that challenged the materialist worldview dominant in science since the 17th century. Investigations into the nature of the most fundamental particles of the material world revealed a different order of reality where the previously 'universal' Newtonian laws of physics did not apply.

Carl Jung confirms this notion of an underlying reality that is the foundation of our world's apparent multiplicity:

Undoubtedly the idea of the Unus Mundus [one unitary world] is founded on the assumption that the multiplicity of the empirical world rests on an underlying unity, and that not two or more fundamentally different worlds exist side by side or are mingled with one another. Rather, everything divided and different belongs to one and the same world, which is not the world of sense but a postulate whose probability is vouched for by the fact that until now no one has been able to discover a world in which the known laws of nature are invalid. That even the psychic world, which is so extraordinarily different from the physical world, does not have its roots outside the one cosmos is evident from the undeniable fact that causal connections exist between the psyche and the body which point to their underlying unitary nature... The background of our empirical world thus appears to be in fact a unus mundus.

From the time of Rene Descartes and Isaac Newton, Western science has maintained a materialistic worldview—the world is fundamentally a world of matter, both observable and measurable. In the last century, Quantum Physics revealed a new worldview whereby the basis of our material world is non-material—non-material forms that are a part of a non-visible realm. If these forms are non-material and invisible, why should they be considered as real? The short answer to this question is that they are real because they have the ability to manifest in the real world and have impact; they exist in the form of potentiality.

In 1975, Fritjof Capra (born 1939), an Austrian-born American physicist published his groundbreaking book, *The Tao of Physics: An Exploration of the Parallels Between Modern Physics and Eastern Mysticism,* where he drew a parallel between quantum physics and the teachings of Hindu, Buddhist, and Eastern philosophy. After its first edition the book has since been published in 43 editions in 23 languages. It was especially astonishing in the mid-70s, for a scientist such as Capra, to boldly profess that modern science and ancient mysticism share a common denominator:

We shall see how the two foundations of twentieth-century physics—quantum theory and relativity theory—both force us to see the world very much in the way a Hindu, Buddhist, or Taoist sees it, and how this similarity strengthens when we look at the recent attempts to combine these two theories in order to describe the submicroscopic world... Here the parallels between modern physics and Eastern mysticism are most striking, and we shall encounter statements where it is almost impossible to say whether they have been made by physicists or by Eastern mystics.

Capra states that the purpose of his book is that of an exploration of the link between modern physics and the mystical traditions of the Far East. He begins by illustrating that he does not stand alone in his theory by quoting three of the greatest scientific minds of all times.

The general notions about human understanding... which are illustrated by discoveries in atomic physics are not in the nature of things wholly unfamiliar... Even in our own culture they have a history, and in Buddhist and Hindu thought a more considerable and central place. What we shall find is an exemplification, an encouragement, and a refinement of old wisdom.

—Julius Robert Oppenheimer

For a parallel to the lessons of atomic energy... we must turn to those kinds of epistemological problems with which already thinkers like the Buddha and Lao Tzu have been confronted, when trying to harmonize our position as spectators and actors in the great drama of existence.

—Niels Bohr

The great scientific contribution in theoretical physics that has come from Japan since the last war may be an indication of a certain relationship between philosophical ideas in the tradition of the Far East and the philosophical substance of quantum theory.

                                            —Werner Heisenberg

Capra returns us to the genesis of Western science; the early days of Greek philosophy. Here, in the sixth century B.C., we find a culture whose worldview does not distinguish and separate science, philosophy, and religion. Tracking the evolution of Western science over the course of three millennia, it is apparent how intellectual thought has turned away from its mystical beginnings to develop a worldview that is in sharp contrast. Now, having just crossed the threshold of the new millennium, the new science recognizes the potential of having a new worldview that is essentially mystical. If nothing more, Capra (and a number of his distinguished colleagues) was saying that modern science is increasingly validating spiritual perceptions and mystical beliefs concerning our reality.

The *spiritual scientific worldview* remains in its infancy. Science still maintains a materialistic view of reality, keeping a tight grip on its materialistic bias. Although there are a number of nonmaterialist scientists who are continually emerging, for the most part, science does not recognize any reality except physical reality.

Also, initially, materialist neuroscientists not only denied the existence of a Soul, they often regarded the mind as an illusion created by the brain. Neuroscience, the study of the brain's functions and the nervous system, is a field that has been around for over a century. Although, according to the

Society for Neuroscience, it was not established as a unified discipline until 1971. For most of its history, neuroscience learned about brain function by studying the brains of animals. Yet it became apparent that the human nervous system was far more complex than those of lesser animals.

Human brains not only functioned as lesser animals to achieve sight, hearing, eating, body movements, etc., the human brain was also involved with such things as language and moral reasoning. Originally these concerns were kept under the umbrella of philosophy. Recently, however, a new field emerged, Cognitive Neuroscience, which consists of contributions made in part by psychology and philosophical reasoning. The term, *cognitive neuroscience*, was coined in the late 1970s by Harvard, Princeton, and M.I.T. Professor George A. Miller (1920-2012), who was the recipient of the National Medal of Science, and by Michael Gazzaniga (born 1939) professor of psychology at University of California, Santa Barbara, and elected to the National Academy of Sciences.

The field of Cognitive Neuroscience was a reaction to the 20th century's stimulus-response approach of behaviorism, which, at best, came up short in explaining mental abilities and processes related to knowledge, thought, evaluation, reasoning, judgment, decision making, memory and the like. This was the start of the modern scientific study of the mind. This revolution that began at Harvard led to the founding of Cognitive Science, including experimental psychology, linguistics, computer science, artificial intelligence, and neuroscience. At this point, neuroscience was no longer just the study of the brain; it also included the study of the abstract concepts of mind, intelligence and knowing. While behaviorists did recognize the existence of thinking, they identified it as a behavior, and were reluctant to view unobservable mental thought processes as worthy of scientific study. The new *cognitivists* argued that thinking impacts behavior and therefore cannot be considered a behavior.

Psychologist George A. Miller, along with colleagues Jerome S. Bruner, psychologist, (born 1915), and Avram Noam Chomsky, philosopher, scientist, and author, (born 1928), founded the field of Cognitive Psychology. On September 11, 1956, George Miller recalls leaving the second day of the Symposium on Information Theory held at MIT, *with a strong conviction, more intuitive than rational, that human experimental psychology, theoretical linguistics, and the computer simulation of cognitive processes were all pieces of a larger whole, and that the future would see a progressive elaboration and coordination of their shared concerns.* In his 1967 book, *Cognitive Psychology,* Ulric Neisser (1928-2012), known as the *father of cognitive psychology,* recalls that MIT symposium and its impact on the emergence of modern cognitive psychology and the growing disappointment with behaviorism.

Before the 1980s, interactions between neuroscience and cognitive science were rare, however, after the launch of Cognitive Neuroscience the ground was being laid to integrate with the approaches in neuropsychology and neuroscience. Add to this, advances in modern brain mapping technology such as MRI and PET allowing enhanced research and investigative experimentation.

In his 1995 book, *The Creative Loop: How the Brain Makes a Mind,* Syracuse physics professor, Erich Harth, describes in elaborate detail what it might entail to determine exact brain states:

We would want to know in every millisecond (the time it takes a neuron to fire) which of the 100 million or so neurons are active and which are not. If we denote activity by a "1" and inactivity by a "0," this would require a string of 100 billion zeros and ones every millisecond or 100 trillion every second. To give a running account of the true neural state, I would have to produce in every second something like 110 million books, each containing a million symbols. This awesome record is to be compared with my mental states as they occur.

Dr. Harth's elaborate description of the workings of the human brain gives us a feel for the complexity of what goes into our experience. It is so vast and complex that even the most advanced computer system pales by comparison. Even beyond the intricacies of the brain are those of the mind. At least the brain is an organ that can be examined and analyzed; the mind and its related consciousness remains a mystery. It is through the portal of the mind and the recognition of our consciousness that we are able to gain access to the spiritual realm. In this journey into the discovery of the Soul, the greater part of who we are remains hidden for most of us throughout our entire lives. This is why we say that the spiritual journey begins as an investigation.

Scientific vs. Religious Method of Investigation

In science it often happens that scientists say, 'You know that's a really good argument; my position is mistaken,' and then they would actually change their minds and you never hear that old view from them again. They really do it. It doesn't happen as often as it should, because scientists are human and change is sometimes painful. But it happens every day. I cannot recall the last time something like that happened in politics or religion.

–Carl Sagan

Before we even begin this section comparing scientific and religious inquiry, let's be clear that what follows has nothing to do with Divine design or evolution, nor does it attempt to estimate the age of the planet earth. Rather we will explore the disparity between the current and historic methodology of religious and scientific investigation. This exploration will not include the findings or conclusions of either inquiry, but will examine the investigative styles and strategies of both disciplines.

Examining the discoveries of science over the past millennia, it is doubtful that anyone would challenge that science has come a very long way since the early Greek and Roman civilizations. This is especially apparent if we include medicine and technology under the umbrella of science. Examining the strides made by religion over the same period, the results are far less impressive.

For example, advances that have been made within the lifetime of the average 80-year-old reflect progress from a time when most people did not own their own telephone to modern children carrying pocket devices that connect them globally, offering not only voice, but images and video connection. This same time span has taken us from horse and buggies to manned rockets into outer space, from influenza epidemics killing entire communities to transplanting healthy hearts into those dying from failed ones.

There is no stretch of the imagination that can claim comparable strides made by religion. Such claims would have to address the objectives of transcending man's inhumanity towards his fellow man or the average person putting concern for the wellbeing of one's neighbor over one's own self-interest.

So why have science and technology had such a bountiful run while religion has had to stumble and tire just trying to keep up the façade? Is it because science is based on truer principles and has had greater predecessors? Are the great geniuses of science viewed as giants in comparison to the great sages of religions? Fortunately for us, such is not even close to being the case. The collective spiritual wisdom of humanity's teachers is in no way less than that of our techies and medical greats. There is, however, one glowing difference between these two groups—the methodology of investigation and teaching. For the most part, science works inclusively and with cooperation, while religion has taken on the path of exclusivity and disparity. One doctor's breakthrough surgical procedure becomes the new surgical standard for all doctors; a new microprocessor discovered by one team of engineers will eventually be adapted by all other innovators.

In religion, the greatest saint of one denomination is often not even recognized by other religions. To this day, Jesus is kept tethered to Christianity, Mohammed is followed exclusively by Muslims, and you will rarely find the clergy of either faith studying the teachings of Buddha. These are three of the greatest spiritual minds in human history. Followers claiming insight and transformation in their names are counted in the billions, yet it is not customary for religious followers to study all three. This is never the case with science, medicine or technology. Other than the purely economic incentives to do otherwise, these fields learn and grow from the discoveries by others in their fields.

During the momentous sequencing of the human genome, Francis Collins, director of the Genome Project, recounts how the geneticists and researchers throughout the world, each night, would post their daily findings online to be shared with everyone else. In one glowing report, Collins recalls the jubilation felt by all when such discoveries as the genetic cause of diseases such as sickle cell anemia were discovered. What strides might religion have made over the centuries had there been this kind of cooperation and teamwork?

Religion appears to have taken a similar approach to that of its wicked sibling, politics, in which progress is only acknowledged within the confines of its own party. Like politics, religion should never become an exclusive club representing only its own members. The betterment of humanity is the authentic purpose of religion, politics and science. Yet it is difficult to imagine political parties working harmoniously for the common good, or to even imagine Judaism, Islam and Christianity sharing that sacred piece of real estate in Jerusalem.

When we look at the number of truly great spiritual leaders who have taught throughout human history, we find a relatively small number as compared to the extraordinary number of renowned scientists. The Buddha once said that there have only been a limited number of enlightened beings that lived in this world. Regardless of the exact number, it is safe to say that their recorded thoughts and insights are an invaluable treasure to the rest of us. If there were such a person alive today, we would hope that all people would do their best to promote and preserve his or her teachings, rather than mock this person for not belonging to our exclusive club.

It is human nature to defend our religious beliefs, but it is unbridled egoism to challenge the beliefs of others with little more than personal opinion as our foundation. Those who condemn others to eternal damnation or designate as nonbelievers those who have different views, never recognize that their behavior is scorned by the spiritually gifted. There are far too numerous examples throughout history where people have slaughtered others in the name of righteousness, never recognizing the greater sin in feeling victorious with innocent blood on their hands.

Many adherents to religious doctrine even repress the teachings of their own spiritual greats when they appear inconsistent with current doctrine. As it is, our great teachers have been few and far between. Moses taught for about forty years; Buddha is said to have taught for forty-five years. Most scholars place the time of the teachings of Jesus between eighteen and thirty-six months. Yet the Four Gospels collectively contain only about 2.5-3 hours of direct quotes from Jesus. Even if Jesus' active ministry was only for two years, there would have been considerably more teachings than what is currently presented.

A recent discovery unearthed a rich treasure of recorded teachings of Jesus. These scrolls included the Gospel of Thomas and the Gospel of Mary. Yet this wealth of new information was not made readily available to the public. According to such authors as Michael Baigent, *The Jesus Papers*, allegedly, much of this new cache of spiritual wisdom was confiscated and, in some cases, scrolls were actually burned.

If a discovery were made of Einstein's lost notebooks containing new information about his scientific discoveries, would any scientist choose not to read them or worse yet, have them burned because they do not comport with current scientific theory? What is it about the religious investigation that causes the seeker to care more about protecting what is already known at the cost of new discoveries? This difference between the investigative minds of science and those of religion seems to reflect the different objectives held by each. In science, the ultimate objective appears to be the discovery of truth. It seems that the ultimate objective of many religious leaders appears to be the need to be right, protecting what is already known and accepted—even at the cost of compromising newly discovered truth.

Today's scientists examine the work of their great predecessors, study their teachings and analyze their discoveries before taking the old truth to the next level. A scientist recognizes the obligation to advance the field and add to the discoveries of his or her esteemed teachers. We may be in awe of the great names of science such as Galileo, Copernicus, Newton, Pasteur, Freud, Einstein, Heisenberg, Curry, Watson, Fleming and Salk, but few contemporary scientists would accept that truth stopped with their discoveries centuries ago.

In the grand field of science, even when initial reactions resist the suggestion that its greatest minds might be fallible, ultimately, the scientific community refused to be tethered to such ideas and the quest for scientific truth propelled it forward. Isn't it time for us to recognize that the vast influence of religion deserves the same kind of scholarly approach as science?

Carl Sagan (1934-1996) was an American astronomer, astrophysicist and author of more than 20 books and 600 scientific papers. He received great recognition during his illustrious career, including the NASA Distinguished Public Service Medal in 1977—NASA's highest civilian honor. Sagan was truly a scientist with an open mind concerning the existence of God, and one who often asked the big questions.

> *How is it that hardly any major religion has looked at science and concluded, "This is better than we thought! The Universe is much bigger than our prophets said, grander, more subtle, more elegant?" Instead, they say, "No, no, no! My god is a little god, and I want him to stay that way." A religion, old or new, that stressed the magnificence of the Universe as revealed by modern science might be able to draw forth reserves of reverence and awe hardly tapped by the conventional faiths.*
>
> — Carl Sagan, *Pale Blue Dot*

It appears that both science and religion have let us down. Religion has not instilled the virtues necessary to uplift humanity into the Era of Altruism. Religion has been in conflict with itself, always vying to gain the coveted position of the Only Way to the Divine. This lack of compassion and acceptance of others seems to be at the root of all that is anti-spiritual in nature. Man cannot seem to be right unless making his fellow wrong—it is the way of the ego.

Similarly, science has also let us down by not recognizing the lack of morality of those who govern us. Science was late in recognizing that the momentous discovery of nuclear fission was beyond the maturity of mankind. The failings have reached crisis proportions in the last half century.

Max Planck: Science has Taught Man how to Think
In 1927, Max Planck was the first recipient of the Lorentz Medal for his enormous contributions to theoretical physics.

It was given by the Royal Netherlands Academy of Arts and Sciences. Four years later, during his interview, J.W.N. Sullivan asked Planck: *What do you think is the chief importance of science in mankind?*

He replied: *I put first the part it has played in making men more intelligent. The effort to create science has led men to adopt a certain method of thought... The development of intelligence is the development of the art of successful thinking. Science has shown men that, to be successful, a certain way of thinking is necessary. By pursuing this method one can gain real knowledge.*

Sullivan: *Do you think that mankind has progressed?*

Planck: *Man has progressed in the sense that he has acquired a greater mastery of natural laws. This mastery has necessitated, as I have said, a progress in intelligence, and it has led to great material progress. For all the material advantages of our civilization can be traced, of course, to our mastery of natural laws. Both in intelligence and in material matters, mankind has progressed.*

Sullivan then asked Planck if mankind has progressed morally.

Planck: *No, I do not think there has been any moral progress.*

The moral character of man expresses itself in different ways in different ages. The beliefs that led to witch-burning are no longer held. Man does not, nowadays, manifest his impulses in that way. His growth in intelligence has made such things impossible. But this does not mean that he has a kinder heart. Modern man finds outlets for his impulses along different lines, but I can see no improvement in the moral character he displays. I do not believe that man has progressed morally.

It is not the possession of truth, but the success which attends the seeking after it, that enriches the seeker and brings happiness to him.

In 1944, Max Planck said,

As a man who has devoted his whole life to the most clear-headed science, to the study of matter, I can tell you as a result of my research about atoms this much: There is no matter as such. All matter originates and exists only by virtue of a force which brings the particle of an atom to vibration and holds this most minute solar system of the atom together. We must assume behind this force the existence of a conscious and intelligent mind. **This mind is the matrix of all matter.**

Planck regarded the scientist as a man of imagination and faith, "faith" interpreted as being similar to *having a working hypothesis*. He also said:

Both Religion and science require a belief in God. For believers, God is in the beginning, and for physicists He is at the end of all considerations... To the former He is the foundation, to the latter, the crown of the edifice of every generalized world view.

The spiritual quest is to see reality as it truly is, without it being obscured by collective dogma, personal biases and preconceived notions. While religion has always maintained that truth was its top priority, history has shown numerous examples of the truth being secondary to various political agendas. When religion sought to maintain existing beliefs rather than discover new dimensions of truth, it lost its Soul. As so many spiritual teachers have taught—the purest form of truth is found in the present moment as opposed to those of the past and future.

Fortunately, as religion became institutionalized and compromised by the demands of any large social and political establishment, science picked up some of the slack by conducting its own investigations into the true nature of reality. Although science and religion have often found themselves at odds, we are now at a time where they will both need to recognize and respect one another. Our worldview is shaping into one that could be called *spiritual science.*

Nearly fifty years ago, Grace Cooke, co-founder of the White Eagle Lodge in England, wrote these prophetic words:

The time will surely come when scientists, through their discoveries in the realm of physical science, will be faced with the truth that there is a spiritual as well as a physical universe. And when man discovers the wisdom of studying spiritual science, he will enter the most wonderful, the most beauteous world, for in doing so he will quite plainly see the true way of life, and will naturally develop all the God-like qualities inherent in himself.

— Grace Cooke, *The Wisdom from White Eagle*

In Summary...
This chapter begins a historic inquiry into the development of our materialist, scientific worldview. Science began impacting our worldview as far back as the ancient Sumerians and Greeks, some 4,000 years before the Christian Era. Aristotle is recognized as the first true scientist. Nicolaus Copernicus triggered the Scientific Revolution of the 16th and 17th centuries by formulating a new model of the heliocentric universe. Along with Galileo and Sir Isaac Newton, these scientists overhauled our entire view of society and nature.

The shifting worldview during the Age of Reason, or Enlightenment, was characterized by the continuing face-off between the theories of science and the beliefs of religion throughout the 18th century. By the 19th century, the ideas of the enlightenment philosophers were being expressed by bullets and cannonballs, becoming known as the Age of Revolution.

The 20th century brought with it the greatest scientific contributions in human history—advances in information and communication technology, as well as medical innovations that advanced healthcare. However, the discoveries of 20th century science would also expose the world to horrific weapons of mass destruction and warfare—the new normal of acceptable atrocities. It is here that our collective consciousness became darkened by a century of hostility and violence; world wars and cold wars; government sponsored genocide and military sanctioned rape.

This chapter painfully examines the darkened

nature of the collective consciousness into which we were all born. So often we rack our brains in search of a reason to explain our feelings of anxiety, depression or fear, never recognizing that source to be found in our collective consciousness rather than the events of our individual lives.

Having examined the *content* of the current noosphere, chapter six delves into the *concept* of the noosphere itself. Our understanding of collective consciousness took a quantum leap forward in the first part of the 20th century when scientists Vladimir Ivanovich Vernadsky and Pierre Teilhard de Chardin developed and popularized the philosophical concept of the noosphere. Merriam-Webster's dictionary defines noosphere as *the sphere of human consciousness and mental activity especially in regard to its influence on the biosphere and in relation to evolution.* Teilhard extends this evolutionary process of humans actualizing their potential to a future stage where man will have *far transcended himself —so much so as to require a new name for our species.*

This notion of Teilhard's coincides with the *big question* posed by J. Krishnamurti and Dr. David Bohm as to whether humanity can break free from the conditioning of who we have been to become who we have never been. And, according to Nobel Prize laureate, Werner Heisenberg, this future waiting for humanity's evolution is far grander and infinitely more mysterious. In Heisenberg's words: *Not only is the Universe stranger than we think, it is stranger than we can think.*

As *cognitive neuroscience* emerged into the scientific study of the mind in the 1970s, the stage was set for science to become a partner with religion in guiding the mind toward discovering the Soul. In the words of Nobel Prize laureate Max Plank: *There can never be any real opposition between religion and science; for the one is the complement of the other. Every serious and reflective person realizes that the religious element in his nature must be recognized and cultivated if all the powers of the human Soul are to act together in perfect balance and harmony.*

Part I has been a review of humanity's endless quest for spiritual truth. While science has done an extraordinary job of discovering almost every aspect of the physical world, our collective consciousness remains shrouded in mystery. Part II of this book will navigate the spiritual path to higher consciousness.

PART TWO

In Search of the Soul

While Part One of this book explores the history and evolution of humanity's collective consciousness toward spiritualization (often viewed through the lens of religion, philosophy, psychology, and science), Part Two focuses on our own personal, spiritualization process toward discovering the Soul. It is important to establish and trace who we have been collectively before embarking on an individual quest to discover our true, spiritual nature. Although the experience and teachings of others who have navigated the spiritual waters are invaluable, ultimately it is our direct, personal experience that brings us to Self-realization (discovering the Soul). Here, it is stated by cultural historian (specializing in the religions of South Asia), Alistair Shearer, in his Introduction to *The Yoga Sutras of Patanjali*:

> *The desire to know the Self [Atman or Soul] is implanted deep within each of us... Only when we realize our true nature, and the individual mind becomes infinite, shall we be satisfied. This Enlight-*

enment is the first and last freedom; it is the state of effortless Being.

> *"We shall not cease from exploring*
> *And the end of all our exploring*
> *Will be to arrive where we started*
> *And know the place for the first time."*
>
> —T.S. Eliot, *Little Gidding*

The quest for the Self has enthralled mankind since the dawning of desire. Ancient myths of every culture tell the same story of our search for wholeness. As the mind explores its own depths, it uncovers archetypal images that sustain and guide the journey inward. These are the signposts on the old road home, half remembered from long ago. Each society hands down its stories of the great heroes who have made the journey before us as reminders and examples to those who follow.

> —Alistair Shearer, *Introduction,*
> *The Yoga Sutras of Patanjali*

The passage used by Shearer from the poem, *Little Gidding,* by Nobel Prize laureate Thomas Stearns Eliot, suggests a prevailing theme in the ancient Eastern writings regarding the experience of realizing the Soul—an experience that is both novel and familiar simultaneously—the origin and destination of our journey.

CHAPTER SEVEN

Embarking on the Spiritual Journey

Traditionally, the spiritual journey has been perceived and discussed as the mortal seeking the Divine—man in search of God. Dr. Abraham J. Heschel published his renown book, *God in Search of Man*, in 1955. Here Heschel looks at this quest from a unique angle—*i.e.*, the Divine on a quest for humanity. After centuries of interpretation and manipulation, the ancient scriptures of our ancestors are no longer resonating with many contemporary minds.

Such ideas as religion, immortal Souls, God and the like, separate all too many from their greater potential. Unfortunately, an appropriate lexicon has not yet surfaced to afford such individuals access to their spiritual quest. Even though the topic of this book is *unchurched spirituality* (spirituality outside of the context of religion), the most authentic sources of spiritual wisdom come from the scriptures of the world's great religions and the teachings of the Saints and Sages. Furthermore, even though we rely on religious scriptures and teachers to gain spiritual understanding, it is nonetheless the premise of this book that people can orchestrate their spiritual encounter and arrive at full spiritual realization without depending on religious narratives, dogma, rituals, or the approval of any religious community.

It is the spiritual experience, rather than the expression of the experience, that we seek. Regardless of the words used, a person blocked from recognizing their spiritual nature is like a computer without connectivity. Certainly, there is valuable software and perhaps even a few good games installed on the hard drive, but the computer's functionality without connectivity is sorely limited. The purpose of this chapter is to consider the benefits of getting connected.

The Search for God: Most persons do not even suspect the real existence of God... There are others who, through the influence of tradition, belong to some faith or another and acquire the belief in the existence of God from their surroundings. Their faith is just strong enough to keep them bound to certain rituals, ceremonies, or beliefs; and it rarely possesses that vitality which is necessary to bring about a radical change in one's entire attitude toward life. There are still others who are philosophically minded and have an inclination to believe in the existence of God, either because of their own speculations or because of the assertions of others. For them, God is at best a hypothesis or intellectual idea. Such lukewarm belief in itself can never be sufficient incentive for launching upon a serious search for God. Such persons do not know of God from personal knowledge, and for them God is not an object of intense desire or endeavor.

A true aspirant is not content with knowledge of spiritual realities based on hearsay, nor is he satisfied with pure inferential knowledge.

[The] *True aspirant seeks direct knowledge of spiritual realities.*

Although the aspirant cannot be content with second-hand knowledge or mere guesses, he does not close his mind to the possibility that there could be spiritual realities that have not come within his experience... he is conscious of the limitations of his own individual experience and refrains from making it the measure of all possibilities.

—Meher Baba, *Discourses*

Setting Personal Intention: Initiating the Spiritual Quest

The destination of our spiritual journey is the epiphany declared in Chapter One's opening quote: we are not physical beings *seeking* the spiritual experience; rather we are spiritual beings *having* a physical experience. Gaining this insight, we are able to transcend our limited perception of reality. This includes the limited perception of our *own* identity. Many spiritual teachers refer to this transformative shift as *transcending the ego* or *detaching from self-interest*. The higher rungs of the spiritual ladder are not accessible to those who are anchored in self-interest. The ego, with its predisposition toward self-interest, is a critical mechanism for survival and flourishing in the material world. However, this very same mechanism obscures and impedes spiritual awakening.

Transcending the ego and eliminating any trace of self-interest is unrealistic for most. One should not become discouraged, however, just navigating the path toward transcendence is beneficial and highly liberating. And, just getting the ego leashed brings clarity to our perception, improves interactions with others, and enhances our experience of life. In other words, it is in our best interest to overcome our self-interest.

Prior to embarking upon the spiritual journey, it's prudent to measure the *octane* quality of our fuel. Attitude is the fuel driving the bus. It is a sound practice to keep it monitored. Here are five different attitudes that typically characterize and influence our initial approach to the spiritual hypothesis of being more spiritual than physical. That we are more spirit than flesh may not already be a part of our previous conditioning and this hypothesis may be one that the intellect does even not consider reasonable. Long before we can ascertain the truth about the spiritual hypothesis, we must first determine our attitude *toward its possibility*: **Rejecting the possibility; Resistance to the possibility; Open-minded to the possibility; Acceptance of the possibility; Embracing the possibility**.

These five typical variations of mindset share one common denominator. Each is based on our previous conditioning. In other words, we characteristically react based on who we've been in the past—our previous beliefs, teachings, family religion, education and, to some degree, our DNA. It's human nature to develop deeply rooted thought and behavior patterns as we mature. These habitual thought patterns allow us to make snap decisions without recreating the wheel with every new challenge. If every cloud has a silver lining, and this is the *silver lining* of previous conditioning, let's look at the *cloud*. When deciding whether to take the dish out of the hot oven without a potholder, preconditioning comes in handy. When it comes to deciding whether our true nature is physical and perishable, or spiritual and enduring, previous conditioning is more of a liability. The stakes here are far too high to rely on the image reflected in the rearview mirror.

When deciding on the authenticity of their own spiritual nature, the most common mistake people make is failing to reserve judgment until the question is fully understood. It would be foolish for a person uneducated in advanced mathematics to attempt to answer a question about the Riemann Hypothesis—a problem that has not been solved since Bernard Riemann proposed it in 1859. It is equally foolish for us to attempt to respond to the spiritual challenges put before us by the great Saints and Sages without adequate learning and personal experience. As our Sages have said, *hold judgment of the spiritual until we have attained understanding of it*. Study and learning lead to the understanding that forms the foundation of spiritual realization. This realization takes place during one's personal experience of the spiritual. At the point of true realization, a person is fully capable of deciding *what is truth* and *what is illusion*; not before.

Until we have the clarity brought by personal realization, we are in a state of spiritual confusion—actually double confusion—*i.e.,* being confused, yet unable to perceive our confusion. Through admitting our own confusion, we get past our **resistance** and achieve the more powerful attitude of **openness**.

Certainly, **openness** to the possibility of the spiritual hypothesis of being more spiritual than physical is a higher-octane approach than rejection; however, because attitude tends to be in a state of flux, at least initially, we needn't put too much emphasis on where we currently stand. Each new turn on the learning curve impacts our ability to navigate the path. Like an athlete who brings home Olympic gold, there was that initial dream that ignited the path to attainment. There are no Olympians who have not followed the traditional routine of training and sacrifice prior to achieving the moment of glory. So it is with the venture before us—how we perform is based on intention and effort; the decisions we make today determine who we become tomorrow.

In the physical world, we believe that our results are based on what we do to achieve them. *It is an act of doing that leads to what we have in life.* There's plenty of evidence supporting the accuracy of this widely held belief. Spiritually, what we are **doing** is secondary to who we are **being** in terms of generating results. When we reach the ultimate state of human consciousness, *i.e.,* the consciousness of a spiritual being having a physical life in a material world, we will find ourselves in a reality that has only been known by an enlightened few. Although it has taken centuries upon millennia to reach this critical moment in the evolving collective consciousness that Teilhard called the noosphere, we are arriving at a time when ordinary people can experience what previously was reserved only for extraordinary masters.

There are those who seem gifted in their ability to imagine their spiritual nature and the spiritual structure at its source. Others have had no reference prior to their first taste of the spiritual nectar. Whether it is imagination or curiosity, interest or passion, that initiates our **embracement** of the spiritual—it is steadfast **intention** and unbridled **enthusiasm** that will keep us advancing on course. As with so many worthy goals, we achieve the spiritual experience because we set our intention to achieve it. As we proceed on the path, discipline will transform into enthusiasm.

Responding to the Whispers Within

Whether we call it a quest, a mission, an exploration, a journey, the path, the Way, or some other name, there is an aspect of human consciousness requiring us to turn inward in order to recognize our true nature and purpose. Regardless of how subtle the *calling*, this quest is as serious and resounding as a fire alarm. As with an alarm, if unheard or ignored we imperil our safety. While it may seem unreasonable and overstated that we could miss our very purpose in being because we simply failed to heed an alarm, it is even more mystifying when discovering that the alarm is both inaudible and invisible by design. When you put it that way, you have a valid point. This is precisely why relatively few people answer the call.

Unfortunately, the only way to hear this silent alarm is to search for it. Why would someone search for fire without smelling smoke? Perhaps in response to a trusted advisor declaring, *something's burning!* For now, let our trusted advisors be those explorers who have navigated these waters before us. Their message is initially the same—gain the knowledge left by others to conduct your own investigation. There has yet to be a Sage in history who advised us to remain indifferent and wait for someone else to provide us with the discovery of our own Soul.

Just as great geographic explorers, such as Leif Ericson, Marco Polo, Columbus and Magellan, increased our awareness of the outer world; so too, there have been great explorers of our inner world. These spiritual explorers, as well as the forerunners and founders of the science of human psychology, opened new passages into uncharted, inner territories. Like their geographic counterparts, they left us maps. Regardless of whether referring to the former or the latter group of explorers, we have responded individually to their calling, and paved the way for the masses to respond collectively.

All explores, whether of space, mind or spirit, have a responsibility to those impacted by their discoveries. In the previous century, scientists went from exploring continents and solar systems, to molecules and atoms. With the historic breakthrough of splitting the atom came enormous moral implications concerning how this new science would be put to use. When the awesome power of this discovery was applied to weapons of mass destruction, many scientists expressed concern and overwhelming feelings of guilt.

Can mankind be trusted with such power? Did science put the potential of mass destruction, or worse yet, total annihilation in the hands of those who cannot be trusted with such enormous responsibility?

> *Scientists, therefore, are responsible for their research, not only intellectually but also morally. This responsibility has become an important issue in many of today's sciences, but especially so in physics, in which the results of quantum mechanics and relativity theory have opened up two very different paths for physicists to pursue. They may lead us - to put it in extreme terms - to the Buddha or to the Bomb, and it is up to each of us to decide which path to take.*
>
> —Fritjof Capra, *The Turning Point: Science,*
> *Society, and the Rising Culture*

Capra's words ring as true today as when he wrote them in the early 1980s; the scientist's responsibility is not just intellectual; it is moral as well. Whether we are heading toward the Buddha or the Bomb, toward Enlightenment or destruction, is a decision that rests with each of us and with all of us. This is the *communal* nature of spiritual responsibility; what happens in the community impacts the individual and what happens within the individual impacts the community—the world. There is no greater contribution a person can make to the world than the contribution made by elevating his or her own consciousness.

Charles Darwin recognized the evolutionary patterns in all living species, by scientific observation of the material world. He recognized that species that survive are those that best adapt to their environment. Later, scientist and Jesuit priest, Pierre Teilhard de Chardin, expanded the theory of evolution by adding the non-material aspect of consciousness. According to Teilhard, it is consciousness that is evolving and expanding. The phenomena that we then see in our material world are expressions of that evolving consciousness.

Spiritual Exploration Requires a Moral Compass

Tracking the events of history, we cannot escape the pervasiveness of violence. Like the lower animals, humans have had to fight to survive. From ancient times to this morning's news—wars, killing, conflict and violence dominate the front page of mankind's story. This is the outward expression of the survival mechanism by which we live. In a world of *fight to survive*, tremendous resources are dedicated to enhancing our ability to kill. It appears that in order to kill, we have taught ourselves to hate, and by our ability to hate and wage war, we have survived. The downfall of war, however, is that it does not bring lasting peace. Ironically, these very survival skills of hatred and violence that have sustained us, now threaten us. As we move toward a new era of enlightenment and higher consciousness, we must *unlearn* these dark skills that served our past. According to the spiritual Sages, we will not survive through war and hated, but only when we master their opposites—peace and unconditional love. They taught not only to love our friends and neighbors, but to also love our enemies—admittedly a tall order.

Again, the downfall of war is that it maintains and promotes hatred and hostility. War is the outward expression of violent consciousness; peace is the expression of loving consciousness. We have no chance for world peace until our collective consciousness allows it. In the opening of Genesis, we see that *Light* is created first; consciousness precedes matter. To create a world of peace and compassion, we must first create the necessary consciousness. We were given this power/gift to create our own consciousness; it is our responsibility to unwrap this gift. Although we shoulder the responsibility as individuals, the results of our efforts devolve to us collectively. The events that are currently unfolding are rooted in the consciousness that they express. The past collective consciousness of hostility and violence has brought us to where we find ourselves today. Whether it will define our future is up to us individually.

In the teachings of scripture, each person brings light or darkness into the world; this is the choice we each face. There is no better way to bring light into the world than to take on the *spiritual quest*—the *search for the Soul*. The reason we are not able to access our Soul and the spiritual realm is that their presence is concealed beyond our immediate awareness. When humanity believed that the world was flat and the earth was stationary, it was because the truth was beyond our previous awareness. The key element for greater understanding has always been expanded awareness and elevated consciousness. So it is with the spiritual quest. To gain access to the spiritual realm and discover our inner Souls, we must raise our consciousness.

Our search begins by identifying its three key elements: **The Spiritual Pursuit; The Spiritual Structure; The Spiritual Process**.

We begin by establishing *the spiritual pursuit*. Unless we have clarity regarding the purpose of our spiritual quest, it will be difficult to cultivate the motivation necessary to achieve it. In its simplest terms, the purpose is to discover our individual Soul and then use it as a portal to gain access to the spiritual structure. Although this purpose may be easily stated, it is not so easily accomplished. The premise here

is that there is a part of our being that remains undiscovered or partially discovered. In order to move to the next phase of our existence, it is necessary to realize this hidden portion—and to do so while still in our material form. The spiritual pursuit is the responsibility of all born into this life.

Souls exist within *the spiritual structure*. It is not part of the physical reality that surrounds us as perceived through our physical senses. Although our Sages teach that physical reality is a structure within the spiritual structure, it is best to save this more complex concept for later. It serves our immediate purpose to distinguish the physical and the spiritual as separate dimensions, even though they are both dimensions of the same reality. In other words, Jesus taught over 2,000 years ago: *The Kingdom of Heaven is amongst us.* It is here, although not perceptible—at least not in the same way that the mountains and oceans are perceived.

To fulfill our spiritual responsibility, we will need to familiarize ourselves with the spiritual dimension. This method is used to gain access to the spiritual domain; through understanding the spiritual structure we are able to perceive it. Once perceived, we have entered it. Of course, it is not our body that enters the spiritual dimension; it is our mind, or more precisely, our consciousness. With this purpose in mind, we will explore and familiarize ourselves with the spiritual structure.

After defining the **spiritual quest** and establishing the **spiritual structure** (where our work will take place), we will explore **the spiritual process** employed to achieve our purpose. The spiritual process we will discuss is highly effective; however, it is only a jumping off point. The ultimate process will emerge once you have established a strong connection with your inner core—the Soul. Just as each person has his or her unique mind and personality, so each Soul has its unique aspects as well. The convergence of one's physical identity with his or her spiritual identity will result in an individualized approach for moving forward. In other words, once you meet the Soul, she will teach you the way she wishes to be courted. (Note: Like ships, the Soul is often referred to in the female gender.)

Keep in mind that we are attempting to bring clarity to something that is beyond description or explanation. What we hope is that we will get close enough to the spiritual for it to *accept our efforts and grant us clarity*. One does not learn about spirituality in the way one learns math or biology. Access to the Soul is not through linear learning. It is more through the experiences we encounter as we move through the process. If one recognizes these experiences and responds to them appropriately, they will reveal the intended insights. It will be useful to keep this in mind as we begin the journey.

Accepting the Path of Spiritual Exploration

Defining the spiritual path will be as difficult as any other task we attempt in the remainder of the book. Up to now, our focus has been to recognize and describe the worldview of which we are all a part and which has shaped our individual outlook. It is the collective thinking and perception of all who have lived before us and who now share our current lives. This is our world with its history, its great teachings and its epic disasters. Through it all, we have arrived at this moment, with this mind and this identity.

The challenge is to *drill deep*—to gain access to an expanded version of ourselves and to raise our consciousness—i.e., to climb the spiritual ladder. With broadened consciousness, we will take on a new identity—one which expresses our new consciousness. This expanded consciousness is one that breaks through a self-perception limited to a physical body and mind. This *epiphany* allows for a self-perception that is not limited to the physical beings we believe ourselves to be. Once a person recognizes his or her self to be a spiritual being living an earthly life, the initial objective of our spiritual quest is accomplished. This experience of an expanded self, changes everything; it cannot be forgotten; it redefines what it means to be alive. It is the *New Drug* that songwriter

Huey Lewis sings of that won't make you sick, crash your car, or hurt your head.

This is the defining experience we are all seeking, regardless of whether we recognize our Soul's need to be expressed or not. Until our sacred submarine rises to the surface, we have no choice but to perceive only our physical nature and our material world. Of course, it's only normal that without firsthand experience of our spiritual nature, we are left with the impression that there is nothing beyond the physical. As the great spiritual teacher, Swami Vivekananda, points out, the only way to define the spiritual is through direct personal experience.

With this epiphany, we will know firsthand what Zen Master Suzuki means by *Satori,* and the great Sages meant by the *Mystical Experience.* This altered state of consciousness opens a person to the experience of spiritual ecstasy described by Saint Teresa of Avila—*an apparent convergence of matter and spirit.* Until our physical and spiritual aspects are expressed jointly, we remain uncertain as to our spiritual nature. Once this merger takes place, our life comes under new management.

One might ask, *can a 21ˢᵗ century person take on the quest of ancient prophets, saints and monks?* For most of us the answer is: *Absolutely, what other choice do we have?* If we cannot pursue our spiritual path within the confines of our current living situation, it may be out of reach. Modern people needn't quit their jobs, leave their families, foreclose on their house and kiss their 401k good-bye in order to pursue their spiritual awakening. Our spiritual development requires very little reorganization of our lives. It is about the refinement of our character and the expansion of our consciousness. Even if a life has been enmeshed with illicit, unethical and immoral conditions, a person is free to engage the spiritual process as it will eventually repair all that needs repairing.

After asking the question *can it be done?* the next logical question is: *Should it? Why should a person take on the quest for self-realization? Why should a person feel the need to raise their consciousness?* The short answer is that the path enhances the experience of living in the physical realm. Regardless of who we are and the life we have led, there is only so much that can be achieved within the physical realm. We all face the same physical destiny—aging and death. Even before each of us must face our inevitable mortality, that moment comes when we ask: *Is this all there is?* You reflect on how many times you have been to the fair of life, had your face painted and rode the pony. As a teenager, you rode the roller coaster and shared a kiss in the tunnel of love; later in the grandstands, you watched the horse races while enjoying a beer. Each new stage of life brought greater freedom and privilege, more adventures and experiences until you tasted all the tastes and danced all the dances. Then, in some form, that inevitable question arises: *Is this all there is?*

Be warned however, this is not a 30-minute infomercial to get rich selling real estate or lose weight without dieting. The likelihood of your success pales in comparison to the chances of your giving up. Of the many crowded at the starting gate, only a rare few will be found at the finish line. The journey has many distractions and it is not easy for the subtle whispers of the invisible to break through the clamor of our alluring physical world. If it were easy, our physical nature would have lost its appeal long ago.

While theologians, philosophers, mystics and even some modern scientists have recognized that our reality is comprised of more spiritual than material—more consciousness than matter—it still remains awkward to keep the mind spiritually engaged in our day-to-day experience. Ancient monks retreated into caves to gain access to their inner world. To enter *modern cave dwelling* does not require that we climb the Himalayas or join a monastery. All that is required is proper solitude and inner communion to open the inner gates to the spiritual experience. This solitude can take a variety of forms depending on the mental discipline of the practitioner. Those well-seasoned in the art of meditation have been known to reach their inner cave while commuting to work on a crowded train.

Contentment Is a State of Being; Not a Condition of Having

It is not so much the environment or the conditions that bring you to your spiritual journey, as it is the commitment you have to getting there. In the material world, our success is often based on what we do to attain it. Successful people are skilled at *doing*. We do what it takes to get what we want. This is a fundamental mechanism to gaining more in the material world. We learn to *do* school, to *do* our jobs, and become good at *doing* friendships, and eventually *doing* marriage. What we have in the material world is often a reflection of what we have done.

In the spiritual realm, this mechanism is somewhat shifted. What we *have* is a reflection of who we are *being*. It is our *being* that is the determining factor. The path to spiritual development is a path to enhanced being. Interestingly, however, is that while enmeshed in the process of *doing*, we often lose sight of *being*. People can be totally unhappy, unhealthy and unloved while working hard to have more, thinking that as soon as they get what they want, they will recover their happiness, regain their health and find love. It is nothing less than tragic how many good people have fallen prey to this logical, yet wholly ineffective strategy. Of course, there are those who have attained material success and have also become accomplished at *being*. These qualities are not mutually exclusive. Although, those who are continually *obsessed* with having more, and those who are *obsessed* with the lack of having enough, face similar challenges in *becoming* and *being*. In both instances, the impact is a distraction from our spiritual path. Those who run hard to survive, as well as those who run hard to stay ahead, are both running hard and are unable to *be still*.

To gain spiritual clarity, one must develop the ability to be still. Stillness applies to both body and mind. There are those who can be mentally still while the body is involved in movement. Swimmers, skiers, even runners have claimed to enter a meditative state while engaged in these vigorous activities. Of the two types of activity, mental and physical, stillness of the mind is the more critical. To gain the meditative state, the mind must be at peace, <u>inactive</u> and totally content. The spiritual learning here is: ***to be content is not a function of having; it is a function of being***. In the material, world our identity revolves around physical life where our worth is determined by what we have. In the spiritual dimension, what we have can be a reflection of a self-serving nature—the polar opposite of what we seek spiritually.

This spiritual path, as we are calling it, is to gain access to a "greater" sense of being—our higher self. Achieving this objective, each of us will still be the same person. We will, however, be an expanded version of our former selves. For those who never have had a spiritual experience or have never cultivated religious faith, the idea of an expanded version of self may seem alien and somewhat off-putting. This is to be expected and should not interfere with the overall process. Spirituality is never truly understood until it has been experienced firsthand. That is why our initial objective revolves around this experience. The approach is first conceptual, and then experiential.

The Spiritual Path—Gaining "Eyes Blessed with Vision"

Many of the great Sages of religion have actually compared our existence and relationship with God to a child's game of "hide and seek"—where God has hidden and it's our job to seek and discover. What makes the game more challenging are all of the distractions that God has included to divert our attention away from the object of the game. The desire to find God is seldom felt in people as strongly as the physical desires to which we are *enslaved*. (*Enslaved* is frequently used in scripture to describe our strong attachment to physical desires and ego gratification.)

Spiritual teachers often agree that the demands of our material lives are at the forefront while the impetus to fulfill our spiritual nature is in the shadows, if not eclipsed. It is obvious that survival in this world requires that we pursue the challenges of growth, education, relationships and earning a living. Failure to acquire these basic skills will negatively impact our lives. Seldom do we rank our *spiritual goals* in the same priority as our need to achieve social and professional skills. When a parent is asked, *how is your son doing?* — the reply is most often about his family development and career status. If the response is, *my son has become a very loving and honest human being with compassion for all living things* —the inquirer might well assume, *oh he must be single and unemployed.* Our lives are most often measured by our material accomplishments, regardless of the character qualities we achieve along the way.

According to our Sages, our presence in the material world is intentionally influenced by the allure of the material attractions surrounding us. It is the essence of our mortal existence to be imperfect. For anyone to perceive themself as being perfect, it can safely be assumed that this is a misperception or the result of an overactive ego, as Earth has been blessed with very few perfect beings, if any. One should not view his or her *flawed* nature with shame and embarrassment. It is that flawed nature that provides the basis for the spiritual quest. Without something to be rectified, without the darkness lurking throughout our world, this level of existence would be the same as the level above us. Our Sages teach that it is the mission of our existence in the material world to refine and elevate it. Always keep in mind that our physical existence in the material world is the precise environment for the Soul to achieve that mission.

Individually, the spiritual mission is the same—to discover our personal character imperfections and correct them. Further, each of us has the wherewithal to know the refinement that is lacking and the means to correct it. Even if our character flaws are obscured and we are resistant to recognizing them, if we sincerely wish to take on character refinement, we will admit that we already know our imperfections. Once we stop trying to conceal and disguise them, they will be apparent to us as well as those closest to us.

Physical World Provides Conditions for Spiritual Enhancement

The physical realm is a world characterized by time and space. At its most fundamental level, this is a world of change. No two moments are ever identical in this world. At a bare minimum, our world and all who inhabit it are a moment older with the passing of each moment—there is no escaping it.

Apparently, this is not the case in the spiritual realm. The higher levels of existence are outside the realm of time and space, not made of physical matter—they are unchanging and permanent. Because of this difference, the physical world, which is a lesser world, holds great significance for the higher spiritual realm. To put it simply, a spiritual being, namely a Soul, can enter this world and have access to change. A Soul can have the ability to become enhanced during its time on earth, or conversely, a Soul may also be corrupted.

For some, this discussion may sound like a science fiction novel, but if the reader can set that aside for a while, the idea can be quite compelling. This discussion leads to inevitable questions concerning the purpose of our lives. Although our actions in the physical realm are significant, those same actions have even more significance in the spiritual domain. We stand in line at a popular restaurant for the quality of the meal, not so much for the enjoyable conversation that we have while we wait to be seated.

The Responsibilities of Being a Bodymind

The spiritual texts and commentaries reveal a twofold purpose to our lives—both a physical purpose and a spiritual one. There is clearly a physical purpose that relates to our physical world. This purpose is not the focus of this book, but needs to be addressed as it relates to the spiritual. I would lightheartedly characterize this purpose as being similar to the tagline used in the US army commercials—*be all that we can be*. This purpose fits under the heading of achieving our potential, both in terms of body and mind.

It is worrisome to confront the notion that each of us is actually responsible for our individual body's potential, let alone the mind's potential. Imagine how differently our bodies would age and decline if we actually allowed them to reach their potential. In my career in the field of aging, I have seen people who came close to achieving their full body potential. Their bodies had maintained youth and vitality into their eighth and ninth decades. Of course, most 80 and 90-year-old bodies are a far cry from youthful and vibrant. Today, over 15% of us are diagnosed as chronically ill during childhood and will remain that way throughout our entire lifespan. While some conditions are genetic, in most cases, such illnesses are due to the poor care and treatment of the body.

Beyond the task of maintaining a body's potential is the far greater challenge of reaching the mind's potential. The human brain has been compared to a computer. The computer has been described as the methodical acquisition, processing, storage, access and communication of information. While the brain uses chemicals to transmit information and the computer uses electricity, this basic definition rings true for both.

With its 100 billion neurons, and its trillions of connections, the human brain is essentially a huge computer yet only weighs about three pounds—talk about micro technology. There is one glaring difference between the human mind and the computer—consciousness. The mind functioning within the brain is aware of itself. Whereas computers can detect changes in their environment, there has yet to be any report of a computer having any consciousness of its being (at least at the time of this writing).

Think of all the updates a computer must regularly face, yet they still become obsolete in a few short years. Just imagine if we updated our minds so consistently. For many of us, our mind received its most formative programming during our school years. That programming was often focused on the unwavering requirement to acquire a passing grade. For far too many adults, if we exclude occupational learning, our minds have not been significantly challenged since our school years. This is a long way from meeting the mind's need for daily exercise and expansion.

The human body is a factory that runs on proper nutrition and vigorous movement. Considering that contemporary bodies gain the majority of their caloric intake from convenience and fast foods, and an increasing amount of our movement is derived from activity behind the steering wheel, pounding a keyboard, or operating the remote, it's safe to say that our factories are not running at full production and will likely shut down before their expiration date.

For most of us, reaching our *golden years* is no longer sufficient. The goal, as stated in Psalm 92, is to *grow old still blooming.* Without this experience of *elder blooming*, we are left vulnerable to the ravages of time and the perishable nature of flesh. Without adequate attention to healthful aging, our thin veneer of *gold* will inconveniently peel away leaving raw nerves exposed to the elements.

In all fairness to modern times, the achievements in science, medicine and technology are unprecedented. While there is much to be proud of in the modern achievements of science, medicine and technology, these collective material advances are not the focus of our discussion. Rather, it is the actualization of our personal potential that's being explored.

There is a substantial link between the fulfilling of our physical potential and achieving our spiritual purpose. Again, our focus is directed more toward the latter. Pursuing a spiritual path often appears to go against the grain of our physical nature. Some refer to the first law of nature as *survival of the fittest.* From molecular structure, throughout the plant and animal kingdoms, to the existence of humankind, *the strong eat the weak.* In the case of humans, of course, *eating the weak* is figurative.

However, this apparent law of nature is the opposite of those underlying our spiritual consciousness. From the spiritual perspective, the strong *support* the weak. It is for this reason that some of us are stronger than others, that we might use our strength to benefit those who are less able. For our immediate purpose, suffice it to say that this is the linkage between physical fitness and the spiritual path. Directions to function in this manner appear throughout all scripture, urging those of means to care for widows and orphans, the disabled and the elderly, as well as those caught in misfortune or the victims of hardship.

Jesus is quoted in Mark 10:21, saying: *You lack one thing: go, sell all that you have and give to the poor, and you will have treasure in heaven...* Our Sages refer to our spiritual purpose using a variety of words, but the meaning of their words tends to be very similar:

> **Our spiritual purpose is to break though the obstacles of concealment, connect to spiritual Light, and reflect it into the world.**

This appears so simple and innocent when we see it in such a concise and pithy sentence. Don't be deceived, there is a lifetime of commitment and effort associated with this endeavor. Although, just like the path of getting healthy and fit—it comes with benefits. Briefly, the benefit that tends to keep people coming back for more is that most coveted and often obscure treasure of modern times—happiness. There is great joy associated with being physically fit, psychologically balanced and spiritually attuned.

The massive project of sequencing the human genome provides an apt analogy for understanding the spiritual pursuit. Scientists have recognized that each of us comes into this life with a unique blueprint—DNA. According to geneticists, each of us has what could be called *genetic typos*, which increase our chances of developing certain diseases. Once recognized through a personal genome, people can adjust their lifestyle to compensate for, and possibly avoid, what might have been the cause of a premature death or disability.

The findings of the genome project can be applied to our spiritual quest. We each come into this world with *character typos*. Left undetected and uncorrected, they become a source of great suffering. Even though these *flawed* character traits can negatively impact our life's potential, this is not the primary issue regarding them. These very traits define what needs correcting to fulfill our spiritual purpose. These *flawed* character traits are the obstacles keeping each of us from recognizing our spiritual essence.

Just as many of these *flawed* traits are universal to humans, like our *genetic typos,* many are unique to our individual characters. For example, some people have no problem being faithful in marriage, while others must undertake radical inner transformation to even have a shot at fidelity. Similarly, some people can engage in light social drinking without becoming alcoholics, while others, due to their personal genome, must avoid alcohol like the plague.

Consequently, the spiritual journey begins with the recognition and acceptance that each of us is an imperfect being in an imperfect world. It's taught that this very human condition of imperfection is how the Creator enabled us to be co-creators. Through human imperfections, the world was left undone—incomplete. In every other detail of nature—the earth, the universe, the plants, the animals, right down to the subatomic level—we find perfection. There is a fundamental piece of creation that was left for each of us to finish—our human character. That is to say humanity is the *fixer-upper* requiring each of our personal touches for completion.

Interestingly, many people exploit their *flawed* character traits to get more than their share in the material world. Some have done quite well with their adept ability to deceive and take advantage of the good nature of others. Some of the most important careers in our world—judges, lawyers, clergy, politicians, educators of our young, those in charge of caring for our sick, those in charge of public safety and even those entrusted with the safekeeping of our money—attract some of the most diabolical and corrupt characters. Such people have an uncanny ability to tune out the many warning signals consistently emerging from their conscience, urging them to change their ways before the final buzzer sounds. Unlike Ebenezer Scrooge, we don't all get a night with the spirits to assure us our redemption.

Just as Charles Dickens suggested in his 1843 classic tale, *A Christmas Carol*, there's a great deal riding on our own personal transformation while still in human form. As the ghost of Jacob Marley, Scrooge's deceased business partner warned him: *I wear the chain I forged in life... I made it link by link, yard by yard; I girded it of my own free will...* When Scrooge attempts to placate Marley by responding that he was a good man of business, Marley replies: *Mankind was my business. Their common welfare was my business. In life, my spirit never rose beyond the limits of our money-changing holes! Now I am doomed to wander without rest or peace, incessant torture and remorse.*

The Physical Is Designed to Obscure the Spiritual

It is useful to recognize the design principles of the physical and spiritual domains. The physical domain is designed to distract us from our spiritual mission. Not only are there countless earthly delights waiting to be discovered and experienced, so too, the deck is stacked against us. It's the nature of the human design to crave the pleasures woven throughout the fabric of our lives. It is no coincidence that both the pleasure of chocolate and our craving for it exist simultaneously. We are literally designed to crave the pleasures that surround us. The pleasures of life have the function and purpose of distracting us from our spiritual path.

This is not to say that humans are wrong to engage in the physical pleasures of life. The *wrong* is in allowing them to distract us from our mission. The challenge is to have it both ways. The *beauty* and *music* of physical life can be utilized to inspire us toward our spiritual path. The pleasures of this life are fleeting, yet they reflect the eternal bliss that is our true destiny. They are meant to be enjoyed as an incentive toward what awaits. Keep in mind that the life that we see before us— the world that appears so solid and lasting—is only the corridor leading to the life we are meant to have. The dilemma is that life in the corridor becomes so distracting that we fail to progress toward the gates at the end of the hallway. I find this to be one the most astounding teachings I've encountered during my initial studies: we are not even existing in the life for which we were created. It's been stated in many ways and by many different Sages and Prophets, and almost every one of these enlightened teachers affirms that we are in some sort of preparation phase that will determine what happens next.

Our Bodies do not have Souls; Our Souls have Bodies

The ancient mystical tradition, Kabbalah, and the new science of quantum physics, profess a very similar concept regarding what is apparent and what is concealed. Both science and the spiritual suggest that all we can perceive through our five senses, without benefit of instrumentation, makes up less than $1/1000^{th}$ of a percent of all that exists. The mystics say that the physical portion of creation is but a tiny speck of all that was created. Most is hidden. The task for humans is to bring the hidden into clear focus.

The window into the spiritual dimension is found within. The primary unseen part of creation to be recognized is our own Soul. If there is a part one to our spiritual mission in life, it begins with the recognition that we are spiritual beings having a physical experience—not vice versa.

This one simple adjustment in perspective becomes a total shift in our sense of self. It is sufficiently complex to recognize the notion of an undetected Soul lurking within the human psyche. This new layer suggests that "I" am the stranger visiting on the Soul's turf—not vice-versa. My identity and my sense of self have never imagined that there's a *landlord* on this property where I've been *renting* space. This concept of the Soul being the source of the mind and body and the true custodian of our identity is not an easy adjustment to make. It requires perseverance and effort. Once the shift in perception is attained, it will prove well worth the effort. The greatest *tool* to assist us along the spiritual path is *sensing* of *our own Soul*.

I use the word *sensing* as an interim phase that comes

before *experiencing the Soul*. The stage that precedes the *sensing of the Soul* is the *imagining of the Soul*. Imagination is often the starting point for many spiritual experiences. Just as our bodies are an expression of our DNA, our character is an expression of our Soul. Science has made great strides in linking human abilities, proclivities and abnormalities to our unique DNA. Everything from the color of our eyes to the score of our golf game can be attributed to the particular sequence of our genetic information.

Our Souls also express themselves in our physical world. The Soul itself has no form, but it's nonetheless able to express itself in physical form. If one looks into the mirror, one will see the expression of his or her genes. Looking into identity, one will discover the expression of his or her Soul. In essence, you are the expression of your Soul in the physical world. If your character is prone to doing dastardly deeds, and you believe your behavior is a justifiable means to getting what you want, it is this flawed character trait that offers the Soul its opportunity. The correction of this trait benefits the Soul as well as the person. Less than honorable behavior is a clear indication of our individual duty roster and a glimpse at the core agenda of our individual spiritual mission. This will become the central focus of our later discussion. For now, suffice it to say that the discovery of the spiritual realm requires our own individual effort. Spirituality is not given to us in the way adolescent puberty is provided, without any effort of our own.

Spiritual awakening is an achievement. It is attained by reaching through a multifaceted approach that includes both *learning* and *yearning*. During our youth, we experienced many lasting changes brought on by puberty. Neither learning nor yearning were prerequisites to our maturation—to our voice changing or our hormones raging. The changes of puberty were "automatic updates" programmed into our hard drives right out of the factory. They do not require our interest or participation. Nor are we entitled to any merit when they occur. In this sense, puberty is the polar opposite of spiritual transformation. There is no need to *achieve* puberty to benefit from its transformation, but we must *achieve* spiritual transformation.

It's also no mystery as to the *purpose* of puberty; most people are well aware of where this transformation is taking us. The link between the outcomes of puberty and the propagation of the species has been well documented over the years. However, why we require spiritual transformation remains obscured. There are no free tickets for this ride, and as a result, most people spend the bulk of their adult lives ensnared in the effects of puberty, while they remain oblivious to all that might be available through spiritual awakening.

Just as puberty is the gateway to an entire new life experience, one that dominates our mind and changes the course of our actions, spiritual awakening has a similar effect on us. Beyond the initial stirring of spiritual awareness, comes the more significant spiritual awakening. It is a "tipping point" where the larger part of who we are is suddenly shifted by a relatively small step—that one piece of the puzzle that makes everything else fall into place. Often a person is completely unaware that he or she has been compiling support for this very shift for an entire lifetime; then, without apparent warning—change happens. In hindsight, for many, it seems as if their entire life has led them to this very occurrence. It's common for this moment to also include a glimpse at their very purpose in being. The real question that lies below the surface of all human life is the *how* and *why* of existence.

What Is the Meaning/Purpose of (My) Life?

The Mystical tradition arises in response to the age-old question of meaning and purpose that is embedded in every human psyche. The Sages teach that by pursuing and answering this question, each person brings about his or her spiritual elevation. For most people, this search does not surface until later life, yet some of the greatest Sages began their quests in their youth; they are the exceptions. Youth is typically a time of great distraction—the physical cravings of life are far too dominant to allow for pondering the *bigger questions of meaning.*

Some people intentionally avoid these questions—actually even rebelling against their persistent nagging. Perhaps they wish to avoid the obligations that come with the answers. Of course, there is no real escape from the search for meaning or its discoveries, let alone the responsibilities that come with it.

By the time we realize the purpose of our physical (material) life, we are usually well along the path to fulfilling it. Society sets us on course toward material fulfillment even before we recognize the need. In the material world, each of us must grow and learn our way into good favor. We become a positive force in society, learning the ways of the world and making our contribution. In today's high achievement societies, almost every influencer is pointed in this direction—parents, schools, our peers, our culture, etc. We are defined by how well we respond to society's ever-changing needs.

Unfortunately, we're on our own when it comes to recognizing and aligning with our Spiritual purpose. It is not a requirement imposed upon us, nor is it even a hot topic of discussion in most cases. While there are numerous *tripwires* that activate our embedded spiritual *software*, the message is often subtle and quickly fades from consciousness.

Spiritual Journey is a Quest for Truth

In life, you don't get all the answers at once. First you must absorb and live with one simple truth. Then later you find another truth—one that may seem to conflict with and negate all you previously learned. Then, from that confusion, emerges a higher truth— the inner light behind all you had learned before.

Learning is not the mere acquisition of knowledge and more knowledge. Learning is a process of making quantum leaps beyond the subjective self. No matter how high a summit you may reach, there is always another peak above.

—The Rebbe, Menachem Schneerson

The spiritual journey is a quest for truth—Absolute Truth (a term used by the Buddha that refers to pure truth without a trace of human bias or falsehood). There is a plethora of truths along the way that lead us to Absolute Truth. Many great teachers, preachers, philosophers, scientists, psychologists, physicians and other truth seekers have investigated their respective areas of concentration and provided humanity with their best discoveries. Such gifts should never be taken for granted—they should not be condemned nor derided by those who do not agree. If the truth fits, wear it. What does not feel right for one person should not be tarnished or ridiculed for the next. It could be just what he or she needs to hear to move forward. Some versions of the truth told by others will resonate with our own experience, whereas other versions may not seem valid in the least. Each version is true within the experience of those who tell it, and that alone is worthy of our respect. We are taught that each of us has a unique perspective and therefore, each has his or her own contribution toward the development of the whole.

As in art, the image is truest in its objective form; it is the interpretation that remains subjective. It is that subjectivity that resonates with some, but not necessarily with all. Fortunately, it is not our job to vote on who is right and who is wrong. Our task is simply to observe what is shown and add to the individual puzzle unfolding for each of us. If it does not fit currently, it can be stored for a time when the puzzle is more complete. Keep in mind that for the purpose of our discussion, the quest for truth is in learning to perceive without obscured vision. As the Buddha teaches, when we are able to perceive Absolute Truth, truth without the shadow of falsehood, we will find ourselves in Ultimate Reality, a reality without suffering.

Looking Through the All-Inclusive Spiritual Kaleidoscope

Our investigation covers three key areas of concern, which have challenged human beings since earliest consciousness:

First: Greater understanding of ourselves. Each of us exists as if we are a character in an ongoing play. While we have been this character from the beginning, we still have many unanswered questions regarding who we *really* are.

Second: Understanding the reality that surrounds us. Every generation has spent endless hours and countless lives investigating the reality that surrounds us. Collectively, we have explored every continent, cave, mountain and ocean. We have plunged down to the smallest particles and waves of the atom and have reached out to the furthest corners of the cosmos. We have tunneled and submerged, drilled and launched; we have probed the world of microbes and charted the galaxies. Although we have increased our sphere of influence and understanding a thousand-fold beyond that of our ancestors, spiritually speaking, we have only yet to scratch the surface of who we are and what makes up our world.

Third: Knowing the source of our existence. Regardless of the period in history, or the nature of our beliefs, humanity has not yet fully come to terms with the *source of our existence.* Science developed its Big Bang theory about the beginning of the physical universe; religion maintains that it is God who designed and created all reality. Whichever model forms the basis of our individual beliefs, the bottom line remains the same—there is no way to know what is correct, at least not in the traditional sense of *knowing.* Whatever the individual quest for truth, each of us arrives at our own understanding of *what* we are, *where* we are and *how* we got here. With this understanding, we gain insight into where each of us needs to go from here.

Even Mere Curiosity Can Lead to Self-Realization

The individual investigation begins with the feeling of curiosity regarding our true nature. Curiosity is an embedded trait in the human psyche. It is said that before the serpent tempted Eve to eat the apple, she was already curious about the forbidden fruit. This very human trait of curiosity is a powerful force. As the Hindus recognized, it is rooted in our essential *need to know.* And in Viktor Frankl's *will toward meaning*, he determined that a life that feels meaningless is a life destined for suffering.

The ancient Hindus taught that our *need to know* is second only to our *need to be*—to exist. In other words, our first order of business is survival—to maintain our existence. Once we feel secure in our ability to fulfill our need to exist, we shift focus to our need to know why we exist. Of course, in order to know why we exist, we will need to know a bit more about the nature of our existence; this is where it becomes complicated.

If we perceive our existence to be limited to our physical life in a material world, we'll fall short of recognizing the overarching themes that define the totality of our existence. All of the great Sages have taught some variation of this key point. The life that we are currently living is *not* the life that we were created for—this is merely the preliminary life. This life is the basement level of a high-rise luxury building; however, we were created to live in the penthouse. Our purpose is to get where we belong. There is no elevator or short cut to the top; we can only get there by climbing our way up.

As the great Hindu saint, Vivekananda, taught, nobody can raise your consciousness or purify your Soul but you. How is it that we find ourselves in the basement? Every aspect of our existence is the expression of our consciousness—nothing more and nothing less. When our consciousness rises, there is nothing that can hold us down; not even past karma—consciousness trumps karma. The very purpose of karma is to enlighten us as to who we have been and who we need to be. Even though karma is associated with pain and suffering, its true purpose is not punitive, but corrective—its function is to guide us through the mire. Once the Enlightenment takes place, karma has served its function and we are liberated from its control.

Simply put, our purpose is to undertake the spiritual journey while still in our physical form. Once we have transcended our physical existence, *i.e.*, once the body has died, the benefits of the spiritual quest are no longer available. The plainest statement of this principle is—a Soul cannot gain credit for recognizing its spiritual nature; only a living human being can gain benefit from the recognition of our true spiritual nature. When the final buzzer of our life sounds, there will be no more points added to our score.

Imagine the life of a caterpillar that would stubbornly choose to be an earthbound worm with feet as opposed to a work of art floating through the air. Unlike the genetically imprinted caterpillar that emerges as a butterfly, we are given the option of failure. Our metamorphosis is not the product of involuntary instinct, but the result of conscious effort and sheer determination. Man, through his own obstinate ignorance, can choose a laborious life of misery and death.

This is not the life our benevolent Creator designed for us—a life of continual misery that culminates in endless death. Nor is this life of struggle the result of a Divine decree of punishment for an age-old sin committed by our first ancestors, as we've been led to believe. All of our trials and tribulations stem from our own choices made with our own divinely ordained free will. We are both inmate and jailer in our own prison—never knowing that the keys to our cell are in our own hands.

The statements of this book are but echoes of the words of those once spoken by humanity's spiritual giants. The message is always the same: take charge of our life in the time we have left. Before our time has passed, we must break through the thin shroud of obscurity that hides our true birthright.

Presented in the remaining two volumes and chapters of this book, is an accessible process by which we can open the door to our own spiritual path. It is a tested approach that can unfold enough spiritual experience to allow us to gain confidence and strengthen our faith in pursuing our own spiritual domain before we are blindsided by a harsh ending. Many of us feel used up and obsolete when our later years hold little relevance compared to our youth. This is a shortcoming of our culture and the times in which we were born that brings such meaningless aging. These are not the years of purposeless activity— instead, they are the most meaningful years of our lives. But this only holds true if we accept the mission to explore the very core of our true existence. The process is one of surrender, exploration and spiritual discovery.

Engaging the Spiritual Journey

Whether we recognize it or not, we are all seekers. To be human is to desire and to desire is to seek fulfillment. What is the source of our desires? —deficiency. Desire is aroused when we feel deficient in some area of our lives. Of course, if there is an absence of termites in the rafters of your home, you are probably not experiencing lack. It's the *perceived* deficiency that generates desire—perception trumps reality. Perhaps the reality of this moment is that you lack an abscessed molar, yet it is unlikely you perceive this as a deficiency.

On the material side of our psyche, often called ego, we attempt to fulfill our perception of deficiency by adding possessions to what we lack. We may have a perfectly fine automobile, yet when our neighbor drives up in a shiny new BMW, it could easily cause us to feel that our car is now deficient. This may sound trivial and superficial, yet this mechanism of perceived lack and desire is at the root of all human suffering.

Seeking to fulfill one's desires for what he or she perceives to be lacking in life can become a dangerous game. For most of us, we entered this game before we were even able to walk or talk. Long before we will ever be able to gain freedom from our desires, we must first recognize the nature of this addiction—want and envy.

One might argue that the desire for more is the foundation of accomplishment; without ambition, a person would sink into mediocrity. While this has some validity in the material world, spiritually, it is utterly false. Do we actually think that if we met one of the great spiritual teachers, such as the Buddha or Jesus, that we would come away with the feeling that this was a mediocre person?

The purpose of our spiritual exploration is to find fulfillment aside from any linkage to material gain—to achieve complete satisfaction and fulfillment from who we *are*, rather than from what we *have*. What we have may determine our status in the material world, but who we *are* will determine our place in the spiritual structure. This is not to say that you can't have a rich material life without compromising your spiritual status. Some of the most spiritually gifted people today are also enjoying vast material success; although, this is not the norm. Wealth *per se* is not evil; it is, however, enormously distracting. As we will see, distraction is one of the key elements that obscures our spiritual exploration and dilutes its discoveries. Spiritual accomplishment from a material position of wealth requires great wisdom, the right priorities and true altruistic desire.

It is said that the Soul enters this life with utter clarity of purpose. There is but one goal and it is poised to succeed. As soon as the Soul becomes encased in physical form, it loses its ability to direct the action. The physical form has its own guiding apparatus, earthly desire that drowns out the guidance of the Soul. The only chance the Soul has to achieve its mission is to break through the noise and distractions of the alluring physical form, the hypnotic trance of the material world. To recognize and understand these conflicting mechanisms between the wisdom of the Soul and the cravings of the senses is to begin the spiritual quest.

An Ancient Tale

There is an ancient tale told by the great Sages of the Jewish Mystical Tradition that echoes the point of our discussion concerning the distractions and desires obscuring our earthly mission. It is the story of young King Jonathan who was forbidden to venture out into the untamed forest without proper escorts to ensure his safety. Resenting this restriction on his personal freedom, King Jonathan occasionally ventures out on his own to experience the unencumbered joy of a commoner.

Removing his royal robe and jewels, the young king disguises himself as a lowly peasant. Since the forest was full of wild beasts and bandits, the Royal Guards were never to allow the king to be unprotected in the woods. Deep in the woods, unescorted, the king is confronted by a ferocious lion. Without a second to spare, he seeks refuge in a short sapling that offers little hope of keeping him out of harm's way. As the lion advances, the tree begins cracking from the weight placed on its slender trunk. Suddenly, King Jonathan has a clear understanding of why the Royal Administrators placed such a limiting policy on their leader. Unfortunately, this insight came too late. The consequences of his immature actions were about to prove fatal. Just as the king was forced to confront his fate, he heard the swish of a hunter's arrow sinking fatally into the beast's neck.

The hunter, Joseph, called out to the young king that he was safe to jump from his precarious perch, assuring him he meant no harm. The hunter had saved his life without even recognizing who he had just saved. "You are too deep in the woods to walk out and your horse has been scared off by the lion. Allow me to deliver you out of this dangerous situation," offered Joseph.

King Jonathan leaped up onto Joseph's horse and the two rode off together. During the long ride, the young king told Joseph that he would like to reward him for saving his life. To this, the hunter laughed and said, "Maybe someday you can save my life and we'll be even." The king insisted that he wanted to provide a more tangible expression of his appreciation. Again, the hunter laughed and said that his new friend appeared to be no better off than himself. The king then told Joseph that he was not what he appeared to be, and that he must demonstrate his appreciation or he would never be able to face himself. "Well," said the hunter, "just what do you have in mind?" "For your bravery today, I will make you a wealthy man." This bold proclamation by a young boy only made the hunter laugh again. "Just how much wealth can a poor boy bestow even if he is earnest in his intent?" Jonathan's reply caused the hunter to gasp, "Wealth that will last past your next ten generations." Joseph exclaimed, "You are speaking of wealth that is known only by kings!" Then Jonathan told Joseph his story. Seeing that the hunter accepted his true identity and bowed before him, the king declared, "I will grant you one full hour in the Royal Treasury. All you can carry out within that hour will be yours."

It should be mentioned that a typical peasant would not amass the riches brought by a single royal jewel within his entire lifetime. While the king had tearfully thanked the hunter for saving his life, now the hunter was overwhelmed with gratitude at the prospect of being a rich and honorable man. King Jonathan instructed Joseph to report to the Royal Treasury in one week hence at noon. "The guards will be expecting you." The two men embraced and each felt blessed by what the other had done for him that day.

The following day the king detailed to the Royal Council the events of the previous day. His advisors gasped at the thought of the nearly fatal events of their imperial leader and they applauded the gallant intervention of the courageous hunter. However, this gasp was exceeded by the one they uttered when the king apprised the Council of his promise. Cautiously, the treasury minister mentioned that an hour is a very long time for a peasant to be given free rein in the Royal Treasury. The young king immediately took offense, questioning what the minister thought his royal life was worth. After an appropriate apology, the minister asked if the king might consent to an alternative reward—something less threatening to the Royal Treasury. A man of his word, King Jonathan would not renege on his promise. With this final declaration, the king left the chamber without addressing any other business that day.

The Royal Council was comprised of men with great understanding and extraordinary ability to achieve objectives. Accordingly, they met to plan how they might minimize the impact of their king's hasty decision. "First, we must find out all there is to know about this hunter—his strengths, and more importantly, his weaknesses."

As it turned out, Joseph had only one love greater than hunting—his love of music. Since the first time he heard his mother's melodious voice singing to him in his cradle, he was entranced by all things musical. From childhood, he had pursued his passion for music. He had managed to obtain a few primitive instruments that he learned to play, bringing him soothing relief from his struggles as a hunter. As a poor peasant, he was never exposed to music played on real instruments by real musicians.

Learning these details, the Minister of Treasury devised a cunning plan. From the time the hunter would enter the Royal Corridor to the Treasure Chamber, the Royal Orchestra would play the greatest music the world had ever known.

On the appointed day, Joseph arrived at the gates anxious to enter the great palace. Nobody in his family had ever ventured inside the palace. Fascinated by all the ornate designs and symbols of power, Joseph eventually entered the Corridor leading to the Treasure Chamber. He was greeted by a celestial melody of the Royal Harp; unlike anything he'd ever heard. He stopped abruptly in his tracks. This heavenly sound was followed by another from an expertly played instrument. With each step another instrument began to play until the music reached a crescendo and Joseph became overwhelmed, falling to the ground and weeping in ecstasy. It was as if time stood still. Joseph felt as if he had been transported to a heavenly chamber, about to come face to face with the Divine. He had never heard anything so moving, so penetrating. Yet he knew that he had a mission and even though the music itself was a great treasure, Joseph was now ready to enter the Royal Treasury.

With a spring in his step, he approached the doors of the Royal Treasure Chamber at the end of the long corridor. Burly guards with serious faces crossed their spears before him, ordering him to halt. He explained that he was a guest of the king and was granted an hour in the treasury. The guards told him that he was due to enter an hour ago. The doors had been kept open for him until one hour past noon. Now the doors are closed and his hour is gone. No matter how much the hunter pleaded and promised, the Royal Guards remained unyielding. Joseph had to face the reality that he had squandered his time while being seduced by the heavenly music. He became lost in the melody that was designed to fill his heart and stir his passions—music designed to distract him from his mission and the treasure that was available.

A Modern Message Found in an Ancient Tale:

Here the great Sages make this overarching assertion—*such is life*. We enter life having clarity as to the spiritual mission we have undertaken and the treasure that we are here to capture. But like the beautiful music in the corridor leading to the treasure chamber, the material world is designed to obscure our spiritual exploration and distract us from our mission.

Not only are there countless earthly delights waiting to be discovered and experienced, but the deck is stacked against us. Our very nature has been designed to cause us to crave the pleasures that are woven throughout our lives. It's no coincidence that both the pleasure of chocolate and our craving for chocolate exist simultaneously. We have been designed to crave the pleasures that surround us. Just like the music in the legend, the pleasures of life have the function and purpose of distracting us from our spiritual path.

Be cautioned not to come away from this parable thinking that the lesson is to avoid all earthly delights, as both indulgence and avoidance are extreme approaches. The key is to walk the middle ground—enjoy the fruits of this life without becoming obsessed or attached to them. It is the ability to gain freedom over our desires that holds the key to navigating the spiritual path in a material world. As long as we are attached to our desire for sense-pleasure and for ego gratification, we are mired in a lesser reality—a reality defined by impermanence, death and suffering.

Ultimately, it's a question of priorities; although the music in the chamber was a delight, the priority was to secure the treasure granted by the king. The life we are living may be filled with delight and even opportunities for more, but there is a spiritual agenda that must eventually become the priority.

> *We do not usually know how to distinguish between what is essential and what is secondary. We spend our lives running about here and there after pleasures that are forever eluding us and leaving us unsatisfied. We try to be happy come what may, without wondering whether we are causing anyone else to suffer in the process. We are prepared to do anything to amass and defend our possessions, which are neither lasting nor true sources of happiness.*
> —Dalai Lama, *Daily Advice from the Heart*

We may be concerned that by not striving to have it all, we will squander our time here. There is a fine line between enjoying the taste of chocolate and making ourself sick. The recommended approach is not to avoid the glorious taste of chocolate, but to lose the obsession. The flaw is not in the external behavior; that is merely the expression of the flaw. The flaw is in our attachment to the physical desires of the material world. How we deal with our desires will either build character or accumulate addictions—either move us forward or cause us to stall and slip back. Further, the worst expression of our addiction to sense-pleasures and ego gratification comes when our lust for pleasure becomes the cause of another's suffering.

The Spiritual Journey leads us to the *sensation* that occurs during what is Soften called *self-realization*; *i.e.*, the epiphany that we are more than what we appear to be. While the word "sensation" is not accurate, as it implies an experience through the senses, for now, we will refer to this *sensation* as what accompanies the spiritual experience. While it is a feeling unlike anything found in our physical experience, it is often compared to the intense emotion of falling in love. However, this comparison also falls short since most human love is linked to ego, while the sensation of spiritual awakening is deeply rooted in the Soul.

There is also the comparison made to the expanded awareness talked about by the professors who conducted the psilocybin experiments at Harvard University—here again, close but no cigar. The *sensation* of Self-realization is unique to the human experience. Nothing within our ordinary human experience comes close to defining this *sensation*. Sensations occur all the time in our physical world. However, this *sensation* is one that transcends our physical realm. Through it, we gain the awareness of being more than we perceived ourselves to be.

Self-realization is the expanded awareness that confirms we are more than a physical being. It may come as a spontaneous flash of insight caused by a particularly soulful experience, or it may be the result of a long and determined effort. The former is often unpredictable and usually not sustainable; while the latter tends to be less dramatic, it's far more dependable. For our purposes, we will focus on this latter sustainable variation of the spiritual experience.

The Personal Path—Onward and Upward
True spirituality has one universal guideline—*onward and*

upward. Regardless of the *tests* and *challenges* set before us, we must find a way to persevere. Even when our lives hit rock bottom, spiritual advisors counsel that this is the perfect place for a rapid ascent. Many of us unwittingly choose this form to advance—slipping back in order to leap forward. Even those who commit grievous sins and live lives of self-serving indulgence are but a single experience away from spiritual awakening. Some Souls seek development through suffering, while others employ the mechanism of Enlightenment. The Soul focuses on the outcome and leaves the process up to us.

The spiritual structure is all-inclusive. Everything—the good, the bad and the ugly—all belong. We are not looking for the *best path*; we are uncovering *our own path*. This is an important distinction between spirituality and religion. Religion teaches that the best path has already been discovered and the adherent must learn this path and follow it. Spirituality teaches that the path one needs to follow already exists within the seeker, waiting to be discovered and followed. This is not to say that religion has nothing to offer the spiritual seeker. On the contrary, the guidance offered by religion is invaluable, but ultimately it is the means to an end, not the end itself.

For most of human history, the greatest spiritual teachings came from religions. Our Sages teach that the greatest religion is found in the greatest temple—the temple of the human heart. All spiritual teachings are designed to gain entry into our own temple. The great spiritual teachers are guides leading us to the teacher that resides within. Here religion is not a record from the past, it is responding to the present.

Jiddu Krishnamurti (1895-1986*),* one of the 20th century's greatest spiritual teachers, was once regarded as the new World Teacher. He was raised towards that end throughout his youth in British India. In 1922, Krishnamurti traveled to the Ojai Valley in Southern California and made it his home. During this time, he experienced a spiritual awakening that caused him to rethink his role as a spiritual "leader" connected with any organized religious approach. He subsequently broke his ties with his mentors and the Theosophical Society to become an independent voice:

> *I maintain that truth is a pathless land, and you cannot approach it by any path whatsoever, by any religion, by any sect. That is my point of view, and I adhere to that absolutely and unconditionally. Truth, being limitless, unconditioned, unapproachable by any path whatsoever, cannot be organized; nor should any organization be formed to lead or coerce people along a particular path... The moment you follow someone you cease to follow Truth... Religion is the frozen thought of man out of which they build temples.*
>
> —J. Krishnamurti

Krishnamurti saw a humanity that is seized by fear and restraint— people unable to explore their spiritual depths as they are confined in "cages" of their own making. He recognized the need for a complete psychological revolution in the culture—a shift in the very core that guides humanity—both individually and collectively. From his perspective, humanity is flawed by an inability to be fully conscious in the moment, and without the ability to be present in the moment, we are not fully present in our lives.

Living Life in Real Time Prevents Us from Missing It

This perspective of Krishnamurti is shared by many of the great Sages. One of the most meaningful benefits of the spiritual path is that it conditions its followers to find themselves in real time. Most of us tend to loiter somewhere between our regrets of the past and our dreads about the future. Even if our *cerebral time travel* is not in the negative vein, it still takes us out of the real and into the imaginary. Although imagination is a valued portal into the spiritual, it's not meant to replace the experience of our life in real time. Too frequently, we experience our lives as passing by without any feeling of connection to the action.

Dani Shapiro (born 1962), is an author and professor of creative writing at Wesleyan University. In her book, *Still Writing: The Perils and Pleasures of a Creative Life,* she draws an analogy between the characters created by a novelist and our own characters who are also being revealed to us through our moment-to-moment reality.

We are revealed to ourselves—just as our characters are revealed to us—through our daily actions. When making my son's breakfast, I try to focus simply on cracking the eggs, melting the butter, toasting the bread. It doesn't get more elemental than that. As I drive down country roads taking Jacob to school, I remind myself to focus on the way the sunlight plays on the surface of a pond, the silhouettes of cows in a field. I've learned that it isn't so easy to witness what is actually happening. The eggs, the cows. But my days are made up of these moments. If I dismiss the

ordinary—waiting for the special, the extreme, the extraordinary to happen—I may just miss my life.
                                                    —Dani Shapiro

What an extraordinary insight to discover: **it is possible to miss our life.** It is similar to watching a movie while so engrossed in unrelated thoughts of work or relationship conflicts that the story unfolding on screen is totally lost. In life, there is no remote control allowing us to rewind back to where we stopped paying attention. Even worse, we are actually accountable for what we missed. In other words, there's no piece of our life that's not connected to all of the rest. If we're going through life without being fully cognizant of actions, thoughts, and intentions, we are bound to get lost; and without a trail of bread crumbs to follow back home, we just might stay lost.

In Part I, we looked into the big picture that led humanity to our collective spirituality in the 21st century. Today's spirituality is in real time—it's no longer history. We are in the *now* of pure spiritual experience in present time. What is currently unfolding is *related* to the past but not *defined* by the past. It is far less predictable than anything previously encountered. It's a spontaneous awakening that has the momentum generated by centuries of evolving wisdom and endless flashes of insight. Our great spiritual Sages are alive today through the words they've left. Yet, what is emerging today is unlike anything our ancestors faced; this is the next progression of what they've ignited.

The ideas and explanations covered in Part 1 were expressed by key people throughout a winding journey leading us to this very moment. For our purposes, their contributions are not presented for judgment—not even for analysis.

They are to be observed and noted as pieces of an elaborate puzzle. When all the pieces fit together perfectly, they reveal a big picture—a picture that generates the experience it holds with no need for explanation.

The Spiritual is at the Root of All Human Endeavors
While it may be difficult at first to distinguish the purely spiritual perspective, as it becomes more familiar, it will be easier to recognize that spirituality is at the root of all human endeavors intending to uncover truth. Spirituality is manifesting while scientists seek to discover the cure for cancer. It is also driving psychologists who probe the human psyche to discover the hidden source of depression and anxiety that plagues humanity. It is even manifesting into form when engineers work to discover innovations that will change the way we live. Anytime humans are engaged in the quest to discover the hidden structure of truth and untapped potential (whether science, philosophy, psychology, art, or even technology) they are on the spiritual path of discovery. Spirituality exists in all forms of truth, not just religious pursuits.

When Swedenborg or Emerson, Allen or James, Freud or Jung, Rodgers or Maslow communicated their experience of truth, it allowed us to get closer to our own experience of truth. When Buddha tells his experience of becoming enlightened, or Jesus tells us of his experience of the Kingdom of God, they have provided us with access to our own enlightenment and Divine vision. Conversely, when Archie Bunker exposes his own bigotry and prejudice, it helps us to recognize those same human defects within our own character. As Jung pointed out, we all share the same root system; the growth we provide for ourselves is shared by all.

Resolution of The All-Inclusive Puzzle

The all-inclusive image we describe is one that is currently formulating in our own mind—mostly within the subconscious. It is our goal to bring this image into focus with the clear, bright light of consciousness. As the image emerges, it will have sufficient clarity requiring no further explanation. Some Sages taught that attempts to add explanation to the emerging image actually causes it to fade. As the Taoist say: *the Tao emerges without words and adding words only moves us away.*

Throughout history, our ancient ancestors as well as our immediate predecessors have been adding their best ideas to what has come before. These efforts provide us with the greatest opportunity to contribute our individual pieces to the puzzle. Each generation, in turn, adds to this endless story, a portion based on its absolutely unique moment in time. The emerging picture includes not only science and philosophy, but draws from each deeply personal perspective as well. It unfolds in a kaleidoscope of imagery, expressed in a multitude of forms—art, music, philosophy, design, technology, and yes... even corruption, war, and murder. It is our story, always changing and continually unfolding. For each of us, the most critical part of our story is the part closest to us—the part just now coming into being.

There are as many viewing points as there are people, both living and deceased. Our most common denominator as a member of the human race is carried out through the unique experience of each of our particular lives. There are those whose interpretation of their time on earth is written and read for centuries to come, while others are barely remembered within their own families. However, from the spiritual perspective, there is no common life. Every life holds the single most important piece to the puzzle, because without every piece, the puzzle remains incomplete. Even the guy living under the freeway overpass holds the key to eternity. Without his tormented story, without his daily unfolding challenge coming to its proper conclusion, humanity remains incomplete. That's how it is with *absolute eternity*; it can only be absolute if every last morsel is included.

Our Sages teach that each person comes into this life with a challenge to overcome; a correction that needs to be made. Each of us is equipped with the perfect DNA to solve this challenge. It is free will that determines the degree of drama, suffering or joy necessary for each life to unfold. Like a cosmic video game, all of the scenery and images are just part of the show. It matters not whether we are born into poverty and addiction or wealth and recognition. The challenge we each face is to discover our spiritual core and solve our unique and personal mystery. The task is the same. The circumstances that appear to be advantageous are no less distracting and obstructive than those which appear to be disadvantageous. In spiritual terms, great wealth and abject poverty, breathtaking beauty and base homeliness, are equal obstacles needing to be overcome.

Spiritually, there is but one purpose to this life: to learn the lessons it offers in order to advance. Viewed through the spiritual lens, we see that each individual life is unique in all of creation. Our physical nature and material surroundings offer great opportunities for spiritual advancement, yet for the most part, we remain oblivious to both the meaning and the purpose of our 70–80-year lifespan in the physical world. The most complex mechanism imaginable, the human psyche, comes from the factory without an owner's manual. While religion and philosophy have spent centuries trying to come up with one, 21ˢᵗ century humanity continues to operate in the dark—blind to our spiritual nature as well as our spiritual mission.

This is not to discount the countless wonderful and fulfilling experiences to be had along the way. These experiences will only serve our spiritual path if we're able to navigate our way through them without becoming distracted and lost. With more distraction and disruption than Alice had in Wonderland, it's unlikely that we will randomly arrive at the finish line having accomplished all that's required to graduate.

Distractions are characteristic of the external world, and disorganization is characteristic of our inner world. To navigate our way through life's labyrinth of blind alleys and hidden tripwires requires proper directions, intense concentration and steadfast intention. The following chapters will provide appropriate directions and skill-based instruction. For now, each of us must distinguish our intention and establish our commitment. Once begun, the spiritual quest will inspire deeper commitment, stronger intention and generate personal enthusiasm. Like the flight of a rocket, however, the greatest thrust is required for the launch. Once the proper altitude is reached, it is able to cruise with little effort.

With the spiritual quest, the largest effort is required to get things off the ground. This initial stage is characterized by the struggle between doubt and faith. There is no proof available to appease the skeptic as to the validity of the spiritual realm. If you ask why there is no proof for modern humanity after thousands of years of spiritual inquiry, it is because the instances in which proof has been presented have been few and far between. They are well documented in various scriptures and the testimonies of many mystics. However, this kind of proof does not satisfy science as sufficient empiric data, nor would it stand up in a court of law. The skeptic looking for *bona fide* proof finds religious scripture and the writings of ancient mystics to be nothing more than rumor and hearsay. So why is the most important question on the most important topic, *i.e.*, the nature of our existence, left without proof? The simple answer is that the spiritual realm and our spiritual nature are not provable within the same system that demands empiric evidence. Further, such inability to prove is inherent in the design.

I appreciate the frustration this answer generates. We would all prefer to have indisputable evidence of our destination before we embark upon our spiritual journey. In fact, having such evidence would be a game changer—the game is one of faith-based inquiry as distinguished from a search for evidence. How worthy would the seeker have to be if he or she were simply following the evidence showing the existence of the Soul, of the spiritual realm and even of the Creator?

The design of faith-based inquiry requires both faith and the manifestation of that faith. Imagine the faith that guided the saints and martyrs to put their lives on the line for their beliefs. If they were simply fools with overactive imaginations, it's doubtful that billions of followers would still hold them in such reverence. Modern leaders are challenged to maintain credibility for their respective terms in office, while the great spiritual leaders have been cherished for generations.

Don't despair. While there may be no discernible proof available—*i.e.*, no empiric proof that could be shown on the late news for the world to judge and analyze—there is, however, all the proof needed to satisfy those who seek with a sincere heart and pure intent. Once you complete the *initiation* phase of the mission, you begin to develop your spiritual *chops* and you will be given insights to satisfy your curiosity. When curiosity blossoms into true interest, and later into unbridled passion, we will be rewarded with sufficient clarity and understanding that we will recognize as irrefutable.

Such is the nature of spiritual truth—it is personal proof found in the eyes of the beholder. Hence, it cannot be shown to others, unless they are at a similar stage in their spiritual development. Once satisfied that you grasp your personal spiritual truths, you will find that any attempt to communicate your spiritual experiences to those who are skeptics is likely to produce reactions and judgments so negative as to wobble your own certainty. This is especially true if your intention was to impress them or gain their admiration.

Even with pure motives and wishing only to assist others in finding the truth that you discovered, there's a danger of back sliding. Unlike ordinary speech, spiritual communications are of a sacred nature and have many qualifications. If you direct a lost man to the destination he is seeking, the only relevant consideration is whether your instructions get him to that destination. When you encounter a man who is spiritually lost, trying to provide him with the benefit of your experience can send him further away from his own spiritual path and may even cause you to hit a pothole in your own road to Self-realization.

As with so many things in life, timing is key. Many children raised in religious households are more prone to spiritual rebellion than those who were raised in a secular environment. When people are in spiritual resistance, the harder you push them toward embracing spirituality, the further you push them away.

Being Co-Creator

What then is our spiritual mission? —in a word—transformation, individual and collective. As human beings we require transformation, and we exist in a world that requires transformation. Transformation will be covered in-depth in the following chapters on the spiritual process. For our immediate purpose, suffice it to say that in the material world, we are motivated by our self-serving nature—*what's in it for me?* Even when it appears that we are giving to others, on closer examination, it is often done with some underlying self-interest. In spirituality, any self-serving intent will diminish the positive effects of our actions. For example, taking on transformation for the benefits we will derive, will negatively impact our efforts and the outcome. While our work toward changing the world may have its rewards, focusing on those rewards diminishes our spiritual credibility.

One might legitimately ask, *If the Creator wanted us to have a more noble character, why weren't we created with one?* What is the purpose of our being imperfect creatures in an imperfect world? In order to understand the answer to this question, the reader needs a certain degree of spiritual insight. Our discussion is focused on cultivating that spiritual insight. It is a bit premature to provide the full answer at this stage. However, a threshold version can be stated now: The imperfection that we see in ourselves and in our world allows us the benefit of becoming *co-creators*—to become God's partner. The Creator allowed imperfection in creation so that *we* could have the spiritual opportunity of making a contribution to creation. Refining what is imperfect and correcting what is wrong in our world is the essential work of creation; it is the work of our Soul—in other words, transformation. This is the expression of the sacred spiritual experience.

Many Sages have observed that the life we are currently living is not the existence we were created to have. Some actually refer to this life as *the corridor* that leads to the intended life. This life is regarded as temporary in an imperfect world, designed for us to hone ourselves for the next level. The behavior manifested throughout our world is clearly inappropriate for the more perfected world at the next level.

Taking even a brief, unbiased look at the reality surrounding us, confirms that this world is not the highest reality an omnipotent Creator would have created. The daily newscasts are clearly not what the Buddha described as Ultimate Reality (*Nirvana*), nor the vision of heavenly delight that Jesus promised, nor the World to Come foretold by the Hebrew prophets. Rather, our world appears to be the proving ground, or test kitchen, designed to get the recipe right before the meal is served.

The ancient and historic debate emphasizes this point: How much or how little should a person engage in the *pleasures of life?* There are clearly those spiritual teachers who advise a life of austerity and asceticism. There have even been teachers who suggest that human suffering is not sufficient on its own and requires additional pain and self-imposed suffering.

These are extreme steps that may have some merit within certain practices, but for our purposes the middle ground may be our best path. The hunter in the ancient tale could have walked through the corridor leading to the treasure chamber fully cognizant of the beautiful music, feeling inspired by the music without stopping to indulge in it. This was a pivotal moment for the hunter. After this day, his reality would have been far more pleasurable than he had ever dreamt. The beauty of the music could have been ushering in his new reality, not replacing it.

The line is drawn where our indulgence in pleasure and gratification interferes with our ability to gain spiritual clarity. When the distractions of our desires and the needs of our ego obscure the yearning of our Soul, they have cost us too much. Oddly, the experience of spiritual awakening is one of life's greatest pleasures. In order to achieve this awakening, it may be necessary to eliminate, or at least reduce, our indulgence in lesser pleasures and pursuits for a time. In this way, the effect of abstaining from fleeting pleasure brings lasting pleasure.

The legend of the young king and the hunter illuminates the dilemma in which we all find ourselves—that which is spiritual and meant to be discovered is concealed, and that which is material is both apparent and highly attractive. Along with the intrinsic draw of earthly delights, is our own embedded desire for them. This is the true challenge set before those who aspire to climb the spiritual mountain; we must go against our very nature—walk away from what we are programmed to desire in order to grasp what is indescribable and concealed.

The Non-Missional Nature of the Spiritual Mission

At first glance, this illogical statement makes no sense. Upon closer examination, one will begin to understand. The nature of our mission is to get to the place where there is no mission. Missions, quests, searchings, goals, objectives, and the like, are all deeply rooted in the material world; they are an expression of the mind, or more precisely, the ego. They all involve action and desire, which are both products of the physical world. This is not to say that the outward expression of spiritual awakening is not worthy and necessary. Ultimately, that outward expression of acceptance of the spiritual is what will drive the elevation of the material world to a higher level, one in which the Supreme Light can enter. The central intent of this book, however, is to focus on the inner awakening. Clearly the mission is to bring the Supreme Light into the world. To do this, we must be in the world while becoming the Light. The force needed to transform the world is cultivated by individuals awakening themselves. Although the outward mission may appear to be the transformation of the world, it can only take place through transforming oneself. The Supreme Light is only able to travel through an authentic channel; one that is, itself, made of the Light that runs through it.

Spiritually speaking, truth, enlightenment, Nirvana, Heaven, even God, cannot be found through the typical channels of our physical life. These spiritual concepts are best characterized as ineffable, and all attempts at description only serve to confuse the rational mind; at the same time, descriptions diminish access to experiencing them. Again, the spiritual dimension is best understood when viewed through the spiritual lens—*i.e.*, direct experience. In light of this requirement, it is best to reserve judgment of spiritual tenets until they are recognized and understood within the context of spiritual realization—direct personal experience.

The 17th Century German mystic, Father Angelus Silesius (1624-1677), a Catholic priest, poet and physician, advocated the pursuit of God through direct experience led by intuition, instinct and insight. In his work, Cherubinic Wanderer, Silesius writes:

As long as you feel yourself to be a distinct individual, you still carry a burden. As long as you have knowledge, and thus are a subject observing objects, you still carry a burden... God is the purest nothing. He does not exist in the realm of human knowledge... God lives in supreme light. There is no path that gives

access to that light. You yourself must become that light; only by becoming supreme light can you see God...The Rose is without 'why'—she blooms because she blooms. It pays no attention to itself, nor does it ask whether anyone sees it.

—Father Angelus Silesius

The message of Father Silesius is echoed in one form or another in the works of many of the world's great Sages. Within this message lies the core of the human dilemma. To be free of the burden we all carry, we must first recognize that our perception of reality is, in fact, subjective, even though it seems objective. It exists only for us; others see their own subjective reality. To glimpse into non-subjective reality is our first step into *becoming supreme light.*

Having said this, and recognizing the futility of any attempt to describe it, perhaps we can gain some clarity of what lies ahead. The spiritual dimension is a *state of being;* it is not a location or the result of certain actions. We cannot desire our way onto the higher rungs of the spiritual ladder, the same way we desire a promotion at work. Not even our beliefs or our prior conditioning provide the key to higher consciousness. To *be* on the higher spiritual plane, we must achieve the *state of being* found on the higher spiritual plane. From there, we will be able to navigate the spiritual realm.

The topic of navigating the spiritual path is explored after the topic of *setting our intention.* It is intention, or human will, that supplies the personal power needed to begin the spiritual process leading into the spiritual structure. *So, if the mission is not a mission, what is the basis of this spiritual process?* It is the spiritual awakening itself, which brings us into a new level of being; a wondrous realization that will undoubtedly redefine who we are and the reality that surrounds us. The idea of a mission or an assignment produces a counter-productive mindset. The way we approach this awakening will have a bearing on our progress. Using the word "mission" here is only for purposes of communication. Thinking of this new approach to life as a "mission," suggests that it requires our full attention and the need for an initial commitment to see it through.

If you have concerns about the level of your commitment or your willingness to provide sufficient attention, put your worries to rest. If you are sincere in your approach and your intent is pure, the process will draw you in. Like falling in love, the spiritual experience is intoxicating and there is a point where we lose control—that is the very point where things get interesting. Spiritual awakening is the only true antidote for physical aging and psychological depression—growing old without spirituality is tantamount to being ill without medicine.

Reaching Spiritual Puberty

In Chapter Four, we presented Jung's idea that somewhere between the age of thirty-five and forty, people move into what he called a second puberty—one not centered on sexuality, but on spirituality. This spiritual puberty, intuits the launch of the spiritual exploration. Unfortunately, unlike the puberty of adolescence, our hormones and emotions do not secure guaranteed spiritual transformation.

In our contemporary culture, at the age Jung designated for spiritual puberty, most people are engrossed in their family and careers. It is the time when they enter their peak earning years. Because many now delay the start of their families, at ages 35 to 40, they are also in the midst of child-rearing. With these demanding distractions, it is a rare person indeed who might also detect and respond to the soft inner calling of the Soul.

In terms of maturity and focus, our lives may be divided into four quadrants. In the first—birth through our teen years, life is all about growth and education. Most of our consciousness is focused on physiological and psychological development. In the second, 20's and 30's, we are usually defined by higher education, the start of a career, a primary relationship and family development. This is when a "professional" identity is formed, along with our "social" identity as spouse and parent, citizen and neighbor. During the third quadrant, 40's and 50's, our children are becoming mature enough to be on their own and our careers are well established. Even though many may be launching new careers and some even new families, for the most part, life takes on a much more *reflective tone*. This reflection is triggered by the realization that our life is half over.

From here it is only a short step to the fourth quadrant, 60 to 80 and beyond, when questions as to our meaning and purpose begin to take the forefront. At this point, largely characterized as undefined in modern culture, are the years that are not as tied to the material world as were the younger years. In this quadrant, most people retire from their careers and cut back in their roles as consumers; they also pay less tax to the government and receive more benefits. For many, it is the time of a second *identity crisis*—we are no longer who we were and we have not yet recognized who we are becoming. And it certainly doesn't help to see that aging person in the mirror as someone you'd prefer not to be.

If each of these twenty-year spans of our lives were viewed as separate movies, each would have its own distinct style, soundtrack, wardrobe, dialogue and perhaps even cast. The inner feelings that harmonized with our first quadrant will not be the ones to harmonize with our concerns in the third. Although each of us is the same person in each quadrant, each is also very different. Values have changed as well as priorities. So too have our activities—some because of physical necessity, while others because of a maturation along the way.

Our modern scientific worldview leans heavily toward the material perspective. Within this view, it is difficult to realize that the fourth quadrant is the most important phase of life. Not just significant, but adventurous and fulfilling. How can this be possible, when most people in the fourth quadrant feel so insignificant and incomplete? It is because we are transitioning out of the material and into the spiritual. If you haven't navigated your way through *spiritual puberty,* you'll feel just as awkward as a pimple-faced kid with a cracking voice at his first dance. Without an emerging spiritual identity nurturing the entire being and informing every spec of consciousness, one is left with only the ghosts of the past and anxiety about what lies ahead. Youth, health, beauty and ambition, are the mainstays of corporeality. As they lose their luster, they are meant to be replaced with experience, wisdom, compassion and transcendence. Without these new avenues of change to travel, one is left with failing support structures, confusion as to why they no longer work and no guidance for where to turn. Like Tarzan letting go of his swinging vine with no other to grab, one falls fast and hard.

In the fourth quadrant, spiritual exploration comes into play with the objective of bringing ourselves into a new spiritual identity. This exploration is similar to the *spiritual puberty* referred to by Carl Jung. However, unlike adolescent puberty given by nature, here we must take the initiative ourselves. The purpose is to have the *mystical experience* that completes our fourth quadrant and to have it during the time we are still alive. In a *mystical experience* one feels firsthand the true nature of reality, or, as Buddha put it, clarity and truth as to the way things are. Unlike scientific truth or accurate historical reporting, this truth cannot be told to us by others; we must experience it for ourselves. This key spiritual tenet is echoed by many teachers: Spiritual truth cannot be taught, it can only be discovered and experienced directly. As stated by Aldous Huxley in the Forward of Krishnamurti's *The First and Last Freedom*:

> *Truth cannot be given to you by somebody. You have to discover it; and to discover, there must be a state of mind in which there is direct perception. There is no direct perception when there is a resistance, a safeguard, a protection. Understanding comes through being aware of what is. To know exactly what is, the real, the actual, without interpreting it, without condemning or justifying it, is, surely, the beginning of wisdom. It is only when we begin to interpret, to translate according to our conditioning, according to our prejudice, that we miss the truth. After all, it is like research. To know what something is, what it is exactly, requires research—you cannot translate it according to your moods. Similarly, if we can look,*

observe, listen, be aware of what is, exactly, then the problem is solved.

This truth is not found in the intellect; rather it's felt in the heart—the intuitive voice of inner consciousness. It's more inspirational than educational. A *mystical experience* opens the gateway to the whole spiritual realm. Once encountering its loving touch, one no longer feels anxious about the future or depressed over the past. One becomes aware of how the system works; as the body ages and deteriorates, the Soul emerges with a grand new sparkle, polished from years of human endurance.

As we have previously stated, the purpose of our physical life is far more related to the advancement of the Soul than to any worldly achievements. The purpose of the puppet is to express the puppet master. While our time of the flesh is fleeting, it provides tremendous opportunities for spiritual advancement. Such advancement may often conflict with opportunities for material achievement. The very behavior that is advancing our material life is frequently a hindrance to our spiritual progress. While this doesn't have to be the case, it typically is. It is rare to find a person who can keep his or her material life and spiritual life advancing simultaneously and in harmony.

One of the greatest aspects of the Buddha's genius was his understanding of the human dilemma—being both physical and spiritual. He recognized how the mind is both a benefit and a barrier to Enlightenment. We depend on the mind to navigate along the spiritual path, yet that same mind is often ruled by hungry desires. Even after coming to know the spiritual path, the mind is easily led astray by the endless pursuit of sense-pleasure. Until free of these unquenchable thirsts, we remain vulnerable to suffering.

In his compassion, the Buddha would say: *It is hard to be born as a human being and hard to live the life of one. It is even harder to hear of the path and harder still to awake, to rise, and to follow.* His advice was simple in form, yet challenging. The Buddha saw how people were heavily under the influence of their own minds. He taught the importance of reining in the mind and gaining control over its wanderings. He encouraged us to purify our own minds until they are able to distinguish what is right, true and good, from what is wrong, false and evil. Being at the effect of our desires is a guaranteed path to destruction. He proposed moderation in all things and, most of all, he emphasized the importance of doing no harm in word or deed.

When asked how to purify our mind and refine our behavior, the Buddha simply stated: *Seek the deepest consciousness.* Each individual is the expression of his or her consciousness. This is true for our culture, as well. The world is a reflection of our collective consciousness. The disorder and chaos running rampant throughout the world today is a reflection of the internal disorder and chaos of the individuals in each culture. By gaining control over the mind and raising individual consciousness, each of us is able to eliminate chaos from manifesting. This individual accomplishment, in and of itself, is a significant contribution to all humanity.

This is the process referred to by the phrase, *being called to the spiritual path.* This *calling* is meant for all people, yet few actually perceive it and even fewer respond. The Daily Word is a monthly publication of the Unity Church, a worldwide Christian organization founded in 1889 by Charles and Myrtle Fillmore. It has been in publication for over 90 years and each day it provides a new spiritual message for its 600,000 subscribers. On June 29th, 2015, the daily affirmation was titled, *Answer the Call.*

> *I answer the call to follow the spiritual path. While I appreciate material things, I know things we buy do not satisfy our souls. I may become aware that my restlessness is a form of "spiritual poverty." I vow to turn this around by embarking on a spiritual quest. I open my heart and soul and prepare for growth. More than anything else, I want to experience God more deeply. My spiritual quest is the most rewarding journey of my life. As I travel the path, I put what I learn into practice. I incorporate spiritual truths into my consciousness and they become the foundation of my life.*

Charles Fillmore established the basic principle of the Unity Church, that the true church is *a state of consciousness in mankind,* and each person is a unique expression of God. In ancient times, only Saints and Prophets heard and responded to the *spiritual calling.* Today people from all walks of life give testimony to being *called* onto the spiritual path. A note of caution—too much emphasis on the notion of a *calling* can lead to misperceptions and distractions. It is best to explore one's spiritual nature as the natural progression of who he or she has always been; as puberty was a natural passage during adolescence, so too is spiritual puberty the natural next step.

The Grand Awakening
While the overall mission is not easily expressed in words, by using analogies, we are able to bring some form and identity to the indescribable. One common analogy used by Sages to

describe the initial phases of Self-realization is *awakening*. This is an appropriate term as we really do not know we are sleeping until we wake up. Do dreamers really know they are dreaming? Utilizing the distinction between being asleep and waking up provides a suitable model for spiritual awakening. No sooner do we open our eyes, going from sleep to wakefulness in the morning, that we are keenly aware of the dominant state of consciousness held by being awake.

For purposes of illustration, imagine this typical state of awareness familiar to us as being awake has yet another state of consciousness that has a heightened experience of clarity. In other words, imagine the material world and our physical existence as being the dream state, and we are attempting to awaken into a clearer and more fully conscious state. According to those who have navigated the process of spiritual awakening, the dramatic shift is even greater than the variation between the dream state and being awake.

Just as our morning awakening brings with it a more vivid reality than our time asleep, so too, this spiritual awakening brings a heightened perception of reality. While our physical reality is vast with mountains and valleys, rivers and oceans, stars and galaxies, it pales in comparison to the next level of reality—the hidden or spiritual reality. If you are trying to decide whether there can be a greater reality than this one that we currently perceive—relax. There is no current data or conditioning within our intellect to make that decision. The intellect works from previous experience and conditioning. Without previous experience of the spiritual realm, or earlier conditioning, we cannot help but be left with serious doubt.

A useful approach to such a challenging notion is to start by contemplating the vastness and complexity of our known physical universe. Also reflect upon how limited and tethered our personal perspective and understanding is of that universe—even from the expanded collective perspective of all of modern humanity. It would be arrogant to suggest that we hold the ultimate truth on whether there's more than meets the eye on this topic. Having suggested this contemplation, the proper approach for exploring the possibility of a spiritual reality that exceeds the physical, is to approach with an open and accepting mind. Granted, it is difficult to accept such a concept with no physical proof to convince the intellect. Spiritual "evidence" is an oxymoron like jumbo shrimp or an original copy. The evidence we seek is only found within our individual, personal experience and stems from intuition and faith—two terms that are seldom used in response to a need for proof. More than the organs of perception, it's the heart that leads the spiritual inquiry. The heart detects spiritual presence the way a Geiger counter detects radiation.

The quest to discover spiritual identity commences the moment the intention (human will) is set in place. When one generates the proper intention to have a spiritual awakening, the awakening has already begun. If one were to commence the spiritual quest without setting an intention, his or her quest would then drive toward the first objective of achieving intention.

Knowledge and understanding impacts the human will/intention. It is not likely that one will place spiritual realization at the top of his or her life priorities without a proper understanding. Because understanding of spiritual awakening most often comes as a result of experiencing it, and experiencing it is dependent on our understanding, one is caught in a dilemma at the outset. However, the teachings of the great Sages provide support. Studying their knowledge and understanding contributes to our own.

Perception vs. Reality

On the physical plane, our reality shapes our perception. However, from the spiritual perspective, our perception shapes our reality. Both of these statements appear to hold a certain degree of truth. Of course, we would agree that the object being viewed determines what we perceive. On the physical plane, if that object were an apple, we would see an apple. From this perspective, it's the apple that determines what we will perceive and experience. Alternatively, on the spiritual plane, it's the subject doing the viewing more than the object being viewed that determines the perception and experience. As the Buddha taught, the unenlightened mind does not actually see true reality; rather it perceives the mind's perception of reality. In other words, the reality we perceive through our senses is interpreted through the mind, via the brain, which is heavily influenced by previous conditioning. Our reality is not objective; it is highly subjective. This is particularly true when it comes to our experience of the reality that surrounds us.

The mind is nothing if not pliant; it is reshaped and adapted to every new idea, new occurrence and emotional reaction. Each experience, thought and feeling we have ever had has worked its way into our brain's conditioning. This conditioning determines how we experience the world. As you might imagine, much of this conditioning is flawed by previous faulty conditioning and misperception. A single frightening event can impact perception relating to similar events throughout life. A young boy can be bitten by a dog and the adult version of that child still perceives all dogs through the lens clouded by that early experience.

Given that the purpose of spiritual exploration is to gain clarity of our true nature and the nature of true reality, and given that our mind (through the conditioning of the brain) is the main instrument of perception, we must address the need to recalibrate this instrument used for our research. This recalibration is a significant shift for the mind. From one's earliest awareness, the brain's primary function has been self-serving—pursue pleasure while avoiding pain, accept support while resisting threats. As the ego develops, this function quickly includes keeping the person's ego safe from threats. In performing this task, the mind will manipulate our perception of reality in order to keep us safe and to satisfy our insatiable egos. The mind can completely alter its perception of truth in order to fulfill these tasks. This is an admirable function in the material world where competition and survival are a priority. In terms of spiritual awakening, however, where it is critical to see things as they truly are, the mind's conditioned predisposition to find the potential threat in every occurrence, renders it flawed and untrustworthy. The quest for truth will be fatally compromised by a mind programmed to perceive threat in every situation and to bolster ego after every encounter. One of the main teachings of the Buddha is to free the mind from the ego's obsessive attachments to all that it desires. We will never be able to gain clarity with a mind enslaved by fears and desires.

Be forewarned: Gaining the mind's liberation from the brain's conditioning and desires is a complex and difficult task. It requires great patience and steadfast intention. Fortunately, we can make enormous spiritual strides even before we succeed in breaking free of our attachments. Just gaining insight into the way our own mind functions and conducts its form of manipulation is a monumental achievement. The Buddha also points out that being subjected to this form of conditioned mental tyranny causes much human suffering.

In the Buddhist scripture Anguttara Nikaya (one of Buddha's 10,000 teachings found in the five collections of the Sutta Pitaka), the Buddha addresses this issue of the undisciplined mind: *It is necessary to cultivate some discipline of mind, for an undisciplined mind always finds excuses to act selfishly and thoughtlessly. When the mind is undisciplined, the body is also undisciplined, and so is speech and action.*

This self-serving nature of the mind is a design feature that provides the survival mechanism. It's not unlike the survival mechanism found in all lesser species—similar in kind, yet different in degree. Like the lesser animals, man's nature seeks to provide for his own needs and desires without concern for others. (In fact, everything that is not the person himself or herself is seen as exactly that—other.) In the spiritual realm, an entire mechanism exists rooted in the exact opposite—altruism. Here people are able to experience empathy and compassion for their fellow human beings as well as all living things.

They are willing to go without in order to meet the needs of others. Such thinking goes against the nature of the intellect—particularly the ego. We will explore this further in the discussion of the *spiritual process* in the chapters ahead. Shifting of our ground of being from egoism to altruism is fundamental in awakening our consciousness and introducing the mind to its counterpart—the Soul. One cannot even imagine his or her identity after a shift from the self-serving agenda of the ego to the altruistic nature of the Soul. Prior to experiencing such a shift, the very lens of our imagination is a product of the intellect, thus coloring our perception by the obvious biases of the ego.

It's not through the intellect that we come to know the virtue of living in accordance with our altruistic spiritual nature.

Rather, this comes from pure experiential insight. It is often while navigating the spiritual path that we come to experience our authentic, altruistic nature. In this way, our insight is no longer intellectual or conceptual, it is experiential.

As the Buddha taught, *beneath it all there is one experience that is the same for everyone.* This experience is often identified as some variation of what we call happiness. It may be, however, that the notion of happiness associated with a unifying spiritual experience is only the byproduct of something even greater—something that defies definition. It is this experience that we are in search of, and finding this experience is the purpose of this book. In Anguttara Nikaya, the Buddha points out, that this form of true happiness is the result of the committed life: *There are two kinds of happiness. There is that of an uncommitted life of sensual pleasures, and there is that of a committed life, one going forth to a new consciousness. Of these, the happiness of going forth is greater.*

In one degree or another, we are all in search of the underlying experience. It is achieved through determined spiritual exploration. Because it's difficult to search for something unknown and undefined, we'll use the Buddha's simple phrase to reference the treasure we seek. We seek the clarity to see things as they really are. The 11th century Buddhist master, Atiśa, said it as: *The greatest wisdom is seeing through appearances.*

The spiritual quest is an exploration of truth—truth that is unadulterated and uncorrupted in its expression as well as its interpretation. In order to explore pure truth, one must begin without pre-conclusions. As Krishnamurti puts it, *Knowledge must be set aside to understand truth.* The approach is similar to the scientific method of searching out truth—we're not looking to prove what we already know, but to discover that which is not yet known. Conclusions previously held will skew new discoveries. We live in our own separate reality where perception is impacted by the brain's previous conditioning. The conditioning takes the form of filters which interpret what the senses perceive, delivering to the mind interpreted reality. What the mind thinks is based upon the interpreted information it receives.

Removing the Filters to Gain a Blank Screen

In the first part of this book, we focused on earlier world-views—all that has led to this moment in the current world-view. Many celebrated teachers have impacted and altered the worldview—teachers of religion and philosophy, teachers of science and psychology, teachers of the heart and teachers of the mind, teachers of enlightenment and teachers of compassion. Some have improved our collective perception of truth, while others have obscured it. All, however, share a common thread—they have all influenced our collective experience of reality.

Fortunately, it is not our task to analyze and judge each individual for the validity of his or her work; this has already been a major endeavor throughout history. Our objective is far less involved. It is simply to observe the ideas that have shaped and led us to our current worldview. Nor is it our task to accept or reject the beliefs that are held by others. Our job is to hone our observational skills so as to perceive both collective consciousness and the consciousness found within us. What then follows is the crystallizing of our thinking and the emergence of our own beliefs. It may appear that long ago we achieved this objective of self-discovery. As we have repeatedly indicated, however, all of our *programming* is somewhat distorted by human ulterior motives and hidden agendas. Some ideas have been imposed from outside influences, while most are rooted in our own incessant drive for greater pleasure and enhanced gratification.

The process of achieving a *blank screen* does not require the dismantling of current beliefs; it is merely a process of allowing a new moment of experience, unencumbered by existing beliefs and judgments. This unencumbered moment is akin to the early experiences we all had when first arriving in this life. Babies and children look at the world without imposing personal perceptions. The world is full of mystery and wonder. Adults have lost this innocence and purity of perception. Most adults perceive a reality that aligns with what we have dictated it to be. Infants look to their surrounding reality with eyes not tainted by years of faulty programming—their mental filters not yet installed.

Throughout life, we accumulate a variety of *filters* that alter our perception of our surrounding reality. The many life lessons and years of education generate these filters that shape the way we perceive and experience the world. For example, those who have been hurt and betrayed in previous relationships have a far different take on love than those who have enjoyed only fulfilling relationships. People who have been swindled have a far different view of investments than those who have prospered by them. Have these life lessons helped or hindered those who have built their beliefs around them? A case can be made either way. Often life lessons or filters provide a valuable service allowing us to be more circumspect when entering a new relationship or investment. On the other hand, when attempting to experience the spiritual path, they obstruct our view and can prevent us from experiencing life's greatest gifts.

Our filters become increasingly problematic when we

allow others to construct them. While the others may be worldly experts, each of us is the leading authority on our own life. Science teaches that the reality we perceive is a mix of what is objective and what is subjective. In other words, our perception of the world does not separate the observer from the observed. As in art, beauty is in the eye of the beholder. So too, perception is in the eye of the beholder.

Keep in mind, our spiritual perception has been influenced by centuries of our material, scientific worldview. For many in that worldview, spirituality is synonymous with superstition. The mechanism that allows the mystical experience in the 21st century, requires a very delicate balancing. Unless we are able to clear our perception and purify our mind of centuries of dogmatic filters and decades of predisposed biases, it is unlikely that we will gain access to objective reality.

Until we've had a glimpse into objective reality, we're stuck in a view of reality that is sourced by the mind simply reflecting upon itself. Our understanding is the product of our mind's previous conditioning. This is the primary reason why transformation is so challenging for many people—it requires a fundamental shift in thinking from that which has roots deeply embedded in previous conditioning. The brain, specifically the ego, goes to great lengths to preserve what it has determined to be truth. Number one on the brain's list is the preservation of what the senses and the ego desire. Whatever the senses crave, the mind finds a way to provide.

Achieving Purpose over Pleasure

Nearly a century ago, the three Viennese schools of psychotherapy recognized that the *human will* is driven by the pursuit of pleasure, power and meaning. From the spiritual perspective, these three drivers are in sequential order. After our innate will to survive, we are on a quest for pleasure. Linked to the survival of the species, sexual pleasure is the strongest drive. Our drive for power and recognition begins to dominate as we mature and become more educated. Not until power and recognition have had their lengthy run does the quest for meaning and purpose begin to arise. It is this third phase that is most linked to spiritual awakening.

It is not easy to separate oneself from the brain's cravings and previous conditioning. The mind is the seat of our identity—or so it seems. For the purpose of illustration, imagine our minds as employees of our company. As with any employee, management must continually observe and evaluate the mind's job performance. As is the case with employees who have their own agendas, management must continually bring the mind back into alignment with the company's mission. If we have an employee who is more committed to socializing than doing the job, we have a problem.

This is precisely the case with the undisciplined mind— it has its own agenda. Worse yet, its primary agenda is not in our best interest. Without installing current upgrades, the mind is tethered to the brain's antiquated beliefs that are in dire need of updating. Painful experiences during adolescence might be steering the mind's vital decisions today. When making current choices, the trials and tribulations that were important during the teenage years, should be regarded as ancient history.

Beyond the brain's previous conditioning, the mind has another agenda that consistently demands adherence. When confronted with a decision that involves sense pleasures, the undisciplined mind manipulates to choose pleasure over purpose. The mind is very childlike in this regard. A child choosing between steamed vegetables and ice cream is unlikely to select the health benefits of the veggies over the sensual delight of ice cream. This is why children require adult supervision in their decision-making. Long after we have left the nest, many of us allow pleasure to guide the direction of our mind. Even though we may be well grounded in knowledge and have purpose, the influence of pleasure is still far too seductive over restraint of mind.

The mystical Sages taught that the purpose of the physical realm is to allow individuals the power of free will. It is free will that gives us dominion over our choices in life—at least in theory. In actuality, we are not truly free until our wisdom is able to override our drive for pleasure and power. As long as we are slaves to our desires, we are vulnerable to suffering.

The method to overcome this incessant human dilemma will be considered more deeply in the chapters ahead regarding the *spiritual process*. At this point, we are only exploring how this dynamic can influence our perception and direct our choices. The mind, and its process of perception and interpretation, influences every aspect of our experience. As the Buddha has said, we cannot be in touch with reality until we are able to overcome the sway of our mind's perception. Fortunately, there is a more powerful force that brings the mind into the sacred fold of our spiritual purpose—the Soul. The Soul is a word used to describe that part of the spiritual realm that is embedded within us. Like all spiritual concepts, the Soul is ineffable; any words used to describe the Soul will fall short and lead to misunderstanding. Even saying that the Soul is embedded within us is misleading. It causes the Soul to be imagined as an organ like the gallbladder, when in fact, it's the Soul that is manifesting the body and the mind. It is taught that the only way to gain knowledge of the Soul is through direct, personal experience. Words, whether spoken or thought, are part of the material world; experience can bridge the material into the spiritual.

Through quickening the Soul, one is able to override the control that sensory desires and ego gratification have over the mind. Although psychology has provided valuable insights into the workings of the mind, for our purposes, one must ultimately gain his or her understanding by going within. Whether by observation and reflection or mindfulness and meditation, it is through inward exploration that one discovers the spiritual realm.

Like Columbus on his mission to discover a distant shore, each of us must explore to arrive at the shore where the Soul resides. Through the mind, we come to discover the Soul, however, because of the mind, we are also distracted from our discovery—it is the instrument of spiritual discovery as well as that which obscures it. In this regard, the mind is both our ally and our foe. Consequently, the first stage of spiritual exploration focuses on the mind itself.

To Think Is to Create

To be effective in our discovery process, we need to hone our skills of observation and develop our mental discipline—i.e., mindfulness. Let's be perfectly clear. We will not be able to discover the presence of the Soul without first discipling the mind. And, we will not be able to discipline the mind until we become aware of how the mind operates. Only then can we assert control over its operations—overruling its automatic programming. This programing, or previous conditioning, has come to pass gradually over a lifetime. The *uninitiated* mind is not working toward our spiritual development; it is conditioned to be protective, focusing on material gain, physical pleasures and ego gratification. Once we become aware of how the uninitiated mind is programmed, its self-serving predisposition becomes apparent.

It's entirely logical that the uninitiated mind will try to sabotage progress on the spiritual quest if it senses a threat to the pursuit of pleasure and power. For example, if a person who enjoys smoking is reading an article about its health hazards, he or she may find it difficult to remain focused on the article and may become easily distracted. Such a mind might provide reasons to doubt the validity of the article or resonate with opposing views that invalidate the data. This is not because the mind isn't wise enough to know the risks. It is because the mind has an alternate agenda—pleasure. If smoking provides pleasure, the article is likely to be viewed as a threat to that pleasure. Until the mind decides that smoking poses a greater threat than the loss of pleasure, it will sabotage attempts at quitting. As long as the desire for the pleasure of smoking exceeds the desire to quit, the person will remain a smoker. Even if the person joins a smoking cessation program and runs the cigarettes down the garbage disposal, the mind will find that vulnerable moment to start smoking again. The mind works for the benefit of the behavior that holds our greatest desire. Because the mind has control over our perception of reality, it is possible for a smoker to see no harm from smoking. Our mind will provide a rationalization and justification for what brings us pleasure, albeit fleeting and often harmful. This process will continue until one perceives the *game the mind is running*, and sets his or her *intention* to take back control.

To gain an unbiased glimpse of the mind in action is difficult enough, but it pales in comparison to actually gaining control over our mental activity. The Buddha taught that an undisciplined mind has little chance at Enlightenment. Without discipline, the mind will take us to all the wrong places and arrive at all the wrong conclusions. This is precisely what the mind has done throughout our lives—wrong behavior justified and even rationalized into being right. In order to make the wrong seem right, the mind has had to adopt many false beliefs and faulty biases.

As with a bookkeeper who is embezzling money, we must take charge and scrutinize every action that employee takes. However, most of us never considered the need to scrutinize the workings of our own mind. Putting the mind under a microscope is an ongoing practice in spiritual awakening, which we refer to as *mindfulness*. Vigilant supervision is the only way to recognize the mind's behavior patterns and gain a modicum of control.

Perhaps the most essential lesson regarding the workings of the mind is one taught by spiritual teachers from ancient times to the present: ***To think is to create***. We cannot distinguish the creative process from thought itself; they are essentially one and the same. Every thought carries with it an effect, thereby opening pathways for action. While some of these effects are so inconsequential that they are hardly noticed, others are so influential that they actually change the course of our lives—impacting our careers, relationships or even our health. Depending on the frequency with which a thought occurs, the intensity of our reaction and the amount of time we commit to it, a recurring thought pattern can completely alter our lives.

It is easy to imagine the damage a powerful recurring thought can have if based on falsity and dishonorable intention. Because the ego is self-serving above all else, its motives in spiritual terms are almost always detrimental. A mind that has not been initiated toward spiritual awakening is egoistic, material driven and hell-bent (no pun intended) on personal gain through its *"me first"* mentality.

Because the mind has the ability to color our perception of reality and control our sense of right and wrong, we may never have a clear glimpse at its veiled manipulations. Even the most horrific criminals, such as molesters and murderers, have rationalizations that justify their abhorrent behavior. It is contrary to the nature of this egoistic mind to be driven by concern for others. People who have concern for others before their own self-interest have embraced altruism. They have gone against their egoistic nature and transcended the tyranny of their baser desires. This core shift from egoism to altruism is the beginning of becoming a spiritual person.

In *The Spiritual Brain: A Neuroscientist's Case for the Existence of the Soul*, neuroscientist Dr. Mario Beauregard and journalist Denyes O'Leary relate how evolutionary psychology has viewed the spiritual quality of altruism as a brain with faulty wiring:

> *Altruism, or self-sacrifice for people other than one's own kin is usually, though not always, related to spiritual beliefs; for example, Mother Teresa's image routinely appears in articles devoted to studying altruism. Altruism is easier to study than spirituality, precisely because it is a behavior that can be studied apart from a belief system. So how does evolutionary psychology account for altruism? As science writer Buchanan explains in New Science, "In evolutionary terms it is a puzzle because any organism that helps others at its own expense stands at an evolutionary disadvantage."*

Evolutionary biologist Robert Trivers, of Rutgers University, thinks: *"Our brains misfire when presented with a situation to which we have not evolved a response,"* he explains. *In other words, we should be selfish because evolution has wired us that way.*

Are we to believe that whenever one foregoes his or her own personal gain or safety to address the concerns of others that this person is only doing so as the result of faulty thinking? Was Mother Teresa's saintly behavior in saving the world's most needy children evidence of brain damage? By comparison, are those investment brokers who committed securities fraud, swindling thousands of investors out of billions of dollars, to be admired for their healthy self-serving minds? According to the material theories supporting Darwin's premise of survival of the fittest, this may just be the case. There certainly is an overabundance of self-serving egoists who are acknowledged and praised for their achievements regardless of the destruction left in their wake. There are not many blockbuster movies based on protagonists who turn the other cheek in the face of injustice.

Perhaps the mind is designed with two agendas—one serving its animal nature, while the other adheres to the spiritual. We will explore this alternative hypothesis further. It is not that the mind is faulty with its *me first mentality,* only that it is a lesser, more basic mentality. A toddler who is reluctant to share toys is said by many psychologists to be displaying healthy ego development. The same behavior in adults, however, is judged as shameful and selfish. It is not uncommon to observe grown people manipulating others to gain the biggest and best for themselves. In order to develop spiritually, we must cultivate selflessness in place of selfishness. In order to do so, we must train ourselves to be an honest observer of our behavior.

The first phase of our spiritual exploration is vigilant scrutiny of the mind in action. As Dr. Beauregard points out, it is easier to observe behavior than beliefs. While we will need to bring both under close examination, we should start with behavior. The other will follow. Our first objective is to observe the thoughts, words and actions that are manifesting, without defending, condemning, judging or endorsing. From such observations, we will reflect upon the mental activity behind them. We will also want to reflect on the lifetime of previous similar behavior and its underlying mindset.

Much of our current behavior is based on learned responses patterned after previous conduct. Consider how dysfunctional our personality has become under the influence of decisions made, and values formed, decades ago. When reconsidered, might there not be a matured perspective that brings new input into the decision making? The *human computer* that directs our perception and our resulting behavior is sorely in need of upgrades. Most of us are running programming that became outdated along with double-knit bellbottoms.

Unlike artificial intelligence, the human intellect remains committed to its previous programming. Much of that programming came from justifications of previous bad behavior. The mind strongly resists viewing itself as wrong or shameful. Over time, it reconfigures all of our wrongdoing, runs it through the spin cycle of self-justification and turns it into noble acts. Those acts then serve as precedent for future behavior. If lying saved us in the past, it remains our go-to strategy for the future. If we stole on the job, especially if we were not caught, we have precedent for stealing again. Exploration of previous behavior is not about reward and punishment; it is simply a process of scanning our human hard drive for faulty programming needing upgrades.

Spiritual mentality is quite different from our default *Me First* mentality. Creating a spiritual mentality is not an easy transition—especially if you are not convinced it is necessary. The mind has worked feverishly to protect itself and justify previous transgressions. It has even trained the emotions to activate should anyone try to challenge our values and motives. We act as if admitting poor judgment for our past lack of integrity will trigger a massive domino effect that won't stop until our credibility and worthiness is left in ruins. Actually, the process of self-reflection is necessary in order to enhance our credibility and worthiness. No one gets through decades of life without innumerable lapses in judgment and indiscretions. Our spiritual *permanent records* are not cast in marble. It is absolutely available to wipe them clean and have a new start. However, it is only possible if we stop defending our negative actions and begin rising above them.

Creating a Space for Spiritual Exploration

In Chapter Eight, which discusses the *Spiritual Structure,* we explore the process of *creating space* in order to bring about the creation of something new. This is a prevailing theme in the ancient mystical tradition. It is also quite helpful for our purposes at the outset of spiritual exploration. The mystical tradition teaches that within the infinite Divine Light there was no space for the lower form of existence that manifests as physical form. Accordingly, the Divine Light was contracted to make space for the creation of the physical world.

In the ancient Jewish Mystical Tradition, Lurianic Kabbalah, this process of contracting the spiritual Light is called *tzimtzum.* The spiritual Light that was contracted and constricted during *tzimtzum* is hidden within us. One might consider that our individual spiritual exploration is to discover and reveal the hidden spiritual Light within and allow it to shine out into the world. Ironically, the same process is employed to move from the physical into the spiritual, as was necessary to move from the infinite spiritual into the finite material—a space must be created in the material to allow the spiritual to emerge. The intention of that space is to create a silence in the midst of mental noise.

In the words of Dutch Theosophist and author, Dr. J.J. van der Leeuw (1893-1934), associate of Sigmund Freud and close personal friend of J. Krishnamurti, *silence is the fertile ground of intuition:*

> *It is just in these rare silences of our busy lives that the intuition can speak to us; it is only when the illusion-bound intellect with its noisy self-assertion is quiet for a while that the voice of living truth can be heard. The moment of illumination may well be the outcome of years of mental search calling forth... where the untrammeled mind sees the vision and speaks to the mind in prison. But it is always the flash of intuition that shows us the truth and coordinates our laboriously gathered intellectual material.*
> —J. J. Leeuw, *The Conquest of Illusion*

This sentiment was echoed by a contemporary of Dr. van der Leeuw, George S. Arundale (1878-1945), president of the Theosophical Society and early tutor to J. Krishnamurti: *The intuition is a kind of bridge between the future and the present. It is a larger consciousness not yet developed or ful-*

filled, any more than the consciousness of mind or emotions is perfected and fulfilled.

The required mental space begins more within than anything external. It is actually inward and external, simultaneously, but the more dominant process takes place in the mind. As spiritual teachers have taught for centuries, controlling the breath allows for controlling the mind. Gradually, one recognizes the endless blather of the mind as mental clutter obscuring sacred treasures. The treasures are more than spiritual knowledge; they include a vast array of experiences unknown to the conscious mind. A wealth of insight and understanding beyond mundane thinking is deep within the unconscious. (More on accessing the mind's control center in the chapters ahead.)

For the most part, our daily awareness is based upon what is observed in the moment and how it correlates with what we experienced in the past. A deeper awareness comes when one turns the mind inward on itself. What we commonly think of as *mind* will merge into what is often referred to as *Soul*. Once the mind recognizes the Soul, our perception, and indeed our identity, are permanently altered. In this moment, we realize the profound truth previously referred to from the spiritual scientist, Pierre Teilhard de Chardin: *We are not human beings seeking a spiritual experience. We are spiritual beings having a human experience.*

Investigation into Our Spiritual Nature

Whether a person is well versed in religion or not, whether believer or nonbeliever, the obligation remains the same for us all—to use the time we have left to conduct our own investigation into our spiritual nature. Like scientists seeking new discoveries, we must do our best to approach this inquiry with an open mind. To seek truth, we must be willing to recognize our own falsehoods; to become right we must accept that previously we may have been wrong. This is a no-brainer for medical researchers. If the research we currently have is correct, we'd already have the cures we are seeking. Scientific research begins with the premise that there is new ground to be broken—new truth that is currently unknown.

Beginning an investigation with the premise that we are out to prove what we already know, the project becomes self-limiting and adds subjectivity to an objective inquiry. Investigating to prove what we already know is less about investigation and more about manipulation. The business practice of conducting studies designed to prove what is advantageous for the products being sold, is all too familiar. If there's a financial incentive for the research to prove a particular result, those results will be tainted. So it is with spiritual investigation; to be authentic we must investigate without ulterior motives and personal biases.

Volume Two, Chapter Nine, introduces the threefold spiritualization process. In this chapter, we examine the significance of this inquiry. It is to understand the very nature of the reality in which we find ourselves. One of history's greatest minds, Albert Einstein, stated in his book, *Out of My Later Years*: *There can be no right action without understanding. The essence of all understanding lies in experiencing the very being of the object to be understood.*

This premise is equally applicable to what we are calling the spiritual. We must explore it from the inside looking out. There are no teachers, religious scriptures, books, or sacred rituals that can substitute for one's personal experience of what is meant by the spiritual. This wisdom is already hidden within us and must be illuminated and brought into our consciousness. The discovery process is highly sensitive and comes about gradually through persistent investigation. As Socrates pointed out some 2400 years ago and captured in Manly P. Hall, *Collected Writings, Vol. 2*, Sages and Seers, *The Mystical Figures of Jakob Boehme:*

> *Socrates said that understanding must be coaxed or persuaded to come forth out of its hidden retreats within the soul... we never release man by pressing our opinions upon him, even if those opinions are themselves true. We must lure a reluctant consciousness to reveal its own purpose, thus leading the creature to a condition of sufficiency.*

Methods and Motives Matter

The most direct path to having the *spiritual experience* is to engage in activities that move us closer to it. At the same time, we should avoid activities that move us further away. In Chapter Nine, dealing with the *spiritual process*, these *approach and avoidance* activities will be clarified. While we already know the activities in each category, our inner mechanism has a way of deceiving us ostensibly in order to preserve our free will. In the end, we must simply *identify* the right activities and have the intention and discipline to *make* the right choices. Although this task is simple to say, it is not so simple to carry out.

There is nothing simple about the *spiritual process* or self-mastery. There's also nothing quick and easy about becoming a great artist or musician, or cultivating an advanced understanding of physics or mathematics, or developing any number of athletic abilities. It is part of being human. We are all raw material waiting to be refined and shaped into something extraordinary. Any life that is not at least partially engaged in the process of refinement becomes fertile ground for depression and emptiness leading to deterioration and decline.

There is a fundamental difference between achieving mastery in a material endeavor as compared to achieving spiritual mastery. Some people training to become a masterful musician or athlete may have the dream of riches and fame. This dream can actually serve as a strong motivator to keep them on track during endless hours of striving and practice. Conversely, with spiritual advancement, spirituality must be for the sake of spirituality alone—no ulterior motives. The introduction of any form of self-serving motivation will compromise our progress. In other words, only when spirituality is for its own sake does it resonate with the highest chords.

Many spiritual teachers have recognized, however, that if one initially is incentivized by self-serving motivation, it may be better than allowing one's spiritual efforts to wane. The thought is that even if one initiates his or her spiritual pursuit with dreams of gaining honor and recognition, this lesser motivation will eventually evolve to a purer and more appropriate form as the process unfolds. In other words, spiritual elevation is its own reward.

Initiating Spiritual Exploration through the Power of Observation

The *spiritual quest* is a tall order, but less daunting when broken into realistic steps. For now, just recognizing how the whole mechanism works is a big bite to swallow. The initial phase of our spiritual pursuit is thorough and vigilant observation. Achieving this phase should easily be within our grasp. After all, we've all been engaged in our lives for quite a while. Now it's time to recognize the strategies and patterns we've been following in the game of life. We start by seeking answers, through the lens of unbiased observation, to a series of questions each of us must formulate for ourselves: *Am I willing to cheat in order to win? Am I a team player or do I seek acknowledgement only for myself? Do I appreciate the opposing team for its role in making our team better players? Do I even understand the rules that will determine whether we win or lose?*

Most people cannot even begin to look at their own behavior through an impartial lens. As uninitiated, egoistic players, it is in our design to exaggerate our pluses while obscuring our minuses. In this scenario, a winning score will not produce a true win as it is not a true score. It is not the product of impartial judgment. The game is being won in our own world, but only because we are playing by our own rules. Occasionally, we are able to convince a few others to humor us with flattery, but this praise is seldom an inroad to truth and is a deterrent to betterment. Put differently, in a game where you are rule maker, player, coach and score keeper, how valid is your merit?

Keeping this in mind, we initiate an impartial observation of how we play the game. More than on any other playing field, spirituality is one game where how we play and the rules we follow, rather than the final score, determine whether we are winners or losers. The Buddha taught his monks and nuns that the first step toward transformation of negative behavior patterns into positive is the step of *observation*. Well before changing our actions, we should fully observe our negative patterns to determine what led to them.

The spiritual tenet of vigilant observation provides the key to opening the door to all spiritual practices that follow. Our lives are a constant struggle between our human wisdom and our animal desires. However, beyond these two facets, is the observer—the eye of the Soul. At the core of vigilant observation is a most fundamental spiritual teaching—*identify with the observer rather than the observed.* Those who practice observation eventually recognize that there are three components at work: First, there is that which is being observed—our outward behavior. Second, there is that which is expressing our behavior—our inner character. Third, there is that which is observing both outward behavior and inner character—the *detached, unbiased* observer.

While close scrutiny of our behavior, and the character traits at its source, is a substantial challenge, this task pales compared to the impact of discovering the unbiased observer. When one encounters the observer within and recognizes it as the true core of his or her identity, it is a total game changer. Most people identify themselves as the *doer* in life. It is our most physical form—our outward actions. The *doer* is who is reflected back in the mirror and is who demands so much attention throughout the day. If life were a Monopoly game, the *doer* or *smaller self* would be the Scottie dog that moves from square to square based on the roll of the dice. The *larger Self* is the roller of the dice and the hand that moves the Scottie. Of course, in real life, the playing pieces have been given free will over their moves while the *larger Self* simply observes. When one shifts consciousness from the playing piece to the observer, from *smaller self* to *larger Self,* a whole new game emerges.

Behavior Change is the Result of Character Change

The Sages taught that what needs our attention is not so much our expressed behavior, but rather the causal character behind the behavior. One who has cultivated an honest character does not lie or cheat. A dishonest person cannot to be trusted, even when behaving honestly. The purpose behind constant vigilance is ultimately character refinement. Of course, it's important to change negative behavior into positive. Fully recognizing and exposing our bad intentions is the decisive inner step before we approach any outward change. Changing the negative trait within, which is the source of our negative behavior, manifests in the outward expression of our behavior. Therefore, discovering and refining the inner trait that is the source of stinginess or lying is a far greater accomplishment than outwardly forcing insincere behavior that reflects generosity or honesty. It is the realm of our *being* (character) that is the true source of our *doing* (behavior).

We can readily notice how fully attached we are to our bad behavior even though we intellectually recognize that it is clearly wrong. People do not smoke because they think it is a good idea; it is an attachment to the pleasure of a negative behavior in which they indulge. If we were to trace the decision to smoke back to where it originated, we would find the character trait that influenced this bad choice. The flawed character trait that allows smoking is the source of many other bad choices.

We all have flawed character traits that lead to choices we know are not right. The perceived benefit of smoking outweighs an ambiguous potential danger lurking in the future. After all, the *pleasure* is happening now, while the impending harm is somewhere in the non-reality of an elusive future. It all boils down to one basic problem: ***The temptation to choose what's wrong is stronger than the wisdom to choose what's right.***

This is always the underlying issue concerning bad behavior. The person spinning on the bathroom floor after a night of over-indulgent drinking is far wiser *after* suffering the consequences. Similarly, it is a far wiser person who faces the reality of a bad diagnosis from his or her cardiologist. The experience of suffering is the ignorant man's greatest teacher. "If I only knew then what I know now" is so often our realization after foolish behavior. Ironically, we often *did* know then—we simply chose to ignore truth in favor of desire. Why? Because choosing what we desire includes the immediate gratification of experiencing some form of sensory pleasure. The only reason we would ever choose the mistake over the truth is to satisfy unrelenting desire.

Within those painful moments of newly faced truth, we finally acquire the willpower we lacked during a reckless past. Wisdom will always correct our intention and strengthen our will, making discipline more accessible. When we struggle with faulty intentions and diminishing willpower, it's the result of wisdom failing to override what tempts us. Feeding our wisdom and strengthening our mental discipline reinforces the stand it takes against our blind physical desires—or in the language of the Bible, *the desires of the flesh*. In the words of Romans 8:6:

> *The mind governed by the flesh is death, but the mind governed by the Spirit is life and peace. The mind governed by the flesh is hostile to God; it does not submit to God's law, nor can it do so. Those who are in the realm of the flesh cannot please God.*

Spiritual Exploration Leads to the Spiritual Experience

The heart of our discussion here is to provide greater clarity and access to what is meant by the *Spiritual Experience*.

This will not be easy. It is difficult, if not impossible, to even define this experience. Remember the words of Loa Tzu and consider that the true meaning of this experience is beyond explanation. The only way to know this experience is to experience it. At this point, it is recommended that we not attempt to describe the experience to anyone other than those who have had a similar experience. Any such attempt runs the risk of not only being misunderstood, but also being judged harshly or worse yet, diminishing the experience of the initiate, rendering it more difficult to repeat.

Simply put, the *spiritual experience* is the experience of our spiritual nature. Often, we *feel* the experience of our thoughts, and we certainly *feel* the various experiences of our body; the *spiritual experience* is when we *feel* the experience of our Soul. The Taoists suggest that we leave that which is spiritual in the spiritual realm. Bringing it into the physical realm of description and reaction can hamper further progress. The proper way for the *spiritual experience* to enter the physical world is by the outward expression of our inner relationship with our Soul, *i.e.,* our behavior. When the dominating relationship with our inner being is that of ego, it is apparent in our behavior. Conversely, when the Soul is dominating, this too, is outwardly apparent. In Chapter Eight, we discuss the *spiritual structure* and focus more on the Soul vs. ego mechanism.

The *spiritual experience* is *the epiphany* referred to in the title of this book. Once the experience of our Soul is brought into consciousness, we are no longer the same person. Every aspect of our identity is altered by this single realization. While many trusted teachers and celebrated teachings have contributed to this discussion, ultimately, it will be your own definition and description that serves you best. Other people who have gone down this path before can assist in our discovery, but our own experience is undoubtedly the most personal and unique, not to mention the most fulfilling.

Each person's experience of *spiritual reality* may be similar, yet not identical to that of others. For this reason, we should not try to have another person's experience. We study the experiences of the Sages and great teachers only to gain insight into the challenge, but never to replace our experience with theirs—it won't work anyway. That each person has his or her unique *spiritual experience* illuminates the profound equality of all humanity. We each have access to the immense *spiritual experiences* that are characteristic of the Saints and Sages.

After having our own *spiritual experience*, we can benefit greatly from the wisdom and guidance available from those who have come to know their own *spiritual experience*. Although they bless us with their words, we should always keep in mind that words are not the end game; it is the experience that follows that we must hold in highest regard.

Even the word *spiritual* carries with it a variety of images—as well as trunk loads of baggage. There are clearly those who shy away from anything identified as *spiritual, sacred* or *divine*. You would not want to miss this opportunity because words got in your way. Rather, consider that the fundamental nature of this experience is one that can be described as an **expanded sense of self**—a dimension of our existing identity that is beyond the physical and psychological.

Consider the expanded capability one has using a computer that is connected to the World Wide Web as compared to using a typewriter. Not only does the computer type words, it corrects spelling and grammar, and connects us to the worldwide web that brings a library of information. This comparison is analogous to using our human capabilities as a body and mind as compared to the full spectrum of body, mind and spirit. There is a whole world of unlimited experience awaiting our spiritual awakening.

The Promise...
In the ancient Hindu scriptures, we find a *promise* echoed throughout most all religious teachings. In the Bhagavad Gita, it is told to Arjuna by Sri Krishna, as a promise made by the Divine to all who are human: *Those who perceive My presence within their physical, astral, and spiritual bodies, their hearts united to Me, retain their perception even at the time of death.* (7:30)

The Bhagavad Gita is an ancient conversation between God and humanity. It reflects the great love existing between the Creator and the created. In this single verse is found the promise that those who achieve the spiritual quest needn't fear their moment of death. Here we find all the justification we need to use our worldly time in pursuit of the spiritual. The great Hindu yogi, Paramahansa Yogananda, explains this ancient verse:

Death is the "final Exam" for which all life is a preparation. To leave the body consciously is a blessing not accorded to many. Most people slip back into the after-death sleep. One's experiences prior to death may be painful, but death itself comes as a relief, and is without pain. Mainly, whatever pain people experience at the time of death is mental: the fear above all of losing the body, to which they've grown not only accustomed, but attached—very often to the point of identifying with it as their real self... Death is an ordeal

everyone must face... The consciousness one brings to
death determines his [or her] future existence.

Yogananda goes on to say that death is an ordeal everyone must face. It is met with the sudden realization that the
entirety of all one has ever known is about to be lost. This
relinquishment includes all the people one has known, the
work one has set in motion and all that must be left undone.
This has been the only home we have known for a lifespan. It
holds our footprints and our stories, and for some, the echo
of our memory will continue to linger on. In that moment,
we face the sum total of our virtues and vices—the good and
the bad, the beauty and the ugliness—that we leave in our
wake. For most people, this moment is too raw and too real
to face, and we can only recoil from its weight back into sub-
consciousness.

If, on the other hand, we have spent our lives cultivating
our spiritual nature, there is another option. True, the flesh
will not continue regardless of how much we have trained
for this moment. All that is physical, including our thoughts
and feelings, will cease to exist in the world. For those who
have found an identity beyond the physical, there remains
that identity through which to navigate the corridors of
death. It is only the flesh that must face the eventuality of all
matter, while the consciousness that has *always been*, will
always be. This is the promise found locked in the ancient
Hindu Scriptures as well as the ancient Hebrew Scriptures,
the Gospels and the Koran. The benevolence of the Creator
would be stained with our blood if we were only given a brief
moment to enjoy creation, albeit marked by toil and suffering, then followed by endless, dreamless sleep. The promise
is that nothing will ever be taken from us without the option

of something greater to replace it. However, we are unable to exercise this option unless we have previously made the appropriate spiritual investment.

In Summary...
Regardless of the terminology used to describe the subject, the spiritual hypothesis remains the same. The human entity exists within three dimensions. The most apparent of the three is the physical dimension of the body. On a more subtle level, the human exists within the psychological dimension of the mind. Few would dispute the existence of body and mind. The spiritual hypothesis declares that beyond the physical and psychological lies the spiritual dimension. Just as the subtlety of the psychological is greater than that of the body, the subtlety of the spiritual is all but entirely concealed—yet completely accessible. Unlike the physical and psychological, the spiritual remains hidden unless *intentionally* accessed. This book challenges the reader to discover the Soul that dwells yet within the body, by gaining access to its distant shore—*Self-realization*. We do not arrive at this revered destination without first setting our intention to get there—*Bon Voyage*.

CHAPTER EIGHT

Recognizing the Spiritual Structure

Chapter Eight is intended to familiarize the reader with the *spiritual structure*—to make its acquaintance and develop a working relationship. This is not an easy task as there are no legitimate definitions, descriptions, images nor any forms that are suitable for this purpose. All words and labels fall short of authenticity when it comes to the spiritual structure. As the Taoists have said for centuries, *if you can put it in words, it's not it.* As a matter of fact, the very term *spiritual structure* is an oxymoron—the spiritual is the polar opposite of structure. However, this idiom is generic and vague enough that we may avoid the emotional tripwires embedded in centuries of more traditional, religious terms. Consider it a *working title* to serve our purpose for the moment. The only way to gain a more authentic perception of the spiritual structure is to enter it.

Of course, even the notion of *entering* the spiritual structure is misleading as we can't enter a space that we already occupy. More precisely, nothing exists outside of the spiritual structure. The Sages taught that what we perceive as our physical lives and our material world are mere expressions or shadows of the spiritual. Our bodies are the garments that the Soul chose for our current adventure, and our lives are the stage where the drama unfolds. So the phrase *entering the spiritual structure* is used as a metaphor. A more precise statement would be: *recognizing the true nature of reality*. But that's quite a mouthful with many moving parts. And without many of those parts already in place, it would be easy to reject such a statement as lofty and overreaching. Given that we already exist within this infinite spiritual reality, Chapter Eight is designed to shed some light on our spiritual surroundings.

The Universe, both visible and invisible, is a Spiritual System. Man is a part of this Spiritual Order, so indivisibly united with It that the entire Cosmos is (or may be) reflected in his mind. Evolution is the awakening of the soul to recognition of its unity with the Whole. Material evolution is an effect, not a cause. This reverses the popular belief, declaring that evolution is the result of intelligence, rather than intelligence being the result of evolution.
—Ernest Holmes, *The Science of Mind*, 1938, p.337

That there are matters we don't understand is obvious—how could the finite intellect of an inherently subjective mortal being, imprisoned within the confines of time and space, be expected to fathom the

infinite wisdom of the Creator? The great wonder is
that there are matters we can understand.
—*The Rebbe*, Menachem M. Schneerson

What the Spiritual Structure Is Not

We begin by describing the indescribable spiritual structure, by discussing what it *is not* in order to gain some idea of what it *is*. Unlike the physical structure, the spiritual does not add up—it is not under the intense tyranny of mathematics. According to English mathematician, logician, and noted philosopher, Alfred North Whitehead (1861-1947), *"All science, as it grows toward perfection becomes mathematical in its ideal."* Mathematics is the lexicon of science; quantitative as opposed to the qualitative nature of the spiritual. Our physical reality is made up of measurable units of time, space, matter and energy. Huston Smith captures this materialistic scientific view of reality in his book, *Forgotten Truth:*

> *A spatio-temporal state of affairs is a spatio-temporal state of affairs... a number is a number, and number is the language of science. Objects can be larger or smaller, forces can be stronger or weaker, durations can be longer or shorter, these all being numerically reasonable. But to speak of anything in science as having a different ontological—as being better, say, or more real—is to speak nonsense.*
> —Huston Smith

Professor Huston makes a vital point in this discussion; from the material scientific perspective, that which is not observable and measurable simply does not exist. Although limited and biased by its own beliefs, science has dominated

425

our perception of reality for the past few centuries. Only recently has the "new" science begun to recognize the possibility of existence that is more than meets the eye. The *spiritual structure* is not covered by the natural laws of material science, as it is neither physical nor material in form. It is not a part of time and space, or a measurable force. For those who hold an exclusively material worldview, the spiritual structure does not exist and to speak of it "is to speak nonsense." When materialists demand physical, mathematically sound evidence of the spiritual structure, there is nothing available to satisfy their uninitiated request—there are no numbers to add together that prove the existence of the spiritual structure, the presence of the Soul or God. Just as science speaks in numbers and religion speaks in words, the spiritual communicates its authenticity through direct experience.

This initial description leaves us at an enormous disadvantage. How can something exist, yet not exist within the context of time and space? This is a fair question asked by those who view their own existence as being only physical and only within the context of the material world, where existence is reflected through time. Within the context of time, we must include the process of change, as every moment reflects a different image of reality. However, once we transcend the physical nature of reality, there is no need for time—we have entered the domain of the spiritual—the domain of the Soul; the changeless eternal.

How does one enter the realm of the eternal and experience the spiritual structure? Throughout the ages, only two portals into the eternal have been widely discussed. The first is apparent—death. When the body and brain cease to function, we are in the eternal realm. The senses of the body and the perceptions of the mind are the main forces that keep us grounded in the physical world. When these forces are no longer functioning, we are no longer attached to physical reality. For our purposes, this first approach is not recommended for finding the spiritual structure.

The second portal into the eternal is through communion with the Soul. While the Soul is embedded within our human form, it exists in both the physical and the spiritual; the material and the eternal. When the Soul is realized, a person experiences his or her eternal root. In that moment, people become aware of their true essence extending far beyond their familiar lifelong identities. For most of us, this first glimpse into the spiritual realm is like a flash of lightning; although brilliant and intense, it is quick and fleeting. It's almost always initially perceived as something that has *happened*, as opposed to something *happening*.

This is characteristic of all events occurring on the material plane; they are mostly viewed as having happened. It is difficult to recognize the happenings of the present moment as they are so quick in passing. There is no mechanism of time in the spiritual structure—no past and no future; only now. Comparing the physical with the spiritual, in our physical lives we experience the present moment as just that—a moment. Before we can even recognize that it is here, it has already passed.

On the spiritual plane, the now is eternal; beginningless and endless. Accustomed to experiencing existence in momentary, fleeting sound bites, our first whiff of infinite experience can be overwhelming to say the least. This is why we often experience spiritual moments in the form of memories. Before we can even respond, these moments are in our past. If truth be told, this is the same process by which we experience our physical lives—through the rearview mirror.

It's unfortunate how this *rearview living* leads to a life that is not experienced. This is a pattern that causes life to be experienced through memory rather than in real time. It is a difficult pattern to break, but well worth the effort. Much has been written on the topic of *living in the now* as it is invaluable to finding true fulfillment. More pertinent to our discussion, is that the now is also where we have the greatest access to the spiritual structure.

Time, and the sequence of time, is an essential ingredient in the design of the material world. Without its two siblings, space and matter, there would be no need for time. These are the defining characteristics of the material world: time and space; energy and matter. It is a challenge to even think of physical reality without thinking within the structure of time, space, energy and matter. The corollary to these four essentials is change. All things physical are in a continual state of change.

Along with change, another key characteristic of the material world is impermanence. On some level, existing in physical form and dwelling in the material world, we are aware of our own impermanence, not to mention the impermanence of all we love. According to the Buddha, this awareness is a key source of all human suffering. It can be quite depressing just to think about; which is why we tend to bury these thoughts deep within our subconscious.

We're like children delighted by our time in the toy store, dreading that moment when we'll be called to leave. However, imagine that the toy store is located in the middle of Disneyland. What if when we leave the toy store, we find ourselves getting on the Star Tours ride? —arguably one of the best rides ever conceived.

This is the nature of the spiritual structure, it underlies the physical structure; and by comparison, the physical structure appears as an illusion. The Buddha taught the need to break our attachment to the toy store lest we miss out on the real action. Those who can't break their attachment to the physical are prodded along by the sting of suffering. Without the merciful aid of suffering, the human caterpillar will never leave the cocoon of physicality and enter the spiritual Disneyland of butterflies.

This brings us to a very important distinction and a key characteristic of the material world that is not present in the spiritual structure—suffering. There is no need for suffering in the spiritual structure as we have already arrived. Unlike the threat commonly employed by many religions, spirituality holds only one purpose for suffering, to keep its recipient moving toward spiritual awakening. In the physical world, punishment may appear to be the purpose of suffering, but this is only concocted to fit the narrow view of our limited perception. In the big picture, suffering is actually the result of our attachment to all that keeps us from evolving toward Enlightenment.

Another important distinction between the material and the spiritual is the concept of limitations. The spiritual structure is neither limited nor limiting, while everything in our material world revolves around limitations. Time is limiting, as are space and matter—not to mention the overwhelming limitations generated by impermanence. Although science and technology have made enormous advances in overcoming some of our major limitations, these innovations only scratched the surface compared to the limitless spiritual structure. For example, compared with our ancestors, it would appear that we have overcome our limits of speed and distance. We have the ability to sit in one part of the world while viewing the events taking place thousands of miles away. We can even communicate with loved ones on the other side of the world from the comforts of our own homes, and view them as we speak. Such achievements pale in comparison to the non-spatial/non-temporal reality of the spiritual structure.

The Glossary of No Definitions

Language itself is a necessary limitation of our physical reality. Without words, we would certainly have a difficult time communicating. Words were one of the first innovations of our cave dwelling ancestors. Yet words impose enormous limitations as well. For the most part, these limitations go undetected in our material lives. We name a table a table and a chair a chair and these labels are adequate when we think or communicate about a dining room set. However, words hamper our spiritual awakening. When we label something that is as unknowable as the Soul or we provide a name for the indescribable spiritual experience, we limit our understanding of the inherent truth, replacing it with a label. As we come to know the Soul by its name, the definition of that name constrains our actual experience of the Soul.

Such is the case with the spiritual structure. The word *spiritual* is defined as *relating to the Soul or spirit*; two more words that have no true meaning within the material world. The word *structure* is defined as *something built or erected; an orderly system of parts functioning as an orderly whole.* This definition gives us a glimpse into what might be meant by the spiritual structure, but given that we cannot define the Soul or spirit, and that there are no parts or structures in the spiritual realm, other than infinite Oneness, our terms feel like misnomers. At best, they are *place savers* allowing communication about an indescribable idea, knowable only through direct experience.

The Buddha taught that man found it necessary to name everything he observed within his reality in order to refer back to it. He pointed out that this was an effective technique for communication. Although now we are left with words rather than the true experience of all that exists. The wisdom of the Buddha is echoed in the words of the 9th century Ch'an Buddhist monk, P'u-yuan of Nan-ch'uan (748-834), who stated it simply; *"What has a name is subject to limitations."* Within these teachings, we are told that the spiritual is known through personal experience as opposed to the intellect. This is as accurate a guideline as any and one that serves our purpose.

Knowledge that is rooted in the intellect, but lacking personal experience may serve in the material world, yet it is a significant obstacle to spiritual advancement. True spiritual growth is less about learning what others have discovered and all about making our own discoveries. All that we need is already within us; our challenge is to drill down into it. This isn't to suggest that there is no benefit in learning from the wisdom of others; rather to say that the experience of others provides a limited benefit to the spiritual seeker— however, it does prime the pump. Nobody but you can raise your own consciousness, tenderize your heart, purify your mind, or refine your character. Yet others can be invaluable when it comes to inspiration and guidance. It's like the old adage; *you can lead a horse to water...*

Setting aside the unique models of science and technical knowhow, our spiritual knowledge, both individual and collective, is found in books, teachings and personal experiences rooted in the past. It is what we have previously learned and stored in our memory. It is what has collectively been concluded as truth and is now tradition. This kind of knowledge has value, especially in the case of science and technology, but it hampers spontaneous spiritual experience. For spiritual discovery, we need our minds to be fresh and free of conformity; unburdened by tradition. In the words of the great 20th century spiritual teacher Krishnamurti:

To follow another, however learned or noble, is to block all understanding... thought originating from the past must inevitably cloud the perception of that which may be called truth... a mind caught in tradition cannot perceive what is true... Put away the book, the description, the tradition, the authority, and take the journey of self-discovery.
— J. Krishnamurti, *Commentaries on Living*

Following this approach toward self-discovery, let's look at several examples of words we should liberate from our current definitions. First on this list is the biggest word of all—*God*. Ironically, in order to gain an experience of God, we must first dissociate ourselves from the word God. The truth is that we are unable to conceive, let alone define God. Like truth, God must be discovered anew in our moment-to-moment experience. Although God defies definition, She doesn't defy experience. (If you are put off by God being referenced in the feminine, this further illustrates the point being made.) As Krishnamurti puts it, we have both the word and the feeling that the word describes. The word comes from our memory while the experience is taking place in the moment. If the word is allowed to define our true experience, we have lost what is real in preference for some lesser idea stemming from knowledge, albeit inadequate knowledge.

Right alongside the word God is the word *Soul*. As with the word God, the only authentic way of knowing about the Soul is through personal experience. While it can be useful to look into the experiences of others in order to gain inspiration and guidance, there is no substitute for "feeling" our own Soul. The quest for self-discovery involves the portion of our psyche that includes the Soul. If your first reaction is that you don't even know if you have a Soul, remind yourself that you also do not know that you don't. The operative words are *don't know*. Rather than filling this *blank space* with words, leave it blank and wait patiently for the space to become filled by the experience of the Soul. Rest assured, when the time is right and your inquiry sincere, the Soul will provide the appropriate experience. It is the experience rather than knowledge that leads to spiritual understanding.

Another important word from our *Glossary of No Definitions* is *spiritual*. It's easy to conclude that spiritual is the opposite of material—pertaining to spirit. For our purposes, it is preferable not to regard spiritual and material as opposites, rather approach them as two aspects of the same idea— the material is its form and function while the spiritual is its essence and experience—two sides of the same coin. No number of words can provide you with the spiritual experience, just as no words will describe this experience once you've had it.

The ineffable nature of the spiritual is by design. While initially viewed as troublesome and frustrating, once you have crossed the threshold separating the two dimensions (material and spiritual), you will recognize that they are actually two aspects of the same reality. This recognition is the epiphany providing the portal into the spiritual structure. Or, more precisely stated, once you experience the spiritual aspect of yourself, you will know it's always been there and needs no introduction.

The words for *God*, *Soul*, and *spiritual* have always seemed somewhat otherworldly. This next word, however, has always been considered an intricate part of the material world—*love*. Although we talk of love, we sing about it, write about it, even profess our love to those who arouse our experience of it, we are unable to fully comprehend the phenomenon of love; especially spiritual love. It is said that the closest we mortals come to spiritual love is the love of a mother for her child. This is not to say that a father does not love his child, but it is the mother who *suffers to bring forth life*. The role of the mother to create new life is far more involved than that of the father. A father's contribution to life rarely requires the *selfless suffering required by the mother*. Even the father's role of provider is more voluntary than that of carrying the child and giving birth.

Physical love is often nothing more than strong feelings of desire—the urge to possess what we want. Just as it is difficult to imagine *wanting* without there being an object of our desire; it is not easy to imagine *loving* without there being an object of our attraction. This is not to say that physical love and spiritual love are of a different kind; they merely differ in quality and degree. Spiritual love initially stems from the experience of expanded perception. Once a person gains a glimpse into the spiritual structure, he or she discovers the extraordinary hidden aspects of our existence. The responding feeling is one of awe, wisdom, and unconditional love. However, our common worldly definition of love barely scratches the surface of the true meaning of spiritual love—one of the foundational pillars of the spiritual structure.

Spiritually speaking, our goal is objectless love. When love has an object, it can easily turn to frustration and pain; or worse yet, jealousy and hatred if the object of our love disappoints us, doesn't love us back or remains unattainable. These are characteristics of desire—not love. In such circumstances, it is the object that controls the love—not the subject. When love originates from the object of desire, rather than from the subject expressing that love, it is the object that arouses this feeling. Without the object of our desire, the feeling of love would not arise. Hence, this love is conditional; it is dependent on the object that originally brought it into being. Should those conditions change, the feeling of love may cease to exist; possibly even be replaced by opposite feelings. From the spiritual perspective, this is love that is fleeting and illusive. The conditions existing in the material world are characterized by their tendency to change—and to change often. If our love is reliant on the changing world *not* changing, it is as dependable as a *candle in the wind.*

Can there be love without an object? Yes, but it is not the love most familiar to us; it is spiritual or Divine love. It is called Divine because it reflects the love present within the spiritual structure and is associated with the love attributed to God and the great Saints and Sages. Although this love is accessible in the material world, it is rare. It is love that is given without the condition of anything being given in return. In fact, the benefit of such love is even greater for the giver than the recipient. Hence the age-old spiritual adage *it is better to give than to receive.*

Objectless love emerges from within; it is not controlled by the external world. It is more about *who we are* rather than *what we want.* To achieve this state of love without an object of our love is sublime; it is without condition. Here the feeling of love that was dependent on an object evolved into the feeling of love that is not dependent on an object. Love transformed from being expressed as *I love you,* to simply being expressed as *I love.* We love as a function of our state of being. In this way we actually *become* love—loving is a quality of our character.

In spiritual terms, this evolution of love takes one more transformation and is expressed as *I am love.* At this point we are no longer just expressing love, we *are* love. It is what we are made of and there is no external condition required. There is also no internal condition required for us to express love, it is simply who we are, without dependence on any arousal of the senses.

These are the three variations of love: love that requires an object to be aroused, love that is aroused without requiring an object and love that needs no arousal as it is who we are. Those who achieve this third level of love become a part of the spiritual structure. The spiritual structure is made of this third level of love; albeit a love that is indefinable in worldly terms. To further differentiate the two, a key ingredient in spiritual love is wisdom. This certainly distinguishes it from physical love.

Actually, the more precise description of this key ingredient in spiritual love is *Light.* This Light is referred to in the Book of Genesis 1:3. It is composed of both the light of loving-kindness and the enlightenment of wisdom. This brings us to yet another word to be included in our *Glossary of No Definitions—Light.* There is no definition in our lexicon that comes close to what is meant by *spiritual Light;* the very substance of the spiritual structure. The Light that embraces both loving-kindness and enlightenment is Light that is reflected by the warmth of the human heart and the brilliance of mind. It is this Light that we are here on earth to cultivate and it is radiated by the Soul. The Light accumulated by each Soul determines its place in the spiritual structure. Perhaps the greatest of all miracles in our material world is that we have access to this spiritual Light. Some Sages go so far as to say that Light is a defining force of the spiritual structure the way gravity is a defining force of the physical structure. However, there is no gravity in the spiritual structure, while the world is filled with Light for those who know how to access it.

Recognizing and Observing the Spiritual Structure

It is difficult, at best, to recognize and observe the spiritual structure. Unlike a bridge or a building, this structure is not available to the senses—our *go-to* source for recognition and observation. The five senses are dependable when dealing with the physical structure, as both the senses and the structure are made of the same substance—matter. However, the spiritual structure is not made of matter, and as a result our five senses fail us.

The spiritual structure is made of something far more subtle than matter—consciousness. Consciousness can neither be seen nor heard; it can't be smelled, tasted, or touched, therefore rendering our typical *windows* of observation useless. This leaves only *direct* experience available for recognizing and observing the spiritual structure. We say *direct* here because we have no use for the sense organs that reflect light or resonate sound to the brain; there are no buds, cones, or sensors employed in this process.

Consciousness is perceived through a *quasi*-sixth sense that provides our awareness with the necessary input. For those who have yet to rely on *intuition* for normal perception, this discovery process will be both a challenge and a delight. To be effective at sensing the spiritual structure, we must suspend those personal biases and beliefs that prevent its recognition. It is easy to dismiss intuition and conscience as taking a backseat to logic and reason. The more we deny the pangs of conscience and the voice of intuition, the less they have to say. To gain a clear perception of the spiritual, we must rely heavily on intuition; without it, we have no service dog or cane to guide us through the dark.

We do have one important faculty that is initially useful in recognizing and observing the spiritual structure—imagination. This is not to say that the spiritual is imaginary or illusive, only that it exists in nonmaterial form. To rely solely on our physical senses to familiarize ourselves with that which is nonmaterial is an exercise in futility. We can start by imagining the spiritual structure before we are actually able to recognize its existence. Whatever means brings us to experiencing the spiritual structure serves the purpose. These spiritual imaginings, however, are not true to form because the spiritual is formless. They are only tools to bridge the gap between the workings of the mind and the nature of the Soul. Many observers have felt a profound connection to the spiritual by simply gazing at Michelangelo's painting of the Sistine Chapel or Velazquez's oil painting, *Christ Crucified*. While these depictions are invaluable contributions to humanity's spiritual vision, they cannot replace the hidden visions in the mind, waiting to be revealed.

One method employed by the brain to grasp the unfamiliar is to associate the unknown factor with a similar known factor. This technique has both advantages and disadvantages. On the plus side, we gain some awareness of the unknown by comparing and contrasting it to something already familiar. On the down side, we often gain a false or inauthentic representation of the truth—we compromise the exactitude of our understanding in order to gain some semblance of familiarity. Although using our imagination to gain awareness and intimacy with the spiritual is beneficial, if the imagining obscures the true experience, we've gone too far.

There are many concepts in our material existence that bridge into the spiritual realm. For example, the concept of God exists in the lexicons of all languages. From the most primitive to the most sophisticated of our species, the word God is associated with a familiar idea. If you were to say "God blessed me with a healthy newborn baby" in any language, you would be understood. In our earthly world, the word God is easily recognized and communicated. However, the true meaning of God does not exist in the material world. At best, our worldly understanding of God is a superficial misrepresentation of God. The true definition of God is unavailable, so we are left with our limited impressions. Over time, these impressions are often shared, analyzed, and argued into widespread beliefs. The players on the blue team all agree with the blue team's definition of God, while the players on the green team share a completely different belief. Eventually, people forget that this concept of God is not rooted in anything more than opinion that became popular over time and handed down through generations.

Although these *hand-me-down* beliefs have served us well, the obvious problem with this worldly belief structure is that it is built on a faulty foundation. Instead of having a tiny and limited, yet *true* understanding of God, we are left with a vastly opinionated belief leaving little room for authentic experience. Simply stated, we have settled for a well-defined and traditionally accepted *label* for God rather than a unique and personal *experience* of God. The former being useful in communication with man, while the latter is essential for communion with God.

For our purpose of recognizing the spiritual structure, it is best to first understand that our impression of the spiritual realm consists primarily of age-old, traditional ideas. While these ideas may hold elements of truth, they are mostly based on opinions, myths, and ancient folklore that became popular over time. The popularity is due to people needing something to satisfy their curiosity while having neither the time nor inclination to seek the truth for themselves.

It serves us best to forego such limiting impressions of the spiritual in order to gain direct access to our own experience. Or, as many of the great Sages suggest: *stop telling reality what it is.* Our nature is to fill in the blanks in our spiritual inquiry regardless of whether the answers are correct. We will be taking the opposite approach. A blank space is much better than a limiting or faulty answer. The blank space prompts us to look deeper rather than accept a partial or false impression. It is human nature to form opinions and biases prematurely. Such preconceived notions hinder progress and prevent true discovery, while a blank space allows us to be open to the possibility of a future we do not currently hold or even anticipate.

The spiritual structure begins where words leave off—in silence. In our modern world of noise, silence is a rare commodity and may initially be somewhat intimidating. This is especially true if we include the clamor of our mental chatter. To enter the spiritual chamber, we must first pass through the corridor of silence. It is easy to mistakenly believe that this silence is empty—quite the contrary. The silence is actually filled with content that does not resonate with our physical and mental senses. In the physical world, it is common to see, hear, smell, taste, and touch throughout our day. Each encounter has three elements—the sense organ, the external object sensed and the brain's response. For example, it is not the eye that does the seeing. While it is the organ used to make contact with the object, it reflects the data back to the brain. The brain is the mainframe of all the senses, where the raw data is processed, interpreted, evaluated in terms of posing a threat, and even qualified as being good or bad. At this point, the brain also decides on the appropriate response to its findings. All this is taking place in the blink of an eye. It is the same for the ear and all other sense organs. Just imagine the amount of data being processed as we walk through a mall or go out for a night on the town. Additionally, in terms of accuracy, the mind is only as good as its previous conditioning, including DNA, intelligence, experience and education. One simple misunderstanding or misperception can spiral into untold misery. Even a person, who has cultivated keen senses and clear perception, falls prey to errors in judgment. The everyday playing field of our contemporary life is nothing less than an onslaught of external stimuli from the moment we wake until the timer turns off the TV after we have fallen asleep.

All this worldly stimulation and response pales in comparison to *sensing* the spiritual structure while withholding interpretation and judgment. This is the initial formula for perceiving the spiritual structure—imagining it, sensing its presence and preventing the knee jerk reactions of interpretation and judgment. Certainly, there are the typical questions: *How do we see or hear something when there is no external object involved? Can our mind still make a conscious con-*

nection without an object? Can we see the invisible or hear the silent? We can when we learn to see and hear that which is already within us without need of anything external. Imagine the wonder and amazement, after our birth, when we first heard or saw the external world. We were clean slates with no anticipation of what our futures held. Many have referenced the spiritual awakening as being born again. It is a fitting analogy providing we allow the presence of wonder to guide us where it will.

To Perceive the Spiritual Structure, We Must Enter it

In this chapter we investigate the spiritual structure from every available angle, recognizing that all angles and views are flawed at best. The spiritual structure defies all description and is unavailable for viewing. It is known only through direct experience. Both the means and the end of attaining this direct experience are explored throughout the remainder of this book. This chapter is designed to familiarize ourselves with the structure that we intend to enter. The wisdom provided by the Saints and Sages of religion, the knowledge of modern and ancient philosophers, along with the teachings of the yogic masters and the discoveries of modern scientists, are more than ample to make an impression on the willing mind.

In her 1981 book of meditations, *The Still Voice*, Grace Cooke continues the teachings of White Eagle on the topic of entering the spiritual structure through the portal of silence:

In Silence you enter the temple of your soul, and hold sweet communion with God. All the truth and wisdom to which you have attained in your many lives on earth goes to build the temple of your soul, your higher self. When you enter the silence, when you withdraw from the clamor of the outer world of man and the outer world of your own mind, and enter into the deep, deep silence of your innermost, you are entering the temple of your own soul. And there you hold Holy Communion...

These words are echoed by many spiritual teachers through the centuries. Spoken in the vernacular of religion, they are meant to provide a bridge between the mortal and the Divine. Like all spiritual teachers, Cooke must find words to explain the ineffable. She selects terms that are representative of her own experience and previous conditioning. Her words may not be the words you would have chosen, but this needn't obscure the truth they hold. The incessant blathering of the mind is the very mechanism that prevents us from sensing the spiritual. There is no doubt that the mind will not enter the spiritual structure until it is stilled and learns the approach of silence.

Three Essential Instruments of Discovery

When we take on the spiritual journey, we take on the quest for Truth—the truth about ourselves, our universe and the Source of reality—our God. In order to conduct our investigation, we have three essential instruments of discovery. They are the same three components that make up our being; i.e., our **body with its senses**, our **mind with its intellect** and our **Soul with its consciousness**. Each component requires additional explanation.

The body, or physical aspect of our threefold being, is the most familiar. Although we all have been in possession of a body since birth, for the most part, it remains a mystery. The complexity of the body's brain and nervous system, the array of organs, its beats and breaths along with countless cells working endlessly to serve the whole is a wonder beyond any of the world's most sophisticated manufactured counterparts. Although much has been written about the discoveries for optimal body performance, most of us still operate on what "tastes and feels good. When our overriding desire for pleasure is assigned the role of VP of Operations, we are left on a collision course of premature aging and premature death.

The **mind, or psychological aspect** of our being, is the second component used for the spiritual quest. The mind is both physical and psychological. Its physical form is the brain, requiring the same kind of care as any organ of the body. In its psychological form, the mind is more mysterious, with more unknown than known. A number of our teachers profess that the mind not only determines our thoughts and identity, it also plays a key role in determining the reality in which we live. It follows that developing the health of the brain and enhancing the performance of the mind not only improve the body, but also the reality that surrounds us. When the mind improves, everything improves. From the perspective of a physician or a psychologist, both body and mind are far more complex than what's recognized by their naive owners.

Unlike the body, the mind does not have clearly delineated boundaries. Difficult as it is to keep the body from overindulging in its desires, it pales in comparison to disciplining the mind. The mind has been called the bridge to the Soul. Thus, in order to achieve spiritual advancement, we are dependent on mental discipline. To even begin to benefit from all that the mind has to offer in this regard, we must develop our skills of focus and concentration; i.e., mindfulness. It would be difficult to overestimate the power of focused concentration. Most of us allow our minds to run their course without supervision and discipline. It is problematic for such undisciplined minds to have control over their own remote control. Picture a computer operating in the same way. Imagine sitting before a monitor, gazing at the random display of endless websites without control over where it takes you. Many minds are like computers that display countless pop-ups, continually distracting and redirecting their focus.

Listen to the words of the Buddha on the topic of the undisciplined mind:

This mind is like a fish out of water that thrashes and throws itself about, its thoughts following each of its cravings. Such a wandering mind is weak and unsteady, attracted here, there, and everywhere. How good it is to control it and know the happiness of freedom—And yet how unruly still, how subtle the delusion of thoughts. To quiet them and master them is the true way of happiness. Putting a bridle on the wandering mind, single-mindedly the seeker halts his thoughts. He ends their darting waywardness and finds peace.

—Buddha, Dhammapada

These words of the Buddha are echoed by many of the great spiritual teachers; a mind that is well organized, aware and focused has the power to transform our existence into something far beyond our currently perceived limitations. The panorama of possibilities is endless and the range of experience runs from our image of hell to our image of heaven. According to some of history's greatest geniuses, the *motherboard* that determines our reality is found within the mind.

The **Soul, or spiritual aspect**, is the third component used to discover the spiritual structure. Through recognition of the Soul, the human experience takes its greatest leap forward. The disparity between the Self-realized and the unrealized individual is comparable to the disparity between Homo sapiens and all lesser species. Think about the magnitude of this statement and the magnitude of its implications. It is within the capacity of humans to *evolve* ourselves into a higher species—and, without the assistance of death to achieve this transcendence. That is to say, the person we currently are, and the life we are currently living, has access to a highly advanced experience in a greater reality. This whole transformation takes place without a single change other than in our perception. We jump from ordinary perception based on self-interest and the pursuit of pleasure and power, to an expanded perception based on the higher consciousness of the Soul. This is the distinguishing feature of the next level of the evolving Homo sapiens; a spiritually awakened, higher consciousness being. Although very similar to our current species, the next evolution will have a higher degree of perfection. These humans will be more perfect physical specimens possessing a higher degree of physical and nutritional fitness. They will also be psychologically advanced, having higher degrees of virtue and morality. Perhaps the most important distinguishing feature will be found in the spiritual aspect—mortals fully aware of their immortal essence— humans driven by Soul rather than sensory cravings and ego gratification. This newly advanced life form will be a more authentic expression of Truth than that which roams the world today.

These determinant traits are already present in our current species, yet tragically obscured for most of us. Dr. David R. Hawkins, M.D., Ph.D., conducted extensive research in the human body's innate recognition of that which is true and that which is healthy regardless of the test subject's opinion or knowledge on the topic:

> *Man's two basic types of operational faculties, reason and feeling, are both inherently unreliable, as our history of precarious individual and collective survival attests. Although we ascribe our actions to reason, man in fact operates primarily out of pattern recognition; the logical arrangement of data serves mainly to enhance a pattern-recognition system that then becomes "truth."*
>
> *...Kinesiology is now a well-established science, based on the testing of an all-or-none muscle response stimulus... this kinesiologic response reflects the human organism's capacity to differentiate not only positive from negative stimuli, but also anabolic (life-threatening) from catabolic (life-consuming), and, most dramatically, truth from falsity...The test itself is simple, rapid, and relatively foolproof: A positive muscle reaction occurs in response to a statement that is obviously true; a negative response occurs if the test subject is presented with a false statement.*
>
> —David R. Hawkins, *Power vs. Force*

Spiritual Awakening Leads to an Expanded Sense of Self

Without recognition of the Soul, our mortal lives eventually become tedious, hopeless, and even cruel. The tendency for our lives to be over before we actually understand them or the miraculous opportunities they hold, in and of itself, is inescapably depressing. It is the Soul that erases the scars and dries the tears of our superficial fears and limited perception. Even a brief glance through the lens of the Soul brings a warm and healing wash over our open sores and raw nerves. These initial flashes that come through the channel of the Soul cause us to recognize that we are not just a body with a mind, but a Soul that has manifested a body with a mind. This realization is the foundation of a new and more authentic identity. We do not identify ourselves as a body with a Soul, rather a Soul with a body. Some compare this sensation to that of *coming home*. Our first encounter with the Soul is akin to reuniting with an old friend we have missed. Even before we are able to recognize the design principles of the Soul, we recognize our Soul as our true identity.

The threefold aggregate of the human entity (body—mind—Soul) is both interconnected and interdependent. Improvement of one leads to improvement of the other two. Conversely, the detriment of one leads to the detriment of the others. One glaring exception to this rule is the case of one whose body is aging and dying. Under proper conditions, for some truly wise and blessed individuals, as their body shuts down to pass away, their Soul becomes enlivened. Instead of the typical anxiety over the pain and depression associated with aging and death, they feel exhilaration and joy. These people have a practical, working relationship with their spiritual nature; they have come to know their own Soul as their true identity. Through the enhancement of the bodymind and spirit relationship, we identify with the Soul more than the flesh, which is destined to perish.

We needn't wait for an entire evolution of the human species to experience the perfection awaiting our descendants. Because humans are a self-evolving species, each of us has the wherewithal to become an advanced version of our current self. Certainly, it's no secret that by enhancing our nutritional and physical fitness, we become healthier, more youthful and even more attractive. This improvement is easily recognized as an *advanced version* of our previously unhealthy, aging, less attractive self. It is also well known that a person can become more virtuous and moral; more ethical and honest. Although less common, there are even those individuals awakening to their spiritual roots and becoming an expression of their spiritual essence. These are but a few examples of people achieving an *expanded version* of their former selves.

Self-evolution is happening all the time. As babies, this process begins involuntarily at birth. At first, we are unable to sit up without support. Eventually, however, we evolve from sedentary to crawling; from standing to walking, to riding a bike and driving a car. Each step is an evolution bringing higher degrees of independence. This is similar to the experience of people who achieve advanced physical skills or highly developed intellect. They can excel in sports, create art, perform surgery, or design new technologies. Others cultivate greater understanding and accumulate vast knowledge in math or science—further examples of expanded versions of lesser selves.

As we become more familiar with our spiritual nature, we develop a comparable *expanded sense of self*. A person who gains access to their spiritual core becomes an expanded version of their former self; elevated beyond that same person whose Soul was previously obscured. Once the third component of the body-mind-spirit entity comes online, our personal power takes a quantum leap. We are no longer the same person, nor will we ever be again. This is only the beginning of a transformation that makes the caterpillar's makeover pale by comparison.

Until we are conscious of it, our spiritual development advances concealed and undetected. There is no greater liberation than that of shedding the bonds of physical exclusivity. To recognize who we are beyond our perishable self, is to recognize our imperishable Self. As a drop and the ocean are one and the same, the evolving consciousness we carry within and the infinite consciousness to which it belongs, are one and the same. For the purpose of illustration, we are calling this infinite, omnipotent consciousness the spiritual structure. And to gain access, we must become an expanded version of our current self.

Ironically, the initial reaction to our expanded identity with greater personal power can either lead to further growth or be the cause of our first setback. It is not uncommon for individuals who have just had their first encounter with their spiritual nature to fall hard. One reason for this backslide is that both the expanded identity and the greater sense of power often wind-up igniting and inflating the ego. If we succeed in stirring of the Soul, our response should be one of humility and unconditional love. If the ego becomes involved, it will initiate the opposite—a swelling of pride and a sense of self-importance. Regardless of which response follows the initial awakening, it must be faced honestly and without self-deception.

How we respond to these momentary flashes of spiritual awakening is as important as the initial experience itself. It is the way we perceive and recall such moments that ultimately defines our identity and influences our behavior. Also, our response to these elevated moments determines whether they remain isolated or are followed by further similar experiences. Because our response has such an enduring influence, we must not simply react; rather we must orchestrate a response that supports reoccurrences. Remember, before the spiritual light remains a constant beam, it first flickers like a fluorescent bulb with a faulty starter. The Buddha compared these flickering moments of spiritual insight to flashes of lightning.

In the gloom and darkness of night, when there is a sudden flash of light, a person will recognize objects; in the same way, the one with a flash of insight sees according to reality.

— Buddha, *Anguttara Nikaya*

Upon experiencing flashes of insight, the rational mind recognizes that something out of the ordinary has just occurred and it immediately seeks to define the experience in rational terms. Holding back this knee jerk reaction allows the intuitive mind to recognize the extraordinary occurrence as something grand that will eventually define itself. The Zen masters refer to this as the *indefinable definition*. This type of *knowing* is at the root of all spiritual encounters. It is *knowing* without benefit of definition or belief—knowing that is pure experience.

Knowing without definition allows the experience to reoccur freely. If your mind immediately generates a rational construct around your spiritual experience, further experiences may not fit within this logical construct, making their reoccurrence unlikely. If you need a reaction to direct yourself, use the one that encourages further and grander spiritual awakening—gratitude. Be grateful for the immense honor bestowed upon you. You have been touched in a similar way to that of the great Sages. This is the only true path; the path that is not based on outward conditions. While faith and belief may have brought you to this moment, your experience exceeds anything produced by the intellect. Here, knowing exists beyond the limitations of belief and reason.

All that we have learned and trusted has fulfilled its function to bring us to this moment. Now we must remain open to the discoveries patiently awaiting our spiritual awakening. If we foolishly impose prerequisites and beliefs on this moment, we stifle the spontaneity of the experience. In other words, don't make the mistake of directing what is unfolding; let *it* direct what unfolds. In this way, we are able to recognize that we are in the presence of ultimate knowledge and pure love; or in Buddha terms: Absolute Truth and Ultimate Reality. There's nothing in our past that we can add to this experience. There is nothing that can improve upon it. Conversely, there is much that can diminish it. Ours is to simply be grateful for the expression of the love and wisdom we've encountered and to reflect back sincere gratitude and devotion in order to maintain the experience that has emerged.

Ten Key Obstacles Blocking the Spiritual Structure

Naturally there are many *uninitiated* questions that surface regarding the spiritual structure and the mystical experience; most of which revolve around the inquiry into why things are the way they are. They are called *uninitiated* questions because they are asked from the rational perspective. From the spiritual perspective, *why* is not only irrelevant, it's a distraction. Our challenge is to recognize the true nature of *the way things really are*; questioning *why* simply muddies the water and obscures our vision.

Asking the Buddha why we must suffer until we overcome our attachment to worldly desires, or asking Jesus why the humble are more worthy of heaven than the arrogant, appears foolish. The great Sages taught humanity *to see things as they really are*—this need to know *why* was irrelevant. It's even been suggested that our concern with *why* is a way of delaying, or avoiding altogether, the responsibilities of spiritual awakening.

Having said this, perhaps we can provide a partially satisfying explanation as to why the spiritual is the way it is. The physical plane is designed in a precise manner to fulfill its purpose—to provide the Soul with the experience that is not available on the spiritual plane. This is achieved by conditions found only on the physical plane: time, space, cause and effect, impermanence, vulnerability, suffering, etc. From this perspective, the imperfections of our world and those who dwell in it are, in fact, perfect in terms of fulfilling their necessary functions. Remember, we are not physical beings attempting to have a spiritual experience; we are spiritual beings who gain benefit by having a physical experience. Our physical lives and the material world exist for the benefit of the Soul, not vice versa. Once we come to terms with this truth and have the epiphany for ourselves, the spiritual realm is no longer beyond our reach—the buzzer sounds, the lights go up, and we get to move on, having passed our initiation.

It is a bit premature to discuss winning the game before we even see how it's played. The recognition of the spiritual

structure and the experience of having a Soul are inseparable. When you are recognizing the structure, you are having
the experience; when you are having the experience, you are
seeing the structure. The two exist as one. You can only see
the structure through the window of the Soul. The windows
of the body—eyes, ears, nose, taste, and touch—are not tuned
to such subtle form.

Before venturing into the process of seeing the spiritual
structure, let's explore what obscures it. There are ten common conditions that hamper our ability to recognize the spiritual structure. This is not to suggest that there are *only* ten—
rather to suggest that these are ten fundamental obstacles
typically encountered. The journey into the discovery of the
spiritual structure is fraught with obstacles and blind alleys.
And because of this, we must familiarize ourselves with these
key obstacles: ***Complacent Spiritual Ignorance; Inner
Psychological Conflict; Obstinate Doubt; No Clear
Definition; Unfamiliar Ground; Disguised Nature;
Inflexible Beliefs; Endless Distractions and Restlessness; Unyielding Desires; Overwhelming Clutter.***

First Key Obstacle: Complacent Spiritual Ignorance
This is not permanent, inherent ignorance, rather the lack of
spiritual understanding and awareness that we must overcome. What complicates this particular brand of ignorance
is our complacency about it. All people are ignorant of the
spiritual structure prior to first experiencing it. There are,
however, those who recognize their ignorance and rather
than justify it, they ignite their passion to overcome it. Others
refuse to accept their ignorance as a problem, while declaring
that the spiritual does not exist.

On this topic, the Buddha states: *A fool who recognizes his own ignorance is thereby in fact a wise man, but a fool who considers himself wise—that is what one really calls a fool.* The sentiment of the Buddha is echoed by one of the

world's most revered philosophers and influential sages—Confucius. This great Chinese teacher lived around the same time as Buddha and taught: *Real knowledge is to know the extent of one's ignorance.* In many ways, the path toward enlightenment is a

process of discovering our own spiritual ignorance and bringing it out into the bright light of day. There's no denying that there is darkness in the world. This darkness is most often rooted in ignorance. To remove the darkness of ignorance and replace it with the light of awareness is a noble act by any person, especially when done for the sake of humanity. Needless to say, this is not an easy task; as Confucius taught: *You are what you think.*

Why is our own spiritual ignorance so difficult to detect? Because our ignorance is there by design. It's not stupidity or our incapacity to perceive truth that keeps us in the darkness of ignorance. On the contrary, very smart people are ignorant of the spiritual structure and their own spiritual nature. In fact, the stronger and more cunning the ego, the more persistent our ignorance prevails. Ego is the mechanism that maintains our separation from the spiritual. The Buddha provides valuable insight into the machinations of the ego to maintain the obscurations of ignorance:

Lifetimes of ignorance have brought us to identify the whole of our being with ego. Its greatest triumph is to inveigle us into believing its best interests are our best interests, and even into identifying our very survival with its own. This is a savage irony, considering that ego and its grasping are at the root of all our suffering.

Yet, ego is so terribly convincing, and we have been its dupe for so long, that the thought that we might ever become egoless terrifies us. To be egoless, ego whispers to us, is to lose all the rich romance of being human, to be reduced to a colorless robot or a brain-dead vegetable.

As long as we are unable to distinguish between perception that has been altered and censored by ego, and that which is unobscured perception, there's no hope of gaining even a glimpse into the spiritual structure. Until we recognize the mechanism of ego at work, filtering thoughts and adulterating perception, we remain imprisoned by our own ignorance while the spiritual waits for our awakening. For humanity to overcome the obstacle of spiritual ignorance, it must be willing to engage the process of awakening. This ubiquitous, spiritual ignorance continues to haunt our world and prevent us from claiming our destiny. One reason man has had to endure the effects of his own ignorance throughout history, is the complacency he feels regarding it.

The path toward awakening is not for the faint of heart. It requires endless effort and daily persistence, and initially we exert ourselves without any hint of benefit. Like the prospector who trusts his map, the spiritual seeker must endure endless hours of searching, driven by blind faith alone. Only those whose passion is in finding what is hidden, and knowing what is yet to be known, will last throughout the search. Once filled with new awareness, the seeker will recognize the degree of ignorance that needed to be overcome.

Second Key Obstacle: Inner Psychological Conflict
Conflict within human psychology is the single greatest condition leading to our recurrent hostility and violence. This is as true on the individual level as with collective humanity. As a species, we are conflict driven. In asking why there has never been a period of world peace, teachers such as Krishnamurti assert that our violence is the expression of our conflicted and hostile psychology. The external expression of inner conflict and hostility is violence, intolerance, hatred and the suffering associated with these conditions.

By nature, we are conflicted beings—we are born in conflict, conceived in conflict; and we live and die in conflict. The act in which we were conceived is a blend of both physical and spiritual conditions. Our time of birth is characterized by intense suffering and miraculous joy. Our entire lives are marked by our conflicting nature of being both physical and spiritual simultaneously. At a very young age, we become introduced to the product of unresolved conflict—resentment and hostility. How we learn to cope with our conflicted nature and the limitations of fulfilling our desires determines the degree of our hostility and regret. It can go by many names, but the feelings are the same—bad. The more resentment and acrimony we cultivate, the more we are at the effect of its poison. Bitter people tend to remain bitter, until one day they feel justified in expressing their hostility; usually at the cost of generating even greater conflict and more hostility.

The Buddha recognized the disturbing nature of these disruptive emotions and referred to them as *kleshas,* or afflictions. Within the teachings of Buddhism, there are elaborate explanations of how these *afflictions* gain control and alter our perceptions. For our purposes, let's simply take a sampling from this swamp water in order to familiarize ourselves with the culprits. In his book, *The Essence of the Heart Sutra,* The Dalai Lama lists a number of these *afflictions*: greed, anger, hatred, jealousy, pride, vengeance, dishonesty, shamelessness, inattentiveness and the like.

These are expressions of our underlying nature, rooted in conflict psychology, that make up our overall temperament. These conflict driven thoughts and emotions become our experience of reality. A great deal of our unhappiness and suffering is not the result of external circumstances, as we tend to believe, but rather the result of our minds' interpretations of all that we encounter. The spiritual process leading to spiritual realization is short circuited when the mind reacts to external conditions with conflict temperament. Exacerbating this situation is the tendency of the mind, in a state of conflict, to continually feed the fire of discontent with one topic after another.

The ego is notorious for holding onto previous betrayals and injustices to have at the ready, once the mind enters another tirade of conflict. At this point of drama, all of the old files are brought out in order to expand the size and intensity of the triggering conflict. Your car's air-conditioner failing on the hottest day of the summer will undoubtedly trigger conflict emotions. Once your conflict temperament is released, it's a hammer looking for a nail—anything is fair game. And, if there's not enough ammunition taking place in the present moment, the ego can dredge up years of fertile compost that was only assumed buried in the past.

A mind under the influence of conflict interprets its world as a battlefield. Its weapons of mass destruction include all of the harmful emotions listed above by the Dalai Lama, and then some. This is where most of us live most of the time—in a reality that is formed by *kleshas* (Buddhism, a *klesha* is a negative mental state that clouds the mind, causing suffering and the conditions for suffering to arise). In addition to the utter misery and anguish resulting from this phenomenon, we also lose our connection to all things spiritual, including the Soul and the spiritual structure.

The 8th-century Buddhist teacher, Shantideva, reminds us in his renowned work, *Entering the Path of Enlightenment*:

> *...encountering adversity, in itself, does not necessarily lead to a disturbed mind; even amid adversity, the principal cause of our unhappiness is our own undisciplined mind under the influence of kleshas. Failing to understand this principle, we allow ourselves to be controlled by the mental afflictions; in fact, we often embrace and reinforce them, for instance by adding fuel to our anger.*
>
> —Dalai Lama, *Essence of the Heart Sutra*

The importance of this point cannot be overstated. If a person gains this insight alone and nothing more, it is well worth the time and effort. All the great Sages, and many contemporary teachers, make this same point: **We all live in a subjective reality of our own making.** Only those who have attained a high degree of insight and realization have been able to see beyond the limitations of their own conditioning. What we perceive as reality is actually our mind's unique *interpretation* of reality. Because all of us have our own DNA, parents, education, past experiences, etc., we also have our own interpretation of what the mind perceives to be real. No wonder we're so caught in conflict! The very core experience of what we perceive to be reality is different from that of the person standing next to us. By this fundamental recognition, it follows that in every situation we encounter; it's our attitude and perception that determine the "reality" we experience.

In practical terms, this means that all our joys and sorrows, our pleasure and anguish, are the result of our own mind's interpretation of our daily lives. It's only natural to believe that our depression, pain and suffering are coming from the external circumstances that make up our life. It would naturally follow then that by changing the external circumstances, we would change our experience accordingly. This is sound logic, except when we stop to consider that our experience, albeit joy or suffering, is not coming from external circumstances, but from our *interpretation* of the external circumstances. Additionally, the mind's tendency toward negative attitudes and perceptions that lead to negative interpretations, which trigger negative emotions, ultimately result in bad choices and negative behavior. Once this cycle is completed and we have behaved poorly, this precise action causes a new cycle, which ultimately fosters more harmful emotions, reinforcing our already damaged perceptions. According to our Sages, this cycle of bad reactions is the common denominator of the human condition. For a person to achieve lasting happiness, and consequently, for humanity to achieve peace and goodwill on earth, we must go against our very nature.

It would be a very rare human being who could immediately cease from all of these destructive emotions gaining control over his or her perception. Typically, it's a gradual process from awareness to cessation. For now, all that is required is to recognize this mechanism of harmful emotions and the ill will they provoke. Most importantly, we must identify these *afflictions* as obstacles which prevent our perception of the spiritual structure.

For now, it is not as important that you recognize *your* particular brand of poison, as it is that you recognize that all poisons obscure the vision of the spiritual structure. Even when these nasty emotions are justified, they will hurt you nonetheless. This is what is meant by the power of forgiveness. Forgiveness is the antidote to this cadre of poisons; the benefit is far greater to the forgiver than the forgiven. We will explore these obstacles more closely, and the methods of releasing their hold on us, in the following chapters dealing with the spiritual process.

Third Key Obstacle: Obstinate Doubt

Although the obstacle of doubt is rooted in ignorance and conflict, it is so prevalent and destructive that it requires its own category. The Buddha views doubt as being rooted in a negative attachment to one's past and future. Most often, we are unwilling to allow the possibility of a future that is beyond our experience of the past. Thus, our doubt prevents us from perceiving the spiritual structure, as it is nowhere to be found in our past.

Whereas the physical structure is governed by the principle of *seeing is believing,* the spiritual structure is governed by *believing is seeing.* Perhaps the most famous example of this spiritual tenet is that referred to in the Gospels involving one of the Twelve Disciples—Thomas. Although the other disciples gave testimony to seeing Jesus when he came to them after the Crucifixion and Resurrection, Thomas refused to believe until he could see the wounds of a living Jesus and touch them for himself. When this moment came true for Thomas, he believed and was told by Jesus to "stop doubting." Then Jesus told him: *Because you have seen me, you have believed; blessed are those who have not seen and yet have believed.* (John 20:29 NIV)

This scripture suggests that one who gains vision through believing is looking in the spiritual domain, while those who require seeing in order to believe are seeking evidence in the physical world. What is even more disturbing is that doubt often becomes skepticism, which is a natural proclivity toward an overall attitude of doubt. Skepticism is the formidable obstacle constructed by doubt, keeping the spiritual structure obscured. While the skeptic may avoid appearing gullible and foolish, this benefit is at the cost of missing what needs to be seen. In the words of the 18th century teacher and spiritual master, Rebbe Nachman of Breslov: *Better to be a fool who believes everything than a skeptic who believes nothing—not even the truth.*

Skepticism is rooted in the ego, which insists that anything that is not observable through the senses does not exist; as if man were the ultimate judge over the boundaries of infinite reality. Gravity cannot be observed by the senses, yet everyone would agree that it exists.

Fortunately, we are not required to *accept* the spiritual hypothesis in order to embark upon its journey. It is only necessary to accept the *possibility* of the spiritual. Most of us do not believe anything without confirming for ourselves. Even if a neighbor phones to say that we have a flat tire, typically we run out to see for ourselves. The spiritual hypothesis is no different. Belief and faith are worthy attributes, but no substitute for our personal experience of truth. Until we have personal confirmation, doubt and uncertainty undermine our exploration of the spiritual structure. Even if we are unable to eliminate doubt completely, we should be aware of it as an obstacle. In that way, we do not reinforce it.

Fourth Key Obstacle: No Clear Definition or Description

An inherent source of confusion in the quest to know the spiritual, is that it defies definition or description. This alone can leave us discouraged. It is like the statement made by United States Supreme Court Justice Potter Stewart when he was ruling on which pornographic material was considered obscene and requiring censorship, versus which material was to be protected by the First Amendment. The judge said he might not be able to define what obscenity is, but "I know it when I see it."

So it is with the polar opposite topic under discussion here; we may not be able to define the spiritual structure, but *we'll know it when we're in it*. This is how the spiritual is defined—by experiencing it. This is not to say that we cannot benefit from the descriptions and findings of others, just to note that our own experience may not resemble the experience of others. It is useful to remember that this experience is one of an *expanded sense of self*, and because all of our "selves" are unique, all of our experiences will also be unique.

Fifth Key Obstacle: Unfamiliar Ground

As if indefinable were not challenging enough, the strange and alien nature of the spiritual domain adds to its complexity. Part One of the book sets the context of this challenge. Our modern worldview is grounded in science and reason and has little room for the mystical. Even references to God are often awkward when initiated in unfamiliar settings or in random conversations. In today's world, all things spiritual have been relegated to a category which is only appropriate within a narrow context.

To enter the spiritual structure and achieve the spiritual experience, we must *crack the shell* formed by our modern worldview. The experience itself is contrary to what our modern times perceive as normal. Not to say that our modern scientific/technologic and rational perception is wrong, just to say that it limits our spiritual perception. The truth that it holds is correct within the context of the material scientific view. If, however, we intend to expand our perception to include the realm of the spiritual, we must break through the confines of the natural and embrace the supernatural.

It is quite normal for people to fear encounters with the unknown. The process of spiritual awakening is usually not a sudden experience. Although it can be initiated suddenly by near death experiences, the miracle of child birth and periods of grieving, etc., typically, it comes on gradually over time. With each new step, we gain some control over our pace and direction. For most people, the passion for more rather than the fear of too much drives us forward. It is our familiarity that accelerates our progress.

Brother Lawrence, who served as a brother in the Carmelite monastery in Paris during the latter part of the 17th century, taught the virtues of "The Practice of the Presence of God." This was a technique he developed whereby he would *practice* being in the presence of God; he would talk with God as if they were in a relationship—sometimes mentor; sometimes best friends. In this way, Brother Lawrence developed familiarity with God and the spiritual structure.

There is not in the world a kind of life more sweet and delightful than that of a continual conversation with God. Those only can comprehend it who practice and experience it.
—Brother Lawrence, *The Practice of the Presence of God*

Even within the sacred walls of his monastery, the experience of being in the continual presence of God was unusual and required practice—how much more so in our modern lives. It takes courage and conviction to cultivate such a practice, but no less so than with any other worthy goal. On this topic, the scriptures (1Timothy 4:15) provide us guidance: *Put these things into practice, devote yourself to them.*

Sixth Key Obstacle: Disguised

The obstacles of no clear definition and unfamiliarity are only the beginning of the factors undermining our ability to perceive the spiritual structure. The next obstacle is one that further frustrates our ability to recognize the spiritual structure—*it's disguised*. It's not that the structure isn't here; not even that it is invisible—it's simply camouflaged. It's somewhat like viewing anamorphic art where images are hidden in the painting and can only be seen when viewed a particular way. Once the eye experiences seeing the hidden image, we are able to find it more easily. Sometimes we can even point it out to those unable to see what's hidden. First, we need the knowledge that we are viewing anamorphic art. Second, we need the understanding of how to view this type of art. Then we need the experience of seeing what's hidden beyond what is readily apparent.

Distinguishing between what is real, and what is apparent, dates back to our earliest recorded history. Almost all religions have teachings that revolve around the notion that the spiritual realm is real and within our reach, yet remains obscured. Perhaps one of the most frequently quoted examples is found in the Gospels attributed to Jesus:

Once, on being asked by the Pharisees when the kingdom of God would come, Jesus replied, "The coming of the kingdom of God is not something that can be observed, nor will people say, 'Here it is,' or 'There it is,' because the kingdom of God is in your midst."
(Luke 17:20-21)

Buddha confirms that just by naming or labeling objects and phenomena, we are, in fact, *disguising* their true essence. By learning what the name means, we assume that we know what the object is; while, actually, the name refers to all objects of the same type, even though each individual object has its own unique experience. In this way, naming is a form of deception within its limited and abbreviated definition; as such, it obscures the spiritual structure.

Disguising what is real can be brought on by the phenomenon of *apparent appearances*. In other words, what is *apparent* is not necessarily what is *real*, and what is *real* is not necessarily *apparent*. Consider such optical illusions as mirages. We see a wet surface on the desert sand or on a hot stretch of highway due to the refraction of light from heated air. Upon approach, the wet disappears.

Another example of that which is apparent not being real is given in the Eastern teachings of *maya* (literally *that which is not*). A Hindu parable tells of a man walking in the jungle at dusk, where he comes upon a six-foot snake in a bush alongside the path. Surprised and frightened by this deadly intruder, he changes the direction of his course. It's later discovered that the six-foot deadly snake was nothing more than a long piece of rope lying in the brush. So what was real? It cannot be said that the snake was real; but it also can't be said that the rope was real. After all, the reaction of the observer was not that of a person who stumbled upon a rope lying on the ground. The rope was real but not apparent, while the snake was unreal yet apparent.

This analogy is useful in understanding the nature of *spiritual disguise*. The spiritual structure is real, but not apparent. This shouldn't be difficult to comprehend. Nevertheless, any difficulty one might have in grasping the *real but unapparent* nature of the spiritual, will pale by comparison to the difficulty grasping the *apparent but unreal* nature of the physical. Even the most seasoned meditators and the spiritually advanced find it difficult to get their arms around this profound and ancient spiritual concept.

Like the rope and the snake, the obstacle of disguise that obscures the spiritual is nothing more than our own misperceptions and misinterpretations. We are unable to recognize the forest through the trees, just as the fish doesn't recognize it's in water. The difficulty in perceiving the illusory nature of the physical world stems from the concept that the illusion is merely an expression of the dominant spiritual structure. When, in the bright light of day, the snake is revealed to be a rope, anxiety and fear melt away. So it is with spiritual teachings regarding the misperception of the physical plane; once seen as it truly is, the cause of fear and human suffering melt away.

Seventh Key Obstacle: Inflexible Beliefs
Given that our beliefs are one of the most sacred and cherished aspects of our identity, it is not easy for us to relinquish

their hold, in order to gain clarity. It is not being suggested that the various religious and scientific beliefs that people hold dear are incorrect or unjustified, only that these beliefs tend to cause static in the spiritual connection. Beliefs of any kind obscure our experience of the spiritual. When connecting to the spiritual, we must let go of the inclination to direct the action. We want to see what the spiritual unveils rather than telling the spiritual what it is.

Our spiritual exploration is one in which we *ask* the spiritual structure to reveal itself. It is important that we not project anything onto the screen prior to the screen revealing its own content. As the ancient Sages would say: *Don't tell reality what it is... Don't tell God who He is.* Be humble, it is the only way you will ever fit through the eye of the needle. Big egos have been compared to camels (or in contemporary terms, a Buick) driving through the eye of a needle.

A humble person waits patiently, with love and gratitude in the heart, to gain a glimpse into that which is beyond comprehension. An arrogant person will lose this rare opportunity by attempting to direct the action. Our beliefs are precious and deserving of reverence, but their entire purpose has been to bring us to this moment—the moment of spiritual revelation. All the truth and insight accumulated over the years will be validated by this spiritual encounter. Any beliefs that become nullified have served their purpose; remaining tethered to them will only hold you back.

Beliefs rooted in the world's great religions and taught by humanity's Saints and Sages, will not be threatened by entering the spiritual structure as they are made of the very same substance. While the religions of the world appear to be separate and unique from the physical perspective, they lose their exclusivity in the name of unity within the spiritual structure. All the Prophets, Saints, and Sages repeat the same messages, albeit flavored with their own personal reflections and expressions. Looking down that very same pathway, you will come away with your own unique version of the Absolute.

September 11, 1893 was a much different day than September 11, 2001. Rather than the religious intolerance and conflict that reared its ugly head on 9/11/2001, 9/11/1893 marked the opening ceremony of the first World's Parliament of Religion held on the shore of Lake Michigan in Chicago, Illinois. Over four thousand people gathered in the Hall of Columbus to honor the ten great world religions—Confucianism, Taoism, Shintoism, Hinduism, Buddhism, Jainism, Zoroastrianism, Judaism, Christianity, and Islam—and particularly that which bonds them together in unity.

If the Parliament of Religions has shown anything to the world, it is this: It has proved to the world that holiness, purity and charity are not the exclusive possessions of any church in the world, and that every system has produced men and women of the most exalted character. In the face of this evidence, if anybody dreams of the exclusive survival of his own religion and the destruction of the others, I pity him from the bottom of my heart, and point out to him that upon the banner of every religion will soon be written in spite of resistance: "Help and not fight," "Assimilation and not Destruction," "Harmony and Peace and not Dissension.

—Swami Vivekananda, Opening Address

The chasm between these two 9/11 days, separated by over a century, is the separation between conflict and resolution; disease and healing; the expression of hatred and that of love. In one case we witness the power of conflicting beliefs, and in the other we recognize the prospect of the enlightened consensus of all beliefs. People killing one another to uphold religious beliefs is as irrational as killing in the name of peace. Although one might make a logical case for such counterintuitive behavior, there is no historical evidence that this rationale has ever achieved its objective.

All religious beliefs have a common denominator and are rooted in harmony and unity as opposed to conflict. What they hold in common, is the link to spiritual truth. The contradiction enters where human ego has adulterated spiritual truth to feed its need to be exclusively right while condemning other beliefs as categorically wrong. Humanity has spent its bloody history trying to make the latter approach outweigh the former. The Hindu spiritual teacher, Vivekananda spoke on this topic often:

> *Every religion has a Soul behind it, and that soul may differ from the soul of another religion. But are they contradictory? ... I believe they are not contradictory—they are supplementary. Each religion takes up, as it were, one part of the great universal truth... It is therefore addition, not exclusion... System after system arises, each one embodying a great idea... This is the march of mankind. Man never progresses from error to truth, but from truth to truth—from lesser truth to higher truth—but never from error to truth.*
> —Vivekananda, *The Complete Works of Swami Vivekananda*

Perhaps one of the best metaphors regarding beliefs came from the Buddha who told his followers to use his teachings and the beliefs contained within them, as a *raft* whose sole function is to get the spiritual traveler to the distant shore of realization. Once this mission is accomplished, the *raft* should be left on the banks rather than hoisted up onto one's shoulders and carried up to the higher peaks.

He offered additional advice to those who were about to embark on their spiritual quest:

Accept my words only when you have examined them for yourselves; do not accept them simply because of the reverence you have for me. Those who only have faith in me and affection for me will not find the final freedom. But those who have faith in the truth and are determined on the path, they will find awakening.
—Buddha, *Majjhima Nikaya*

It is important to distinguish what is being expressed here, from what might be inferred. It is not that *your* beliefs will obscure the spiritual structure; rather that *all* beliefs present an obstacle. It is not because these beliefs are not true or that they present conflict. It is because they are a distraction from the pure experience of their truth. The language of religion is found in words the way the language of science is found in math. The language of the spiritual is found in the pure, clear light of experience.

Eighth Key Obstacle: Endless Distractions and Restlessness

In addition to its *ineffable quality* and the *disguised nature* that obscures the *spiritual structure,* there is another glaring obstacle. This obstacle has more to do with *us* than the experience itself. The spiritual experience we seek is obscured and we, the seekers, are *distracted and restless.* As if obscuration weren't overwhelming enough, the trifecta of *disguise, distraction,* and *restlessness* sets the stage for what lies ahead.

What are the distractions that could possibly take us off course from finding the hidden treasure? In a word—life. Our entire corporeal life and the whole material world is a symphony of distractions. From the moment we open our eyes each morning, we are distracted by our hunger for nourishment, followed by an endless to-do list that spans the full extent of our waking hours. Life is not a spectator sport. It requires full participation—growing up, becoming educated, finding a career and fulfilling its demands are just the beginning. Add to this the greatest of all human distractions, sexuality, and there is barely time to find the right mate to fulfill the demands and distractions of family life.

Adding to the obstacles of desire and distraction is the background in which these two occur—restlessness. The more restless the mind, the more distracted it becomes. The only power we have over the barrage of endless distractions and the incessant shrieking of unyielding desires is in disciplining the mind to focus and concentrate. When the mind is restless, it has no defense over outer attractions and our inner desires.

Ninth Key Obstacle: Unyielding Desires

Not only is there a never-ending supply of mesmerizing attractions and distractions, but each has its intricately designed counterpart embedded within us—*unyielding desires.* It's not just the ice-cream that is a distraction from our losing weight; it's the combination of the ice-cream and our incessant desire for it that lures us into submission. Our distractions would not be a major obstacle if it weren't for their accompanying attractions. The combination of distraction and attraction is a powerful cocktail that we all tend to imbibe in varying degrees. There is yet a third component to this devastating formula that renders it nearly insurmountable. It comes in the form of a memorable truism: **Resistance brings persistence.**

The most *knee jerk* and logical method of dealing with damaging temptations is to resist them. Unfortunately, we seem wired to desire most what we shouldn't have. Even when we're able to *white knuckle* our way into "just saying no," the volume of our desire is cranked up to deafening decibels. What joy and tranquility can we feel if our inner being is sharing space with a boom box blaring unanswered desires?

This is why we are offered a second truism: **Transcendence trumps resistance.**

Any desire for that which is not wholesome creates a limitation. Of course, our involvement with that which is unwholesome compromises our wellbeing. Even the *desire* for what is unwholesome is itself costly. For example, a person who cheats in marriage has compromised the great benefits a marriage can bring. Even before the action of cheating ever occurs, there exists the unwholesome desire to cheat. The desire alone alters the character of the marriage. Both the hunger for infidelity and the act itself are weakening conditions. Of course, resisting the desire to cheat is admirable. Nevertheless, it limits the marriage from entering the higher levels of fulfillment. While resistance is better than submission, it doesn't overcome the obstacle of the unscrupulous desires that sabotage the marriage. Cravings and their debilitating conditions must be *transcended,* not just resisted, in order to eliminate their control over us. Not surprising, transcendence is also a fundamental key to spiritual awakening. We will explore transcendence in greater depth later.

Tenth Key Obstacle: Clutter

Clutter has a variety of meanings. The most common have to do with disorganization and confusion. Clutter is also synonymous with mess. Clutter even refers to an accumulation of objects overfilling a space. These characterizations are all valid for our discussion of clutter as a key obstacle to perceiving the spiritual structure.

Consider another definition of clutter in the form of radar signal contamination. In this usage, clutter refers to objects that jam up radar signals and prevent clear and accurate observation. The military actually uses clutter to overwhelm the enemy's radar and hide troop, ship, and aircraft movement. If clutter can obscure a battleship, just imagine the job it can do on the soft whispering of the Soul. We can think of clutter as anything that shouldn't be there and that interferes with our mission to detect the spiritual structure and have the mystical experience.

We find such clutter in four areas of our lives:

Environmental Clutter—is perhaps the most common variety of clutter. It is the clutter that surrounds us in life. It can be found everywhere: in our closets, on our desks, in our drawers, under our beds, piled in corners, shoved into garages, stashed in glove boxes and hidden in trunks. Anywhere that we find unmonitored, free space, chances are good that clutter has accumulated there. It can be as simple as an unmade bed or an un-defrosted freezer. It can be as small as the clutter in a wallet or as huge as storage space clutter that's eventually carted off to the dump to join the community clutter. De-cluttering one's physical environment is perhaps the easiest and most accessible.

Physical or Bodily Clutter—is clearly more hidden than clutter in the home, but far more devastating. We accumulate clutter in our bodies the same way we accumulate it in our environment. In its most fundamental form, the human body is a processing plant or factory. It is constantly engaged in production—it reproduces itself cell by cell, moment to moment. All that we do in life externally is dependent on all that we do internally. If our human factory is not running properly, all of our activities are compromised. Our factory functions best when provided with proper building materials. Perhaps even more important is protecting it from the accumulation of stuff that interferes with its performance. What helps and what hinders the functioning of the human body is a topic for another book, and there's no shortage of qualified experts. For the most part, contemporary bodies are suffering greatly from an overabundance of what harms, and a scarcity of what heals. The damaging barrage includes everything from bad sugar, bad fats, bad carbs, nicotine, caffeine, chlorine, alcohol, nitrates, pesticides—it's endless. Even more than your environment, your body should be a clutter-free zone. Unfortunately, over packed arteries are less apparent than a bulging closet.

Mental Clutter—is more hidden than the previous form of clutter, yet far more accessible than the form that follows. Mental clutter may not be as deadly as bodily clutter; nonetheless, it robs us of joy and tranquility while interfering with our spiritual perception. The space that mental clutter occupies might not be as apparent as our cluttered environment, but it's just as cumbersome as a garage so full of junk there's no room for the car. Like the clutter-filled public warehouses through-out the world, mental clutter comes in a variety of forms. Most of us have lost track of our childhood toys and games long ago, but few of us have let go of the scars and resentments of our youth. Who amongst us has forgotten our most embarrassing moments or forgiven our biggest betrayals?

The common thread in all mind clutter is that it *doesn't* belong there and it *does* interfere with spiritual perception. The toxicity of negative thoughts, and their expression as words and deeds, will endarken even the most advanced minds. Negative thoughts trigger our stress response, which, in turn, pollutes the mind while accelerating disease and the aging of the body. As the mind thinks *worst case scenario* thoughts, the body actually experiences them.

Soul Clutter—is the most difficult to detect and the most difficult to remove. This type of clutter is more ethereal than apparent. It accumulates in an area of our psyche that is not easily perceptible, let alone accessible. By the time people are so spiritually advanced that they can *feel* their Soul, they have already eliminated their Soul's clutter. So, for our purposes, it's best to describe the Soul's clutter as that which builds up from our character trait of self-interest; something recogniz-able. In other words, self-interest is the root of Soul clutter.

The Soul is obscured by all self-serving thought and activ-ity. By manipulating others and taking more for ourselves, we give expression to a *me first mentality,* which in turn weighs down the Soul and diminishes its accessibility. The *Golden Rule,* taught by all great religions, is what counteracts our self-serving nature and the accumulation of Soul clutter.

For illustrative purposes, we will describe this character trait as selfishness; that which puts our own interest before others. It is what the Dalai Lama refers to as *exaggerated self-centeredness.* When this mechanism clearly benefits *us* at the expense of *others*, it is far more severe. When we think and act in this fashion, without any feelings of remorse or regret for the pain we've caused, it becomes a deeply rooted character trait. As such, this trait of self-interest has the ability to alter our perception of reality—we view the world as if it exists solely for our benefit. We exist in our own subjective reality. In spiritual terms, this subjective reality is the polar opposite reality that we are meant to discover. These self-serving perspectives are the reason our beautiful world remains tainted by ugliness.

The great Hindu spiritual leader, Swami Vivekananda would often say: *It is only selfishness that causes the difference between good and evil.* Another way to say this is that a self-serving nature is the expression of the ego; when we remove selfishness, our Soul has the room to express itself.

It is more difficult to perceive the clutter of our character within the realm of the Soul, than to see it in our garage. So how are we able to detect this hidden clutter in our internal world? We detect Soul clutter when it is expressed outwardly.

Let's first examine the expression of the uncluttered Soul. We can recognize the outward expression of the uncluttered Soul by its overwhelming feeling of happiness and contentment, accompanied by a profound sense of peace and security. When unburdened by the ego's clutter, the Soul can shine through our physical senses as pure joy—bliss. On the other hand, when the Soul exists amidst spiritual clutter, the outward expression is suffering. For most people, the experience of suffering is easier to detect than our own self-centeredness.

Suffering as an expression of spiritual clutter commonly occurs in three key areas. First is the outward expression of hostility. Hostility is at the root of all violence. This is the trait of the common man—the saints could not be moved toward hostility, nor could they have enemies. This concept is at the root of the teachings of two great spiritual Sages separated by 500 years and 3,000 miles—Jesus and Buddha.

Love your enemies, do good to those who hate you, bless those who curse you, pray for those who abuse you.

—Jesus, Luke 6:27

Hatreds do not ever cease in this world by hating, but by love: this is an eternal truth... Overcome anger by love, overcome evil by good. Overcome the miser by giving, overcome the liar by truth.

—Buddha, Dhammapada 1.5 & 17.3

Second, is the experience of suffering caused by our perception of lack and deficiency. We cannot attain peace and satisfaction as long as our Soul is cluttered with feelings of want, cravings, and lust. There is only one appropriate desire in the spiritual realm and that is the desire for the spiritual; be it higher consciousness, the Soul or God. Until we recognize it is *Ultimate Reality* that we desire, initially we may simply experience the desire for the spiritual awakening that leads to it.

The third expression relates to the second—envy. When we feel a sense of lack, and we think our neighbor has what we crave, a debilitating expression of suffering emerges in the form of jealousy and envy. Jealousy and envy have been deemed the most toxic of all poisons. It drives a person to commit all manner of abominations including infidelity, theft—even murder.

All three expressions of Soul clutter have a common root—anger. When the mind becomes angry, the Soul withdraws deeper into obscurity. When we allow ourselves to become angry, we sink to the epitome of self-centeredness. The reality we perceive is narrow and subjective. We do not see the views and concerns of others, as we are blinded by our own. One who eliminates anger, eliminates the clutter that obscures the Soul.

Remember, the spiritual structure exists at the core of our being. It is not something new that we are seeking. Rather it is something we are attempting to uncover that is mystifying and hidden by obstacles. By removing the obstacles, and by drilling deep into our core, the experience of the spiritual is revealed.

Keep in mind that *seeing* the spiritual structure is not the same as seeing a tree or a hill. In this case, the sense organ, the eye, sees the external object, the tree, and the mind reacts with a mental image—its version of the tree. Remember, the eye does not see the tree; the mind sees it and then renders its own version of it. It is also the mind that *sees* the spiritual structure. However, in *seeing* the spiritual structure, there is no external physical object for the eye to grasp and relate back to the mind.

This is where it becomes complicated and where most people have difficulty remaining engaged in the process. The spiritual structure exists beyond the limitations of time and space. The whole of our physical reality, including our own identity and personality, is deeply rooted in the laws of time and space. *How can we grasp reality beyond the boundaries of time and space?* —By perceiving through our spiritual lens, which is rooted beyond temporal and spatial limitations.

Once a person has experienced their own spiritual core (Soul), he or she has discovered the spiritual structure. To say that a *part* of the spiritual structure dwells within each of us would be illuminating yet somewhat imprecise, since the structure cannot be divided into portions. The measurement of portions is indicative of a dimension governed by spatial characteristics—the physical. The spiritual structure has no such spatial limitations, so it is ultimately recognized as an infinite whole (Oneness). Given the nature of the spiritual, one would not be wrong to say that the *whole* of the spiritual structure exists within us; although this concept might be overwhelming at this point in our discussion and will be explored in a later chapter.

In all fairness, it's overly ambitious to think of grasping such a complicated concept based solely on a first glance. It is best not to draw conclusions, rather to live with it percolating in the mind until it reveals itself. And while you're waiting for its revelation, you might occupy your time by dissolving the obstacles that obscure it. We will explore this spiritual process in the following chapters when we dissect each move toward spiritual awakening and the epiphany that follows.

For now, we only need to begin recognizing the spiritual obstacles that all physical beings must endure; knowing full well that awakening from this fleeting dream is our birthright. Pay particular attention to how often the mind is engaged in thoughts of conflict, and notice the destructive emotions that are associated with these thoughts. While it is normal to feel doubt and confusion about something so revolutionary to your ordinary thinking, try to stay open to the idea that this doubt is unfounded from the spiritual perspective. Given the nature of our modern, materialist worldview, it's only natural to be put off by any phenomenon that has no clear definition and rests on such unfamiliar ground. Not to mention the added complexity that all things spiritual initially appear in disguise.

The requirement of viewing the spiritual structure with no preconceived notions might be a deal breaker for many wise and scholarly people. Take comfort in knowing that most of us have had the same difficulty setting aside our previously held beliefs. Certainly, the truth contained in our cherished beliefs is not compromised by the unspoken truth of the spiritual experience; if anything, it is reinforced. Gaining discipline over our *monkey-mind* thought process brings new clarity at every level while enhancing our ability to perform. Finally, we must recognize that relieving both our inner and outer worlds of the inordinate and unwarranted amounts of accumulated clutter tethering us to the chaos and sheer pandemonium of modern life is, in and of itself, life enhancing.

The Grand Illusion—Concealment
These obstacles are working together with a common goal: *Concealment.* Understanding the nature and necessity of concealment is a key element in understanding and navigating the spiritual plane.

It is not an easy concept to grasp, and even more difficult to make operational. However, if you allow this spiritual principle to *linger in your consciousness* without rushing to judgment, you will eventually recognize its fundamental logic and how so many other spiritual tenets are rooted within it.

What is meant by allowing the concept of concealment to linger in our consciousness? Grasping and understanding this complex, spiritual concept is not likely to happen at first glance. It is gradually revealed through continual contemplation and observation, as opposed to being immediately recognized and accepted. The intangible idea of concealment is unlike practical ideas where their practicality can be immediately recognized and put to use. This spiritual concept is not subject to such worldly criteria as judgment and acceptance. Concealment is a condition that simply *is what it is,* and it's up to us to discover it for ourselves.

Many people believe that the spiritual does not exist as they have had no physical evidence to suggest otherwise. From a worldly perspective, this is logical thinking. From the spiritual perspective, the spiritual defies *physical* evidence because it is concealed from the sense organs. A person does not *discover* the spiritual structure, or *any* aspect of spirituality, the way that one discovers cherries on a tree. The spiritual is experienced through revelation; the experiencer is the receiver of that which is revealed. Something as important and worthy as the spiritual structure would not be determined by sense organs and mere logic; it is not left sitting in plain sight. Its beauty is veiled like the face of a blushing bride or diamonds yet to be discovered.

To grasp the concept of concealment, one must first recognize the nature of concealment, its purpose, and, ultimately, how to transcend it. If we doubt that the spiritual exists because it is concealed, this unsubstantiated opinion alone will keep the spiritual structure obscured. As stated earlier, this is what is meant by *beliefs are obstacles obscuring the spiritual structure.*

By keeping the mind open to the spiritual hypothesis, we provide the conditions necessary to move toward its realization. For those finding it difficult to allow the plausibility of a hidden spiritual dimension, there are techniques that can be employed, such as the *"what if"* technique. In the interim stage of considering concealment, we simply ponder its possibility—*what if* such a dimension actually exists? This way we are not required to go against our grain; we are merely following the path of this spiritual exercise. We are not accepting or rejecting; we are staying open in order to maneuver around this formidable obstacle of judgment and doubt.

Once we are comfortable with the perspective of *what if* the spiritual hypothesis is valid, we pave the way for this idea to take root in our consciousness. We are then able to graduate to the *act as if* stage of the spiritual process. At this stage, we begin to perceive reality *as if* the spiritual hypothesis were actually true. *Would you alter your thoughts and behavior if you believed the spiritual hypothesis were valid? If you were not only a part of this world, but simultaneously a part of an eternal spiritual structure with accountability to a Divine Creator, would you act differently?* For most, this would be a resounding yes. Those who believe in God, and in ideas such as karma and redemption, express their beliefs in their behavior. Even Freud, a confirmed atheist, recognized the value of the *illusion of a God* as a reason for mankind to adhere to its moral compass; that is to say, to allow their *superego* to override the darker cravings of the *id*.

Our Sages taught that we do not arrive at the answer to this age-old question through our rational mind; it is not an equation proven by logic. Allowing for the *possibility* of God will lead to acting *as if* there is a God. This *cultivated* idea of God diminishes the veil of concealment that obscures God. Recognizing the concealment dissolves it. This is a critical point—once you recognize the concealment, you have penetrated it. This eventual access into the spiritual structure begins by opening the mind to its possibility.

This is the pivotal moment in the spiritual quest that all the great Sages acknowledge. We are no longer pushing the boulder up the mountain; we are being pulled upward by a force greater than our own. For those who fear they might be drawn by deception rather than truth, the revelation and its spiritual experience alone will validate its authenticity. For most, it is this precise moment that the true meaning of life is revealed, and we are amazed that we hadn't seen it sooner. Similar to the experience people report regarding near death experiences, time ceased while their entire life passed through their consciousness. Although in this instance, we are not leaving life; at last, we are fully engaging in it.

As the ancient Hindus taught, every person craves to understand the meaning of life and his or her particular purpose in it. Even this primordial craving, characteristic of all who enter this world, becomes obscured by the symphony of earthly desires and fears that accompany our daily lives. Those who awaken their craving for meaning are either in voluntary pursuit of it, or their lives are concluding and they suddenly face the possibility of leaving this life without answers to its most fundamental questions: *what* and *why*.

The *Grand Mystery* is by no means solved; we simply acquire the piece of the puzzle we came here to get. If this suggests more frustration and further questions, you are partially right. Of course, the eternal future that lies ahead isn't suddenly illuminated within our current state of awareness, but this realization is in no way frustrating. Would a child be frustrated to find that after enjoying a wonderful ride at Disneyland, there are many more to be enjoyed? Mortals tend to view the process of Self-realization as a struggle—a bit of a chore. The only children who view the amusement park rides as a chore, are those who are afraid of them. Their fear robs them of the thrill of the ride; our fear robs us of the thrill of our lives.

Life is difficult by design. As the Buddha so aptly revealed, life is characterized by suffering and anguish that even the most privileged cannot escape. If your life is not difficult, it's only because you have amassed enough transient pleasures to momentarily drown out its wailing, or you have solved the puzzle that you came to solve. However, if your puzzle is not solved, and you are content to be riding the fleeting wave of material success, you may be likened to the hunter in the *Ancient Tale* who blissfully listens to the music in the corridor while squandering his rights to the king's treasure chamber.

Keep in mind that without the condition of concealment, mortals would not experience themselves as separated individuals, there would be no phenomenon of *free will*, and our material world would not exist. The entire physical dimension has but one purpose, that which brought it into existence—free will. Further, there can be no free will in the presence of Divine will. This is the *gift* bestowed upon us by the Creator—the *illusion* of free will brought about by the concealment of Divine will. Some Sages have said that this *gift* is an indication of Divine love for humanity. It is only in our physical existence that the Creator concealed the Divine Presence in order for us to gain access to free will and to be co-creators in what happens next.

Recognizing the Two Levels of Concealment

Concealment is an overarching theme in spirituality. *Seeing through the concealment* is essentially what is meant by spiritual awakening and Enlightenment—i.e., *seeing things as they really are*. Tradition has it that there are two levels of *concealment*, one deeper and more obscuring than the other. There is an ancient parable that provides some clarity on this point.

In the parable, two men are walking along a path in the woods. They are approaching a large stone wall where bandits are hiding, waiting to ambush and rob the travelers. Neither man can see the bandits behind the wall that conceals them. However, one of the men knows that the bandits are there while the other does not. At both levels of concealment, the bandits are not *visible* to either of the men. At the first level of concealment the bandits are not visible, and there is no *awareness* of their presence. This is known as *double concealment*; the bandits cannot be seen and their whereabouts is also hidden. Alternatively, at the second level of concealment, the bandits are still not *visible*, yet their presence behind the wall is *known*. This awareness of their presence makes this *single concealment.*

Knowing that the bandits are behind the wall, even though they are not visible, provides an enormous advantage. Similarly, the spiritual structure is concealed and is not evident to the senses. Yet there are those who know it exists even though they can't see it. This is *single concealment* as compared to those who cannot see the spiritual structure and have no awareness of its existence—*double concealment.* And, so it is for us. We are each walking along our life's path. We recognize what is apparent to our senses as being reality. For the most part, we plan our actions in relation to what we know to be true in this apparent reality.

Both science and scripture report that the vast majority of reality, over 99.9%, is concealed from our senses. Even something as well-known as germs is still not perceivable to our five senses, yet we all agree that they exist and can significantly alter our reality. Using a restaurant's restroom during flu season is a gamble for a person with no awareness of germs and the need to wash their hands before eating. These *bandit-germs* are hiding in double-concealment waiting to ambush unsuspecting diners, while those aware of their presence wash them away.

The same is true regarding the existence of the spiritual structure, which is also concealed from our five senses. Like the hidden bandits, or the germs carrying the flu virus, we must recognize the possibility that the spiritual may exist. And just like the people who realize that bandits lurk behind walls, or that disease is linked to germs, once we recognize the possibility that there is a spiritual purpose linked to our material life, we must adjust our thoughts and actions accordingly.

Investigation Penetrates Concealment

At the outset, most essential is the investigation into the possibility of the spiritual structure itself. Throughout human history, many highly qualified people have made this investigation and reported their findings. Once we decide to undertake the investigation, we must study their teachings for ourselves in order to find our own experience of truth. This truth must be based on an open-minded inquiry, and our truth barometer should be our Soul's arousal to what we discover. Try not to be limited in your search for truth by the boundaries of your existing belief system.

Remember the teachings of the Buddha on the importance of beliefs. He taught his followers that his teachings are merely a *raft* whose purpose is to deliver them to the distant shore. Although the raft must be authentic, it is not the raft that is significant, rather the destination. If we arrive at our destination, the raft has served its purpose.

Throughout history, humanity has become more and

more attached to the raft than the destination. Some of us are so invested in our raft that we have forgotten that there is a destination. Here we would do well to take a lesson from science. Scientific inquiry is less invested in the experiment than the outcome—less invested in the process than the results. The theories of science are critical, but they do not overshadow the relevance of the experiment's results. Unlike science, many religious inquiries have no intention of making new discoveries. Their sole purpose is to reinforce existing, sometimes ancient and sometimes altered, beliefs.

Beliefs, like biases, are the *filters* that alter our under-standing of truth. It is the aim of the ego to tenaciously protect previously held beliefs and biases, even if they fall short when confronted with something new. This is the ego's inherent need to be right. And it becomes threatened by any challenge to whatever version of truth it currently holds. Ironically, these beliefs are often not even our own per-sonal experience of truth. Instead, we are invested in a truth handed down by parents, teachers and previous generations. We generally hold beliefs that are typical of the culture and family in which we were born. This process is not intrinsi-cally wrong, except when we are unable to break free from the tether of previous conditioning in order to form our own individual perspective.

It is human nature to defend and protect our existing beliefs, but this tendency is the underpinning of why religion has not advanced at the same rate as science and technology. If a religious belief is rooted in truth, there is no chance of its obsolescence regardless of how often it is tested—of this our Sages are emphatic. Essential spiritual beliefs and his-torical religious events are in no danger of being diminished by modern interpretation and direct spiritual experience. It is the practice of contemporary reflection on existing beliefs that breathes new air into their meaning and keeps them from becoming relics of the past.

The Mystical Roots of Concealment

As we explore the mystical source of the spiritual structure, we must keep in mind that *mystical* does not threaten the *literal* meaning of scripture, it expands on it. Mystical, by definition, is beyond human comprehension; it has levels of understanding that reach beyond the surface. As far as the human mind can grasp, the mystical extends further. This is what is meant by scripture having infinite wisdom. At best, we can grasp only as much meaning as we are capable of understanding. This concept is expressed in one of the great parables of Jesus:

> *A farmer went out to plant his seed. He scattered the seed on the ground. Some fell on a path. Birds came and ate it up. Some seed fell on rocky places, where there wasn't much soil. The plants came up quickly, because the soil wasn't deep. When the sun came up, it burned the plants. They dried up because they had no roots. Other seed fell among thorns. The thorns grew up and crowded out the plants. Still other seed fell on good soil. It produced a crop 100, 60 or 30 times more than what was planted. Those who have ears should listen and understand.*
>
> —Matthew 13:1

All scripture and sacred teachings have a mystical component. This is especially true of scripture that is divinely inspired, such as the Koran, Gospels, Torah, Vedanta and the writings of the Prophets, Saints and Sages. Many of the great teachings are told in parables that leave the depth of meaning up to our depth of understanding. Regardless of what is being said, all spiritual teachings have a common denominator: bringing the seeker closer to the spiritual structure.

So it is with our discussion of *concealment,* which is a condition of the spiritual structure. There is no way to grasp the spiritual structure without coming to terms with its concealment. Since ancient times, people have asked the fair and honest question: *If there is a Soul, if there is a God, and if there is a spiritual plane of existence, why am I unable to see them?* The simple, yet honest answer is that they are concealed from sensory perception. While true, this answer leads to a follow-up question: *Why?*

When we ask the question *why,* we move from double concealment into single concealment. In order to probe into *why the spiritual structure is concealed*, we must first accept the *possibility* that it exists. When we *know* that it exists, our experience of the spiritual structure takes on new meaning as the *concealment* begins to dissolve. Eventually we arrive at the place where not only is the spiritual structure revealed, we recognize that we are a part of it.

To probe into the mystical root of *concealment,* we consult the teachings of one of the oldest of scriptures—the Torah (referred to by some as the Old Testament). The Torah is set in time about 3300 years ago during the Israelite exodus from Egypt, as told in the book of Exodus, one of the five books of the Moses. The Torah consists of 79,847 words and 304,805 letters. Each letter has a numeric value that lends itself to mathematical equations relevant to interpretation of the Torah. The word *Torah* is often mistakenly thought to mean law, when, in fact, it comes from the word *Hora'ah* which means *instruction*—instructions on entering the spiritual structure.

Moses Maimonides (1135-1204), is recognized as one of the greatest Torah authorities in history. His masterpiece work, the *Mishneh Torah*, is a 14-volume composition codifying Jewish Law. According to Maimonides, the most fundamental principle set forth in the Torah, is that God exists and requires all humans to *do* certain things and to *not do* other things.

Many important works on the Torah have only recently been translated into English. Some of the words and phrases that were originally put down in Hebrew have no English counterparts. The Hebrew alphabet is made up of 22 letters. Each letter has a variety of meanings before it is even put into words. Each letter also has a numeric value that is interpreted through mathematical calculations. Deeper meanings of the Torah are found beneath the literal surface. Within those deeper meanings, the Jewish Mystical Tradition is illuminated. On this *mystical* level, we may find many answers to assist us on our spiritual journey.

One of the earliest records of the Jewish Mystical Tradition is known as *Kabbalah*. The translation of the word *Kabbalah* from ancient Hebrew into modern English is *to receive. Kabbalah* refers to our ability *to receive* infinite Divine Light into our limited human perception. All spiritual growth requires an enhanced ability *to receive.* Herein, we find the source of our greatest spiritual challenge—our inability *to receive* that which is present for us in the here and now. All spiritual seekers, regardless of the path we choose, begin at the same place—correcting our inability to receive what is readily available. Again, some of the greatest barriers that prevent our ability to recognize and receive this Light are our own personal biases and beliefs. It should be noted that within spiritual teachings, *Light* and *Truth* are often one and the same and used synonymously.

Kabbalah recognizes at least four levels of meaning that emerge from the study of Torah. These four levels advance from the most apparent and literal interpretation, to the most concealed and mystical meaning. The deepest mystical level is referred to as *infinite wisdom*. At the mystical level, *infinite wisdom* speaks directly to the Soul rather than through the ear.

The Hasidic Master, Rebbe Levi Yitzhak of Berditchev (1740-1809), teaches that when we look at the written Torah, we first see black letters written on a white background. A great deal of time and effort goes into reading the words made up of these black inked letters. However, the Rebbe goes on to say that the more profound story is not that which is written in black letters, but is made up of the white "letters" occupying the space *between* the black letters. The black letters are the visible letters making up the visible words, while the white "letters" are not visible, yet their meaning is germane to understanding all that is being communicated.

Here again we encounter the profound theme present throughout all spiritual writings: All that we are able to see is meant to bring us to an understanding of that which cannot be seen. The lesson is to train the mind to see the mystical beyond the apparent. The Rebbe points out that perception is a matter of focus; by altering our focus, we can yield new understanding. Most importantly, the end goal is the awareness of our choice of focus. We then gain the possibility of seeing both the apparent and the concealed at the same time.

For those who have read the words of scripture exclusively on the literal level, looking again through the lens of the ancient mystical traditions will yield new insights. One should not mistakenly think that the *mystical* and *literal* understandings of scripture are contradictory—they are actually complementary. On the literal level, the story of the Book of Genesis is that of the first created humans, and their encounter with a very persuasive serpent that led humanity into centuries of punishment and suffering. Many religious sermons have attempted to make sense out of a loving and benevolent God that punishes billions of people for a lapse in judgment committed by their original ancestors—two people whose DNA was Divinely configured.

It is not our purpose to challenge the literal teachings of religion on original sin or any other tenet; rather to expand our exposure to the spiritual teachings found on the mystical level of interpretation. There have been debates regarding the text of the Bible since the earliest of times. With all due respect to those discussions, our focus is not concerned so much with ancient history, as with modern spirituality—which, according to the mystical tradition, spirituality has no history as it has no past. Spirituality exists outside of time and space, in a constant and endless state of *now*—the infinite present. What we think of as past and future are the result of our physicality in a material world. Any insight into the spiritual structure conveyed by scripture is relevant to the moment we encounter it. It is about you and me personally, in the very moment we now exist.

With this in mind, we begin exploring the mystical track of Torah to gain broader understanding of the opening chapters of Genesis regarding creation and *concealment*. Interestingly, the big debate that has been raging over the past few centuries concerning creation is all about *how it took place*.

Spiritually speaking, the bigger question is not *how*, but *why it took place*. The more profound question that the mystical tradition concerns itself with is: *Why* were we created, and *what* is the meaning of our existence?

These are the mystical questions, and their answers are cloaked in the veil of *concealment*. The phenomenon of *concealment* is pervasive throughout the spiritual structure— hidden from our senses and obscured even from our thoughts and imaginings. Consequently, the first challenge on the journey to the spiritual structure, is gaining understanding of the nature of its *concealment*.

According to the mystical tradition, *concealment* began prior to creation and was extended to humanity on the first day that the first humans took center stage. It was through the *restriction* of Divine Light that the necessary space for the physical plane was provided. The physical, which is characterized by impermanence and imperfection, is a lesser state of existence than the Divine level. This *restriction,* in and of itself, was a form of *concealment*—the concealing of Divine Light. Once an empty space in the infinite Divine Light was made available, the process of creating a more dense form of existence began—this being the physical universe.

Although this original example of *concealment* is pertinent; it is the *concealment* related to mankind that we are attempting to illuminate. This is the *concealment* that all humans face every moment of our daily lives, and it must be clarified if we are to progress toward spiritual understanding. Therefore, we must trace *concealment* back to its beginnings in order to recognize its purpose. The *purpose of concealment* is linked to understanding the *purpose of creation* itself. As our ancient mystical Sages taught; without *conceal-*

ment, there could be no physical existence. Let's consider these mystical principles as they have been taught over the centuries.

According to the ancient *Kabbalah,* creation had but one purpose. Before we consider the *purpose* of creation, we'll first consider the *Source* of creation. Impossible as it is to describe the ineffable Creator, *Kabbalah* provides some insight. Prior to creation, all that existed was eternal Divine Light—limitless, unmanifested potential. As discussed earlier, this Light consists of all the positive attributes primarily rooted in wisdom and loving-kindness. Of course, spiritually speaking, there is no difference between love and wisdom; they are one and the same. Spiritual love is the expression of spiritual wisdom; or, as often taught through religion, to know God is to love God.

Within this serene, omnipotent eternal Light of unmanifested potential, the idea stirred to make something manifest. *But what? What could possibly be lacking?* The simplest explanation given is this: *the infinite Giver had no receiver.* Within the teachings of *Kabbalah,* the Creator is sometimes referred to as the *Will to Bestow.* Even from our worldly perspective, if our will or inclination is to give, there must be someone or something willing to receive. This is it. If you blinked, you may have missed it. This is the most simplified version of the *purpose of creation—**The Creator, who is characterized by the will to bestow, created a creature whose nature is characterized by its will to receive.***

There are few among us who have not recognized this universal trait in ourselves—the love of receiving. If someone is to win the lottery, I would prefer it to be me. If some fan is going to catch Babe Ruth's 714th world record, homerun ball, let that someone be me. If one of the eighty-eight contestants will be crowned Miss Universe, let it be me. Anytime someone is going to win, while someone else loses, it's a safe bet we want to be the winner. If this is not your nature, and you prefer the joy of winning to be bestowed on others, consider yourself a rare and spiritually advanced person. As for the rest of us, we're hardwired to crave receiving in whatever form it takes. To advance spiritually, it is our own human nature that we come up against.

What was given to our original ancestors on the dawn of creation was the infinite Divine Light for which the Creator is known—unbounded delight; unlimited goodness. The definition of Divine Light is beyond the scope of this book—perhaps any book. Divine Light may be *imperfectly* described as all that makes life worth living: the beauty of nature, the wisdom of the Sages, the compassion of the Saints, the unconditional love that we feel when we seek nothing in return. Creation was not about providing something for the Creator, rather for bestowing *everything* upon the creatures.

According to the mystical meaning found in scripture, the original creatures, Adam and Eve, were the first vessels to receive Divine Light, and their idyllic home was the *Garden of Eden.* They were perfect beings in a perfect world—people and nature—a reflection of the Creator's handiwork, in a form only partially imaginable by modern minds. All that existed was the manifestation of Divine Light without the hint of darkness or evil, as these *opposing* conditions were yet to be released.

As ancient mystical tradition explains, these recipients of unbounded delight found themselves in a state of infinite bliss. Soon Adam and Eve were overwhelmed in their limited ability to receive what was being given. This led to a uniquely human experience—shame. Not the shame of being naked; that came later. It was the shame that many of us have known as well, the same shame we feel when we are always on the receiving end and have done nothing to warrant such gifts. In ancient times this was referred to as the *bread of shame*. This type of shame stems from the trait of human nature that recognizes the *restriction on enjoyment from an underserved gift*.

Adam and Eve found that they were unable to receive all of the delight the Creator had in store for them. Their ability to receive needed to be enhanced; as they lacked the feeling of worthiness necessary to enjoy all that was being bestowed upon them. Some commentaries suggest that the Creator was surprised by their response, while others hold that the Creator was impressed by it, as it is a commendable quality.

What would allow the newly created creatures to feel worthy of the Creator's unbounded delight? —playing a role in earning what they receive. This solution changed the course of history in order to enhance the vessel's ability to receive. *How could the newly created creatures in their utopian garden, as well as their future, earthly descendants, become worthy of the Creator's gifts?* Gaining worthiness was not readily available within the ideal state of perfection found in the *Garden*. Worthiness is associated with perfecting that which is imperfect. Thus, the need for an imperfect world became the genesis of the physical structure that is the basis of our material world and current existence.

But what mechanism could be devised to provide for the necessary experience of worthiness? —the mechanism of *free will*. And it remains operational to this day. It is the fundamental process present in all humans from the earliest cave dwellers to modern humanity. By granting humans the ability to choose light over darkness, they can earn the benefits of their choices. *But how can such a lowly creature as man have free will in the presence of Divine will?* Divine presence had to become *concealed* from the awareness of the human creature in order to allow for the experience of separation and free will.

This was no trivial matter, given that the newly created creatures were made in the image and substance of the Divine. Therefore, before there could be *concealment* and *free will,* there needed to be *separation* and *individuation.* In this regard, scripture speaks of eating the fruit of the *Tree of Knowledge.* Unlike the traditional interpretation where this first act of free will is viewed as a foolish and sinful act of rebellion, the mystical explanation holds this action as a calculated choice to release darkness, the antithesis of Divine light, into the world. In order to choose Light over the dark, goodness over evil, there must be darkness. And the attraction of the darkness must be worthy of the challenge.

Not only is the dark side attractive, tempting and seductive; mortals are designed to crave what the darkness has to offer. This is the *virtual reality* into which we are born. There is only one game in town and it cannot be won without first being recognized. The reason this life is fleeting and impermanent is that we are not meant to be stuck here for eternity. We are here on a mission. Once we gain the merit we came to achieve, it is time to return to the *Garden.*

We will explore the *process* of gaining this merit in the chapters ahead. The purpose of this chapter is to gain an understanding of the *concealment* that obscures the spiritual structure. In order for the physical structure (including separation and free will) to exist, the spiritual structure (including the Soul and the Creator) has to be concealed. Without the physical structure, there is no means to earn our stripes and enhance the Soul's capacity to receive. The Soul cannot have the experience it needs without being embedded into human form. There is no other way for a spiritual entity such as the Soul to experience vulnerability, fear and suffering; i.e. darkness. These are distinctly human experiences. By the same token, there is no way for a physical being to feel insecure, afraid, and anguished, unless our spiritual nature is concealed.

Concealment Allows for Free Will

In quick summary, the newly created creatures were unable to fully benefit from the purpose of their creation, i.e., being on the receiving end of *boundless delight*, without first feeling they played a role in earning such wondrous rewards. They and, in turn, all of their descendants, could not earn merit without having free will. They could not attain free will in the presence of Divine will, thus needing the experience of *separation* from the Oneness. In order to have the experience of separation, one must be removed from perceiving Divine presence; this can only be achieved by Divinely initiated *concealment*.

The challenge concerning this *concealment* is that it has rarely been penetrated. Even when it has been penetrated, and revealed by those Sages who serve humanity as beacons of light, we resist their message. It is not that their message lacks wisdom and strength; it is that their message is profoundly threatening to that part of the mind, the ego, whose nature is to remain separated and obscured from the spiritual structure. Here *ego* refers to the part of the mind that separates our identity from others. It is our self-serving ego-consciousness that is the antithesis of the altruistic Soul. The ego grounds us in our physical life and is rooted in the material world.

It could be said that the sum of our body and mind make up our identity or *ego*. Many religious systems use the term *ego* to describe that portion of the human personality that is solely out to serve itself. And because these very same religious systems do not promote the self-serving nature represented by the *ego*, it is most often portrayed in a negative light. There are also similarities found in the term *ego* as it was defined by Sigmund Freud—that part of the personality which mediates between the demands of our unconscious desires, the *id*, and our overarching moral compass, which he named the *superego*.

The ego is not the enemy of the Soul; they work in concert. Remember, from the perspective of the Soul, having a physical form and existing in a material world is a miraculous adventure. It was not a simple process drawing the curtains on a greater reality, in order to exist in a lesser reality; to conceal the spiritual structure, in order to reveal the physical.

One Mystical Glimpse into the Spiritual Structure

In order to bring us closer to understanding the concept of spiritual concealment and how it provides us with human existence and free will, we turn to one of the great works of the ancient Jewish Mystical Tradition—the *Tanya*, written in the 18th century, by Rabbi Shneur Zalman of Liadi (1745-1812), founder of Chabad Hasidism. Perhaps Rabbi Zalman's greatest attribute is that of a spiritual beacon; he had the ability to lead others in such a way as to allow them to approach the spiritual realm. Within this text, ancient scriptures are communicated and illuminated.

According to the mystical teachings of the *Tanya*, a spiritual seeker who has yet to overcome his or her egoistic inclinations is known as a *Beinoni* or intermediary—part physical and part spiritual. Since the time of Babylon, dating back to the 23rd century BCE, we have struggled with what this means. With each new civilization, humanity moved further away from the notion of man being both spiritual and physical in one life form. From Babylon to Persia, from Greece to Rome, and finally to our modern Western Civilization, history has witnessed the evolving idea that our physical entity is dominant. For many, the spiritual portion of our unique makeup is relegated to a compartmentalized form of religion brought out only on holidays and special occasions. Today, it is a rare person who experiences his or her physical and spiritual nature equally, let alone a person whose spiritual side is dominant. The blessed few who do, attest to how extraordinary this experience can be.

Rabbi Zalman took twenty years to complete his foundational work. The *Tanya* was first published in 1797, and has been discussed and digested every day since. By nature, the words of all authentic, sacred texts have the ability to alter the experience of the reader. This notion is clearly reflected in the scripture of Torah, the Gospels, the Koran, the Tao, the Upanishads, the Dhammapada and other teachings of Buddha, as well as the writings of the Saints and Sages throughout history. The *Tanya*, articulating the hidden meaning of the Torah, is just such a text. When read with a clear head and a receptive heart, its teachings stir the Soul. One caveat, like all similar texts, the language of the *Tanya* is mystical, requiring thoughtful and continual reflection and contemplation.

The theme of the *Tanya* deals with the journey of the Soul—its descent into the physical world and its ascent out of it. The greater our insight into the *technology* of the Soul, the more we are able to facilitate its *mission*. This is considered our true purpose in life—to serve the spiritual mission that surrounds us. The information gathered into the *Tanya* by Rabbi Zalman, is taken from the teachings of his teachers and from the teachings of his teacher's teachers. It is not merely one man's reflection or understanding, rather the insights and understandings of many dedicated predecessors searching for the same truths. In turn, it is the obligation of any who find a glimpse of clarity to share that understanding in order to broaden the understanding of others.

Because of its mystical nature, we begin by examining an excerpt from the *Tanya*, in small chunks, along with some insights to assist the reader. Then we will consider the quote in its entirety:

"Creation is to be understood as a descent from the first Source..."
The first Source refers to God as Creator. By definition, the *first Source* has no predecessor and no beginning; it has always existed. This is a very difficult concept for us to comprehend within our temporal existence. In our world, we are limited by the natural laws of time. *How can anything exist beyond time?* Since time is necessarily linear it must have a beginning. Thus, an infinite God is already beyond our comprehension. To create a physical world with the limitations of both time and space, the Divine Light had to *descend*—to literally become a lesser Light, so to speak.

"... giving rise to a series of worlds, from the most sublime to the progressively more material, as they are further removed from their Source."

All mystical texts agree that our world is not the world that is closest in proximity to the Divine. We will not deal with the notion of "a series of worlds," at this juncture. For our purpose here, suffice it to say that the worlds referenced here should not be thought of as other planets in the universe. Rather, they are more like other dimensions existing simultaneously. The concept of heaven is that of a world existing in closer proximity to Source/God than our world, but not distant from us. More accurately, if the mind becomes clear and the heart becomes pure, heaven is perceived during this life. Throughout scripture, we are told of saintly beings that merited a glimpse into this heavenly dimension while living a mortal life.

"This process produces in the created beings a state of separateness from God/the Source."

As already discussed, the whole process of physicality is necessary to produce the *concealment of the Spiritual Structure*. This *concealment* allows for the perception of *separation* between the spiritual and the physical—the Creator and the created. Without such *separation* there can be no *free will* in humanity. Humans cannot experience *free will* in the presence of God. The greatness of *Divine Will* overcomes any *lesser will,* such as that of mankind. Man needs *free will* in order to choose good over evil—Light over darkness. Through this choice, made within our own *free will*, we are able to merit the "unbounded delight" that we were created to receive. This is the choice made by Adam and Eve in the Garden for their descendants.

The Talmud teaches that *to truly know something, we must first experience its opposite.* Therefore, to fully experience the Light, we must first know darkness; it is the darkness that illuminates the Light; it is the suffering that distinguishes the great experience of joy. It has been said that darkness and evil were created to allow for the full experience of Light.

"The degree of materialization and separateness, of which the created beings become aware, increases with their distance from the Source of their emanation."

Remember, spiritual distance is not measured in terms of *proximity* but, rather, in terms of *similarity*. One becomes closer to God by becoming more like God; as God is holy, so are those who come to know God. All of the Saints, Prophets and Sages possessed godlike qualities. These qualities were not *given* to them; they were *earned* through exercising their own *free will*. It has often been said that even among ordinary people; every choice we make either brings us closer to our spiritual nature/God or adds to our distance from God. This is why there are no small choices—no mundane moments.

"Those beings which are nearest to their source retain a higher degree of coalescence and unity..."

This statement refers to the *similarity* mentioned above. Through our free choice, we move our Soul closer or further from its goal—closer or further from God.

"... those further removed from their source receive a greater measure of Independence and Separateness..."

As discussed earlier, the experience of *independence* and *separateness* is the goal of the ego. We cannot serve two masters. On a moment-to-moment basis, we are either serving our ego or we are serving our Soul. Our feelings of *separateness* can actually serve as a barometer to gauge how far we have strayed from our Source. Separateness is also linked to the experience of *uncertainty*, *aloneness* and *depression*— particularly as we age. This inner turmoil and suffering is not meant as punishment, rather, it is a guide to lead us back on track. As we age, we are increasingly aware of the limited time remaining to achieve our spiritual mission. Hence, the inner turmoil becomes stronger.

> **"At the lowest stage of this process of emanation, there emerges a realm of (almost) complete separateness..."**

Some have referred to the almost complete separateness as *Hell on Earth* where a person is prone to commit all manner of contemptible behavior. The daily news provides ample examples of people living their lives at the *lowest stage of the process of emanation*. In such a state, people are able to act without regard for any *moral compass*; they are maintaining the greatest *separation from Source* and operate to serve the baser desires of the ego. At this degree of separation, we do not necessarily experience bad feelings over our *aloneness*; instead, we may actually feel good based upon our temporary delusion of freedom.

*"It is inhabited by existences which are
termed kelipot ('shells'), because in them the
Infinite Light which brought them into being
is completely eclipsed by their outer shell."*

Kelipot (Hebrew תופילק) is one of those terms that do not translate easily into English. Again, it is challenging to bring ancient Hebrew terminology into modern English. And the mystical nature of *kelipot* renders the challenge even more difficult. The Jewish Mystical Tradition, specifically Kabbalah, divides everything in this world into two sides. One side, which is that of *kelipot*, is rooted in impurity (also called darkness or evil). The other is the side of *"Kedushah"* (Hebrew השודק—holiness). Literally, the *kelipot* is the "hard shell" that *protects* darkness from being infiltrated by Light or holiness. Every thought, word and action has its root in one side or the other; there is no in between. It is taught that both sides extend from the will of God. In this world, we experience most effectively through opposition and contrast, holiness is elevated by its contrast with impurity and evil. Both of these terms deserve far more appropriate description, but in the name of brevity, I leave them as stated.

Now that we have dissected this illuminating quote from the *Tanya*, we'll read it through in its entirety.

*Creation is to be understood as a descent
from the first Source giving rise to a series
of worlds, from the most sublime to the
progressively more material, as they are
further removed from their Source.
This process produces in the created
beings a state of separateness from God/*

the Source; the degree of materialization and separateness, of which the created beings become aware, increases with their distance from the source of their emanation. Those beings which are nearest to their source retain a higher degree of coalescence and unity; those further removed from their source receive a greater measure of Independence and Separateness. At the lowest stage of this process of emanation, there emerges a realm of (almost) complete separateness.

It is inhabited by existences which are termed kelipot ('shells'), because in them the Infinite Light which brought them into being is completely eclipsed by their outer shell.

—Rabbi Shneur Zalman of Liadi, Tanya (1797)

What the *Tanya* provides in the brief statement above, is the foundation of both the physical and the spiritual structure. It also implies the process by which one is able to move between the two. We drill deeper into this process in the following chapters addressing the *Spiritual Process*. Until then, we must first clear the way for what follows. If your mind is already racing as to how anyone can claim to know intricate details of creation and spiritual evolution—you ask a fair question.

The language of the *Tanya*, like all sacred texts, is mystical; it is not mathematics. Its purpose isn't to provide proof of what it claims, but to point us in the direction where truth is to be found. Millions of people have benefited from the sacred teachings of Rabbi Zalman. The spiritual wisdom contained in the quote above, is authentic and has passed the test of time, dating back far beyond the life of the rabbi. His teachings are the echoes of his teachers and those who came before them. They cannot be proven or nullified as is possible with scientific theory. The process suggested in these teachings can be engaged in and its truth experienced. From this vantage, you will be able to decide for yourself.

The concealment is recorded in all religions and in the words of most spiritual teachers. Whether it is called maya, illusion, deep sleep, the mysteries of heaven, the secrets of spirit, or simply confusion and ignorance; it points to the hidden that needs to be revealed. As with the parables taught by Jesus, the meaning will be found within the listener.

And the disciples came and said to Him, "Why do You speak to them in parables?" Jesus answered them, "To you it has been granted to know the mysteries of the kingdom of heaven, but to them it has not been granted." For whoever has, to him more shall be given, and he will have an abundance; but whoever does not have, even what he has shall be taken away from him....

— (Matthew 13:10-12)

Seven hundred years earlier, the Hebrew prophet Isaiah spoke of the concealment as a deep sleep that blinds mankind from truth. He maintained his prophetic vision for nearly 90 years during a turbulent time in history when idolatry ruled and the tribes of Israel were exiled.

And it shall be, as the hungry man dreams, and behold, he eats, and he shall awaken, and his appe-

tite is un-sated, and as the thirsty man dreams, and behold he drinks, and he shall awaken and behold he is faint, and his soul yearns... Stop and wonder; they became blind and they blinded... For the Lord has poured upon you a spirit of deep sleep, and He has closed your eyes... And the vision of everything has been to you like the words of a sealed book, which they give to one who can read, saying, "Now read this," and he shall say, "I cannot, for it is sealed." And if the book is given to one who cannot read, saying, "Now read this," he shall say, "I cannot read."

—(Isaiah 29:8-12)

Within the ancient sacred text of the Jewish Mystical Tradition, The Zohar (Book of Radiance), a very interesting quote can be found:

When the world was made, a limit was set how long it will function in confusion.

—Zohar

This suggests that the time of concealment is both calculated and limited. It is highly possible, as is suggested in the teachings of the Abrahamic religions, that there is a designated time when humanity will be redeemed from a history of bad choices and faulty perceptions—a time when the veil of concealment will be lifted and Divine Light will once again shine through. It is, however, not entirely clear if this time of collective revelation will be brought about by the efforts of humanity or as a gift from God. Regardless of which path leads to our collective destiny, individually we face the same challenge—to *grab the brass ring* before the final buzzer sounds.

Living Between Two Worlds

As set forth in the *Tanya*, to be on the spiritual path, is to be an *intermediary* existing between our physical, egoistic dimension and that of the spiritually advanced. Our Sages spent every waking hour pouring over the true nature of mankind and how humans are related to God; how the physical is related to the spiritual. Let's review some of the fundamental elements of this relationship and the unique positioning of humanity:

- *Humans exist in two dimensions simultaneously*
- *Humans distinguish between the physical and the spiritual*
- *The physical world is governed by the laws of time and space*
- *The spiritual domain exists beyond the limitations of time and space*
- *The purpose of the physical dimension is to achieve Free Will*
- *To achieve this purpose, the spiritual dimension must be concealed from the physical; there can be no free will in the clear presence of Divine will*
- *The ego dominates the physical dimension in order to achieve individuation and separation from the Divine*
- *The Soul dominates the spiritual dimension to maintain Unity and Oneness with the Divine*
- *On the most fundamental level, every moment of physical life is a choice between upholding separation or moving toward Unity—ego or Soul*

These are the overarching and highly unique characteristics of being human. According to our Sages, humanity is the only level of existence whereby these particular conditions are found. That is to say, our most significant and distinguishing feature is that we are both physical and spiritual entities intertwined. We are comprised of both matter and consciousness—flesh and spirit. And because of this unique composition, we exist in both the material world and the spiritual world simultaneously. We will delve into these overarching elements a little more deeply:

Humans exist in two dimensions simultaneously...

For most people, it is quite a challenge to even recognize the existence of the spiritual dimension, let alone to personally experience living simultaneously in both the physical and spiritual dimensions. Perhaps the most common reason for not experiencing the spiritual structure is found in not knowing what to look for. When Jesus said that the *Kingdom of God is among you*, it wasn't that the spiritual structure couldn't be seen, rather, that we were looking with blind eyes.

The problem is actually twofold; the structure is obscured, and we need to acquire *eyes blessed with vision*. In the beginning of this chapter, we have described some of the key obstacles that obstruct the spiritual structure; the process of acquiring *blessed vision* (spiritual perception) is explored in the following chapters. Before you become overwhelmed and discouraged, remember this: your spiritual nature already exists. It is not our task to *gain* a spiritual nature; merely to *recognize* it. And, as many teachers have taught, before we are able to *recognize* the spiritual structure, we can start by simply *imagining* it.

To be human is to live in the lesser dimension. We

descended into the physical world—in other words; we came from the place we are trying to get to. The task is not to find the lost continent; it is only to follow the breadcrumbs back home. The physical dimension offers countless, invaluable experiences necessary for the Soul's evolution. In fact, these Soul enhancing experiences are why we are here. Regrettably, the very conditions that provide these experiences also cause us to become distracted and lost. According to the Buddha, our desperate attachment to a fleeting, physical existence is perhaps the most tragic and hopeless aspect of our lives; one that is connected to endless anxiety and anguish.

To be human is also to be connected to the higher dimension. Just as we descended to achieve our objectives, we may ascend to gain back our birthright. This is essentially the meaning of the title to this book. The epiphany is coming to know that we are not physical beings *seeking* a spiritual experience; we are spiritual beings *having* a physical experience. While the physical experience has its moments of sheer joy and intoxicating delights, it will never provide us with what we so desperately crave—permanence.

Imagine the sense of security and wellbeing that comes with the realization of permanence. For most of us, it is only through imagination that we are able to plant this seed of eternal existence. This is quite a stretch for us who were born into the most scientific, materialist worldview in history. Words like eternity and immortality are most often associated with science fiction or superstition. This is a common and understandable kneejerk reaction to such incredible notions. Bear in mind, as unverifiable as the existence of our immortal Soul may be, it is no more unverifiable than the notion that it *doesn't* exist. When it comes to the existence of one's Soul, the old adage rings true; *the proof of the pudding is in the eating.* And until you have tasted this delicacy, it is best to hold back judgment.

Humans distinguish between the physical and the spiritual...

Interestingly, those who have yet to experience the spiritual, most often distinguish it from the physical. Even the initial experiences into the spiritual realm suggest this distinction. Yet our Sages taught that this distinction is an illusion, as both are part of a unified whole. Perhaps a more precise way of perceiving this is that the physical plane is a *reflection* or *expression* of the spiritual; matter is an expression of consciousness. Once we experience our spiritual nature, our physical nature becomes far less significant, although far more enjoyable. If this sounds farfetched and even undesirable, remember, our physical nature is fleeting and impermanent. While young, it's easy to imagine our lives as never-ending. This naïve indulgence provides no assurance to those who must confront their imminent expiration date on a daily basis. By the time we enter the fourth quadrant of life (60-80+), it becomes easier to recognize the diminished status of our transitory, physical identity; especially in light of an emerging ageless and timeless spiritual nature. Aging provides most of us all the evidence we need that our physical bodies are temporary and prone to degeneration before they expire. Here again, the epiphany is the realization that it is the Soul that has a body rather than the body having a Soul.

The body and mind are instruments of our physical nature within a material world. With our physical nature and its perceptions, come all of the elements of vulnerability and fear associated with being impermanent. Each moment of our physical lives presents a new reality that is changed from that of the previous moment. We judge these momentary flashes of reality as being better or worse than the previous, but they all share one common thread—each new moment brings us closer to our inevitable, physical demise. If we are able to bridle our thoughts and keep them from wandering too far into that quandary, we may be able to sustain a somewhat secure perspective. When the body begins its unavoidable decline, and the thin veneer of invincibility peels away, we can no longer remain aloof to our approaching finale. Life's culmination can be nothing short of utter anguish without the promise of spring's new buds at the end of a daunting winter.

The physical world is governed by the laws of time and space, while the spiritual domain exists beyond the limitations of time and space.

Why would spiritual beings, i.e., Souls, descend into a physical reality in order to engage the conditions of time and space? It is not so much time and space that benefit the Soul; but the condition expressed by time and space—change. Time and space are the consequence of a changing reality. We cannot be in one place at one moment and another place in another moment, without passing through time and traversing space. It is change that makes the physical dimension attractive to the Soul, as the spiritual dimension does not include the phenomenon of change. Without change, there can be no temporal or spatial variations.

Embedded in physical form with a mortal life, the Soul is able to benefit from the changes that occur during this life. Again, the rationale for the Soul's adventure in corporeality is to enhance its ability to receive the *unbounded delight*

(Divine Light) that marks the purpose of its creation. *What enhances the Soul's ability to receive Light?* —the experience of its opposite, darkness. And as all mortals come to realize, there is no shortage of darkness at play in the physical world.

The spiritual structure is not dependent on opposing polarities, as is the physical. The spiritual structure does not require darkness to illuminate the Light; it does not require evil to recognize goodness. A realm of unchanging, unbounded delight is as foreign to humans as a realm of impermanence and suffering is to the Soul. Without change there can be no choice; without choice there can be no free will; and without free will there is no opportunity to choose good and renounce evil—Light over darkness. This single act of choosing Light over darkness brings worthiness to the vessel and enhances its ability to receive. It was the lack of feeling worthy of all that was being bestowed upon it, that caused the original vessel to shatter, separate and descend into the physical structure. Here, worthiness is *achieved* through using human free will to choose the Light over darkness; altruism over egoism; unity over separation.

With this purpose in mind, the Soul enters the physical dimension as a physical being. Physicality is characterized by such limiting phenomena as time, space and matter. As a result, the Soul is able to experience the *dark* qualities of vulnerability and suffering; insecurity and fear; imperfection and impermanence. This is quite a contrast from its home in the spiritual dimension, characterized by unlimited, infinite, eternal Light, without a trace of darkness. Every aspect of the physical world is distinguished by diversity, while the spiritual structure is characterized by Oneness. Each of us is an expression of Oneness developing our own unique identity. Within our unique identity, lie the opportunities that are brought about by change. *What are these changes made available on the physical plane?* —to become more like the Light that brought us into being.

Each unique personality, or ego-identity, has areas of *darkness*, or *flaws*, necessitating change or correction, in order to resemble the Light. As changes are made, through exercising our own free will, the Soul gains merit and becomes *worthy* of the delight that awaits. According to the ancient mystical traditions, it is this *unbounded delight* being bestowed on creation that is the purpose of creation. Although worthiness was not a requirement of the Creator, it was a self-imposed necessity of the creature.

By design, the ego is the opposite of the Soul. Just as the physical world is, by design, the opposite of the spiritual. These opposing polarities are not enemies; they complement one another. Without the ego, there can be no experience of separation and individuation, which is critical in achieving the Soul's ultimate objective on its earthly mission. As Darwin pointed out, without the profound inclination toward serving and preserving oneself, the human species would not have survived.

When viewing the physical world through a human lens, we are struck by its imperfections. Based on all the inhumanity within humanity, some even question the existence of God. However, conditions such as greed and envy; suffering and cruelty; are also self-imposed. Viewed through the lens of the Soul, our world is perfection within its apparent imperfection. This is the ideal environment for the Soul to do its work and gain benefit. The anguish caused by viewing the world through the human lens is rooted in fear. It's only human to sense that we are under the oppression of time, restrictions of space and the impermanence of matter. We see time fleeting past and the evidence can be found in our own aging bodies; time passes while matter deteriorates. Our foolish perception of endless time and permanent wellbeing is merely a fantasy of youth. Only the Saints and Sages feel confident and enthused about meeting their maker. For the rest of us, the prospect of accounting for our time spent in this life arouses consternation.

Only when viewing through the lens of the Soul, are we able to see the big picture. When it comes to the Soul, the darkness and imperfections within us, and within our world, provide grist for the mill. The Soul did not descend into our reality to find perfection; it exists in perfection. The darker the room, the brighter the flame shines. Only here, in our darkened, grief stricken, imperfect world is the Soul able to do the work of the Creator. This is the perfect setting for angels to earn their wings—our boot camp for building character. The Sages taught that the only portion of this life that travels with us beyond the grave is the character traits we have developed. Compromising one's character for personal gain is the single greatest blunder a person can make during this life. This is the warning expressed by the Golden Rule of all religions and cultures, both modern and ancient. Doing toward others as you want done to you is the epitome of a moral and ethical character. The refinement of character enhances the Soul's capacity to receive.

The purpose of the physical dimension is to achieve Free Will. Therefore, the spiritual dimension must be concealed from the physical, as there can be no free will in the clear presence of Divine will.

Understanding the purpose of the physical world brings many other spiritual properties into focus. Without understanding the purpose of this life, we are at a terrible disadvantage in achieving that purpose. Sadly, so many of us spend most of our lives providing for our lives. We grow in stature and knowledge; we accumulate and contribute; we receive love and give love—all worthy endeavors. Yet, for the majority, the single most important mission requiring our undivided attention often passes under our radar. As a reminder, let's review the mystical model of creation:

The purpose of creation is to provide a recipient, or vessel, to receive the Creator's bestowal of unbounded delight. The newly created vessel was unable to receive all that was being bestowed; its *cup runneth over*. The obstacle preventing the vessel from its unlimited capacity to receive was the first feelings of shame. This shame was rooted in the vessel having not merited the delight being bestowed. The original vessel, the Soul, needed to feel worthy of such a gift. The mechanism created to offer the opportunity for feeling worthy is *free will*. Through *free will,* the Soul can choose what is right and overcome what is wrong; good over evil. For the spiritual Soul, made in the image of its Creator, to gain *free will* would require experiencing itself as separate from the Divine will of its Maker. This could only be achieved by concealing the spiritual structure. The mechanism created to conceal the spiritual structure is physicality. The physical body is able to conceal the spiritual Soul from itself by focusing on its five senses and ego-based identity. The material world conceals the spiritual structure by keeping the *bodymind* entranced in the hypnotic allure of physical distractions and sensory cravings. Hence, the purpose of the physical dimension is to achieve *free will* for the creature by concealing the Creator.

The ego dominates the physical dimension in order to achieve separation and individuation from the Divine, while the Soul dominates the spiritual dimension to maintain unity and Oneness with the Divine.

The ego is not a precise mechanism—not easily defined or located. Often referred to as a part of human intellect, perhaps it is most accurately described as our self-serving nature; our unique personality. Spiritually speaking, the ego is the opposing force of the Soul. The Soul is rooted in *unity* with the Creator, while the primary function of the ego is *separation* from the Creator. Keep in mind, the purpose of the physical experience is to achieve free will, and the ego is an essential ingredient in this process. It is the ego that brings about separation and individuation in humanity. Without a self-serving, individual personality, we would cease to be physical beings in a material world.

By dominating every aspect of our physical nature, the ego dominates the physical dimension. The mind cannot conceive, nor can the senses perceive, without the ego acting as a filter. In this way, each of us exists within a reality of our own making; our ego designs the reality we experience. This is the phenomenon of *subjective reality*. We assume that we are all looking at the same reality; however, we're not all *experiencing* the same reality. Perception is not an objective mechanism. Perception is *manufactured* by the conditioning of the main organ of perception: the mind. And the main instrument in conditioning the mind is the ego, at least from the perspective of the physical dimension.

As we engage the process of quickening the Soul (spiritual awakening), the ego becomes threatened. The ego recognizes that it's no match for a fully engaged Soul, so it employs the tools of distraction and desire to keep the mind from focusing on the Soul's agenda. Its need for gratification is intensified as the threat becomes more real. Ancient Hindus portray this tug-of-war in paintings depicting the opposing polarity of mortality and immortality; ego and Soul. At our most fundamental level, this is the dance we all perform. Day in and day out, we use our gift of free will to strengthen or weaken the forces that bind and tug at us. All that we are, and all that we become, is directly related to this continual effort pitting our physical and spiritual natures against one another.

> ***On the most fundamental level, every moment of physical life is a choice between upholding separation or moving toward Unity—ego or Soul.***

When we peel the onion back to its core, what remains

is the choice between unity with the Creator and separation. We sustain our position in physical reality by rejecting the spiritual—either we cling to the **Tree of Life** or we continue eating from the **Tree of Knowledge**. *What causes a person to remain attached to a life of misery and suffering, rather than returning to the Garden?* — delusion and ignorance. It's not our fault. In the words of the Buddha, we have yet to see things as they really are.

What is real is concealed and what is apparent is highly alluring. Like the mule chasing the carrot tied to a stick, we've yet to discover the illusion of permanent fulfillment in an impermanent life. Each step closer to the carrot is another step further away. If we remain blind to this futile mechanism, like the mule, we will prolong the chase until we are drained of energy and run out of time.

This is the realization that leads to Self-realization. It is so simple, yet so difficult to grasp. *Why, if it's so obvious, are so many of us hoodwinked into chasing the carrot into a gulf of anguish when a sea of ecstasy awaits us? Why is a loving parent deaf to a child's misconduct? Why is a trusting spouse so blind to a cheating partner?* We do not hear or see what is real; rather, we hear and see what we desire to hear and see. All of our perceptions are filtered through a self-serving ego motivated by pleasure and gratification. Until our subjective reality is bridged to the spiritual structure, truth remains obscured by an impenetrable veil of concealment.

Concealment of the Spiritual Structure Provides for the Physical

The Taoist Master Lao Tzu taught that the path of perception must be free of the senses to gain insight into that which is concealed: *To merge with Tao, turn away from your senses. The light of pure consciousness hides in formlessness.*

The phenomenon of *concealment* allows the uniquely physical combination of conditions to exist and work in harmony. This *concealment* is so vast and all-encompassing that even the Creator is obscured from the physical realm. A person existing in the physical realm cannot perceive the spiritual structure without opening their spiritual lens. Through the *lens of the Soul,* humanity gains access to the spiritual structure.

The spiritual dimension is concealed in the physical world so that we may discover it individually. That is to say, something cannot be discovered if it is already apparent. For example, if our purpose is to discover the existence of trees, there is no challenge in that, as trees are *not* concealed. Through the discovery of that which *is* concealed, we *pass through the gates of the spiritual realm.* The discovery of our spiritual nature and the spiritual structure are key aspects to discovering life's purpose.

While the discovery of our spiritual nature is an imperative step toward fulfilling life's purpose, it is also what elevates the Soul in its second stage. Ancient mystical traditions hold that the Soul was created in three stages. In the second stage, the Soul is embedded into a physical form within our material world. In the first and third stages, the Soul is without the limiting element of form; explicitly *not clothed in a body.* The difference between the first and third stages is the enhancement that takes place during the second stage while the Soul is embedded in the body, experiencing all of the aspects of a physical life. It is in this second stage that we all find ourselves.

Imagine two overlapping circles. The circle on the left represents our Soul's existence prior to birth, and the circle on the right is our Soul's post-death existence. In this Venn diagram, the center area where both circles overlap, the *vesica piscis,* contains the properties of both circles. Our current level of existence is found in this area of intersection containing both body and Soul; physical and metaphysical; i.e., being both a part of nature and beyond nature. Birth brings us into the middle section, and dying moves us out of it. Birth and death are both involuntary transformations. We are only able to impact our transformation in the span between birth and death. Clinging to existence within the middle section, we will remain in denial that another circle to the right (existence beyond death) even exists. We exist in the intersection of the physical and spiritual. To realize this truth is linked to fulfilling our purpose.

Beyond its role in fulfilling our purpose, discovering one's spiritual aspect is an exhilarating breakthrough. It opens an entirely new dimension of our identity and capability. While modern life is characterized for many as wrought with utter frustration, disappointment and depression, to discover our spiritual essence is nothing less than a critical update to our limited system.

According to spiritual teachings, this new and improved existence is the result of entering a new dimension. Encarta dictionary defines *dimension* as a **level of reality:** a level of consciousness, existence, or reality. *How might one enter a new level of reality?* —by altering one's level of consciousness. Our consciousness is often altered by external circumstances. You could be enjoying a peaceful and happy day gardening when a phone call brings news of an accident in which someone dear to you was hurt. In a matter of seconds, you leave the peaceful, happy dimension and enter one of tension and anxiety.

Your perception and experience of reality have been altered by your awareness of new conditions emerging within your external circumstances. Notice that your reaction is the same regardless of whether the information is correct or not. The ancient Hindu scripture of the Vedanta speaks of *Adhyāsa*, which is Sanskrit for *superimposition, false attribution, illusion, perceptual error.* An example of perceptual error is the *rope/snake metaphor* used in the Vedanta. Under dimly lit conditions, an ordinary coil of rope can be mistaken for a snake. In this situation, a person will react to the rope as if it were a snake. Even though it is the illusion of a snake and the reality of a rope, it is the illusion that causes the reaction. In this metaphor, a person enters a new dimension of fear and panic based on an *adhyāsa*, or misperception.

The spiritual structure is another dimension of reality. It is not separate from the physical structure; it is an extension of it. If we stand with our back toward the sun on a sunny day, we see our shadow. Even though the shadow appears to be separate from the person casting it, the shadow cannot exist without sunlight and the person. In the dimension of shadows, neither the person nor the sun need be perceived. If we expand our perception to include the dimension of the person, we find the shadow only exists due to the person. An even greater perception occurs when we include the role of the sun; without the light source there can be no shadow.

In this analogy, each new dimension is brought about by our expanded consciousness. It is no coincidence that the shadow moves at the precise moment the person moves; they are interrelated. And if the sun drops behind a mountain, the shadow disappears altogether. The shadow is determined by the object that casts it and the light source behind it. So it is with our physical world. It is merely the expression of the spiritual structure—a shadow cast by the *light* shining behind spirit.

In order to enter the spiritual structure, we must raise our consciousness to the level where spirituality is perceived. Humans are comprised of the physical and spiritual intertwined. Our physical aspect is far more apparent and perceivable than our spiritual nature. Few, indeed, doubt their physical existence. On the other hand, for most, spiritual certainty remains questionable, if not doubtful. We believe what is apparent, even when the frightening snake is, in fact, a coiled rope. Our physical nature constantly reminds us of its presence—it's too cold or too warm, it's hungry or thirsty, it's comfortable or uncomfortable. The physical communicates through physical sensation and perceivable thoughts; this provides all the evidence we need to confirm its presence.

Our spiritual nature communicates on a far more subtle level, through consciousness. Even when communication has been successful, it is unlikely that we will recognize its source. Like two friends vying for your attention, one may openly complain of feeling neglected, while the other waits for you to come to your own conclusions. So it is with the ego and the Soul; the ego will always be the squeaky wheel.

A Human Is Like a Computer with Two Operating Systems

To illustrate the competing nature of our ego and Soul (physical and spiritual), consider the following analogy. Humans can be likened to a computer with *two operating systems*, both competing to control the *hard drive.* Imagine how this operating nightmare would play out on your personal computer, and its impact on your productivity. Not to mention the incredible frustration and helpless confusion that would ensue. An efficient computer depends on open passages and free access to arrive at its destinations. If, at every step, it encounters conflicting commands and constant churning, its access to information and its ability to connect will be drastically obstructed.

A similar quagmire is happening within each of us. We have two operating systems both trying to gain control over our cerebral hard drives. This is the source of our collective inner conflict. To be human is to be engaged in the conflict of flesh and spirit, regardless of our awareness of it. Every moment of our lives is processed through this tangled mechanism before it can proceed into sensation, thought and expression. It is tantamount to asking directions on a trip while one person directs you to head east and the other asserts you must go west. Each time you lean toward one, the other reacts unfavorably. It is our job to distinguish between these two aspects of ourselves that provide the constant input giving rise to our daily living.

For most people, the solution to this predicament is to dial down the volume on one in order to follow the other. This is fine, providing the directions you follow are correct. After all, if you're in Middle America intending to go to the Pacific Ocean, directions to head east are not the ones to follow. Of course, even if you choose east, there is that temporary relief in having made a choice, thereby avoiding the anxiety of conflicting input. However, sooner or later you will make the startling discovery that you have spent a lot of time and effort heading in the wrong direction. It's best to find the right course before moving forward, even if it seems as though you are taking time away from your journey.

Let's be clear about the two operating systems vying for control of our hard drives. The two systems are transmitting on different frequencies. Model One operating system, rooted in the physical structure, has an automatic design that speaks to us continuously. It is difficult to experience a moment in life when we are not engaged in the transmission and reception of this operating system. It receives data from the senses, interprets that data, and evaluates it at speeds measured in split seconds. This does not include the input from endless random thoughts banging against our deep-dish receptors, requiring detailed viability reports and our need to take action. Model One is the system most connected to our basic drives toward pleasure, self-preservation, and the propagation of the species. Almost all *human desires* stem from this system. It's a blend of our basic desires for food, shelter, love, sex, etc. as well as the more sophisticated desires associated with *ego gratification*, such as recognition, respect, honor, power, control, and so on, that determine our reactions *to* life and our behavior *in* it. Model One operating system gives rise to the physical structure and appears to be operating on its own with complete autonomy.

Probing deeper, Model One is the main operating system that determines how we experience the world and how the world experiences us. Our reality is based on this system; and this system is based on our previous conditioning, sensory desires, and ego cravings. Literally, the reality we have come to know throughout our lives is less about the *way things really are*, and more about the *way we perceive things to be*. Buddha taught that what we call reality is an illusion—a product of a conditioned mind that is conditioned by our incessant desires.

If its link to our desires were not enough to dominate our view of reality, Model One is also the gatekeeper of our perception and the source of our expression. Its constant voice and narrow, biased view eventually become what we recognize as our entire identity. In short, common man is identified by common man desires—a new take on the old adage "You are what you eat." Only here, "We are what we desire." The uncommon man, the extraordinary human being, is one who manages to break free the domination of sensory based, ego driven desires.

To put in perspective this issue of overcoming one's desires on the path to spirituality, Buddha recognized: ***All suffering is caused by* desire**. The second of the Four Noble Truths of Buddhism.

> *It is not good conduct that puts you on the path to liberation, nor will ritual do it, nor book learning, nor seclusion and solitude, nor meditation. None of these alone can bring mastery or joy. It is desirelessness that does it.*
>
> —Buddha

Model One is so pervasive that it eventually becomes the voice of our identity. For most, life is far too busy and complicated to even begin to distinguish a second operating system; especially one transmitting on a frequency not recognized without committed and sustained effort. "I am my identity" is a fundamental truth of the rational mind; *apparently* indisputable.

The design principle of Model One is fairly straightforward; it begins with the identity as self. It has two fundamental functions: the preservation of life and the pursuit of pleasure, including ego gratification. While these two functions operate within all of us, they manifest in a variety of ways depending on each of our unique personalities. Some personalities go to unethical, immoral, even illegal extremes in the name of self-preservation and ego-enhancement, while others are self-sacrificing in their drive to contribute to others, especially their children and loved ones.

In keeping with the design principle of Model One, this operating system runs all input through a *filter* to determine whether it's a *threat* or a *support* to the ego's self-interest.

This is an inherent operation in the functions of *self-preservation* and *ego-enhancement*. Another distinction that needs to be made is what the ego deems *self-preservation*. To the ego, *self-preservation* goes beyond the customary definition of preserving life and limb, to include preserving its reputation and defending its character. Something as simple as a person challenging the validity of our ideas can appear threatening to the ego. Consequently, our judgment is based on *perceived* threats or *perceived* support that ultimately may or may not be accurate.

The primary mechanism employed by Model One in dealing with *threats* and *support* is the process of *judgment* and *evaluation*. The ego's judgment is constantly activated; it's analogous to a radar screen detecting everything entering its range. Someone innocently pays you a complement and your ego mistakenly judges that person harshly. A friendly greeting at the office such as "Good morning, you sure look nice today" might be filtered by the ego as "Is she suggesting that I usually don't look nice?" Of course, when the ego feels threatened, the judgment filter is already twisted toward perceived threats. Here again, inaccuracy is not uncommon.

A second design principle of the Model One operating system, utilized for maintaining *self-preservation* and *ego enhancement,* is *manipulation* and *domination*. The ego deals with the barrage of perceived threats by manipulating and dominating others while, at the same time, avoiding their domination. It engages in a constant struggle to gain and maintain the upper hand. We see illustrations of this process within any group dynamic, especially office politics and social interactions, where egos tend to feel most vulnerable. People will go at each other, both openly and covertly, to prevent being controlled by others or made to appear wrong.

Occasionally people resort to reckless behavior just to protect and enhance the ego. This behavior is often rooted back to early childhood where toddlers defiantly touch a hot stove simply because they were sternly warned not to.

Once the ego has gone on its rampage to be right and to dominate, it moves into phase two of its operation—*self-justification*. This is the obvious result of the ego recognizing how inaccurate it has been in its attempt to be right. To justify its false position, the ego will often fabricate some semblance of the truth. This is akin to a chronic liar telling an endless stream of lies in an attempt to cover-up the original lie—all the while, failing to recognize how obvious this scheme is to others.

Observe how often you, and those around you, are engaged in ego driven perceptions and behaviors such as: manipulating the truth in order to be right, manipulating others to be in control, and spewing endless self-justification to excuse inaccurate, self-serving statements and their corresponding bad behavior. Such responses follow our knee jerk evaluations and judgments as to what poses a threat, and what is considered support, for the ego's *campaigns*. Herein lies the work of the ego and it is a 24/7 job. Take note, every thought, word and deed performed by the Model One operating system is rooted in its continual, self-serving pursuit of pleasure and power to gratify the ego.

In addition to being devastating to our spiritual progress, this ego mechanism is potentially unhealthy physically; it keeps us in a perpetual state of anxiety and stress. Furthermore, this mechanism is psychologically damaging. It prevents the nurturing condition brought about by a mental state of wellbeing and peace. Overactive egos constantly perceive enemies and threats—both human and circumstantial.

The egoist mindset perceives others as the enemy because it is constantly attempting to dominate them; when they do not comply, they are viewed as threats.

Obviously, this is not a sound basis for nurturing relationships. It is difficult, at best, to nurture mutual love and respect, while having to maintain the status of always being right and dominant. This fundamental design feature of the ego sheds light on endless flawed relations and countless social disasters. While our self-serving, ego-based identity is perhaps the single greatest factor contributing to the survival of our species, it is also the single greatest obstacle to *peace on earth, goodwill toward mankind.*

The Ego Mechanism Determines Our Reality

This ego mechanism, or self-serving personality, is perceived by the individual as vital to its overall identity—forming its self-image. The conditioned mind serves as the filter through which we perceive our self and our reality. For most people, there is no identity other than the one provided by the ego, and no other reality than the *subjective reality* of the ego— the physical plane. Even those of us holding strong spiritual beliefs find it difficult, if not impossible, to view the spiritual structure through the lens of the ego.

The ego constructs its own self-image and its *owner* attempts to live up to it. If that self-image is overly-exaggerated, it can have a devastating impact on a person's personality, making it difficult to achieve harmony with others. *Self-justification* can dominate one's thought process and often be the primary topic of one's conversations, painting the self as right at all cost. We see numerous examples of people going to extreme measures, including violence, to *save face* and preserve the ego.

The self-justification mechanism is so important to the ego that it will actually *stockpile* incidents, accolades and accomplishments into a sort of *self-justification file* for future use. If some event or argument evidenced the ego being right in the past, it will be utilized again and again in support of its current campaigns, as though these scenarios serve as legal precedent. Just imagine the interference this all brings to our ability to have effective communication, loving relationships and harmonious interactions.

Because the ego, the *Model One operating system,* is perceived to be our *only* operating system, it has the potential to dominate one's total *airspace*; becoming the only voice we hear from within—our most trusted advisor. For most, our entire identity is being formed by this highly judgmental and overly biased perception, driven almost exclusively by self-interest. Whenever we are having difficulty with relationships (our spouse, children, parents, siblings, neighbors, bosses, co-workers, friends, etc.), look no further than the ego-based identity for the source of the problem.

Souls Mate; Egos Clash

As a rule of thumb: **Souls mate, while egos clash.** This doesn't just apply to romantic relationships, as all relationships share a Soul connection. The very nature of the Soul is to form connections and contribute to others; this is how the Soul is nurtured. So often we identify a new relationship with the *Soul connection* experienced when first meeting someone of interest. As the relationship develops, whether friendship, romance or business, we inevitably encounter the Soul's evil sibling—the ego. This is the ultimate bait and switch. In place of the nurturing and contributing experience of the Soul, we face the self-serving and manipulative nature of the ego—a total game changer. If our relationships could be entrusted to our Souls, they would thrive—Souls are masters of bonding.

Sadly, only the very spiritually advanced remain exclusively in the Soul's domain. For most, our relationships go from harmonious, soulful bonding, to the discord of the ego's incessant evaluation, manipulation and judgment. The ego's aim to establish itself as always right and always dominant is eventually introduced into our relationships, resulting in discord and endless self-justification. The ego thrives in this chaotic environment; it was bred for battle—a battle it will never win. And the reason it will never win is that the ego's ultimate goal is constructing a world that fits all of its criteria; namely, a world made in its own image. The ego sees fault in all that is not itself. If egos were allowed in paradise, they would find fault with the landscaping.

It's been said that the ego fights its endless battles from two distinct positions—on its feet or on its back. When standing, the ego has full reign of its arrogance: *Things will go my way because I am right and I dominate.* The ego always claims to be the source of its own power and joy. But when that power fails to produce, and the joy is infringed upon, the ego changes its stance to fighting on its back—from an offensive to a defensive position. This is the ego in the role of victim. If there is a loss of power or pleasure, it can only be because some force other than itself is responsible. The ego will do whatever it takes to shed any trace of culpability in its own losses. At its worst, the ego turns against its biggest supporters (family, friends, loved ones, etc.) in order to keep the obvious from surfacing—that it's wrong.

There are many who are actually more effective at manipulating others from a position of the victim, especially if they tap into their own righteous indignation. More than a few good marriages and successful businesses have been brought down by this insidious trait of human nature. The ego's supreme mission is to always be right. So, on those occasions when things are clearly going wrong, it shifts into *damage control* and takes on the point of view that others are the source of the abomination, declaring: *I can no longer endure the suffering brought on by your mistakes...* This simple declaration then justifies, at least in one's own mind, the destructive action about to be taken: ending a marriage, a partnership, relationships, etc. Pushed to its very limits, an ego may actually murder its own body as the ultimate expression of the contrived injustice victimizing it. Suicide might be a last attempt at being right and dominating others, posthumously. It certainly closes the door on any potential retaliation and is the definitive last word.

It's easy to assume that the ego is pure evil, a demon we must destroy. Counterintuitive as it may seem, the ego was given to humanity as a gift. Ego is a kind of armor that protects us along the arduous journey that is our lives. It is unlikely that we would have lasted as long, or survived as well, without the power of ego—*model one operating system.* The ego is motivated to protect us by its undying love of self. In many ways, the ego is like fire—a useful tool until it gets out of control. It is the ego's domination over perception and behavior that causes our experience of separation and suffering.

Within the physical structure, the ego has two roles. First, it is the system that drives the human animal to maintain its life and sustain the future of the species. *Like* the lesser animals, this raw instinct, or as some call it, "animal Soul" provides for our physical life—it animates us.

Secondly, *unlike* the lesser animals, the *animal Soul* of the human has an additional component referred to as ego, or self-serving nature. This far more sophisticated human drive includes our urge for a better life. Within this second role, the human ego pushes us to succeed: to gain wealth and position, education and wisdom, recognition and acknowledgement, myriad pleasures and gratifications. It is our ego that is the source of the *Me First* mentality that is so common within our species. Scripture refers to this characteristic of humanity as *man's natural inclination to serve himself*—and to serve himself first.

Second Operating System

Another role of the Model One operating system is to provide *concealment* for the Model Two operating system—the spiritual structure. Because the Model Two operating system is linked into the spiritual structure, it is veiled in *concealment.* All things spiritual have the characteristic of *concealment* when viewed through the physical lens. In this way, the spiritual structure and the physical structure are separated—or at least appear to be separated. Without separation, the physical structure could not exist. As our Sages taught, it is our attachment to the physical structure that keeps the spiritual structure concealed.

Ultimately, the objective is to bring both of these distinct structures into balance. The *sweet spot* is found in perceiving the spiritual while maintaining the physical. Once we achieve this advanced state of awareness, in which we are attentive to both our physical and spiritual nature, life takes on an elevated experience. Once attained, the Model Two operating system is running our *hard drive.*

There are many obstacles to achieving the ideal shift from the dominance of Model One to the authority of Model Two. One of the most frustrating obstacles is the resistance of the ego to allowing this shift to take place. The ego is deeply embedded in the Model One system, and as mentioned before, it reacts strongly to anything that threatens its control. As we attempt to gain clarity of the Model Two system, the ego will do all that it can to sabotage any progress. The ego recognizes the threat posed by the Model Two system. Consequently, it will *maintain our inclination to serve ourselves;* while *resisting the inclination to serve others—including God.* A simplified version of this spiritual shift is a person going from one prone to take, to one inclined to give. On this point, the Talmud teaches: *"A person should always provoke his good inclination to overpower his evil inclination"* (inclination toward self-interest).

At the very core of our being, this struggle involving our two inclinations rages on without pause. This is the condition we were born into and will someday die out of—all that takes place in between is *window dressing.* The big question we face in determining the validity of our time on earth is

whether we were able to graduate from egoism to altruism—from separation to unity, from being a taker to becoming a giver. Our lives can be reduced to a continual stream of circumstances presenting the choice of perpetuating our inclination toward self-interest or evolving past its domination.

Rabbi Israel Meir Kagan (1838-1933) was known as

The Chofetz Chaim (Desirer of Life), the name of his first of 21 holy books. He took his title from the words of the 34th Psalm: *Who is the man who desires life, who loves days to see goodness? Guard your tongue from evil and your lips from speaking deceitfully.* Rabbi Kagan taught the laws regarding the ethics of speech, particularly the evil talk and gossip that hurts both the speaker and subject. Speech is a fundamental aspect of the third phase of the spiritualization process, expression, discussed in Chapter Seventeen. What we express into the world has consequences. He recognized that there are forces within us all that have the power to hurt or heal; He would often teach his students: *We must always hold the reins of the animal within us.*

In 1907, Rabbi Kagan welcomed Rabbi Yerucham Levovitz as the *Mashgiach* (spiritual supervisor) of his *yeshiva* (Orthodox Jewish college or seminary). As a disciple of the Chofetz Chaim, Rabbi Levovitz is considered to have been a great spiritual leader and ethicist who taught:

It is a mistake to assume that the struggle between these inner forces is one of logic, and that our actions are determined by whichever logic prevails. Not so. The battle is one of sheer force. Whichever force has the greater strength dominates.

This internal *tug of war* is at the very root of human existence. It is the source of the *conflict psychology* referred to in the early 1980s by Professor David Bohm and Spiritual teacher J. Krishnamurti in their dialogues on the future of humanity. To be human is to be composed of both flesh and spirit—matter and consciousness. As such, we are endlessly engaged in the tussle for supremacy of one over the other. We could make a case that all human hostility is rooted in this single overarching conflict as to who we are and who we are becoming. This primary conflict is expressed in myriad forms through diverse personalities. Scripture says that humans were provided the gift of free will, but our will cannot truly be free until this conflict is resolved and our choices are no longer under its influence.

As mentioned earlier, when the two operating systems are in direct conflict, the ego turns to its most desperate measure—that of victim. The ego is strongest and most diabolical when threatened. It will often form unhealthy alliances with others who are also feeling threatened. It is not uncommon for the ego to engage in self-destructive behavior as a means of activating its sense of victimization, thus tapping into another source of strength. At a minimum, the ego *turns up the volume* of its propagandizing. In a world dominated by a "Me First" mentality, is it any wonder that we have such collective chaos and cruelty?

Model Two operating system is far more subtle and hidden; it is not readily perceived, especially given the loud and persistent nature of Model One. This second design requires our effort to actively disengage from Model One's constant input. The *Spiritual Process* to bolster the Model Two operating system will be explored in the remaining chapters. For now, it's important to recognize the distinction between these two mechanisms and the advantage of cultivating a link with the Spiritual Structure.

Model One operating system has many *software programs* working to support its agenda. The sexual drivers in the human psyche alone can drown out the voice of Model Two for half a lifespan, if not longer. Add to this the continual pressure to achieve more and have more. Not only does this operating system urge us relentlessly, but our outer world is designed to intensify our inner drives with a continual barrage of media images, ad campaigns, and new product launches tempting us to acquire more. Since the early days of television in the 1950s, people have been influenced and conditioned (shamed and scared) into keeping up with unrealistic, concocted standards ultimately designed for marketing purposes. Rarely have these shows, or their sponsors, been held responsible and liable for their psychological impact. Modern people are not just burdened by keeping up with the Jones. We are now held to standards set by Hollywood and Madison Avenue regarding what we *do* and what we *have*.

Beyond *doing* more and *having* more, there is also the realm of *being* more. Ultimately, this is where we wish to arrive—*having* more through *being* more. More precisely, we are not so much required to *be* more, as we are required to discover more of our *being* that is not yet apparent. We are pointed in the direction of tapping into the part of ourselves that is concealed—our hidden potential. This hidden potential is beyond the physical and psychological, it includes our spiritual nature. This quality makes us unique to all other life forms. Clearly, there's an enormous variety of species inhabiting the earth, yet humans stand alone in being both physical and spiritual—body and Soul.

Any arousal of the spirit will alter a person's identity toward becoming a more spiritual being. We do not stop being a physical being when we discover our spiritual nature; it's an additional dimension of our psyche. This shift is not just inward; it changes our outward perception of reality, along with how we are perceived by others. At the fundamental level, the spiritual perspective does not view the physical world as all that exists. Awareness of something more is the common denominator of all spiritual people—there is more to us and more to existence. Physical reality is but a mere reflection of the larger spiritual reality, albeit a reflection that hides the source of its reflection—the same way a dream hides the dreamer.

The analogy of the dream world is often referenced in Hindu scripture to illustrate the *unreal nature* of the physical realm as distinguished from the *real nature* of the spiritual. We are only able to recognize the unreal nature of the dream when we are awake. During the dream, we are unaware that we are dreaming. So it is with our perception of the physical; it cannot be recognized as unreal from the perspective of our senses and ego, which are both a part of the physical realm. Only when viewed from outside the physical, i.e., from the spiritual perspective, is the physical world's illusory nature perceivable.

In the dream analogy, if it were the *purpose* of the dream to *conceal* the dreamer, then it would correlate perfectly with the spiritual tenet that it is the *purpose* of the physical world to *conceal* the spiritual. Because the design of the physical experience is to conceal the spiritual, it becomes impossible to conceive the meaning of the ancient precept that the world is an illusion concealing true reality. Upon spiritual awakening, this impossibility begins to dissolve. Examples of this teaching include the Buddha speaking of the *empty* nature of form, echoing the Hindu scriptures that speak of maya.

Jesus taught that the Kingdom of Heaven is not in a different time or space, but here and now, yet seen only by those who have "eyes blessed with vision." The physical concealing the spiritual is also found throughout the ancient teachings of the Jewish Mystical Traditions. Rabbi Dessler taught that the very purpose of physical time was to provide a veil of concealment.

As previously referenced, living in the 21st century, we were born into an unyielding materialist, scientific worldview. To establish a footing within the spiritualist worldview, so common to our ancestors, we must swim against the tide of modern times. Science has made huge contributions through observing and analyzing all that is quantifiable, yet remains at a loss when it comes to the qualitative state of the spiritual structure. This is not to denigrate science, as the spiritual structure is beyond its range of vision; at least up until now.

Bringing Form to the Formless

At first glimpse into the spiritual structure, there are two common recognitions that emerge. **First**, the spiritual structure reflects the spiritual qualities of the one making the observation. Although the spiritual structure is formless, it projects an experience. This *sensation* is often how a person comes to know they are in its presence, and the *projected* experience is not separate from the person observing. In other words, the spiritual structure is initially experienced as the self perceiving itself, or more precisely, the self perceiving the Self. What stands out most emphatically is the quality of one's character—it's made of you.

If you jumped to the conclusion that the spiritual structure looks like you, this is a common misperception. When we look at ourselves, we see our physical form. From the physical perspective, this is the most apparent aspect of our identity. Spiritually speaking, this *outer garment* of form is not our identity; it is simply an ever-changing, ever deteriorating container housing our true identity. Within the spiritual structure, we are the sum total of our highest virtues minus our self-serving traits—it is this that is reflected back to us. If we are wise and loving, giving and compassionate, we will see a spiritual structure that is quite different from the one seen by those who lack such qualities. For those who have always viewed reality through the lens of their self-serving ego, there will be no trace of a spiritual structure as it cannot be seen through that lens.

Second, recognizing the spiritual structure diminishes the substantial nature of the physical structure. Up until the initial glimpse, the spiritual structure is conceived as ethereal and insubstantial while the physical appears to be rock solid. Like the moment a child first sees the puppet master pulling the strings, this peek behind the curtain of spiritual concealment alters our view of the world and the part we play in it. Now our world is simply viewed as a reflection in the mirror of a far greater reality. As the puppet master is to the puppet, so too is the spiritual to the physical.

Curiously, this life altering realization that diminishes the stature of our physical life and our material world simultaneously enhances our *experience* of it. Somehow the recognition that this fleeting and ultimately incomplete life we are living is not all there is, frees us to enjoy our time here far more profoundly and with far less anxiety. It's as though the puppet recognized that it is not an independent entity, rather it is only responding to the tugging strings of the puppet master. Upon further examination, the puppet discovers that the master and puppet are one. This discovery opens the door to benefiting from our newly found capabilities with unprecedented joy.

This is the epiphany we seek in this life and the realization of this epiphany is the purpose of this book. The intense anguish experienced in the fourth and final quadrant of life (60-80+), while crushed by the deterioration of body and mind, is due to the lack of this imperative realization. It is only the container that is approaching its expiration date; the contents remain fresh and eager to move on. When the body expires, the Soul is liberated. For those whose lives have supported and contributed to the liberation of the Soul, what lies ahead is not to be feared, but embraced.

How can we know that death is more a nativity than a finality? It is not through traditional learning nor teaching that one gains this clarity. No book or seminar can provide this comfort. It comes only through personal experience as one becomes familiar with the spiritual structure. This is not to say that the teachings and guidance of those who have previously navigated these waters are of no value. On the contrary, they are invaluable. This type of outer inspiration leads to inner realization.

In his 1976 book, *Forgotten Truth: The Primordial Tradition*, Professor Huston Smith provides a common description of the spiritual structure found throughout many religions. He reports of multiple spiritual levels that correspond with the multiple layers of the self. According to Smith, we find indications of this 'hierarchical view" of a "tiered reality" within a variety of sources...

...from the multiple heavens of Judaism to the storied structure of the Hindu temple and the angelologies of innumerable traditions, this view was reached convergently and independently, as if by innate tropism, by virtually all known societies....

As long as modernity was captive of an outlook presumed to be scientific, but in fact scientistic [the belief that science alone can explain phenomena], reality was taken to be as science mirrored it. Now that it is apparent that science peers down a restricted view-

finder, we are released from that misconception.
The view that appears in a restricted viewfinder is a
restricted view.

—Huston Smith, *Forgotten Truth*

The Future of Humanity; Is there Evolution of Consciousness?

This notion of a restricted view is discussed from the scientific perspective by American scientist Dr. David Bohm (1917-1992), protégé of Albert Einstein, and often considered the most significant theoretical physicist of the 20th century. He was also influenced by his friendship and work with J. Krishnamurti, who Bohm met in 1959 and with whom he maintained close communication, particularly regarding the human brain and the interconnectedness of mind and matter.

On June 11, 1983, two of the greatest living minds of our time, one from science and the other from theology, sat down in Brockwood Park, England, to discuss the future of humanity. J. Krishnamurti, referred to by many as the "New World Teacher," and the celebrated scientist Dr. David Bohm, looked at the current state of humanity and the history from which it emerged, to provide their insights into the future.

It was important to both men that their assessments take the whole of humanity into consideration, not simply the developed countries and advanced cultures. Without a moment's hesitation, it was clear that all of humanity, from the beginning of time to this very moment, has been hopelessly caught in a perpetual pattern of thought and behavior that has led to unspeakable violence. Human history is unquestionably stained by the blood of wars, terrorism, racial intolerance, misogyny, starvation, ecological and economic disasters, as well as a cadre of cruel and corrupt leaders unable, or unwilling, to change the course of events.

They decided that there must be something inherent in the human psyche that is responsible for this abhorrent behavior, otherwise man would have moved on centuries ago. We certainly cannot claim any great progress toward worldwide peace and goodwill in the years following their conversation. Bohm actually questioned whether he would choose to become a scientist if he were to make that decision today. As he put it, *science does not seem to be relevant to this crisis.*

There is no doubt that science and technology have advanced at a remarkable pace throughout human history. However, these great advancements become dangerous unless there are equally great advancements in human psychology and morality. Without comparable psychological advancement, the instruments of advanced science and technology become dangerous to humanity. Without repairing the disorder in the human psyche, Bohm said "the rest is useless."

The big question remains, can the consciousness of mankind be changed over time? This question is complex. Time is irrelevant to the consciousness of mankind. It is, however, relevant in terms of the actions of man. Both men agreed that the future of mankind will not be determined through actions in time, but rather through the consciousness of mankind, consciousness that is whole—undivided and inseparable.

As pointed out in the *Tanya*, and now echoed in this dialogue, it is the lower form of humanity that does not recognize the illusion of separation and individuation. Due to previous conditioning, people experience themselves as separate individuals, when, in fact, we are interconnected by the same consciousness. As Dr. Bohm put it, *the consciousness of mankind is one inseparable whole.* However, from our earliest child-hood, we cultivate the distinction between mine and yours. Growing up, we become rooted in the conditioning thoughts of *my* family, *my* community, *my* country and so on. These conditioning thoughts are a part of our memory—our past. Krishnamurti makes the point that knowledge is also rooted in our past, as it is the outcome of our past experiences. Both men agree that thoughts, experience and knowledge rooted in our past are limited in scope and are affected by time.

This issue of a limited memory manipulating our current perception is all-encompassing. Dr. Bohm and Krishnamurti question whether it is *even possible* to perceive something directly, without memory entering into the perception. *Is there nothing that can stop memory from impacting our perception?* Our memory is not only impacting our percep-tion of the objective external world, worse yet, it is literally creating our subjective inner world—our self-image. Most of what determines how we act in the world is based on how we have acted in the past. If we responded to previous situations in a self-serving, greedy fashion, we will likely respond to cur-rent situations in the same manner. Only when we are able to rationally recognize the activity, or expression, of our limited memory on our current perception, are we able to break free of it.

Bohm and Krishnamurti then shift their inquiry beyond the individual, and focus on the whole of humanity. Here the overarching question is whether humanity is even capa-ble of living without conflict. Can we have peace on earth? It seems that what is true for the individual is also true for col-lective humanity. Conflict is an inherent trait of human psy-chology—it lives within our thought process. For a person to achieve true peace of mind, or for humanity to achieve peace on earth, we must move beyond our limited thoughts and embrace the activity of our highest form of intelligence. Limited thoughts are born out of limited memory, which is the source of conflict. To have a memory that is devoid of conflict is tantamount to having a world history devoid of conflict. Of course, both memory and history are rife with conflict.

Conflict, hostility, violence and the like, are a part of our collective past and our individual memory. As such, they are a part of our conditioned thoughts. Like a computer, humans are programmed to operate from memory. As Dr. Bohm and Krishnamurti point out, there is, however, a faculty of the mind that is free of such programming and limitations— intelligence. *If I have always been self-serving in the past, am I destined to be the same in the future?* The answer is yes, if one remains unconscious and ignorant of these inner traits. Through new knowledge and greater intelligence, we have the ability to delete our selfish programming and upgrade to generosity. In this way, it is no longer memory determining identity, i.e., *who I am, is who I was*. Rather, a new identity emerges through new intelligence as *I am who I choose to become*. This is intelligence operating one's free will to choose beyond the pre-conditioned programming of the past.

We have wars today because the pattern of conflict that has dominated the past five thousand years continues to program the collective thoughts of current humanity. Dr. Bohm explains that it is this memory/programming of our past that interferes with our intelligence. He goes on to say that there are those who believe that through the incessant suffering brought from the repetitive expression of faulty conditioning, i.e., wars and violence, mankind will eventually learn from its mistakes and gain the necessary intelligence to break free of our conflict programming. To this, Krishnamurti responded, if the ego of mankind were able to dissolve or become purified by our continual warfare and endless suffering, history would have shown evidence of this possibility before now. Those who believe that intelligence and compassion can emerge from endless conflict, arrogance and cruelty are sorely mistaken.

As long as memory and history alone define us, we remain imprisoned in our faulty conditioning. Alternatively, just as suffering is common to all humanity, so too is evolving consciousness. The suffering of one is registered in the collective consciousness of all humanity. And the compassion of humanity for the suffering of others is the result of a higher intelligence than that expressed throughout history. Even during the lives of our most sacred Saints and wisest Sages, the whole of humanity took little note and was not dissuaded from the futile strategy of ending conflict with greater conflict.

The world is me, I am the world, remarked Krishnamurti, adding that *the world is not different from me*. These words have an almost *bumper sticker* simplicity, yet they hold the key to everything. Here, the spiritual leader expresses his strongest emphasis while insisting that every human being needs to gain the deep and profound experience of these words. *You must feel this, it is not just a verbal statement, it is an actuality.* Deep contemplation is required to realize this ancient truth: *I am my brother's keeper.* If this spiritual law were to come alive in the hearts and minds of all humanity, it would be a first.

This describes intelligence that is beyond the conditioning of previous experience. It's not to say that the words spoken by Krishnamurti were original. They are the words of the Saints and Sages of all religions. The teachings of Jesus and Buddha, Moses and Mohammed, have been known for centuries, but their words are yet to be realized on a grand scale. So far, the righteous lives of the spiritually inclined have not hit the *tipping point* where critical mass has the ability to influence those in resistance.

The end of human cruelty and suffering will not be the result of yet another conflict with bigger fists and more deadly weapons. We cannot alleviate hatred and intolerance with more hatred and intolerance. When the ignorance and hostility of war are replaced with the wisdom and compassion of peace, we will have collectively turned a very important corner. In spite of so many generations beyond the caves, humans still haven't overcome their primordial, psychological conditioning toward conflict and hostility, the consciousness of lesser creatures ignorant of the spiritual structure.

As the earlier quote from the *Tanya* points out, our physical existence is based on the experience of separation, individuation and self-interest. Everything about us suggests that we are deeply rooted in this perception—you are you and I am me, and those people over there are certainly not us. This common perception is a universal misperception; it is an expression of previous conditioning and pervasive spiritual ignorance. The spiritual experience of Oneness and Unity requires at least a slight easing of the grip brought by this overarching mirage. Again, to gain any glimpse into the spiritual structure, we must go directly to it without any words, beliefs, conditioned reactions, or memories of the past influencing our perception. When separation and individuation no longer define us, clarity and compassion will. Spontaneous intelligence replaces previous conditioning as our guiding light. The ultimate byproduct of this higher consciousness is that conflict and suffering are no longer required to direct our activity. This alone is worth the price of admission.

These spontaneous thoughts that emerge out of higher consciousness are the perfect setting to gain clarity and freedom. This is the path toward higher consciousness, both individually and collectively. There is no individual vs. collective consciousness separation. When an individual raises his or her consciousness, it *is* a collective elevation as well. It is movement toward what Teilhard called the *Omega Point*—the *tipping point* where critical mass is reached and the entire game is shifted. In terms of our current discussion, the whole of humanity will then be moving toward peace and away from conflict for the first time in human history. Warfare between people and the destruction of nature will no longer be tolerated. Human compassion and peace will replace intolerance and violence. An apocalyptic event will not be necessary for the redemption of humanity; we will have achieved it through Enlightenment and transformation—tragedy averted.

Disparity Between Real and Unreal

Questions regarding what is real and what is unreal have been a mainstay of human inquiry for centuries. Every civilization has had its version of this discussion and, depending on the times, the dialogue would either lean one way or the other— quantitative or qualitative, mathematical or mystical. There's never been a time when science and superstition shared common ground. Yet, we may now find ourselves on the brink of just such a time—science and the spiritual sharing precepts that render each indistinguishable from the other.

Over 2,500 years ago, the Buddha taught a profound lesson regarding the disparity between the real and the unreal. This lesson is echoed throughout the mystical teachings of many great Sages. Simply stated, what we consider to be real is determined to be real through interpretation. The lens through which we view reality determines our perception. The eye reflects the light and the mind provides the image. This process is not the same as a camera's rendition of reality, as the camera's lens is not conditioned by DNA and previous photos. The camera's functioning is based on its lens and the object being viewed, while human functioning adds a third component—conditioned interpretation. The Dalai Lama echoes the Buddha's teachings:

All sensory experiences of the external world arise through the coalescence of three factors: a sensory faculty, an object, and our mental perception. This perception of an external object then gives rise to a subjective evaluation... On the basis of this projection, we may then develop a strong emotional reaction.
　　　　　—Dalai Lama, *Essence of the Heart Sutra*

The Buddha also referred to the "emptiness" of things that appear to be real and how they come into being and then cease to exist. They only *appear* to be independent with intrinsic nature, when, in fact, it is the observer who provides form. This notion of matter being empty and without form remained an esoteric idea for centuries until modern physics recognized its validity.

In the appendix of his 1965 book, *The Special Theory of Relativity*, theoretical physicist David Bohm puts a scientific spin on the ancient Buddhist teaching regarding the disparity between that which is real and that which is unreal within physical reality. Twenty-five years later, Professor Bohm reinforced this notion on Dutch TV following his presentation at an international symposium entitled "Art, Science, and Spirituality in a Changing Economy." He discussed the role of perception when it comes to our experience of reality:

I wrote a book on Special Relativity with an appendix which I devoted to Perception... According to Relativity, everything was related to the way that you interacted with it, to observe it... the point about Perception is that it's a dynamic process... We're constantly doing things and seeing what happens...

Bohm uses the example of a solid circle being built where people could walk around it and perceive it from different angles. From some angles, the circle appears to be stretched into an oval. So, what is appearance and what is real? The ellipse, or oval, is only an appearance, while the circle is the true essence. This became settled science for quite a while.

Bohm explains that scientists later proclaimed that the circle is not the true essence either, as it is made up of many atoms. Observing the solid circle at a more fundamental level, we find that *it is mostly open space with atoms moving there.* In other words, the solid circle itself is but an appearance, and the atoms are the essence.

For a materialist, the idea of atoms being the fundamental building blocks of physical reality still supported their rational beliefs. However, Bohm points out, new scientists came along saying that these atoms are not the essence of our physical world, as they are also made of smaller objects. When the atom is split open, it is mostly empty space—thus atoms, too, are appearances. Even the atom's electrons and protons are made of quarks, fields and so on. From all of this Bohm concluded:

You see, they're looking for a "Theory of Everything," but it keeps on receding. So, this suggests to me that everything – even our thoughts – are fundamentally appearances... How things appear to the mind, right? ... "theories" don't give final true knowledge. They give a way of looking at it. The very word "theoria," in Greek, means "theater," it has the same root... And, so, a theory is sort of a theater of the mind that gives insight into the thing. And, therefore, you can say that, fundamentally, Science is involved in a perceptual enterprise, not primarily gaining knowledge. Though knowledge appears, knowledge is a by-product of it, by understanding the thing... In our contact with it, as long as it is coherent, it shows that our understanding is correct. You see we must distinguish between correct appearances and incorrect appearances... they're illusory.

When we first recognized the original structure as a solid circle, were we correct in our observation? What about those who stood close by the structure and perceived it to be more oval than circle? Yet science still determined that both were only appearances. In fact, the structure was not solid at all; it was made up of atoms that were mostly empty space with tiny subatomic particles. It is here that Dr. Bohm suggests: *Our whole thinking process should be called an extension of our perception... And not, primarily, the accumulation of knowledge...* He goes on to say that we must distinguish between thinking and thought, as thinking is an active verb indicating that there is action being done. Thinking is a process of critiquing our own thoughts to determine if they are coherent and valid in accordance with our observations. If we find that they are not, says Bohm, we change them and experiment with others. This is how we arrive at new intuitions and new insights. Whereas "thought" is the past participle—it has already taken place; the action is over and it is now saved in the brain as a file on record, like a computer archive, or mental conditioning.

The Buddha taught that this *mental conditioning* determines our perception, interpretation and experience of reality. This means that *mental conditioning*, more than any external circumstance, is the basis of our reality—our joys and sorrows. The Sages go even further to say that we must make an effort to overcome this *mental conditioning* as it was not formed conscientiously, with full awareness of its consequences.

Two key factors suggest that our *mental conditioning* was not formed with proper care. First, a good portion of our conditioning was formed during our earliest and most immature years. The circumstances leading to this early conditioning are long forgotten, yet it is still directing us from the obscure recesses of our unconscious, making it difficult to access.

Second, our *mental conditioning* is programmed by our incessant need for sensory pleasure and our ego's need for gratification. Since neither of these is a source of ultimate wisdom, desire and wisdom are often at odds. The Buddha went so far as to say that these worldly desires are the very cause of all human suffering and that liberation from their oppressive restraint is a vital step toward Enlightenment. The brain is as susceptible to programming as any common personal computer. Allowing our desires to be our primary cerebral programmer is as irresponsible as allowing our PC to be programmed by hackers.

Distinguishing Between the Brain and the Mind

The materialist view of the distinction between the brain and the mind is that the mind is a function of the brain. Another view states that the brain and the mind are two different things, yet they are deeply rooted in one another and form a relationship. Scientific thinking tends toward the notion that the brain and the mind are the same and cannot be separated. Clearly the brain is a part of the physical world; it can be seen and touched, has form and occupies space. The brain has functions that are vital to human life. It coordinates the movements, senses, thoughts and feelings of the body. The mind is more associated with understanding and awareness. The mind has no form or size and cannot be found in a particular location. Unlike the brain, it is not made of nerve cells and blood vessels; it is considered mental rather than physical.

The brain is highly conditioned by neurophysiologic conditioning, chemically and psychologically, as well as by patterns of previous generations and by the historical and current influences that impact it. All of this conditioning serves as the brain's *programming* as it conforms to certain patterns. As such, the brain exists almost entirely in the past while attempting to modify itself for the future. Certainly, some of this conditioning is necessary. However, the conditioning that determines the psyche, or self, can be harmful and be in conflict with all that is other than the self. Because the brain relies heavily on memory and is subjected to previous conditioning, its thoughts are restricted, limited and often unreliable.

While the brain is understood to be part of the physical structure, existing in and limited by time, the mind exists somewhere separate. The brain is tethered by its conditioning while the mind can be moved and liberated by insight. The brain processes and stores information, which is also limiting; the mind is driven by intelligence. This consciousness and intelligence of the mind allows for insights, while the brain is limited by the scope of its past education and previously accumulated information.

In their book, *The Future of Humanity: Two Dialogues between J. Krishnamurti and David Bohm,* the big question that both men consider is whether the cells of the brain that dominate consciousness are capable of change. It should be obvious, by the centuries of recorded history, that the collective knowledge and thoughts of humanity have not been adequate to overcome the *irrational and self-destructive programme in which the brain seems to be helplessly caught up.* They conclude this idea by saying; *"If mind is limited by such a state of the brain, then the future of humanity must be very grim indeed."* However, Krishnamurti regards the mind as *"being free of the distorting bias that is inherent in the conditioning of the brain."* He goes on to say that *"through insight arising in proper undirected attention without a centre, it can change the cells of the brain and remove the destructive conditioning."*

Responding to Krishnamurti's profound theory, Professor Bohm said the following:

At this point, it is worth remarking that modern research into the brain and nervous system actually gives considerable support to Krishnamurti's statement that insight may change the brain cells. Thus, for example, it is now well known that there are important substances in the body, the hormones and the neurotransmitters, that fundamentally affect the entire functioning of the brain and nervous system. These substances respond, from moment to moment, to what a person knows, to what he thinks, and to what all this means to him. It is by now fairly well established that in this way the brain cells and their functioning are profoundly affected by knowledge and thought, especially when these give rise to strong feelings and passions. It is thus quite plausible that insight, which must arise in a state of great mental energy and passion, could change the brain cells in an even more profound way.

— David Bohm

Although the response of these two men is not entirely optimistic with regards to their inquiry into the future of humanity, the silver lining is the notion of the mind's capability to lead and change the brain through insight. In this instance, the mind is portrayed as a bridge linking the previously conditioned and limited knowledge of the brain to a distant shore where time and conditioning dissolve in the bright light of insight. It's as though this newly acquired insight does not come from the same traditional, linear learning curve that produced previous knowledge. Instead of the lengthy process of building point onto point until the accumulation leads to a logically induced conclusion, insight arrives in the form of an unrestricted light flashing across the horizon of the already known, leaving a residue of new perception. Within this flash of new light, one is able to catch a glimpse beyond the boundaries of what has always been and receive a spark of what might be unprecedented reality. This is the shadow of the spiritual structure.

Recognizing the Spiritual Structure

We are wise to study the dynamics of spirituality in order to awaken our own spiritual identity. Of course, this is not an easy task for reasons we've already addressed. Because the

spiritual structure exists within the spiritual domain, it is not describable in physical terms. The 16th century Carmelite nun, Saint Teresa of Ávila (1515-1582), provides one of the most famous descriptions of the spiritual structure. She was canonized by Pope Gregory XV in 1622. Throughout her life, St. Teresa suffered greatly—first, by the death of her mother when she was just 14 years old, then from severe illness that plagued her throughout her entire life. During her illness she encountered some of her most profound religious experiences.

In her book, *The Interior Castle*, published in 1588, St. Teresa describes her vision of the spiritual structure. In a letter written by one of St. Teresa's confessors, Fray Diego, he describes one of her visions:

> *... a most beautiful crystal globe, made in the shape of a castle, and containing seven mansions, in the seventh and innermost of which was the King of Glory, in the greatest splendor, illumining and beautifying them all. The nearer one got to the center, the stronger was the light; outside the palace limits everything was foul, dark and infested with toads, vipers, and other venomous creatures.*
>
> — Saint Teresa of Ávila, *Interior Castle*

Each of these seven mansions is defined by its particular proximity to God. As we engage in spiritual activity, we are moved through the mansions and become closer to God until we enter the seventh mansion where complete Unity is found.

This spiritual awakening shifts any external situation from surface to depth, from material to spiritual, from body to Soul. Only humans hold such a unique position—existing within two dimensions simultaneously. A great deal of study focuses on this topic. One might even say that *the purpose of spiritual study is to experience oneself in this distinctive situation.* Within our particular equation, the physical and spiritual are intertwined at all times.

However, as stated previously, because the physical is driven by the senses and has the undivided attention of the cognitive mind, the physical controls and establishes the identity of the individual and can actually eclipse all that is spiritual. This point cannot be stressed enough: ***Every human has a spiritual core longing to make connection with the conscious mind.*** While science debates the distinctions between the brain and the mind, spirituality remains unconcerned. The grand epiphany brought by spiritual awakening occurs when the mind recognizes its true source—the consciousness radiated through the Soul. Upon such recognition, the veil of concealment is penetrated and the spiritual structure is revealed.

We do not suddenly *develop* a Soul; we do suddenly *discover* our Soul. As a matter of fact, the word "suddenly" is likely inappropriate as well. There is nothing "sudden" about it. The discovery usually happens over a significant period of time—little by little we make progress in the persistent *drilling* into our inner being. What's true for oil drillers is also true for *Soul drillers,* many dry holes are drilled before we hit a gusher.

This is the nature of *concealment;* just because you glance in the direction of the spiritual dimension does not mean it will be revealed. Make no mistake, however, our Sages say that even a passing glance in the direction of the spiritual is recognized and noted. It is said that a move the distance of the breadth of a human hair toward the spiritual generates movement the distance of miles in heaven—any and all movement counts.

Allow this message to penetrate deeply into your consciousness: every thought, every word, every action taken with the spiritual in mind, brings benefits and provides impetus for the next move. It can be overwhelming to think in terms of *spiritual destinations*—where the spiritual path ultimately arrives. For now, it is best to thoroughly enjoy each new morsel and let it fully nurture you in places that need to be fed. The real goal of spirituality is to be headed in the right direction, i.e., *on the right path.* The journey itself is considered a key destination. It is like a luxury cruise. They call the ports destinations, and it appears that the purpose of the cruise is to arrive at them. Yet the actual time on board the ship, out in the mist of endless ocean with no land in sight, is no less a destination.

Long before arriving at the spiritual destination called *Self-realization,* we discover the utter joy of heading in that direction. As you read a verse of sacred text that answers the exact question troubling your heart and disturbing your Soul, in that precise instant you realize this moment of insight is a destination. Like a traveler lost in the woods, the smallest confirmation that you're heading in the right direction brings new eagerness to your stride.

Life may be viewed as a game where many players erroneously think of themselves as spectators. It is never a valid excuse to say that had you known your role, you would have played much better. It is not easy to recognize that the grand purpose of this life has little to do with *this* life. What happens here is more about what follows on the next level of our existence. As the universe expands, we assume that we will expand with it. Our Sages taught that humans are the only life form for whom Nature does not take responsibility for our expansion and growth. We are responsible for our own progress and refinement.

All animals have brains to keep the machine running. It is the human mind, however, that is responsible for our unique character and circumstances. The body is a manufacturing plant where each organ is engaged in its own contributing process. The brain produces thoughts and feelings—ideas and desires. Desire is the agent of human will; it puts the *power* in *willpower*. We go to great extremes when it comes to attaining the objects of our desires. Danger comes into play when our desires are not rooted in wisdom; this type of desire leads to disaster.

This is made even more complicated by the constant cravings of our physical nature. We are designed to feel the irresistible allure of all things that are sensually pleasing. Satisfying the hunger of our senses and the cravings of our ego can easily be mistaken for our purpose in life. Like the hunter in the corridor of the King's treasury, it is easy to forget one's mission when the distractions are so overwhelming and the pleasures so intoxicating.

As the Buddha points out, it is by design that we are unable to see through the veil of *concealment*. If all that is concealed were visible, there would no longer be the challenge of discovery. Worse yet, the value of discovery would be diminished. As a result, the discoverer would lose the joy of finding hidden treasure. Even something as free as a breath of fresh air becomes invaluable when it is not readily available. The value and the challenge of spiritual discovery are inherently related. Even a flawless diamond would lose its significance if diamonds could be found strewn along the side of the road.

Throughout history, our Sages have spent endless hours and countless lifetimes pouring over and discussing the human condition—always probing for one more truth—one more stone yet unturned. We now have vast libraries of limitless volumes written by a long line of scholars spending their entire lifetime pondering the words of previous generations, *looking with fresh eyes at old bones.* They are always hoping to find that shining idea that penetrates the dark recesses of who we are and what our purpose is. And from it all, the most common conclusion is: *The human being is a Divine Soul encased within a mortal beast.*

The Mystical Legend of Embedding the Soul
There is a mystical legend that dates back to ancient times regarding embedding the Divine Soul into human form at the time of creation. The angels (referred to as spiritual beings without physical form) watched as God created the universe. They applauded every new aspect of creation, from the very beginning to the moment in question. When God created the mountains and the sea, the moon and the stars, the heavens and the earth, the plants and the animals, there was thunderous applause. Then God created man. The angels were overwhelmed by man's unique form and intricate capabilities, the human's enhanced intellect and vast powers of reason.

Next, God took a Divine spark made directly of the substance of God and implanted it in the newly fashioned beast called man, and in place of applause there were only groans and gasps to be heard. God questioned the angels as to their obvious disapproval. The Angel of Truth said that within man, sacred Truth will be turned into lies. The Angel of Love said that man will turn Love into hatred. The Angel of Peace said that man will turn Peace into violence. And so it went, each angel protesting that man would change Harmony into chaos, Beauty into ugliness, Joy into sorrow, etc. And God replied by saying ... *and there within lies the magnificence of the human condition.*

All of the conversions called out by the angels, whereby Divine Light descends into darkness, would take place within the human. Ultimately, however, man would recognize the folly of his ways and seek to restore the spiritual back into his world. When examining our personal history, it is apparent how often our spiritual nature emerges and peeks through. Unfortunately, the pangs of conscience frequently go ignored. These breakthroughs take place on the individual scale as well as the collective—like cream, goodness pushes its way to the top. We see evidence of this repeatedly, and we often recognize goodness when it flares up. Whenever people put their own lives in peril to save a stranger caught in a burning building, or when people send money to help the victims of disasters from around the world, goodness has pushed its way to the top.

On the individual level, there are many spontaneous instances in which we are suddenly swept into experiences of the Soul—moments of deep feeling where we are moved beyond our ego-based experience. Such moments are fostered by seeing great art, hearing music, falling in love or becoming parents; they might also occur in moments of extreme pain and suffering, as in the case of losing a loved one. Because these experiences are random, they can only open the spiritual gate, but unless we commit to sustaining this opening, it's likely to close again.

Even fleeting experiences leave a lingering *imprint* on our consciousness. These impressions are left in our foggy awareness, like a dream that lingers after we awaken. Enriched by their occurrence, we are left a bit wiser, more poised for our next encounter. It is in this way that many actually become indoctrinated on the spiritual path. Without the aid of any organized approach, and without benefit of any religious scripture or ritual, many people *stumble* upon the stirring of their own Soul.

How is this possible? How can a person achieve such a pinnacle without years of climbing the spiritual mountain? Perhaps the answer was best stated by the celebrated 19th century French poet and novelist, Victor Hugo: **All the forces in the world are not so powerful as an idea whose time has come.**

For many 21st century spiritual pioneers, the idea whose time has come is the *enhancement of human technology.* Just as we update and upgrade our electronic technology, so must we upgrade our *human technology.* Once we upgrade to a *spiritual operating system*, we become compatible with all spiritual software. As with electronic upgrades, these, too, can cause frustration and complications until we become used to them. It's the nature of the process. There has been no end to the opinions on why spiritual progress must be so challenging—but all seem to agree that it is, in fact, a challenge. Like electric technology, spirituality also requires *disruption* to achieve advancement. For those of us who resist disruption, we must resign ourselves to a life of mediocrity.

Gateway to the Spiritual Structure

The Buddha taught a simple yet profound truth: Enlightenment is the result of seeing things as they really are. *Do we
need great knowledge and wisdom, a high IQ, and an elaborate education to become enlightened?* Although helpful,
these are not prerequisites. In some instances, these worthy
qualities and conditions may provide their own obstacles to
Enlightenment. What is required, however, is getting past our
mind's previous conditioning. Liberation from our self-imposed biases, beliefs and cravings, is the beginning of clarity.
Once the smoke has cleared and the dust settled, we are left
with a clear vision of the *elephant in the room.*

What is this elephant in the room? It is the spiritual structure. It is here, and has *always* been the true source of reality; we have danced around it from the beginning of time. It is
endless and changeless. It's the very same spiritual structure
referenced in the scriptures of all great religions. Although
their teachings have always pointed to this Ultimate Reality,
religion cannot provide the spiritual structure; it can only
provide the pathway to it. Only you can provide yourself with
this highly personal experience. And by the same token, only
you can deprive yourself of it.

However, the spiritual structure cannot be provided without first being recognized. It is our perception that allows us
access to the spiritual structure, and it is also our perception that continues to tether us to the physical. Access to the
spiritual structure requires a significant shift from physical
to spiritual perception. For those who have experienced this
progression into spiritual perception, it is most often referred
to as *a release from prison.* It's as if we've outgrown our
3-dimensional world the way a butterfly outgrows its cocoon.

For those of us getting on in years, not only are we imprisoned—the prison is burning. We all know how the story ends—physically, we share a common destiny. As physical beings, living in a world of time and space, we all face the same finality. Fortunately, regardless of our degree of spiritual awareness, the spiritual trumps the physical. What appears to be a closing door on this side, is the same door opening on the other side. What we find on the other side of that door, is entirely dependent on how we conducted our life on this side of it.

The ancient teachings of Kabbalah provide a mystical interpretation of the human condition at its most fundamental level. If it were possible to *bottom-line* the circumstances of the physical structure from the perspective of the spiritual, it all comes down to three key elements. The three elements are *ego*, *Soul* and *free will*, which comprise the *Gateway to the Spiritual Structure.* How we navigate our way within this *gateway*, determines whether we are caught in an endless revolving door, or allowed access into the spiritual dimension. This is the sum total of the human condition brought to its most fundamental level.

Within each of us are three essential elements: a transient ego, an eternal Soul, and the free will to choose between them. Spiritually speaking, this is all there is to the physical level of existence. We were given free will to determine whether we continue the self-serving path of separation from the spiritual structure or return to our roots. This is the choice, referred to in Deuteronomy, between light and darkness, life and death. Every thought, word and deed that makes up our time on Earth, is an expression of this recurrent moment of truth. The rest is mere window dressing—the same act with an ever-changing cast of characters and new props added to the stage.

We cannot address the topic of *free will* without considering the necessary condition that allows for free will—*concealment*. The topic of concealment is so fundamental to the mystical tradition, that everything we learn about spirituality is based on this aspect of our reality.

As previously stated, the experience of the Soul is the portal into the spiritual realm. Like any door, part is on the inside and part is outside—and the part of the spiritual experience that is on the outside of the door (existing in the physical world) is our *reaction* to having the experience in question. The *reaction* that accompanies our glimpse into the spiritual domain takes form as a *sensation,* which is experienced as both physical and observable. This sensation is perceived as very real, clearly tangible; it eventually provides a bridge between the worldly and the spiritual. What clearly defines the experience for the person having it is the body's and mind's response. The physical *benefit* to the spiritual encounter comes as the body and mind are changed by it. There is much more to be said about this *bodymind's* response to arousing the Soul, but first there's more groundwork to be laid. The physical response to the *spiritual experience* is infinitesimal when compared to its spiritual counterpart.

What's on the inside of this door is the complete spiritual domain. Our Sages all insist that our true essence is more aligned with the spiritual than the physical. Access to the spiritual domain is our birthright. And unlike Esau, we should not *sell our birthright* for a *bowl of lentil stew.* The Bible story of the twin brothers Esau and Jacob holds a valuable lesson. Esau, driven by his physical nature, sold his *birthright of the firstborn* to his brother Jacob in order to satisfy his hunger with Jacob's lentil stew. Being the firstborn son of the Patriarch Isaac had great spiritual implications, yet all of that had little significance when compared to Esau's hearty appetite.

How imprudent we are when we fail to recognize what we sacrifice by allowing our physical perspective to eclipse our spiritual nature. Of course, how can we be blamed for such a costly blunder when we are unable to see that which is intentionally concealed? It is the concealment of the spiritual structure that makes the game challenging. Without this concealment, there could be no physical dimension, let alone our physical nature. Our Sages teach that God, and all that is spiritual, had to be concealed from the physical world in order to give humanity separation, individuation and free will.

The Topic of Concealment is fundamental to understanding spirituality and it is an overarching theme of this book. We will continue to broaden our exploration into the role of concealment in spiritual development, throughout the following chapters. For now, we simply affirm that concealment of the spiritual structure (including the concealment of Soul and God) provides a sizable obstacle to having the spiritual experience. Don't be discouraged, however. Even the slightest, sincere move toward our spiritual nature opens the door to greater understanding. Even openness to the possibility of the spiritual structure is a giant step toward experiencing it.

A subtle, but important distinction: the spiritual structure is not invisible—simply concealed.

This may cause you to ask: *What's the difference?* Both the invisible and the concealed cannot be seen. The invisible will never be seen—by nature, it is unable to be seen. Conversely, the concealed is merely hidden, and under the right conditions is revealed.

It is not just the experience of the Soul that is concealed; the entire spiritual structure is concealed. We do not see or know the spiritual, as it is *intentionally* designed to be obscured from our physical senses and our rational mind. The more we learn about the spiritual structure, the better we are able to understand it. Understanding is the path to perception. As the psalmist said, we gain "eyes blessed with vision."

It's no coincidence that after so many centuries, and billions of people searching, there is still no clear evidence proving once and for all (1) whether there is a Soul embedded within our human form, (2) whether this Soul continues its experience of existence beyond our physical death and, perhaps most pondered, (3) whether God exists. Still, *humanity* does not have these answers in the way we have certainty that the earth revolves around the sun even though it appears to rise in the east and set in the west. However, *individuals* do know the truth regarding their spiritual nature and the existence of God. Yet these individuals are unable to transfer their *evidence* to others, as it is the result of direct, personal experience.

God has had many fully realized messengers, prophets, Saints and Sages who have enriched us with their profound knowledge. Most of us know their names and have heard their stories; still the spiritual truth remains veiled. *Why are some blessed with knowledge of this truth while so many others remain in the dark?* They looked—and when they didn't find what they were seeking, they kept looking. They refused to give up by declaring that the spiritual doesn't exist.

We will continue exploring this topic later, but for now, there is one important point that may lighten your load and inspire your quest. It has been a beacon, guiding more than a few weary travelers throughout their arduous journey into the spiritual realm: ***That which is concealed yearns to be found.***

In Summary...

Because the spiritual structure cannot be put into words, let alone defined or described, our initial approach is one that familiarizes us with its nature. Our best source for understanding comes from those who have already made its acquaintance. These are the teachings of the great Saints and Sages who developed in themselves the attributes they discovered from within the spiritual structure. In other words, they transformed their own nature to be similar to the nature of the spiritual. This process of becoming familiar and akin to the spiritual structure gains our entry. As its nature is honest, we become honest; as it is forgiving, we become forgiving. There is a gradual transformation of our inner qualities, from self-serving and ego-based, to those qualities found within the spiritual structure. Thus, we are able to enter and navigate our way throughout the spiritual realm. This is the dance of all spiritual seekers.

A life without ever perceiving beyond the physical, leaves us far too vulnerable. Because the physical is apparent while the spiritual is concealed, our perception remains focused exclusively on that which resonates with our five senses. We associate our own identity, and the life we are living, with the physical structure. As we age, the distractions of youth begin to subside. Our preoccupation with coupling and mating; family and career; status and recognition wanes. For those who have matured through the years, even our incessant need to be right and the endless pursuit of more, bigger and better, also seem to level off. While this may leave us feeling bored and depressed, it might also allow the space to ponder that which is hidden behind our previous distractions—the spiritual.

The physical structure is the domain of the body with all its material concerns—joys and sorrows, pleasures and pains. The spiritual structure is the realm of the Soul; it is concerned with life's true meaning and purpose. To be human is to be an expression of a living Soul. However, we are not privy to this ancient spiritual wisdom until we experience it for ourselves. Although there are many seemingly random stirrings of the Soul throughout our lives, these experiences go undetected as being sourced by the Soul; thereby, remaining disconnected until recognized and identified for what they are—expressions of the Soul.

The spiritual structure is most often referred to as being comprised of *Divine Light*. Within the physical structure, the term light is associated with electricity and fire or the sun and the moon. Spiritual Light has a broader meaning encompassing attributes such as wisdom and love. The more wisdom and love we attain, the more Light we radiate, and the more Light we radiate, the more we gain coalescence with the spiritual structure. This is the process that brings the spiritual structure into the physical; it elevates the quality of our lives and evolves collective consciousness. It is this life that fulfills our destiny and our true purpose in being. There is no greater joy than being part of such a worthy cause.

Although the topic of this chapter is recognizing the spiritual structure, any words or images used to describe it fall short of the experience it holds for those who enter it. To enter, we must become one with it. The remainder of this book is dedicated to the *spiritual process* that provides entry into the spiritual structure. There are no shortcuts or gimmicks for a quick entry—with the possible exception of premature death (not recommended). The spiritual process is, today, the same as it was during the time of our ancient ancestors. All that is necessary is good intention, an open mind and a yearning heart. A little enthusiasm doesn't hurt either...

Closing Statements of The Epiphany Volume I: Evolution of Human Consciousness and the Form it Manifests

Having completed Volume I, you have set the foundation for what lies ahead—understanding and distinguishing our individual consciousness from humanity's collective consciousness. Clearly, we each have our own individual consciousness that is the source of how we think and perceive throughout our lives, as well as how we feel, experience, and ultimately, behave within our lives. However, what is not so clear is how our individual consciousness is part and parcel of humanity's collective consciousness. Indeed, we are inescapably influenced, if not dominated, by the totality of humanity's collective consciousness. That is to say, the consciousness of others (in our home, our neighborhood, our culture, our country and even our world) has an enormous impact on our individual consciousness. There are even those rare individuals who have had such an extraordinary influence on our collective consciousness that their influence extends far beyond their lifetimes.

Volume I, Part One, of *The Epiphany* explores the evolution as well as the influence that humanity's collective consciousness is having on our individual consciousness. There are many elements of the collective consciousness that benefit our quest toward experiencing our true nature as an immortal Soul. Each of the renowned Saints, Sages and spiritual teachers have elevated humanity's collective consciousness, thereby beneficially influencing our individual consciousness. The development and expansion of education and religious institutions, along with the enormous progress of science, have had a profound impact on humanity's collective consciousness, not to mention the impact of the studies of philosophy and psychology. Advances in medicine extended the span of human life by over thirty years in the previous century, resulting in additional time and opportunity for the masses to contemplate their lives beyond survival in order to ponder their life's purpose. Add to this the advances in technology (dating back to the printing press, radio, television, etc.) which broadened the individual's access and understanding into greater spheres of knowledge and awareness. And, most recently, the unprecedented expansion of global connectivity. Just imagine the impact that Confucius, Socrates, Aristotle, Buddha, Jesus and others would have had with their own webpage and weekly podcasts.

Also identified in Part One are the adverse elements that have had a profound negative impact on humanity's collective consciousness, consequently having a negative impact on our individual consciousness. David Bohm (one of the most significant theoretical physicists of the 20th century), along with Krishnamurti (recognized as a worldwide spiritual leader), referred to this negative impact as the *conflict psychology* of man. This conflict-driven, collective consciousness has accounted for, and outwardly manifested, centuries of incessant hostility, hatred and violence. Some of the worst atrocities in human history took place as recently as the previous century, in the form of World War II—including mass genocide, nuclear bombing of populated cities, government sanctioned abuse of women and the like. Unfortunately, these have also had an enormous impact on our individual consciousness.

In the early 1980s, when asked, *"What is the future of humanity?"* both Krishnamurti and Dr. Bohm were in agreement. Dr. Bohm stated: *This question is by now of vital concern to everyone, because modern science and technology are clearly seen to have opened up immense possibilities of destruction.* Dr. Bohm went on to say: *It soon became clear as we talked together that the ultimate origin of this situation is in the generally confused mentality of mankind, which has not changed basically in this respect throughout the whole of recorded history...* In essence, the conflict, hatred, hostility and violence has been inherent in the conditioning of man's brain since the earliest days of our species. However, it needn't be a part of humanity's future. Dr. Bohm makes clear that it is *well established that brain cells are profoundly affected by knowledge and thought...* Furthermore, insight and epiphany can give rise to higher states of human consciousness.

Just as collective consciousness influences our individual consciousness, so, too, does individual consciousness influence collective consciousness. Even the average lives of ordinary people are held accountable in terms of what they take and what they contribute to the collective consciousness of humanity. Through the wondrous gift of human *free will*, we decide for ourselves whether we are givers or takers, thereby determining our own karma and destiny.

After Volume I completes the six chapters of Part One, it proceeds to open the door to Part Two: *In Search of the Soul.* Volume I, concludes with the first two chapters of Part Two of *The Epiphany*: **Embarking on the Spiritual Journey** and **Recognizing the Spiritual Structure**; i.e., the journey toward, and the destination of, the spiritual dimension. Volume II begins by introducing *The Threefold Spiritualization Process*; i.e., the process by which we move toward discovering our Soul.

Preview of The Epiphany Volume II: The Spiritualization Process toward Discovering the Soul

The purpose of the next two volumes is *the matching of the immortal Soul and its human mate.* Volume II begins by introducing *The Threefold Spiritualization Process*; i.e., the process by which we move toward discovering our Soul. Spiritualization is the process utilized to invoke spirituality—to purify our spiritual nature from the corrupting influence of our physical, egoistic nature and its material world. The initial approach of the spiritualization process is a relatively straightforward formula: we gather greater knowledge regarding the spiritual to increase our spiritual understanding, which will further our spiritual awareness and expand our spiritual perception toward enhancing our spiritual experience, which leads to spiritual realization—the discovery of our spiritual nature—namely, the discovery of our Soul.

This rendezvous of the immortal Soul and the mortal being is often characterized as having an intimate, almost romantic overtone. This is due to the pronounced presence of *love* and *tenderness* associated with, and experienced

575

during, the encounter. There are three aspects to the development of this moment of spiritual realization. First, we find the intense beckoning of the immortal Soul to be recognized by the human entity. Second, and simultaneously, the mortal heart is yearning to realize the Soul's presence and to become its expression in the world. Thus, becoming a compassionate and altruistic expression of higher consciousness as opposed to the self-serving, egoistic expression characteristic of those operating exclusively under the influence of the lower levels of consciousness which are oblivious to their true spiritual nature. And third, it is critical, throughout the process toward the discovery of the Soul, that the human mind must remain open in order to bear witness to that which is beyond its current knowledge and the boundaries of any previous experience—both real or imagined. Truly, a match made in heaven—literally.

The chapters found in Volume II (and Volume III) of *The Epiphany* will provide the reader with a compilation of teachings and tenets from many of the most preeminent, spiritual masters throughout history. As long as we maintain an open mind and continue cultivating our hungry heart, their words and guidance are more than adequate for us to initiate the spiritualization process.

Of course, navigating the spiritual journey toward discovering the Soul is by no means an easy task. Our human nature is designed and conditioned to be a physical being in a material world. These design principles and our previous conditioning bring about multiple distractions and obstacles that hamper our ability to experience or perceive the spiritual, leaving it hidden behind a veil of concealment.

Fortunately, the ancient Saints and Sages; Masters and Mystics, have taught their followers how to identify and distinguish the obstacles that obscure our spiritual insights from those conditions that pave the way throughout our spiritual journey—thus providing modern seekers with an invaluable map. These teachings are an enormous benefit to those who are persistent and patient enough to comprehend their meaning.

The final two chapters of Volume II focus entirely on the process of overcoming our previous conditioning in order to arrive at the fourth level of consciousness—transcendental consciousness. It is here that the Soul (which is concealed at the lower levels of consciousness) begins to be experienced directly. In simple terms, if we desire to realize the presence of the Soul, it is best to go where such a realization is available. It is clearly not found on the three lower levels of consciousness where the vast majority of us spend the entirety of our mortal lives—sleep, dream and awake. Sleep is where both body and mind are inactive; dream is where the body remains inactive while the mind is active; and awake is where both body and mind are active.

For millennia, the renowned spiritual teachers and sacred scriptures taught of higher levels of consciousness where a person becomes aware of the *Greater Reality* that is imperceptible at the lower levels. Here the mind *transcends* the limitations and previous conditioning of the brain, providing the expanded awareness and enhanced perception necessary to experience that which was previously concealed. This is the beginning of Self-realization or more commonly referred to as the *discovery of the Soul.*

More recently, theoretical physicist and Nobel Prize laureate, Max Planck (1858-1947), originator of quantum theory, used the term *Universal Mind* to describe the consciousness that is the source of our physical world. He states:

*"I regard consciousness as fundamental. I regard matter as derivative from consciousness.... All matter originates and exists only by virtue of a force which brings the particle of an atom to vibration and holds this most minute solar system of the atom together. We must assume behind this force the existence of a conscious and intelligent mind. **This mind is the matrix of all matter.**"*

The objective of the spiritualization process, and that of all spiritual seekers, is to reach the higher levels of consciousness. Here, we are able to perceive beyond the physical structure of life and attain our first glimpse into the spiritual. Once we have reached this coveted and blessed state of awareness, the mind is poised to gain entry into the higher echelons of consciousness. After we have realized our spiritual nature and it becomes the new normal, life becomes an expression of spirit dwelling within flesh. This single shift from *taker mentality* to *giver mentality* is the necessary component for human redemption and humanity's salvation. For the one having this epiphany, it comes with a new identity—that of *a spiritual being having a physical experience.*

Upcoming in...
The Epiphany: Guiding the Mind toward
Discovering the Soul

Volume 2: The Spiritualization Process toward
Discovering the Soul

CHAPTER NINE: *The Threefold Spiritualization Process*
This chapter begins our discussion of the spiritualization process leading to Self-realization and, ultimately, Enlightenment—edification/learning, spiritual realization and Soul expression. Essentially, the spiritualization process is the mechanism that allows us to become more spiritually aware. It awakens us to the three dimensions of the human entity— body, mind and spirit (physical, psychological and spiritual). The fundamental technology of the spiritualization process is that of *evolving consciousness and expanded awareness.*

CHAPTER TEN: *Stage One of the Spiritualization Process: Edification*
While Chapter Nine introduces the Threefold Spiritualization Process, this chapter begins phase one of the process— edification/learning. The way we initiate the spiritualization process is by learning about it. Therefore, stage one of the spiritualization process is edification (spiritual, moral and intellectual improvement), or in religious terms, drawing in the light. It is this process that ultimately aligns our thoughts, conduct and eventual experience with our spiritual nature. Whereas our physical nature is to think and act in order to

579

satisfy our self-interest and sensory cravings, our spiritual nature focuses on evolving our consciousness toward attaining Self-realization—the moment in which the mind consciously recognizes the Soul.

CHAPTER ELEVEN: *Thirteen Operational Elements of the Spiritualization Process*

In this chapter, our explanation of the spiritualization process continues with thirteen bite-size morsels that are more easily digested than the overarching, complex, spiritual tenets explored ahead. The thirteen elements explored in this chapter are called "operational" because they each have relevance to the spiritualization process and, once understood and cultivated, can be put into operation. We may find that many of the elements are already a part of our character, while others may be lacking. The more we understand these elements, the more likely it is that they will become integrated into our character. In this way, we can operationalize these essential, spiritual principles and break free from the previous conditioning that keeps us tethered to a perspective of physical exclusivity while obscuring our spiritual nature.

CHAPTER TWELVE: *Realization I—Obstacles that Block the Path and Conditions that Pave the Way*

This chapter begins the second phase of the spiritualization process—realization. If learning is the process of leading the horse to water, realization is the actual drinking. And, like the old adage, there is little point in being led to water if not for the drinking. Although the pinnacle of realization is Self-realization, there are a variety of spiritual insights and realizations leading to it. For many of us, at our present level of spiritual awakening, Self-realization is not our current concern; rather, it is the *pursuit* of Self-realization that is the focus of our attention. Grand realization of the Soul does not occur in a vacuum, nor does it take place on our own calculated timeline. Impatience and doubt are obstacles on the spiritual path; they are the polar opposite of perseverance and faith, which pave the way. This chapter identifies many key obstacles and explores some of the most fundamental conditions that pave the way toward spiritualization. Remember, ***it is fundamentally the physical that obscures the spiritual***. Self-realization is the confirmation of our true spiritual nature, which exists in the span of eternity well beyond the span of a lifetime.

CHAPTER THIRTEEN: ***Realization II: Liberation from Previous Conditioning***

In the previous chapter, we explored the first two areas of obstruction of the spiritual: first, the distraction caused by our attachment to the physical while the spiritual remains concealed; and, second, the overwhelming influence that self-interest has over our perception. In this chapter, we delve more deeply into the third key area of obstruction—previous conditioning of the brain/mind. Just as a computer both benefits from and is limited by its previous programming, so too, the brain benefits from and is limited by its previous conditioning. Throughout our lives, the brain accumulates a vast array of files. These files include various experiences we have encountered as well as our ensuing emotional reactions along with the beliefs, biases and opinions that subsequently form. These previous experiences form the basis of our perception and the judgments of our current experiences. Even though these files may be useful in determining what is worth pursuing and what should be avoided, this mechanism also keeps us tethered to our past.

Even more important to our discussion, in order to realize our spiritual nature, we must first become free of the previous conditioning that limits the mind's ability to perceive the spiritual. The path toward spiritual awakening and Self-realization is not so much an outward investigation for new facts as it is an inward exploration—a process of uncovering what is already within us. This is where we find our next big challenge: the recultivation of the faculty of observing the internal mechanism—the mind observing the mind (introspection). The challenge is to liberate the mind from the brain's previous conditioning, which has been limiting the mind's perception. The key theme of this chapter is *realization through liberation*. The mind, no longer tethered to the brain's previous conditioning, is free to discover its true destiny—to rendezvous with the Soul.

CHAPTER FOURTEEN: *Realization III: The Inward Journey toward Transcendental Consciousness*
Mysterious as this notion may seem, discovering the indwelling Soul is perhaps the most natural and momentous of all the mind's endeavors. The basic design principle of the psychological (mind) is to provide access to the spiritual (Soul). Of course, there is a great deal of new learning and adaptation that takes place to advance the spiritualization process to this realization. Most of our secular learning and early training focuses on having a physical life in a material world. Throughout this life, however, there are recurrent events and conditions geared toward awakening the mind to its ultimate purpose—accessing higher states of consciousness. It is not so much the process of the inward journey, as it is the fruits of the inward journey that are so significant.

The ancient Sages of the mystical traditions put an

immense significance on our need to awaken and expand our consciousness. Perhaps most succinctly stated by eminent Swiss psychiatrist, psychologist and founder of analytical psychology, Carl Jung asserted: *Who looks outside, dreams. Who looks inside, awakens.* The inward journey toward transcendental consciousness, in whatever form it takes, is a transformative process. Gradually, as we become familiar and fond enough of our inner surroundings, the boundaries between our inner and outer lives become blurred. At such a time, we are most susceptible to that all-important moment when we experience living in two dimensions simultaneously—the material and the spiritual. From this vantage, we are able to realize that we are, indeed, *spiritual beings having a physical experience.*

Later in...
The Epiphany: Guiding the Mind toward Discovering the Soul

Volume 3: Realizing the Soul and Expressing it into the World

CHAPTER FIFTEEN: **Realization IV: Unleashing the Hidden Power of Mindfulness**

CHAPTER SIXTEEN: **Realization V: Accessing and Identifying Sixteen Gates of Entry**

CHAPTER SEVENTEEN: **Spiritualization Process Stage Three—Expression Expressing the Spiritual into the Physical**

Review and Study Guide